9th Linguistic Annotation Workshop 2015

(LAW IX)

Held at NAACL HLT 2015

Denver, Colorado, USA
5 June 2015

ISBN: 978-1-5108-0431-9

Printed from e-media with permission by:

Curran Associates, Inc.
57 Morehouse Lane
Red Hook, NY 12571

Some format issues inherent in the e-media version may also appear in this print version.

Printed by Curran Associates, Inc. (2015)

For permission requests, please contact the Association for Computational Linguistics at the address below.

Association for Computational Linguistics
209 N. Eighth Street
Stroudsburg, Pennsylvania 18360

Phone: 1-570-476-8006
Fax: 1-570-476-0860

acl@aclweb.org

Additional copies of this publication are available from:

Curran Associates, Inc.
57 Morehouse Lane
Red Hook, NY 12571 USA
Phone: 845-758-0400
Fax: 845-758-2634
Email: curran@proceedings.com
Web: www.proceedings.com

LAW IX

The 9th Linguistic Annotation Workshop held in conjuncion with NAACL 2015

Proceedings of the Workshop

June 5, 2015
Denver, Colorado, USA

Order print-on-demand copies from:

Curran Associates
57 Morehouse Lane
Red Hook, New York 12571
USA
Tel: +1-845-758-0400
Fax: +1-845-758-2633
curran@proceedings.com

Proceedings of the 9th Linguistic Annotation Workshop (LAW-IX)
Adam Meyers, Ines Rehbein and Heike Zinsmeister (eds.)

Introduction to the Workshop

The Linguistic Annotation Workshop (The LAW) is organised annually by the Association for Computational Linguistics' Special Interest Group for Annotation (ACL SIGANN). It provides a forum to facilitate the exchange and propagation of research results concerned with the annotation, manipulation, and exploitation of corpora; work towards harmonisation and interoperability from the perspective of the increasingly large number of tools and frameworks for annotated language resources; and work towards a consensus on all issues crucial to the advancement of the field of corpus annotation. The series is now in its ninth year, with these proceedings including papers that were presented at LAW IX, held in conjunction with the NAACL conference in Denver, Colorado, on June 5 2015.

This year's LAW IX has received 35 submissions, out of which 18 have been accepted to be presented at the workshop, either as a talk or as a poster. In addition to the papers, LAW IX also features a panel dedicated to this year's special theme, the Syntactic Annotation of Non-canonical Language. For the panel, we invited researchers who have vast experience with the manual annotation of language resources that can be described as "non-canonical", such as web data, learner language or non-standard language varieties, and who are – at the same time – aware of the problems arising when using the annotated data as training data for NLP tools or when trying to automatically predict syntactic analyses for non-canonical, noisy data. Before the workshop, we presented the panellists with a number of discussion points and asked them to write a short opinion piece addressing these issues. The resulting contributions are part of these proceedings.

Our thanks go to SIGANN, our organising committee, for its continuing organisation of the LAW workshops, and to the NAACL 2015 workshop chairs for their support. Also, we thank the NAACL 2015 publication chairs for their help with these proceedings. Most of all, we would like to thank all the authors for submitting their papers to the workshop, and our program committee members for their dedication and their thoughtful reviews.

Special Theme: Syntactic Annotation of Non-canonical Language

This year's LAW especially invited contributions addressing the special theme Syntactic Annotation of Non-canonical Language, and also features a panel dedicated to this topic. But what exactly does "non-canonical" mean? In the literature, we find different definitions that vary depending on the background and research interests of the respective research groups. Hirschmann et al. (2007), who focus on the analysis of learner data, use "non-canonical" as follows.

> "'Non-canonical' [...] refers to structures that cannot be described or generated by a given linguistic framework – canonicity can only be defined with respect to that framework. A structure may be non-canonical because it is ungrammatical, or it may be non-canonical because the given framework is not able to analyse it." (Hirschmann et al., 2007:1)

Dipper et al. (2013) use the term "(non)-standard" instead of "(non-)canonical" but emphasise that they do not intend a normative, prescriptive reading but simply refer to "de facto standard language found in newspaper texts". This definition, however, raises the follow-up question of what exactly is meant by standard, as the criterium "appears in newswire" seems to be a bit vague. A possible interpretation of standard could be transcribed as everything that observes the (grammar) rules of the standard language variety. This approach allows us to better operationalise which structures are included and which are considered to be non-canonical. However, this definition is also not without problems. A minor problem is caused by new constructions that are used by many speakers of the language community but still considered to be ungrammatical by a large number of native speakers. But, and this is the more severe problem, how do we handle languages where we have more than one standard (e.g. British/North American/Australian/... Standard English) or where no standard exists at all? The latter is especially relevant for oral languages that have no script. Furthermore, the notion of a standard is often used to refer to the most prestigious variety of a language. As a result, language attitude also comes into play, making it even harder to arrive at an objective definition of what standard means.

While these topics have mostly been discussed in the theoretical linguistics literature in the areas of socio-linguistics or dialectology, other terms used to refer to non-canonical language in NLP include low-resourced languages and noisy data. The term "low-resourced languages" simply refers to any language for which no or only small-scale language resources exist. This means that, with respect to the definition given above, low-resourced languages can, but do not necessarily have to be non-canonical. We are not aware of any clear-cut definition for the term "noisy data". Usually, noisy data refers to text that contains spelling errors, abbreviations, non-standard words, missing punctuations, missing case information, and phenomena typical for spoken language, such as disfluencies or fillers. The term "noisy" does not distinguish between 'real' noise which was inserted unintentionally in the data (such as spelling errors, OCR errors etc.) and language features that fulfil a certain function and thus are part of the language system (but are, admittedly, challenging for NLP systems). An example are fillers which are often used as strategic devices for turn-taking and also fulfill pragmatic functions in the discourse. We would prefer to think of the latter as non-canonical (with regard to the rules of the standard variety) instead of noise.

Having shed some light on what we mean by non-canonical language, we now briefly discuss why we think this to be a relevant topic for a panel. When the first linguistically annotated corpora were built, research mostly focussed on written text from the newspaper domain. Meanwhile, also other corpora are available, including spoken language, learner data, or historical texts. The advent of Digital Humanities has further advanced this trend, and many projects exist that work with data from domains other than newspaper. Especially data from the social media has attracted lots of attention, and many new corpus projects are now under way. The new projects follow different approaches, some using existing annotation schemes as they are, others extend and adapt existing schemes to the particularities of their data, and others again invent their own scheme for annotation. Concerning the granularity of the annotations, we can also find a huge range of detail. Some use rather coarse-grained label sets while others aim at very fine-grained distinctions.

This again brings us to the question of the reliability of the annotations. There have been discussions of whether it is worthwhile employing expert annotators, given the time requirements and high costs, or whether one could achieve similar results with untrained annotators. Also, and this has been in the focus of last year's LAW: "The good, the bad, and the perfect: How good does annotation need to be?" The answer to this question is closely related to the next one: What type of annotators do we need? Is crowdsourcing reliable enough, and can it be employed efficiently for treebanking?

We think that future work on the linguistic aspects of non-canonical language as well as on processing it will benefit from a discussion on best practices for the syntactic annotation of non-standard language.

As panellists, we invited Ann Bies (LDC), Aoife Cahill (ETS), Barbara Plank (CST, University of Copenhagen) and Nathan Schneider (ILCC, University of Edinburgh), and presented them with the discussion points below.

- What are the factors that lead to the adoption of a totally new annotation scheme rather than using an existing annotation scheme?
- How do you decide on the granularity of the distinctions you choose to annotate? Give examples.
- For building new resources for NCLs, is it still worthwhile to invest a huge amount of time and human labour for manual annotation, considering that the annotators spend most of their time making arbitrary decisions, and that the aim of building 'high-quality resources' for NCLs might not be realistic?
- On a related note, what are the considerations when choosing the level of expertise of the annotators? When is crowd sourcing appropriate? When do we need linguistic experts?
- Can the concept of "gold annotations" be applied to non-canonical languages where the inherent ambiguity in the data makes it hard to decide on the "ground truth" of an utterance?

The resulting papers are part of the proceedings. We would like to thank the panellists for their insightful contributions and hope that this will foster future discussions on that matter.

Adam Meyers, Ines Rehbein and Heike Zinsmeister, program co-chairs

LAW Co-chairs:

Adam Meyers, New York University
Ines Rehbein, Potsdam University
Heike Zinsmeister, University of Hamburg

Organising Committee:

Stefanie Dipper, Ruhr University Bochum
Chu-Ren Huang, The Hong Kong Polytechnic University
Nancy Ide, Vassar College
Lori Levin, Carnegie-Mellon University
Antonio Pareja-Lora, SIC & ILSA, UCM / ATLAS, UNED
Massimo Poesio, University of Trento
Sameer Pradhan, Harvard University
Manfred Stede, University of Potsdam
Katrin Tomanek, VigLink Inc.
Fei Xia, University of Washington
Nianwen Xue, Brandeis University

Program Committee:

Collin Baker, UC Berkeley
Ann Bies, LDC
Archna Bhatia, Carnegie Mellon University
Marie Candito, Université Paris Diderot - INRIA
Özlem Çetinoğlu, University of Stuttgart
Christian Chiarcos, University of Frankfurt
Markus Dickinson, Indiana University
Stefanie Dipper, Ruhr University Bochum
Tomaž Erjavec, Josef Stefan Institute
Kilian Evang, University of Groningen
Pablo Faria, Universidade Estadual de Campinas
Jennifer Foster, Dublin City University
Andrew Gargett, University of Birmingham
Kim Gerdes, Sorbonne Nouvelle, Paris 3
Nizar Habash, New York University Abu Dhabi
Udo Hahn, University of Jena
Chu-Ren Huang, The Hong Kong Polytechnic University
Nancy Ide, Vassar College
Aravind Joshi, University of Pennsylvania
Varada Kolhatkar, University of Toronto

Valia Kordoni, Humboldt University Berlin
Sandra Kübler, Indiana University
John S. Y. Lee, City University of Hong Kong
Els Lefever, University College Ghent
Lori Levin, Carnegie-Mellon University
Amália Mendes, Universidade di Lisboa
Anna Nedoluzhko, Chareles University Prague
Kemal Oflazer, Carnegie-Mellon University, Qatar
Lilja Øvrelid, University of Oslo
Alexis Palmer, University of Stuttgart
Antonio Pareja-Lora, SIC & ILSA, UCM / ATLAS, UNED
Massimo Poesio, University of Trento
Sameer Pradhan, Harvard University
James Pustejovsky, Brandeis University
Arndt Riester, University of Stuttgart
Benoît Sagot, Inria, Université Paris 7
Nathan Schneider, Carnegie-Mellon University
Djamé Seddah, Université Paris Sorbonne & INRIA's Alpage Project
Kiril Simov, Bulgarian Academy of Sciences, Sofia
Anders Søgaard, University of Copenhagen
Caroline Sporleder, University of Trier
Manfred Stede, University of Potsdam
Joel Tetrault, Yahoo! Labs
Katrin Tomanek, VigLink Inc.
Reut Tsarfaty, Weizmann Institute of Science, Israel
Yulia Tsvetkov, Carnegie-Mellon University
Andreas Witt, IDS Mannheim
Fei Xia, University of Washington
Nianwen Xue, Brandeis University

Panellists:

Ann Bies, LDC
Aoife Cahill, ETS
Barbara Plank, University of Copenhagen
Nathan Schneider, University of Edinburgh

Table of Contents

This page intentionally left blank.

Workshop Program

Friday, June 5, 2015

8:45–9:00 ***Opening Remarks***

9:00–10:30 ***Session 1***

Oral Presentations

9:00–9:30 *Scaling Semantic Frame Annotation*
Nancy Chang, Praveen Paritosh, David Huynh and Collin Baker

9:30–10:00 *An Analytic and Empirical Evaluation of Return-on-Investment-Based Active Learning*
Robbie Haertel, Eric Ringger, Kevin Seppi and Paul Felt

10:00–10:30 *Annotating genericity: a survey, a scheme, and a corpus*
Annemarie Friedrich, Alexis Palmer, Melissa Peate Sørensen and Manfred Pinkal

10:30–11:00 ***Coffee break***

11:00–12:30 ***Session 2***

Poster presentations

Design and Annotation of the First Italian Corpus for Text Simplification
Dominique Brunato, Felice Dell'Orletta, Giulia Venturi and Simonetta Montemagni

On the Discoursive Structure of Computer Graphics Research Papers
Beatriz Fisas, Horacio Saggion and Francesco Ronzano

Semantic Annotation of Japanese Functional Expressions and its Impact on Factuality Analysis
Yudai Kamioka, Kazuya Narita, Junta Mizuno, Miwa Kanno and Kentaro Inui

A Qualitative Analysis of a Corpus of Opinion Summaries based on Aspects
Roque Lopez, Thiago Pardo, Lucas Avanço, Pedro Filho, Alessandro Bokan, Paula Cardoso, Márcio Dias, Fernando Nóbrega, Marco Cabezudo, Jackson Souza, Andressa Zacarias, Eloize Seno and Ariani Di Felippo

Friday, June 5, 2015 (continued)

Developing Language-tagged Corpora for Code-switching Tweets
Suraj Maharjan, Elizabeth Blair, Steven Bethard and Thamar Solorio

Annotating Geographical Entities on Microblog Text
Koji Matsuda, Akira Sasaki, Naoaki Okazaki and Kentaro Inui

The Annotation Process of the ITU Web Treebank
Tuğba Pamay, Umut Sulubacak, Dilara Torunoğlu-Selamet and Gülşen Eryiğit

Part of Speech Annotation of Intermediate Versions in the Keystroke Logged Translation Corpus
Tatiana Serbina, Paula Niemietz, Matthias Fricke, Philipp Meisen and Stella Neumann

A Hierarchy with, of, and for Preposition Supersenses
Nathan Schneider, Vivek Srikumar, Jena D. Hwang and Martha Palmer

Bilingual English-Czech Valency Lexicon Linked to a Parallel Corpus
Zdenka Uresova, Ondřej Dušek, Eva Fucikova, Jan Hajic and Jana Sindlerova

Correction Annotation for Non-Native Arabic Texts: Guidelines and Corpus
Wajdi Zaghouani, Nizar Habash, Houda Bouamor, Alla Rozovskaya, Behrang Mohit, Abeer Heider and Kemal Oflazer

12:30–14:00 ***Lunch break***

14:00–15:30 ***Session 3***

Panel

Balancing the Existing and the New in the Context of Annotating Non-Canonical Language
Ann Bies

Parsing Learner Text: to Shoehorn or not to Shoehorn
Aoife Cahill

Non-canonical language is not harder to annotate than canonical language
Barbara Plank, Héctor Martínez Alonso and Anders Søgaard

What I've learned about annotating informal text (and why you shouldn't take my word for it)
Nathan Schneider

16:00–18:00 ***Session 4***

Oral presentations

16:00–16:30 *On Grammaticality in the Syntactic Annotation of Learner Language*
Markus Dickinson and Marwa Ragheb

16:30–17:00 *Across Languages and Genres: Creating a Universal Annotation Scheme for Textual Relations*
Ekaterina Lapshinova-Koltunski, Anna Nedoluzhko and Kerstin Anna Kunz

17:00–17:30 *Annotating the Implicit Content of Sluices*
Pranav Anand and Jim McCloskey

17:30–18:00 *Annotating Causal Language Using Corpus Lexicography of Constructions*
Jesse Dunietz, Lori Levin and Jaime Carbonell

18:00–18:10 ***Closing***

Scaling Semantic Frame Annotation

Nancy Chang, Google, ncchang@google.com
Praveen Paritosh, Google, pkp@google.com
David Huynh, Google, dfhuynh@google.com
Collin F. Baker, ICSI, collinb@icsi.berkeley.edu

Abstract

Large-scale data resources needed for progress toward natural language understanding are not yet widely available and typically require considerable expense and expertise to create. This paper addresses the problem of developing scalable approaches to annotating **semantic frames** and explores the viability of crowdsourcing for the task of **frame disambiguation**. We present a novel **supervised crowdsourcing** paradigm that incorporates insights from human computation research designed to accommodate the relative complexity of the task, such as exemplars and real-time feedback. We show that non-experts can be trained to perform accurate frame disambiguation, and can even identify errors in gold data used as the training exemplars. Results demonstrate the efficacy of this paradigm for semantic annotation requiring an intermediate level of expertise.

1 The semantic bottleneck

Behind every great success in speech and language lies a great corpus—or at least a very large one. Advances in speech recognition, machine translation and syntactic parsing can be traced to the availability of large-scale annotated resources (Wall Street Journal, Europarl and Penn Treebank, respectively) providing crucial supervised input to statistically learned models.

Semantically annotated resources have been comparatively harder to come by: representing meaning poses myriad philosophical, theoretical and practical challenges, particularly for general purpose resources that can be applied to diverse domains. If these challenges can be addressed, however, semantic resources hold significant potential for fueling progress beyond shallow syntax and toward deeper language understanding.

This paper explores the feasibility of developing scalable methodologies for semantic annotation, inspired by three strands of work.

First, **frame semantics**, and its instantiation in the Berkeley **FrameNet** project (Fillmore and Baker, 2010), offers a principled approach to representing meaning. FrameNet is a lexicographic resource that captures syntactic and semantic generalizations that go beyond surface form and part of speech, famously including the relationships among words like *buy*, *sell*, *purchase* and *price*. These rich structural relations provide an attractive foundation for work in deeper natural language understanding and inference, as attested by the breadth of applications at the Workshop in Honor of Chuck Fillmore at ACL 2014 (Petruck and de Melo, 2014). But FrameNet was not designed to support scalable language technologies; indeed, it is perhaps a paradigm example of a hand-curated knowledge resource, one that has required significant expertise, training, time and expense to create and that remains under development.

Second, the task of **automatic semantic role labeling (ASRL)** (Gildea and Jurafsky, 2002) serves as an applied counterpart to the ideas of frame semantics. Recent progress has demonstrated the viability of training automated models using frame-annotated data (Das et al., 2013; Das et al., 2010; Johansson and Nugues, 2006). Results based on FrameNet data have been limited by its incomplete

Proceedings of LAW IX - The 9th Linguistic Annotation Workshop, pages 1–10,
Denver, Colorado, June 5, 2015. ©2015 Association for Computational Linguistics

lexical coverage (since the project is ongoing) as well as the relatively limited amount of annotated data. More impressive results have been based on PropBank (Palmer et al., 2005), a semantic resource whose frames are more lexically specific than those of FrameNet. PropBank frames are generally more tightly linked to surface syntax (and thus afford less generalization across words), but are relatively simpler to define and annotate, as reflected by its greater coverage and amount of annotated data. It seems natural to investigate whether a comparable amount of FrameNet data would yield equally good performance (along with the further benefits of frame-level generalizations).

Third, a handful of studies from the relatively new field of **human computation** suggest that some aspects of frame annotation may be amenable to non-expert curation, such as made possible by crowdsourcing platforms like Amazon Mechanical Turk (AMT) (Hong and Baker, 2011; Fossati et al., 2013). These findings are not altogether surprising: frame semantics purports to capture generalizations that depend on everyday, non-specialist language use. Frame annotation should therefore not require the same level of training as, for example, syntactic annotation. On the other hand, while competent speakers of a language are assumed to make implicit use of frame-like structures—i.e., understanding who did what to whom and other kinds of relationships implied by a specific expression—they do not explicitly annotate semantic information as a natural part of everyday language use. Thus, unlike translation—which (some) humans do rather naturally—frame annotation is unlikely to occur in the wild, and will likely require more instruction than a typical AMT task.

These three strands together suggest that frame semantics is a promising option for meaning representation; that larger-scale frame-annotated data could drive ASRL models; and that the task of frame annotation may be amenable to crowdsourcing methods. We take these strands as a starting point for exploring how richer human computation frameworks can support scalable frame annotation, focusing in this paper on one part of frame annotation (the **frame disambiguation** task).

In the remainder of the paper, we first describe relevant previous work in more detail (Section 2). We then introduce a novel **supervised crowdsourcing** framework that adapts previous work by introducing multiple kinds of feedback and supervision (Section 3) and describe experiments using this framework to crowdsource frame disambiguation (Section 4). Finally, we discuss results and future avenues suggested by this research (Section 5), in particular the possibility that non-experts can be efficiently and effectively trained to perform tasks requiring an intermediate level of expertise.

2 Background

In this section we briefly describe the target representation of semantic frames, the FrameNet resource, the frame disambiguation annotation task, and some relevant past human computation efforts.

2.1 Frame semantics

A **semantic frame** (or simply **frame**), as developed by the late Charles J. Fillmore (Fillmore, 1976; Fillmore, 1982), is a conceptual gestalt that represents a generalization over similar scenes—typically corresponding to events, relations, states, or entities. Frames are structured around a set of semantic **roles**, also called **frame elements** (FEs), corresponding to participants in the scene.

The key theoretical insight of **frame semantics** is that the meanings of most words (and other constructions) can be understood in relation to the semantic frames they evoke. The much-discussed Commercial Transaction frame, for example, has FEs for the Buyer, Seller, Goods and Money; and it is associated with a set of words, or **lexical units** (LUs), that **profile** (or highlight) different FEs or sets of FEs (e.g., the verb *buy* is typically expressed along with the Buyer and the Goods FEs, while the noun *price* is mainly associated with the Money).

Frames vary considerably in complexity and level of granularity. Moreover, individual **lemmas** (or words) might be associated with multiple frames. For example, the lemma *like* (as a preposition and verb, respectively) is associated with two frames:

- Similarity: *Skiing is LIKE windsurfing.*
- Experiencer focus: *I LIKE looking in windows.*

The same lemma with the same part of speech can also be ambiguous, as in the case of *century*:

- Measure duration: *CENTURIES of farming have shaped our countryside.*
- Calendric unit: *By the 13th CENTURY....*

For simplicity, the examples above do not show the FEs defined for each frame and how they relate to different parts of the text, but a fully frame-annotated sentence would include that information.

2.2 FrameNet and frame disambiguation

FrameNet is a lexical resource for English based on frame semantics, in development since 1997 (Fillmore and Baker, 2010; Ruppenhofer et al., 2006). It includes nearly 1,200 frame definitions; 200,000 manually annotated examples; and about 13,000 LUs linked to specific frames.

The frame annotation process traditionally employed by Berkeley FrameNet combines **frame creation** with **lexicographic frame annotation**, where annotators select sentences from a corpus containing a lemma illustrating a frame. A separate **full-text frame annotation** process attempts to annotate all frames evoked by a sentence.

For either style of frame annotation, one must decide whether a lemma used in a given sentence is an instance of a particular frame, or more generally decide which of several candidate frames it evokes. Since the FrameNet project is ongoing (i.e., many frames have not yet been defined), the evoked frame may not even be among the known candidate frames. We call this task **frame disambiguation** (FD), corresponding roughly to word sense disambiguation.

FD is only the first step toward complete frame semantic annotation. The second is **frame element annotation** (FEA), the assignment of FEs to words in the sentence. The output of FEA corresponds to that of ASRL systems like those mentioned above; these systems often make precisely the same division of labor among FD and FEA phases (Das et al., 2013).

2.3 Insights from human computation

Human computation, in particular the use of large numbers of non-expert judgments to complement or substitute for expert judgments, has been well-established for many types of data collection, both commercial and scientific. Several crowdsourcing experiments have explored frame disambiguation and related tasks.

2.3.1 Crowdsourcing for frame disambiguation

The most relevant precursor of the current work is a series of experiments on crowdsourcing frame annotation, in particular the frame disambiguation task, using Amazon Mechanical Turk (AMT), reported at LAW V (Hong and Baker, 2011).

The target sentences consisted of unannotated sentences from the FrameNet database, plus a few annotated sentences for measuring annotator accuracy. Several task designs were tried:

- frame choice: Workers choose from a list of candidate frames, plus "None of the above".
- simplified frame names: as above, but with FrameNet terms rewritten for non-experts.
- frame sorting, with randomly chosen gold exemplars: Workers see a list of sentences and "piles" corresponding to candidate frames, each with a starter gold exemplar. They sort sentences into the appropriate frame pile (and freely recategorize sentences if desired).

Several experiments were run with the last design, varying the qualifications of the workers and the pay rate, over words with varying degrees of ambiguity.

The results showed that AMT workers could perform the FD task fairly well, that accuracy varied across lemmas (and did not depend only on the number of candidate frames per lemma), and that in a few cases, workers strongly (and correctly) disagreed with gold data. These studies suggest that crowdsourcing for FD is feasible at least on a small scale (about 6 lemmas with a maximum of 5 candidate frames per lemma). The current study adopts and extends many components of that framework to support larger-scale validation of the approach.

2.3.2 Crowdsourcing for WSD

Despite the optimism expressed in Snow et al. (2008) (which included a limited WSD task) and the 2010 Workshop on Creating Speech and Language Data with Amazon's Mechanical Turk (Callison-Burch and Dredze, 2010), relatively few large-scale studies have investigated crowdsourcing for WSD. An important exception is Kapelner et al. (2012), who paid workers to disambiguate 1,000 instances of 89 ambiguous lemmas using the OntoNotes senses (Pradhan et al., 2007), which are relatively coarse. They found that (1) rephrasing the sense definition improved accuracy, (2) more frequent words were resolved less accurately, and (3) annotators who spent more time per item were less accurate. They also found that all the workers were roughly equal in ability, and those who answered more items did not get more accurate, i.e. there was no measurable practice effect, contrary to the findings of Chen and Dolan (2011), who paid more for better work and tried to retain the more accurate workers.

2.4 Other crowdsourcing for semantics

Few precedents exist for crowdsourcing complex semantic tasks. Bernstein et al. (2010) describe Soylent, a word processor that uses workers on AMT to help writers improve their text. They used a find-fix-verify pattern to iteratively evaluate and refine the quality of tasks like text paraphrasing and summarizing. DuoLingo (von Ahn, 2013) turns translation into an educational game, and translates web content using its language learners.

Freebase is a large human curated collaborative knowledge base (Bollacker et al., 2008) of structured data. The schema for Freebase includes types and relationships that are human curated and validated via large scale crowdsourcing (Kochhar et al., 2010). A key methodological finding from this work was to focus on reproducibility as a key criteria when collecting semantic judgments from human annotators (Paritosh, 2012).

3 Supervised crowdsourcing

The findings discussed above provided promising ways of accommodating some challenges of the FD task. Our goals in extending the FD crowdsourcing framework were twofold: (1) adapt previous efforts to accommodate larger-scale annotation; and (2) incorporate multiple kinds of supervision, broadly construed. We discuss each of these below.

3.1 Scaling up frame disambiguation

We adopted the basic frame-sorting paradigm of Hong and Baker (2011), organizing tasks around specific lemmas. In each task, a set of sentences (each including the target lemma) was presented along with a set of candidate frames (each known to be associated with the target lemma).

Several challenges arose in expanding from these small-scale experiments to less constrained conditions: The 32 lemmas used for our pilot study typically had 3-4 candidate frames but in some cases as many as 10, necessitating an interface that could flexibly accommodate the need for detailed frame definitions within a limited space—while trying to avoid sensory overload that would likely detract from performance. Figure 1 shows a screenshot of the task user interface.

Another problem came from the need to adapt a resource designed for experts for use in a non-expert context. The prose used in FrameNet frame definitions varies considerably in the degree of technical jargon employed—perhaps as much as annotators varied in their appreciation or effective use of those definitions. Hong and Baker (2011) found improved performance with replacing just the frame name with a more easily interpretable title.

Given the impracticality of abridging the frame definitions for each task, we chose to show them unchanged, but to also provide more example uses and related words for each frame to de-emphasize the technical definitions. (We also explicitly warned annotators about the technical jargon and directed them to focus on example uses.)

Finally, we anticipated that a broader range of lemmas would make the task more difficult in various ways. The potential for more candidate frames per lemma raises the chance of ambiguity and similarity among frames. It also seemed likely that there might be cases that fit none of the presented candidate frames for a lemma, either because the appropriate frame had not yet been created or because the lemma in question had not yet associated with that frame. We thus included extra choices corresponding to these failure modes ("None of the above" and "I can't decide"), as well as a way for workers to indicate uncertainty or provide additional comments.

As a general principle we also tried to design the simplest interface and instruction materials possible given the nature of the task and the other constraints above. The final guidelines, defining semantic frames for non-experts and introducing them to the task and UI, are 4 pages—longer than a typical crowdsourcing task, but much shorter than materials for expert annotation. These focus on mechanical aspects of the UI and keep terminology and defini-

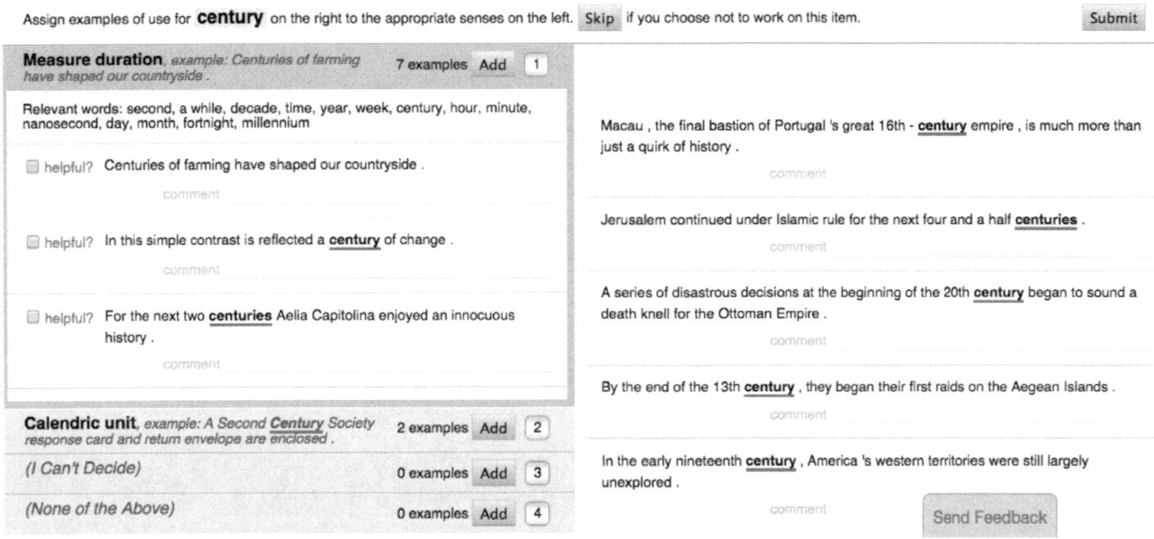

Figure 1: Frame identification task interface for the lemma *century*. Candidate frames (here, **Measure duration** and **Calendric unit**) are shown on the left, each featuring typical examples of usage with the target lemma. The frame definition (not shown in figure) as well as other related words are also available. The examples to be classified are on the right side of the screen.

tions to a minimum.

3.2 Incorporating supervision

In moving to the middle ground of task complexity, we made two broad assumptions that informed how supervision could be introduced.

First, we assumed that the task was complex enough to need some training time, and that annotators with practice and experience would perform better. We thus required a crowdsourcing platform that would allow us to main a relatively stable annotator pool. In contrast to crowdsourcing platforms based on an open marketplace—where anyone is potentially eligible for any task, and no continuity across tasks or workers is guaranteed—we made use of a platform that tracks individual annotators' history and allows some form of communication between task designers and annotators.

This interactive potential of our platform was crucial to our iterative design process: at every stage we were able to conduct small pilot studies that yielded useful qualitative feedback. More broadly, the fact that the same annotators would be working on multiple tasks allowed us to expect and plan for improved performance over exposure to the task—which in turn made it more worthwhile (for both the designers of the task and the annotators) to invest in some amount of training.

Second, we assumed that some gold data would be available for our task. (In our case, it was easy to draw this from the available FrameNet data.) Gold data allows us to follow both conventional wisdom (that people learn best by example) and common practice in (supervised) machine learning of providing explicit training examples of the task being learned. (We have relaxed this assumption in subsequent experiments.)

We use gold data in both *exemplar* and *real-time feedback* form. We lead by (and with) example, by prominently featuring several sentences illustrating each candidate frame. The task UI also allows a mode in which annotators are given explicit positive or negative feedback (in the form of happy or sad faces) indicating whether their frame choice matches the gold data; annotators are allowed to change their frame selection as many times as they would like to. Crucially, we discovered (as in previous work) that gold data occasionally included mistakes, or was potentially ambiguous or uncertain. We thus included explicit means for annotators to indicate disagreement with the apparent gold data (as shown in Figure 3.2), an option that turned out to be quite useful.

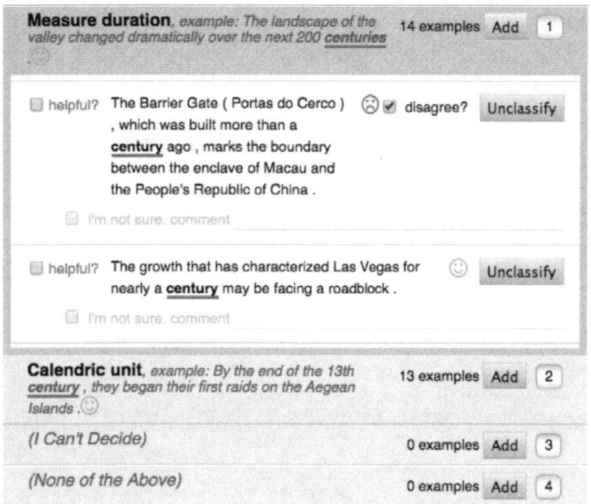

Figure 2: Close-up of task UI used with feedback. Green smiling and red frowning icons indicate correctness of an annotator's selection with respect to the correct (gold) answer, but annotators are allowed to indicate disagreement with the feedback.

4 Frame disambiguation experiment

To investigate how frame disambiguation can be accomplished at scale and with feedback, we used the frame-sorting design and UI described above in several annotation experiments. Below we describe the basic experimental set-up and methodology, followed by our evaluation metrics and results.

4.1 Methodology

We chose lemmas from existing gold examples from FrameNet's full-text annotations, further restricting ourselves to examples from the American National Corpus. We chose 32 target lemmas (occurring in a total of 881 sentences) which satisfy the following conditions:

- At least 15 occurrences in the corpus.
- More than 1 candidate frame for each lemma. The actual number of candidate frames per lemma ranged from 2 to 10 (average 3-4).
- At least 3 examples of the lemma's use in each candidate frame.

The first restriction above (15+ occurrences) was made purely to create tasks of a reasonable size for evaluation; tasks with significantly fewer occurrences have been run with no effect on results.

The second restriction was intended to focus the task on *disambiguation* among multiple frames rather than simply *validation* of a single frame (though other experiments included validation cases). Note that of the current 10K lemmas in FrameNet, 1900 (19%) are polysemous (i.e., associated with more than one frame). These lemmas are thus relatively more ambiguous than the average lemma in FrameNet.

The final restriction, on the number of exemplars available to be shown for the task, was made to facilitate the testing of the feedback condition. Note that more general versions of the task could be run with fewer (or even no) exemplars, or expert annotators could supply those needed.

4.1.1 Experimental design

We used a 2x2 within-subjects factorial design. The lemmas were randomly split into two equal batches (n=16): *No Feedback* and *Feedback*. In the *Feedback* condition, the annotators received real-time positive or negative feedback in response to their sorting actions, based on whether their action matched the gold answer, while no such feedback was provided for lemmas in the other condition. Each annotator performed the task for each lemma, and each lemma was presented with the same type of feedback to all annotators. Each lemma was presented to at least 7 annotators. In both conditions, the annotators were allowed to undo and change their sorting, and every annotator action was logged.

The annotators were randomly allocated to two equal-sized groups: Group 1 and Group 2. Annotators from Group 1 were presented the *Feedback* batch of exemplars before the *No Feedback* batch; and annotators from Group 2 were presented *No Feedback* before the *Feedback* batch. This gives us fully counterbalanced, within-subjects data for comparison of performance across conditions.

4.2 Analysis

We focused our analyses on how **accuracy**—that is, correctness with respect to gold data—varied based on two factors:

Feedback. This is the main dimension we varied across experimental conditions. We compare the difference in performance acrosss *Feedback* and *No Feedback* conditions. We further distinguish the

Feedback condition into two subcategories: Since the task UI allowed annotators to change their selection (potentially in response to gold feedback), we were able to record each frame choice and thus track how well annotators in the *Feedback* condition performed on their first choice for a given item (which we call the *Pre Feedback* condition), as well as what they eventually settled upon (which we call the *Post Feedback* condition).

Number of annotators. We also compared accuracy across different numbers of annotators, ranging from 1 to 7 annotators.

We measured accuracy of the chosen frame against the gold-annotated frame. Our resolution policy was to require a threshold of 75% inter-rater agreement as the minimum for which a resolved answer would be considered usable.

4.3 Results

Figure 3 shows the mean accuracy for the three possible feedback conditions, and Figure 4 shows precision results for different numbers of annotators per lemma (n=1 to 7).

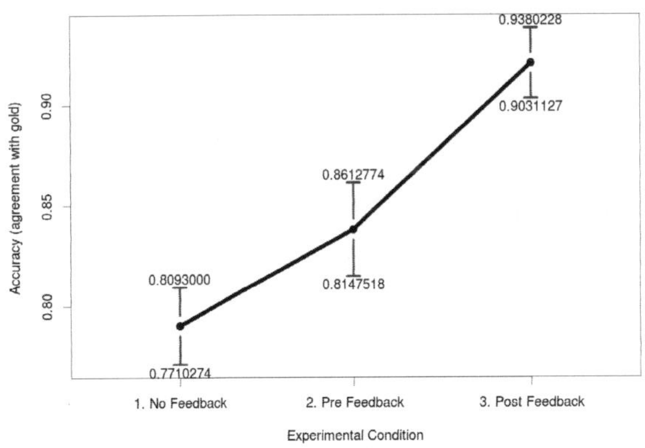

Figure 3: Mean annotator accuracy across three experimental conditions: (1) *No Feedback*, for annotators who received no feedback. (2) *Pre-Feedback*, the accuracy of annotators' first response **prior to** receiving feedback based on gold data. (3) *Post-Feedback*, the accuracy of annotators' final response after receiving feedback, and after any number of revisions. Note that the Post-Feedback accuracy is significantly less than 1.0, showing that annotators have developed strong enough opinions to disagree while learning via the same gold data.

Figures 5 and 6 show individual annotator responses for two lemmas, *like* and *century*. These were both typical in exhibiting a fairly clean division of responses between the candidate frames: i.e., the usages were straightforward to disambiguate. The latter example also includes a panel displaying individual responses, including annotator's disagreement with feedback and frame selection history.

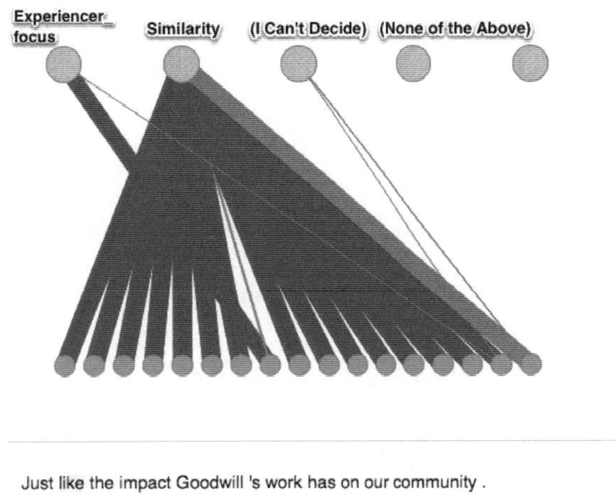

Figure 5: Results for the lemma *like*. The nodes in the top row correspond to candidate frames (Experiencer_focus and Similarity) and three problem conditions("I can't Decide", "None of the above", and an unmarked "Other"). The nodes in the bottom row correspond to classified sentences; lines between nodes in the top and bottom rows represent annotator choices, with thicker lines corresponding to more annotators making that choice. This situation was typical: most sentences had a strong majority for one of the two expected frames, with a few outliers expressing indecision or otherwise disagreeing with the crowd. The red line highlights the results for the single sentence shown below.

We discuss our findings below: Findings 1-3 concerning the effect of feedback, and Finding 4 concerning the effect of number of annotators.

Finding 1. Feedback improves annotator accuracy. Unsurprisingly, we found that feedback improved accuracy: the mean annotator accuracy in the *No Feedback* condition was 0.78, *Pre Feedback condition* was 0.81, and *Post Feedback* condition was 0.92. All differences are significant ($p < 0.0001$). Figure 3 shows the differences between means across the three conditions. In addition, feedback decreased variance in annotator behavior significantly, i.e., the annotators had converged to more

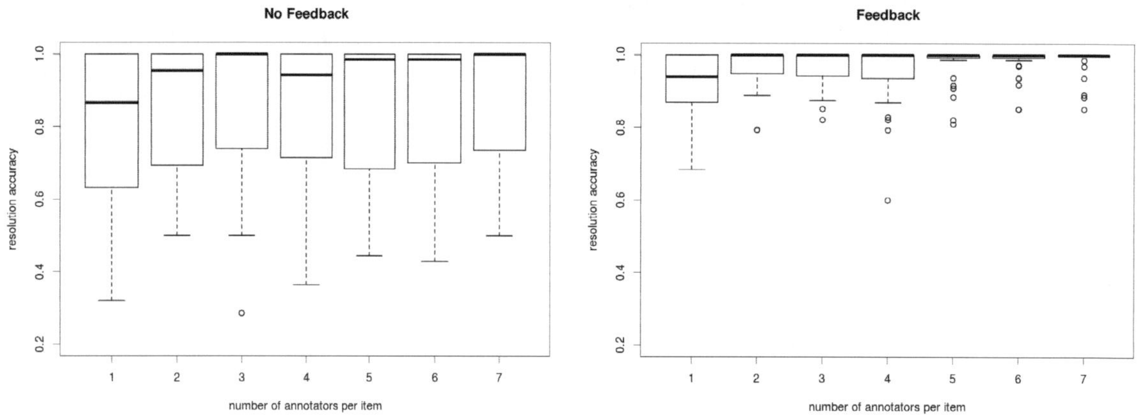

Figure 4: Accuracy of resolutions by number of annotators, in the *No Feedback* (left) and *Feedback* (right) conditions. Box and whisker plots show median (marked by a heavy bar) and variance (indicated by box size) of accuracy across all lemmas. The resolutions are computed by combining independent answers from multiple annotators using a plurality threshold of 0.75.

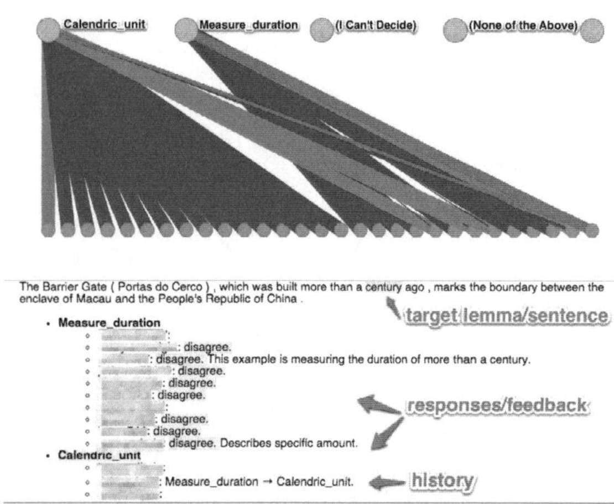

Figure 6: Results for a task with lemma *century*. The responses for individual annotators (names masked) are displayed below, showing that many explicitly disagreed with the gold feedback (some providing additional justification). Note that the history of choices made is shown in one case, also suggesting some uncertainty. This example was one of several that further investigation revealed to be an error in the gold data.

reliable performance. Figure 4 shows two box and whiskers plots of resolution accuracy by number of annotators. There is much wider variance in annotator behavior in the No Feedback condition, as indicated by longer boxes and whiskers.

Finding 2. Feedback works even with imperfect gold data, and can be reliably used to correct it. Our crowdsourced resolutions were significantly *better* than the gold data that was used to train the annotators. In all conditions, annotators were allowed to change their responses; thus, those in the feedback conditions could in theory have performed at 100% accuracy by adhering strictly to the feedback. We were surprised to find, however, that the average accuracy even with feedback was less than perfect—an indication that annotators sometimes chose not to adhere to gold data. We were aware that there might be some errors in the gold data, and allowed and encouraged the annotators to disagree with the feedback.

To investigate cases in which the annotators reliably disagreed with the gold, we asked experts to manually validate gold data for sentences with a resolved answer from the crowd, which was 385 sentences (87.10%). (Recall that we required agreement of 0.75 to be considered resolved.)

Table 1 shows the proportions of validated accuracy of resolved judgments. We found that in most cases (93.77%), the crowd (correctly) agreed with gold. But in some cases (4.94%), the crowd disagreed with gold that turned out to be incorrect. In other words, the crowd was nearly always vindicated when they strongly agreed that the gold was incorrect—and they were overall correct 98.70% of the time.

	number	percent
Correct resolution, valid gold	361	93.77
Correct resolution, invalid gold	19	4.94
Incorrect resolution, valid gold	2	0.52
Incorrect resolution, invalid gold	3	0.78

Table 1: Accuracy of resolved judgments (total 385) based on validated gold data. The top two lines reflect all cases in which the crowd was correct, either in agreement or disagreement with gold data. The bottom two lines reflect very rare cases of incorrect crowd resolutions.

This finding suggests that a richer framework can support crowdsourced semantic annotations even with imperfect data; even better, reliable crowdsourced signals might be an effective avenue to the discovery and correction of imperfect gold data.

Finding 3. Even first responses improve with feedback. Figure 3 shows that the *Pre Feedback* condition was significantly better than the *No Feedback* condition: that is, there seemed to be a boost to performance even on annotator's first guesses (before receiving any feedback). This result suggests that feedback may have had effects that spread beyond the current item, such that subsequent items were learned faster. One possible explanation for this apparent learning based on prior feedback is that there may be increased attention due to the expectation of feedback, such that the annotator homed in more quickly on the correct concept. These hypotheses need further examination.

Finding 4. More annotators produce better results. Unsurprisingly, more is better: resolution accuracy increases with the number of annotators in all conditions. The mean resolution accuracy is higher in the *Feedback* condition, which is as expected since per-annotator accuracy is higher in that condition. In fact, performance was fairly high (in both conditions) with as few as three annotators, but variance in resolution accuracy was significantly lower in the *Feedback* condition, further establishing the effectiveness of feedback. This difference is important, since both mean and variance affect crowdsourcing cost in terms of redundancy required.

5 Discussion and future directions

Our challenge was to devise effective and scalable ways of training annotators to perform the relatively complex task of frame disambiguation. In this paper we have leveraged insights about human learning, in particular the value of exemplars and feedback (early, often and even imperfect), to create a novel crowdsourcing approach suitable for more complex tasks. A key feature of this approach is that it emphasizes examples over explicit instructions, tapping into the cognitive capacity to learn deeply from a limited amount of data. It further exploits supervision, particularly in the form of real-time feedback.

We demonstrated that real-time feedback can substantially increase mean annotator accuracy and dramatically increase inter-annotator agreement. Our experiments also showed the surprising result that even feedback based on imperfect gold data is effective for training annotators—and that they can learn to produce resolutions of higher accuracy than the gold data they trained on. This suggests that we can train annotators with tarnished gold, and as part of that process even improve the gold data.

Besides being valuable in its own right as a version of word sense disambiguation, this task is also a small step on the road to full frame semantic annotation. We are currently piloting the task for the next step toward full frame annotation (frame element annotation), applying the same principles of feedback and supervision.

More generally, the supervised crowdsourcing paradigm developed here explores a useful middle ground of expertise, one we believe to be suitable for many semantic annotation tasks too complex for standard transient crowdsourcing. An effective way of producing such data on a large scale using faster, less expensive methods has great potential for easing the semantic bottleneck and facilitating progress toward richer natural language understanding.

Acknowledgments

We gratefully acknowledge support from Google in the form of a Google Faculty Research Fellowship to Collin Baker. On the FrameNet team, we thank Michael Ellsworth for insights on the annotation process and gold data validation, and Warren McQuinn for gold data validation. At Google, we thank Binbin Ruan and Xiaoming Wang for their help on the UI, and Dipanjan Das, Michael Tseng, Russell Lee-Goldman, Ed Chi, Jamie Taylor, Eric Altendorf,

John Giannandrea and Amar Subramanya for useful discussion and feedback.

Thanks also to the reviewers for very thoughtful, constructive comments. Any opinions or errors are those of the authors alone.

References

Michael S. Bernstein, Greg Little, Robert C. Miller, Björn Hartmann, Mark S. Ackerman, David R. Karger, David Crowell, and Katrina Panovich. 2010. Soylent: A word processor with a crowd inside. In *Proceedings of the 23nd annual ACM symposium on User interface software and technology*, pages 313–322. ACM.

Kurt Bollacker, Colin Evans, Praveen Paritosh, Tim Sturge, and Jamie Taylor. 2008. Freebase: a collaboratively created graph database for structuring human knowledge. In *Proceedings of the 2008 ACM SIGMOD international conference on Management of data*, pages 1247–1250. ACM.

Chris Callison-Burch and Mark Dredze, editors. 2010. *Proceedings of the NAACL/HLT 2010 Workshop on Creating Speech and Language Data with Amazon's Mechanical Turk*, Los Angeles, CA, June. ACL.

David L. Chen and William B. Dolan. 2011. Building a Persistent Workforce on Mechanical Turk for Multilingual Data Collection. In *Proceedings of The 3rd Human Computation Workshop (HCOMP 2011)*, August.

Dipanjan Das, Nathan Schneider, Desai Chen, and Noah A. Smith. 2010. Probabilistic Frame-Semantic Parsing. In *Proceedings of the North American Chapter of the Association for Computational Linguistics Human Language Technologies Conference*, Los Angeles, June.

Dipanjan Das, Desai Chen, André F. T. Martins, Nathan Schneider, and Noah A. Smith. 2013. Frame-Semantic Parsing. *Computational Linguistics*, 40(1).

Charles J. Fillmore and Collin F. Baker. 2010. A Frames Approach to Semantic Analysis. In Bernd Heine and Heiko Narrog, editors, *Oxford Handbook of Linguistic Analysis*, pages 313–341. OUP.

Charles J. Fillmore. 1976. Frame semantics and the nature of language. *Annals of the New York Academy of Sciences: Conference on the Origin and Development of Language and Speech*, 280(1):20–32.

Charles J. Fillmore. 1982. Frame semantics. In *Linguistics in the Morning Calm*, pages 111–137. Hanshin Publishing Co., Seoul, South Korea.

Marco Fossati, Claudio Giuliano, and Sara Tonelli. 2013. Outsourcing FrameNet to the Crowd. In *Proceedings of the 51st Annual Meeting of the Association for Computational Linguistics (Volume 2: Short Papers)*, pages 742–747, Sofia, Bulgaria, August. Association for Computational Linguistics.

Daniel Gildea and Daniel Jurafsky. 2002. Automatic Labeling of Semantic Roles. *Computational Linguistics*, 28(3):245–288.

Jisup Hong and Collin F. Baker. 2011. How Good is the Crowd at "real" WSD? In *Proceedings of the 5th Linguistic Annotation Workshop*, pages 30–37, Portland, OR, June. ACL.

Richard Johansson and Pierre Nugues. 2006. A FrameNet-based Semantic Role Labeler for Swedish. In *Proceedings of Coling/ACL 2006*, Sydney, Australia, July 17-21.

Adam Kapelner, Krishna Kaliannan, H. Andrew Schwartz, Lyle Ungar, and Dean Foster. 2012. New Insights from Coarse Word Sense Disambiguation in the Crowd. In *Proceedings of COLING 2012: Posters*, pages 539–548, Mumbai, India, December. COLING.

Shailesh Kochhar, Stefano Mazzocchi, and Praveen Paritosh. 2010. The anatomy of a large-scale human computation engine. In *Proceedings of the acm sigkdd workshop on human computation*, pages 10–17. ACM.

Martha Palmer, Daniel Gildea, and Paul Kingsbury. 2005. The Proposition Bank: An Annotated Corpus of Semantic Roles. *Computational Linguistics*, 31(1):71–106, March.

Praveen Paritosh. 2012. Human computation must be reproducible. In *CrowdSearch*, pages 20–25.

Miriam R. L. Petruck and Gerard de Melo, editors. 2014. *Proceedings of Frame Semantics in NLP: A Workshop in Honor of Chuck Fillmore (1929-2014)*, Baltimore, MD, USA, June. Association for Computational Linguistics.

Sameer Pradhan, Eduard Hovy, Mitch Marcus, Martha Palmer, Lance Ramshaw, and Ralph Weischedel. 2007. OntoNotes: A Unified Relational Semantic Representation. *International Journal of Semantic Computing*, 1(4):405–419.

Josef Ruppenhofer, Michael Ellsworth, Miriam R. L. Petruck, Christopher R. Johnson, and Jan Scheffczyk. 2006. *FrameNet II: Extended Theory and Practice*. International Computer Science Institute, Berkeley, CA. Distributed with the FrameNet data.

Rion Snow, Brendan O'Connor, Daniel Jurafsky, and Andrew Ng. 2008. Cheap and Fast — But is it Good? Evaluating Non-Expert Annotations for Natural Language Tasks. In *Proceedings of the 2008 EMNLP*, pages 254–263, Honolulu, HI, October. ACL.

Luis von Ahn. 2013. Duolingo: Learn a language for free while helping to translate the web. In *Proceedings of the 2013 International Conference on Intelligent User Interfaces*, pages 1–2. ACM.

An Analytic and Empirical Evaluation of Return-on-Investment-Based Active Learning

Robbie Haertel, Eric K. Ringger, Paul Felt, Kevin Seppi
Department of Computer Science
Brigham Young University
Provo, Utah 84602, USA
robbie.haertel@gmail.com, ringger@cs.byu.edu,
kseppi@byu.edu, paul.lewis.felt@gmail.com

Abstract

Return-on-Investment (ROI) is a cost-conscious approach to active learning (AL) that considers both estimates of cost and of benefit in active sample selection. We investigate the theoretical conditions for successful cost-conscious AL using ROI by examining the conditions under which ROI would optimize the area under the cost/benefit curve. We then empirically measure the degree to which optimality is jeopardized in practice when the conditions are violated. The reported experiments involve an English part-of-speech annotation task. Our results show that ROI can indeed successfully reduce total annotation costs and should be considered as a viable option for machine-assisted annotation. On the basis of our experiments, we make recommendations for benefit estimators to be employed in ROI. In particular, we find that the more linearly related a benefit estimate is to the true benefit, the better the estimate performs when paired in ROI with an imperfect cost estimate. Lastly, we apply our analysis to help explain the mixed results of previous work on these questions.

1 Introduction

In active learning (AL), a sample selection algorithm sequentially chooses instances, or "samples," to be labeled/annotated by an oracle. Each annotated instance results in a measurable benefit, such as an increase in model accuracy, and incurs a specific cost, such as the time needed to obtain the label. Unfortunately some AL research has ignored the fact that instances have varying costs. Decision-theoretic approaches (e.g., Liang et al., 2009) can incorporate per-instance cost but typically ignore it during experimentation, due in part to the difficulty of subtracting cost from benefit when they are measured in different units (Donmez and Carbonell, 2008; Haertel et al., 2008). Return-on-investment (ROI) is a cost-conscious technique that avoids this requirement by selecting the instance x^* having maximum net benefit *per unit cost*, i.e.,

$$x^* = \arg\max_x \frac{benefit(x) - cost(x)}{cost(x)}. \quad (1)$$

This approach to AL was independently proposed by Donmez and Carbonell (2008), Haertel et al. (2008), and Settles et al. (2008); in addition, Tomanek and Hahn (2010) evaluated the effectiveness of ROI. Unfortunately, the published results regarding the usefulness of ROI are mixed. In addition, despite its intuitive appeal as a practical cost-conscious algorithm, there has been little theoretical justification for the ROI approach to AL.

The purpose of this paper is to provide an initial theoretical analysis of ROI that, in turn, allows us to identify the conditions needed for the successful application of ROI in a practical environment. We also empirically assess the degree to which violated conditions affect the overall performance of ROI and shed some light on the previously published results. The paper is organized as follows: related work is presented in Section 2. Section 3 examines the conditions under which ROI would be optimal. Section 4 discusses the experimental methodology. Section 5 experimentally assesses the extent to which

Proceedings of LAW IX - The 9th Linguistic Annotation Workshop, pages 11–20,
Denver, Colorado, June 5, 2015.

the conditions hold in practice – but outside the context of AL – while Section 5 explores the overall effect on AL. Finally, Section 6 presents our conclusions.

2 Related Work

The essence of active learning is to select the next "best" instance to be annotated. Naturally, the question arises: which sample selection function is optimal? Cohn et al. (1996) derive a solution for selecting the instance that minimizes model variance. A related class of solutions based on optimal experimental design uses Fisher information to select the optimal instance (Zhang and Oles, 2000). However, these approaches fail to account for problems in which instances are not equally costly to annotate.

Decision theory offers an elegant framework for (greedily) selecting the next best instance based on the utility of the instance and considering variable query costs. Some examples include Liang et al. (2009), Anderson and Moore (2005), Margineantu (2005), and Kapoor et al. (2007). In this framework, the optimal instance is the one with maximum net utility, that is, utility minus cost. However, this approach requires that utility and cost be measured in the same units. This requirement is particularly problematic when heuristics (such as entropy) are used to approximate expected utility.

Another approach, borrowed from the financial industry, is return-on-investment (ROI) (Donmez and Carbonell, 2008; Haertel et al., 2008; Settles et al., 2008). ROI is related to the decision theoretic approach (Haertel et al., 2008); however, unlike the decision theoretic approach, ROI does not require conversion between units of utility (benefit) and cost. ROI has explicitly been employed with mixed results on a variety of tasks. Donmez and Carbonell (2008) show positive results with ROI on face detection, letter recognition, spam detection, and high revenue detection tasks but do not evaluate ROI using variable instance costs. Settles et al. (2008) evaluate ROI on entity-relation tagging, speculative text classification, and information extraction. They limit themselves to an N-best approximation to entropy for the sequence labeling tasks, but in this study ROI does not outperform basic AL. Haertel et al. (2008) show positive performance of ROI on English part-of-speech tagging. Finally, Tomanek and Hahn (2010) find that ROI slightly outperforms two new cost-conscious algorithms when an appropriate benefit function is used.

3 Theoretical Analysis of ROI

The purpose of this section is to provide a bottom-up theoretical explanation of ROI. The analysis also provides a framework within which we can explain why in some previous work ROI has succeeded while in other work it has failed. This section examines Area Under the cost/benefit Curve (AUC) as a suitable objective function and then enumerates a set of conditions that, if true, would lead to ROI maximizing AUC. Within the context of a bottom-up derivation of ROI, the assumptions introduced are somewhat strong, but we dedicate the remainder of the paper to analyzing the degree to which they hold in practice and their effect on practical results.

We begin with a brief set of definitions. AL algorithms sequentially select instances from a set of unlabeled instances $\mathscr{U}$ ("the pool"). As an instance $x \in \mathscr{U}$ is annotated with label y, it results in a measurable benefit and also incurs a specific cost. For the purposes of this section, we follow previous work in assuming a single annotator and in recognizing that the benefit and cost of obtaining a particular annotation may depend on previously obtained annotations. Thus, we define *total benefit* and *cumulative cost* to be functions ($b(\cdot)$ and $c(\cdot)$, respectively) of a sequence of labeled data $L = \langle (x_1, y_1), \ldots, (x_n, y_n) \rangle$. For simplicity, we assume that the cost to annotate an instance is independent of its place in the sequence, although it can be shown that this assumption has no bearing on the final analysis. Therefore, $c(L_{1 \ldots i}) = \sum_{i'} c(L_{i'})$.

All previous work of which we are aware evaluates AL using cost/benefit curves or some derivation thereof. Cost/benefit curves (a generalization of standard learning curves) parametrically plot $b(L_{1 \ldots i})$ against $c(L_{1 \ldots i})$ for $i \in \{1, \ldots, |L|\}$. Rather than focusing on a single point, these curves capture the performance of algorithms over a range of costs. AUC represents the expected benefit across the full range of costs and generally speaking algorithms with higher AUC are more desirable. Note that Settles and Craven (2008) and Baldridge and

Osborne (2004) use AUC to evaluate AL algorithms.

We now formally define AUC. Assuming linear interpolation between discrete neighboring points, AUC is the sum of the area of the right trapezoids defined by adjacent points on the curve. Let $a_i(L)$ be the area of the ith trapezoid:

$$a_i(L) = \frac{1}{2}\left[c\left(L_{1\ldots i}\right) - c\left(L_{1\ldots i-1}\right)\right] \cdot \left[b\left(L_{1\ldots i-1}\right) + b\left(L_{1\ldots i}\right)\right] \quad (2)$$

(where $c(\emptyset) = b(\emptyset) = 0$). Then, the AUC defined by the sequence L is:

$$auc(L) = \sum_{i=1}^{|L|} a_i(L). \quad (3)$$

Maximizing AUC using AL can be seen as a sequential decision problem in which each decision consists of selecting an instance for annotation. The optimal instance to select given previous annotations L, will depend on the decision's effect on the next decision, and the effect of the second decision on the third, and so forth, until all decisions have been made. To account for this recursive dependence, we must consider entire sequences of decisions. Note that if we do not allow instances to be selected more than once from $\mathscr{U}$ we will eventually choose every instance and the number of decisions per sequence is $N = |\mathscr{U}|$.[1] Additionally, since the actual annotations that the oracle will provide are unknown, they must be considered in expectation, represented with random variables Y_i. Given a sequence of already annotated data L, one approach to maximizing AUC in expectation that accounts for this recursive effect of decisions is (see Haertel et al., 2008 for a decision-theoretic variant):

$$x_1^*, \ldots, x_N^* = \underset{x_1, \ldots, x_N}{\arg\max} \; \mathbb{E}_{Y_1 \ldots Y_N | x_1 \ldots x_N, L}\left[auc\left(L \oplus \langle (x_1, y_1) \ldots (x_N, y_N) \rangle\right)\right] \quad (4)$$

where $\oplus$ represents sequence concatenation. Although finding the optimal sequence in this way accounts for the effects each decision has on successive decisions, in fact, the sequential decision process protocol requires only the first instance in this sequence, viz., x_1^*. We then append x_1^* and the oracle's annotation for the instance y_1 to L. The result is an updated belief reflected in the expectations (via the new L) used to select the next instance.

We now derive ROI from equation 4 under the following conditions:

1. The covariance of cost and benefit is zero.
2. The cost and benefit of each instance are independent of the order in which instances are annotated.
3. Each random variable y_i (i.e., label) is conditionally independent of all other $y_{j \neq i}$, given x_i and L.
4. Cost and benefit are exact up to a scalar constant.

The reader is reminded that we do not necessarily presume these conditions to hold in practice; we briefly discuss their practicality herein and later empirically examine the degree to which they hold.

First, while it is conceivable that cost and benefit have zero covariance in some annotation problems, there are certainly cases where there may be some correlation. This correlation is especially evident in structured prediction problems, e.g., "larger" instances (e.g., long sentences) will tend to contain more information but be more costly. However, to our knowledge, the amount of correlation in such cases has not been studied previously. Second, although cost may be independent of annotation order (as implicitly assumed by previous work, e.g., Settles et al., 2008), the benefit of an instance will, in fact, usually depend on the order in which it is annotated. Consider, for example, a pool of instances in which there are several similar instances (e.g., the same word in the same context with the same part-of-speech). By annotating one of the instances, the model will likely learn what it needs from this single instance and therefore the benefit of annotating the others is greatly diminished. Third, the conditional independence assumption is similar to the assumption that benefit is independent of the order in which instances are annotated, but applies distributionally and is more mathematically precise. Finally, optimal (exact) benefit estimators are computationally intractable. While some approaches are optimal for the last decision and perform very well (e.g., Roy

[1]This limit is rarely reached in practice due to budgetary constraints, however, such a constraint does not affect the current analysis. One simply performs computation as if they were going to annotate all instances, but then only selects the best instance, repeating the process until the budget is exhausted.

and McCallum, 2001), these approaches are impractical for structured prediction tasks; we will examine the effectiveness of several heuristic benefit estimators in our empirical examination. Similarly, although cost is sometimes knowable *a priori* it often is not. However, Settles et al. (2008) showed that cost can be reliably learned in practice.

While we defer the question of the degree to which these assumptions are violated in practice to our experiments, we proceed with the analysis as if they were true to better understand the theoretical underpinnings of ROI. In the context of maximization, the scalar constants allowed by condition 4 can be ignored. The linearity property of expectations allows us to move the expectation in equation 4 inside of the sum in equation 3. The first condition then allows us to move the expectation further into the area calculation so that equation 2 becomes (omitting expectation indices for brevity):

$$a_i(L) = \frac{1}{2}\left(\mathbb{E}\left[c\left(L_{1\ldots i}\right)\right] - \mathbb{E}\left[c\left(L_{1\ldots i-1}\right)\right]\right) \cdot \left(\mathbb{E}\left[b\left(L_{1\ldots i-1}\right)\right] + \mathbb{E}\left[b\left(L_{1\ldots i}\right)\right]\right). \quad (5)$$

Condition 2 implies that $b\left(L_{1\ldots i}\right) = \sum_{i'=1}^{i} b\left(L_{i'}\right)$; applying linearity, we obtain:

$$\mathbb{E}\left[b\left(L_{1\ldots i}\right)\right] = \sum_{i'=1}^{i} \mathbb{E}_{y_{i'}|x_{1\ldots i'}, y_{1\ldots i'-1}, L}\left[b\left(L_{i'}\right)\right] \quad (6)$$

(idem. for cost). Finally, condition 3 implies that:

$$\mathbb{E}\left[b\left(L_{1\ldots i}\right)\right] = \sum_{i'=1}^{i} \mathbb{E}_{y_{i'}|x_{i'}, L}\left[b\left(L_{i'}\right)\right] \quad (7)$$

(idem. for cost). This result allows us to compute the expected cost and benefit of each instance once per iteration of active learning (as is common outside of decision theoretic frameworks). Because these quantities can be computed independently of one another, we can represent each instance x_i by a line segment with fixed width and height—the expected cost and benefit, respectively, according to the current model—and statically compute the area using these line segments.

It can be proven that, under these conditions, the sequence $x_1^*, \ldots, x_N^*$ that maximizes AUC is the sequence that is in non-strict slope-non-increasing order.[2] This is precisely the ordering provided by ROI (see equation 1). Thus, under these conditions, ROI is optimal. (Recall that typically only the first element x_1^* is annotated, models are updated, then the process repeats).

4 Experimental Methodology

In this section, we describe our methodology for empirically assessing the degree to which the conditions of Section 3 hold in practice and define what we mean by practical contexts. Space constraints limit our experiments to a single task: English part-of-speech (POS) tagging on the POS-tagged Wall Street Journal text in the Penn Treebank version 3 (Marcus et al., 1993).

For this task, we employ Maximum Entropy Markov Models (MEMMs) to model the distribution of tags given words, $p(\mathbf{t}|\mathbf{w})$. The model choice is motivated primarily by the speed of retraining. AL typically begins with a small set of randomly selected instances: we use 100 instances annotated "from scratch" (i.e., without AL). However, we do account for the cost incurred by annotating the seed set using the cost simulation described below. Each experiment is run 5 times with a different random seed. For TVE (a committee-based approach; see below), we use a committee size of 5 and train all members in parallel. We additionally score instances in parallel, using 4 threads; the remaining processors are used for training the cost model, evaluating benefit, and garbage collection. For non-committee methods, we found that extra scoring threads do not improve results. All simulations are run on dual hex-core Intel Westmere 2.67 GHz CPUs equipped with 24 GB of RAM.

4.1 Active Learning Simulation

We are interested in empirically testing ROI outside of the clean mathematical environment implied by Section 2. However, the number of experiments we performed necessitated running AL in simulation. Nevertheless, we employ various techniques to keep the simulation as true-to-life as possible.

Most importantly, each time we select an instance for an annotator to annotate, we simulate the length of time the annotator will need to annotate the instance (i.e., the cost) using Ringger et al.'s (2008) linear cost model derived from user study data. This

[2]A detailed proof sketch is provided by Haertel (2013).

model assumes that instances are pre-annotated using an automatic annotation model, and the task of the annotator is to correct the errors from the predictive model. The length of time required to annotate a sequence **w**, pre-annotated with hypothesis tags **t** and true tags **y**, is:

$$cost(\mathbf{w},\mathbf{y},\mathbf{t}) = \alpha + \beta \cdot |\mathbf{w}| + \gamma \cdot \sum_{i=1}^{|\mathbf{y}|} \mathbb{1}(y_i \neq t_i) \quad (8)$$

The sum represents the number of tags from the pre-annotation that the annotator changed. We estimate the parameters of the linear model ($\alpha = 50.534, \beta = 2.638, \gamma = 4.440$) using the user-study data from Ringger et al. (2008). To add noise to the simulated cost, we generate a random deviate from a shifted Gamma distribution having mean equal to the time predicted by the model, a variance of 5063.35 (the empirical variance of the user-study data), and a shift of 10.0 (near the minimum time). We chose a (shifted) Gamma distribution because the data from the user study appear to be Gamma distributed; as an added benefit, the generated values are guaranteed to always be positive.

In our experiments, we simulate the scenario in which annotators request instances to annotate on demand, e.g., by requesting work on a crowd-sourcing service; we call this annotator-initiated AL. This AL contrasts to the alternative in which the algorithm spends time determining the next instance to be annotated and then sends the instance to an annotator to perform the work. We call this latter paradigm learner-initiated AL. The usual implicit assumption in learner-initiated AL is that no cost is incurred between the time the machine sends a request to the annotator and the time the annotator actually starts the work. This assumption is unrealistic, despite being the approach to AL simulation in previous work; real annotation projects are annotator-initiated (e.g., crowd-sourcing). The "Parallel No-Wait" active learning framework introduced by Haertel et al. (2010) follows the more true-to-life annotator-initiated paradigm and provides the guarantee that annotators never need to wait for an instance. We further extend the framework by scoring instances, training the cost model, and training the tagging model in parallel.

Realistic annotation environments also often involve multiple annotators (cf. Donmez and Carbonell, 2008). We take an incremental step towards allowing multiple annotators by assuming that all annotators are infallible and have the same distribution over the amount of time to annotate any given instance. Under these circumstances, each instance needs to be annotated only once, and annotators are interchangeable. We simulate in real time 20 tireless oracles who continuously and simultaneously annotate instances for 50 hours each. In contrast to learner-initiated AL, this represents the *worst* possible case for the no-wait framework since models are maximally out-of-date. Thus, this simulation provides an empirical lower bound on the AUC.

4.2 Cost Estimation

The denominator in ROI is an estimate of the cost to obtain a label for the instance being scored. This estimate is not to be confused with the simulation of annotation times for selected instances, as described in the previous section. The cost estimate (as used in ROI) is computed over many instances to help select an informative instance when the annotator requests one. Once the instance has been selected, we then (noisily) simulate what it would cost for the annotator to annotate it, as described above. For algorithms that estimate cost as the time to annotate an instance, we learn a linear model of the same form as equation 8. The coefficients are learned using the data obtained during AL (ultimately obtained from the noisy simulation). However, since we do not know which of the automatically pre-annotated tags are incorrect during estimation, we must compute the expected number of incorrect tags in place of the sum in equation 8.

The results of our experiments are potentially better than in practice since our cost estimate has exactly the same form as the simulated true cost. However, the results are still useful because (1) the gamma-distributed noise in the true cost has high variance and (2) the estimate is computed in expectation (using the learned model).

4.3 Benefit Estimation

ROI's numerator is an estimate of the benefit of obtaining a label for a given instance. As previously mentioned, optimal benefit estimators are impractical for structured learning problems; uncertainty-based heuristics are typically employed instead. Let **t** represent a sequence of tag assignments for sentence **w**. Drawing mostly from previous studies, we consider the following:

Constant (CONST) assumes all instances have equal benefit.

Approximate Token Entropy (ATE) (Settles and Craven, 2008) approximates the true sequence entropy as the sum of the entropy of the individual marginal distributions $p(t_i|\mathbf{w})$. The marginal distributions can in turn be approximated as $p(t_i|\mathbf{w}) \approx p(t_i|t^*_{i-1}, \mathbf{w})$ where t^*_{i-i} is the $(i-1)th$ tag in the Viterbi best sequence $\mathbf{t}^*$; a beam search can significantly reduce computation.

Monte Carlo Entropy (MCE) uses a Monte Carlo approximation to compute the entropy, i.e., $\mathbb{E}[-\log p(\mathbf{t}|\mathbf{w})]$, using samples taken from $\mathbf{t}|\mathbf{w}$ (the trained MEMM).

N-best Sequence Entropy (NSE) (Settles and Craven, 2008) approximates sequence entropy by computing the entropy of the top-n sequences, where the probabilities are re-normalized to sum to unity.

Least Confidence (LC) (Culotta and McCallum, 2005), in contrast to entropy, is not concerned with the distribution over the entire support, but rather focuses on the best option and its complement (the rest of the support). It is the probability of being wrong, i.e., $1 - \max_{\mathbf{t}} p(\mathbf{t}|\mathbf{w})$.

Negative Max Log Probability (NMLP) (Haertel et al., 2010) is defined as $-\max_{\mathbf{t}} \log p(\mathbf{t}|\mathbf{w})$; it ranks instances the same as LC but with different scores under the assumption that the relationship between probabilities and change in accuracy is logarithmic rather than linear.

Token Vote Entropy (TVE) (Engelson and Dagan, 1996) uses a committee of classifiers trained from bootstrapped samples of the annotated data. For each word, each committee member votes for the tag it predicts for its word; the entropy of the distribution over votes is summed over each word in the sentence.

5 From Theory to Practice: To What Degree Are the Conditions Met?

In this section, we empirically test some of the conditions from the preceding analysis in practical contexts. For the purposes of this work, we are mostly interested in examining conditions 1 and 4. While condition 3 (conditional independence) is assumed in most previous work, we leave quantification of the effects of violating this condition and the related condition 2 to future work.

For these experiments, it is necessary to estimate true benefit and cost. Due to the complexity of so doing, we compute the various metrics along a *passive* learning curve (i.e., without AL). We compute the true cost of each instance as described in Section 4.1. In order to estimate the true benefit of a particular instance at a particular point on the learning curve, we assume that the true benefit of an instance is the change in held-out accuracy that would result from incorporating the instance with its annotation into the training data; we ignore the effects of future choices. We compute the change in accuracy (benefit) by adding the instance and its true label to the training data, retraining the model, and then computing the model's new accuracy on the held-out set. The process is repeated to compute the true benefit of at least 1,000 instances and the statistics noted below are averaged over 5 random initial training sets. We use one standard error as a simple measure of statistical significance.

Is the covariance of cost and benefit zero? Using the aforementioned methodology, we compute Pearson's correlation coefficient (a normalized form of covariance) between benefit and cost. As seen in figure 1a, true benefit and cost have virtually no correlation when model quality is high, and is only weakly correlated in the early stages. Thus, condition 1 roughly holds.

To what extent is the cost estimate a scalar multiple of true cost? Using the technique mentioned above, we produce pairs of true cost and estimated cost at various locations along the learning curve and compute R^2 values of a linear model estimated with the y-intercept fixed at zero. Pearson's correlation coefficient is inappropriate since it would allow for the cost estimate to be shifted in addition to being scaled. An R^2 of 1.0 would indicate that the cost estimate was an exact scalar multiple of the true cost, while a zero would indicate no scalar relationship. We repeat this test with differing amounts of variance in the simulated cost, which allows us to assess the effect of poor cost models (good models will account for most of the variance). The results are shown in Figure 1b. The exponential decay

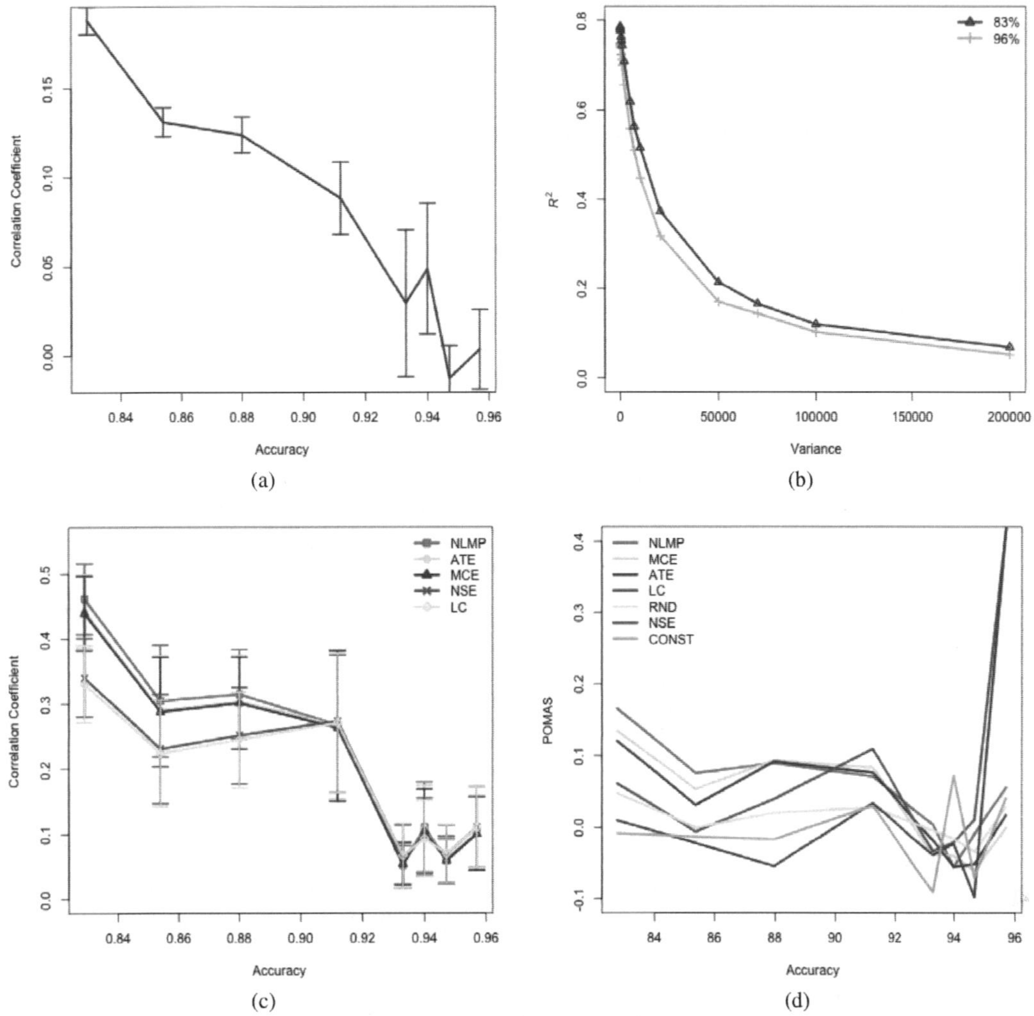

Figure 1: At various points on the learning curve: (a) correlation between true cost and true benefit (b) R^2 values representing the degree to which the cost estimate is a scalar multiple of the true cost, for varying amounts of variance in the noise model at two points on the learning curve (83% and 96%). (c) R^2 values representing the degree to which various benefit estimators are scalar multiples of true benefit (d) POMAS of the top-20 instances. Error bars represent one standard error.

as variance increases underscores the importance of accounting for as much variance as possible in the cost model. We found the R^2 values to be around 0.745 and 0.785 when the variance was equal to that of the aforementioned user study (and the one used through the remainder of the experiments). We note that these numbers may be overly optimistic given the similarity between the model used to simulate annotation times and that used to estimate cost. As a point of reference, Settles et al. (2008) and Arora and Nyberg (2011) report R^2 values for cost models for *different* tasks on the order of 0.3–0.4. Even these values indicate some scalar relationship between true and estimated cost as per condition 4.

To what extent are various benefits estimators scalar multiples of true benefit? We repeat the experiment described for cost, but reporting the R^2 values for the fit between true benefit and several benefit estimators; Figure 1c depicts the results. Although the R^2 values are much worse than for the cost estimate, they are still reasonable. Most of the separation of algorithms (where it exists statistically) occurs during the beginning stages of learning. NMLP has a slight (though not statistically significant) advantage over ATE and MCE while all three are more linearly related to true benefit than NSE and LC. Once the model achieves 91% accuracy, there is no separation. The results suggest that condition 4 holds weakly for benefit estimators.

Are instances with the highest slopes being selected? The success of ROI depends on its ability to select the instance with the highest slope. Using the aforementioned setup, we compute the largest slope of the candidate instances on the basis of estimated benefit and cost and divide it by the largest slope according to the true values; we call this value the Percentage of Maximum Attainable Slope (POMAS). Since multiple instances can be selected using the same model in the no-wait framework, we repeat this procedure for the second highest slopes, etc., for the top-20 slopes and average them. The results are in Figure 1d. The separation between algorithms at the beginning mirror those of Figure 1c. We note that there is ample room for improvement even amongst the best algorithms we tried.

6 Active Learning Results and Discussion

The previous experiments were conducted outside of the context of AL in order to gain insight into how well the conditions of section 2 are met in practice. However, the most direct evaluation is the comparison of the actual quantity of interest, AUC, in the type of practical AL defined above. We compare normalized AUC (expected benefit) for several benefit estimators and two cost estimates and discuss the results in light of the previous section and the theory from Section 2.

Although not predicted by the theory per se, we would expect AUC to decrease with degradations in the cost and/or benefit estimates. First, we compare the AUC when using the true cost in the ROI calculations (thus satisfying one half of condition 4) and compare the results to using estimated cost learned during AL. The results are displayed in Figure 2. Interestingly, when cost is exactly known (perfectly predictable), all estimators–even CONST–readily outperform the random base-

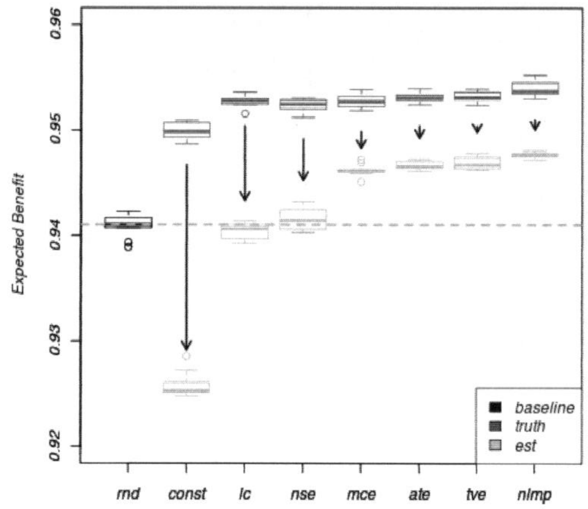

Figure 2: Expected benefit (normalized AUC) for various benefit estimators with true and estimated costs. The median baseline performance (rnd) is depicted as a dashed line and is the same for both experiments. Estimated cost affects the benefit estimates to different degrees.

line. Furthermore, the difference between most of the estimators (except perhaps CONST) is not statistically significant, which suggests that a good cost estimate may be capable of overcoming deficiencies in even very poor benefit estimators like CONST. Not surprisingly, all algorithms perform worse when using the learned estimate of cost during AL (indicated by the downward arrows), even though the MSE of the learned cost models was high–on the order of the variance in the simulated times.

Further support that AUC depends on the quality of estimates comes from the fact that the performance of the various algorithms exactly follows the quality of the corresponding benefit estimate (see Figures 1c and 1d). In fact, LC and NSE do no better than random and CONST does much worse. Upon further examination, we found a common property between these benefit estimators, namely, that most scores fall within an extremely narrow range; i.e., there was very little difference between the (benefit) scores of most instances (CONST being the extreme case). NSE differs from the other entropy estimates primarily in the re-normalization. Due to their nature, structured prediction problems have very large supports which tend to have long tails. Therefore the top-n probabilities grossly underrepresent these distributions and renormalization makes scores very similar to each other—even for instances of differing lengths. Similarly, although LC and NMLP would rank instances the same (before dividing by cost; dividing by cost alters the rankings), the *log* in NLMP produces greater spread in the score. Since the cost estimates are better dispersed, they tend to dominate ROI for these "low-spread" benefit estimators. To illustrate, consider the extreme case of CONST by substituting an arbitrary constant for benefit in equation 1: instances are selected lowest-expected-cost first. On our particular task, this scenario is particularly undesirable as the shortest sentences are nearly always the cheapest but disproportionately information poor (a contributing factor to the non-zero correlation). In more general terms, as the spread in the benefit estimates approaches zero (as in CONST), the cost estimates increasingly become the discriminating factor. While this behavior is correct for perfect benefit and cost estimates, it is problematic when condition 4 is violated.

The results also highlight the fact that expensive scoring algorithms are naturally penalized in annotator-initiated AL. The relatively expensive sampling in MCE leads to slightly lower performance than cheaper entropy estimates (ATE); the relatively cheap NMLP outperforms TVE, which incurs the expense of multiple models.

The mixed results of previous work are explainable based on our analysis. While condition 4 *requires* that cost and benefit estimators be scalar multiples of the true values, our empirical results suggest that better estimates yield higher AUC. We have explained why NSE has poor mathematical properties for structured learning tasks and is therefore expected to produce relatively low AUC, hence the negative results on the structured prediction tasks of Settles et al. (2008). In contrast, the authors report positive results on a standard classification problem using exact entropy calculations, coinciding with our results in which the good (i.e., non-NSE) entropy estimators are good estimators. We have also explained the poor properties of LC for structured prediction; the results of Tomanek and Hahn (2010) present further empirical evidence. Interestingly, they find that exponentiating LC leads to positive results. Mathematically, $exp(\beta(1-p))$ behaves similarly to $-log(p)$ (NLMP) in that they both separate scores that are close together—the former much more so than the latter, especially for probabilities of the very low magnitudes seen in structured prediction problems. This separation gives the benefit estimate more influence relative to cost as compared to LC. In sum, the negative results of previous work are due to poor benefit estimators, in particular LC and NSE; in contrast, positive results are due to better benefit estimators.

7 Conclusions and Future Work

ROI-based AL successfully reduces annotation costs in practice by maximizing the area under the cost/benefit curve. We have provided an initial theoretical justification for ROI-based AL in a bottom-up fashion. We have shown empirically that, for our task, true benefit and cost have little-to-no correlation when model quality is high; cost estimates have a scalar relationship to true cost; similarly for benefit estimates, though to a lesser degree; and the estimators that demonstrated the most scalar relationships to the truth resulted in higher AUC.

Although we focused our empirical analysis on a single task, other studies have applied ROI to several tasks and problem types, and their results are consistent with our analysis. As a result of this work, we recommend that practitioners carefully select their benefit and cost estimators, ensuring that they are "good" estimators for their task as described above. Particular attention should be paid to the cost estimator: even trivial benefit estimators out-performed random with a perfect cost estimator. Also note that estimators (e.g. NSE and LC) that produce scores with relatively little "spread" should be avoided. Future work could consider using a small set of annotated data to estimate how scalar the relationship of the estimators are to true benefit and cost before annotation begins.

Our empirical results suggest that deficiencies in even the best benefit estimators lead to the selection of suboptimal instances. Future work could focus on directly and tractably estimating true cost and benefit for structured prediction problems, and automatically tuning heuristic estimators to match true benefit during AL. Future work may also benefit from investigating a different set of conditions for simplifying equation 4.

References

Brigham Anderson and Andrew Moore. 2005. Active learning for hidden Markov models: Objective functions and algorithms. In *Proceedings of the 22nd International Conference on Machine Learning*, pages 9–16.

Shilpa Arora and Eric Nyberg. 2011. Assessing benefit from feature feedback in active learning for text classification. In *Proceedings of the Fifteenth Conference on Computational Natural Language Learning*, pages 106–114. Association for Computational Linguistics.

Jason Baldridge and Miles Osborne. 2004. Active learning and the total cost of annotation. *Proceedings of the Conference on Empirical Methods in Natural Language Processing.*

David A. Cohn, Zoubin Ghahramani, and Michael I. Jordan. 1996. Active learning with statistical models. *Journal of Artificial Intelligence Research*, 4:129–145.

Aron Culotta and Andrew McCallum. 2005. Reducing labeling effort for structured prediction tasks. In *Proceedings of the National Conference on Artificial Intelligence*, volume 20, page 746.

Pinar Donmez and Jaime G. Carbonell. 2008. Proactive learning: Cost-sensitive active learning with multiple imperfect oracles. In *Proceeding of the 17th ACM Conference on Information and Knowledge Management*, pages 619–628. ACM.

Sean P. Engelson and Ido Dagan. 1996. Minimizing manual annotation cost in supervised training from corpora. In *Proceedings of the 34th Annual Meeting on Association for Computational Linguistics*, pages 319–326.

Robbie A. Haertel, Kevin D. Seppi, Eric K. Ringger, and James L. Carroll. 2008. Return on investment for active learning. In *Proceedings of the Neural Information Processing Systems Workshop on Cost Sensitive Learning.*

Robbie Haertel, Paul Felt, Eric Ringger, and Kevin Seppi. 2010. Parallel active learning: Eliminating wait time with minimal staleness. In *Proceedings of the HLT-NAACL 2010 Workshop on Active Learning for Natural Language Processing*, pages 33–41. Association for Computational Linguistics.

Robbie A. Haertel. 2013. *Practical Cost-Conscious Active Learning for Data Annotation in Annotator-Initiated Environments.* dissertation, Brigham Young University.

Ashish Kapoor, Eric Horvitz, and Sumit Basu. 2007. Selective supervision: Guiding supervised learning with decision-theoretic active learning. In *Proceedings of the International Joint Conferences on Artificial Intelligence.*

Percy Liang, Michael I. Jordan, and Dan Klein. 2009. Learning from measurements in exponential families. In *Proceedings of the 26th Annual International Conference on Machine Learning*, pages 641–648. ACM.

Mitchell P. Marcus, Mary Ann Marcinkiewicz, and Beatrice Santorini. 1993. Building a large annotated corpus of English: The Penn Treebank. *Computational Linguistics*, 19(2):313–330.

Dragos D. Margineantu. 2005. Active cost-sensitive learning. In *Proceedings of the International Joint Conferences on Artificial Intelligence*, volume 19, page 1622.

Eric Ringger, Marc Carmen, Robbie Haertel, Kevin Seppi, Deryle Londsale, Peter McClanahan, James Carroll, and Noel Ellison. 2008. Assessing the costs of machine-assisted corpus annotation through a user study. In *Proceedings of the International Conference on Language Resources and Evaluation.*

Nicholas Roy and Andrew McCallum. 2001. Toward optimal active learning through sampling estimation of error reduction. In *Proceedings of the Eighteenth International Conference on Machine Learning*, pages 441–448.

Burr Settles and Mark Craven. 2008. An analysis of active learning strategies for sequence labeling tasks. In *Proceedings of the Conference on Empirical Methods in Natural Language Processing*, pages 1070–1079. Association for Computational Linguistics.

Burr Settles, Mark Craven, and Lewis Friedland. 2008. Active learning with real annotation costs. In *Proceedings of the Neural Information Processing Systems Workshop on Cost-Sensitive Learning*, pages 1069–1078.

Katrin Tomanek and Udo Hahn. 2010. A comparison of models for cost-sensitive active learning. In *Proceedings of the 23rd International Conference on Computational Linguistics: Posters*, pages 1247–1255. Association for Computational Linguistics.

Tong Zhang and Frank J. Oles. 2000. The value of unlabeled data for classification problems. In *Proceedings of the Seventeenth International Conference on Machine Learning, (Langley, P., ed.)*, pages 1191–1198.

Annotating genericity: a survey, a scheme, and a corpus

Annemarie Friedrich[1] **Alexis Palmer**[2] **Melissa Peate Sørensen**[1] **Manfred Pinkal**[1]

[1]Department of Computational Linguistics, Universität des Saarlandes, Germany
{afried,melissap,pinkal}@coli.uni-saarland.de

[2]Institut für Maschinelle Sprachverarbeitung, Universität Stuttgart, Germany
alexis.palmer@ims.uni-stuttgart.de

Abstract

Generics are linguistic expressions that make statements about or refer to kinds, or that report regularities of events. *Non-generic* expressions make statements about particular individuals or specific episodes. Generics are treated extensively in semantic theory (Krifka et al., 1995). In practice, it is often hard to decide whether a referring expression is *generic* or *non-generic*, and to date there is no data set which is both large and satisfactorily annotated. Such a data set would be valuable for creating automatic systems for identifying generic expressions, in turn facilitating knowledge extraction from natural language text. In this paper we provide the next steps for such an annotation endeavor. Our contributions are: (1) we survey the most important previous projects annotating genericity, focusing on resources for English; (2) with a new agreement study we identify problems in the annotation scheme of the largest currently-available resource (ACE-2005); and (3) we introduce a linguistically-motivated annotation scheme for marking both clauses and their subjects with regard to their genericity. (4) We present a corpus of MASC (Ide et al., 2010) and Wikipedia texts annotated according to our scheme, achieving substantial agreement.

1 Introduction

This paper addresses the question of distinguishing clauses or noun phrases (NPs) that convey information about particular entities or situations, as in example (1a), from those which convey general information about kinds, see example (1b).

(1) (a) Simba is in danger. ***(non-generic)***
(b) Lions live for 10–14 years. ***(generic)***

Making this distinction is important for NLP tasks that aim to disentangle information about particular events or entities from general information about classes, kinds, or particular individuals, such as question answering or knowledge base population. Our present work targets the current lack of a large and satisfactorily-annotated data set for genericity, which is a prerequisite for research aiming to automatically identify these linguistic phenomena.

Krifka et al. (1995) report the central results in semantic theory on *genericity*. Several phenomena have been studied within this research field: one is *reference to a kind*, which is a NP-level property. The form of the NP itself (definite, indefinite, ...) is not sufficient to make this distinction (Carlson, 1977; Chierchia, 1998); the interpretation of the NP depends on the clause in which it appears, see (2).

(2) The lion is a predatory cat. ***(kind-referring)***
The lion escaped from the zoo. ***(non-generic)***

Characterizing sentences are another phenomenon studied under the heading of genericity. They may be *lexically characterizing*, as in (3a) and (3b), or *habitual* as in (3c) and (3d). Habitual sentences describe regularly occurring episodes rather than specific ones. Characterizing sentences as in (3) may relate to a kind (*lions*), or to a particular individual (*John*).

(3) (a) Lions have manes.
(b) John is tall.
(c) Lions eat meat.
(d) John drives to work.

Proceedings of LAW IX - The 9th Linguistic Annotation Workshop, pages 21–30,
Denver, Colorado, June 5, 2015.

Statements about kinds, such as example (3a), are not rendered false by the existence of counter-examples. If we encountered a vegetarian lion, it would still be true that a *typical* lion eats meat. Such sentences have been analyzed as referring to a kind instead of a set of entities (Carlson, 1977), or as containing a 'generic' quantifier (Krifka et al., 1995). Similarly, habitual sentences such as (3d) are not rendered false by exceptions.

As the linguistic manifestations of both generic and non-generic clauses (and NPs) are quite diverse, automatic discrimination between generic and non-generic information is a highly-challenging task, and annotated resources are necessary for making progress. Existing corpora for genericity focus on different aspects of genericity or related phenomena.

In this paper we provide a comprehensive survey of existing resources for computational treatment of genericity (Section 2). Section 3 presents an agreement study for ACE-2005, the largest annotation project regarding genericity of NPs to date, highlighting problems in their annotation scheme.

In Section 4, we introduce a linguistically motivated annotation scheme for marking genericity. We focus both on whether a clause makes a characterizing statement about a kind and whether its subject refers to a kind, eliminating some of the uncertainties in some previously-proposed schemes. Our scheme does not address whether a clause is habitual or not, leaving this question to future work. We apply our scheme to several sections of the Manually Annotated SubCorpus (MASC) of the Open American National Corpus (Ide et al., 2010) and to Wikipedia texts, mostly reaching substantial agreement.

2 Survey: annotating genericity in English

Existing resources treat both NP- (Section 2.1) and clause-level (Section 2.2) phenomena related to genericity. For each approach, we explain the annotation scheme, discuss its relation to theoretical concepts, and describe the data labeled. Table 1 gives a summary.

2.1 NP-level annotations

Section 2.1.1 describes corpora from the Automatic Content Extraction (ACE) program (Doddington et al., 2004); other NP-level approaches are described in Section 2.1.2.

2.1.1 ACE entity class annotations

The research objective of the ACE program (1999-2008) was the detection and characterization of entities, relations and events in natural text (Linguistic Data Consortium, 2000). All entity mentions receive an *entity class* label indicating their genericity status. Of the corpora described here, the ACE corpora have been the most widely used for recent research on automatically identifying generic NPs (Reiter and Frank, 2010). The annotation guidelines developed over time; we describe both the initial guidelines of ACE-2 and those from ACE-2005.

The **ACE-2 corpus** (Mitchell et al., 2003) includes 40106 annotated entity mentions in 520 newswire and broadcast documents. The annotation guidelines give no formal definition of genericity; annotators are asked to determine whether each entity refers to "any member of the set in question" (**generic**) or rather "some particular, identifiable member of that set" (**specific/non-generic**).[1] This leads to a mix of constructions being marked as generic: types of entities (*Good students do all the reading*), generalizations across a set of entities (*Purple houses are really ugly*), hypothetical entities (*If a person steps over the line,...*) and negated mentions (*I saw no one*). Suggested attributes of entities are marked as generic (*John seems to be a nice person*), but a 'positive assertion test' leads to marking both NPs (*Joe* and *a nice guy*) as specific in examples like (*Joe is a nice guy*). Neither of these two cases (*be a nice person / be a nice guy*) is in fact an entity mention; they are rather predicative uses.

The guidelines for genericity were redefined for annotation of the **ACE-2005 Multilingual Training Corpus** (Walker et al., 2006), which contains news, broadcast news, broadcast conversation, forum and weblog texts as well as transcribed conversational telephone speech. In contrast to ACE-2, the ACE-2005 annotation manual[2] clearly defines mentions as kind-referring or not, using the labels GEN (generic)

[1] See "Entity Detection Tracking and Metonymy Annotation Guidelines, Version 2.5.1", available from LDC: `https://catalog.ldc.upenn.edu/docs/LDC2003T11/`

[2] See "ACE English Annotation Guidelines for Entities, Version 5.6.6" (available from LDC) or 2008's version 6.6.

Corpus	Level	Scheme	Amount
ACE-2	NP	generic, specific	40K entity mentions
ACE-2005	NP	GEN, SPC, USP, NEG	40K entity mentions
ECB+	NP	GEN, non-GEN	12.5K entity mentions
GNOME	NP	generic-yes, generic-no	900 clauses
Herbelot & Copestake	NP	ONE, SOME, MOST, ALL, QUANT	300 subject mentions
CFD	NP	GENERIC_KIND, GENERIC_INDIVIDUAL	3422 NPs (131 generic)
Mathew & Katz	clause	habitual, episodic	1052 sentences
Louis & Nenkova	clause	general, specific	894 sentences
MASC	NP, clause	GEN_gen, NON-GEN_gen, NON-GEN_non-gen	20K clauses
WikiGenerics	NP, clause		10K clauses

Table 1: **Survey of genericity-annotated corpora** *for English*, including our new corpus.

and SPC (specific/non-generic) respectively.

The new guidelines also introduce two additional entity class labels for non-attributive mentions. Negatively quantified entities that refer to the empty set of the kind mentioned (*There are no confirmed suspects yet*) receive the label NEG. The label USP (underspecified) is used for non-generic nonspecific reference, these cases include quantified NPs in modal, future, conditional, hypothetical, negated, uncertain or question contexts. USP also covers 'truly ambiguous cases' that have both generic and non-generic readings (*The economic boom is providing new opportunities for women in New Delhi*), and cases where the author mentions an entity whose identity would be 'difficult to locate' (*Officials reported ...*). In our opinion, the latter interferes with the definition of SPC as marking cases where the entity referred to is a particular object in the real world, even if the author does not know its identity (*At least four people were injured*). The breadth of the USP category causes problems with consistency of application (see Section 3).

The ACE annotation scheme has also been applied in the **Newsreader** project.[3] The **ECB+ corpus** (Cybulska and Vossen, 2014) is an extension of EventCorefBank (ECB), a corpus of news articles marked with event coreference information (Bejan and Harabagiu, 2010). ECB+ annotates entity mentions according to ACE-2005, but collapses the three non-GEN labels into a single category. Roughly 12500 event participant mentions are annotated, some doubly and some singly. Agreement statistics for genericity are not reported.

[3] `www.newsreader-project.eu`

2.1.2 Other corpora annotated at the NP-level

The resources surveyed here apply carefully-defined notions of genericity but are too small to be feasible machine learning training data.

The question of whether an NP is generic or not arises in the research context of coreference resolution. Some approaches mark coreference only for non-generic mentions (Hovy et al., 2006; Hinrichs et al., 2004); others include generic mentions (Poesio, 2004), or take care not to mix coreference chains between generic and non-generic mentions (Björkenstam and Byström, 2012). Björkelund et al. (2014) mark genericity in a corpus of German with both coreference and information-status annotations. Nedoluzhko (2013) survey the treatment of genericity phenomena within coreference resolution research; they provide a complete overview. In short, they argue that a consistent definition of genericity is lacking and report on their annotation scheme for Czech as applied to the Prague Dependency TreeBank (Böhmová et al., 2003).

The **GNOME corpus** (Poesio, 2004) is a coreference corpus with genericity annotations; NPs are marked with the attributes `generic-yes` or `generic-no`. Poesio et al. report that their annotators found it hard to decide how to mark references to substances (*A table made of wood*) and quantified NPs. Similar to our experience, they found it helpful to have annotators first try to identify generic sentences, and then determine this attribute of the NP. They report an agreement of $\kappa = 0.82$ on their corpus, which consists of 900 finite clauses from descriptions of museum objects, pharmaceutical leaflets and dialogues.

Coming from a formal semantic perspective, Herbelot and Copestake (2010) and Herbelot and Copestake (2011) describe an approach to treating **ambiguously quantified NPs**. This annotation effort aims to produce resources for the task of determining the extent to which the semantic properties ascribed to a given NP in context apply to the members of that class. For example, the statement *Cats are mammals* describes a property of *all* cats, where *Cats have four legs* is true only for most cats. The scheme, which includes the labels ONE, SOME, MOST, ALL and QUANT (for explicitly quantified NPs), is applied to 300 subject-verb-object triples from sentences randomly extracted from Wikipedia. Annotators are shown the sentence and the triple. κ ranges from 0.88 and 0.81 for QUANT and ONE to values between 0.44 and 0.51 for the other classes.

Bhatia et al. (2014b) present an annotation scheme for **Communicative Functions of Definiteness**, intended to cover the many semantic and pragmatic functions conveyed by choices regarding definiteness across languages of the world. The scheme has been applied to 3422 English NPs contained in texts from four genres. Their typology includes two categories relevant to our survey: GENERIC_KIND_LEVEL applies to utterances predicating over an entire class, like *Dinosaurs are extinct*. GENERIC_INDIVIDUAL_LEVEL is for predications applying to the individual members of a class or kind, such as *Cats have fur*. Across 1202 annotated NPs for an inter-annotator agreement study, the two annotators used the GENERIC_INDIVIDUAL_LEVEL label 45 times and 30 times, respectively, with agreement in 29 cases. Neither used the GENERIC_KIND_LEVEL. The entire corpus contains just 131 NPs labeled with GENERIC_INDIVIDUAL_LEVEL and none with GENERIC_KIND_LEVEL (Bhatia et al., 2014a).

The question of genericity has also been addressed in cognitive science (Prasada, 2000). Gelman and Tardif (1998) study the usage of generic NPs cross-linguistically for English and Chinese in child-directed speech. They annotate kind-referring NPs as generic. They report agreement as the fraction of items on which the annotators agreed at over 99%, but given that their data set has fewer than 1% generic NPs, this statistic does not allow us to estimate how well annotators agreed.

2.2 Clause-level annotations

The two resources described in this section are the only we know of which mark phenomena related to genericity on clauses of text.

Annotating habituality. Mathew and Katz (2009) conduct a study on automatically distinguishing *habitual* from *episodic* sentences. Habitual sentences are taken to be sentences whose main verb is lexically dynamic, but which do not refer to particular events (see for example (3)), and may have generic or non-generic subjects. Their singly-annotated data set, from which they excluded verb types with skewed class distributions, comprises 1052 examples covering 57 verb stems. Their data set is not publicly available.

General vs. specific sentences. Louis and Nenkova (2011) describe a method for automatic classification of sentences as *general* or *specific*. *General* sentences are loosely defined as those which make "broad statements about a topic," while *specific* sentences convey more detailed information. This distinction is not immediately related to the phenomena treated as generics in the literature. Kind-referring subjects can occur in both *general* (4a) and *specific* (4b) sentences; *general* sentences can also have non-kind-referring subjects (4c).

(4) *(a) Climatologists and policy makers, ..., need to ponder such complexities... (**general**)*
*(b) Solid silicon compounds are already familiar – as rocks, glass, ... (**specific**)*
*(c) A handful of serious attempts have been made to eliminate ... diseases. (**general**)*

3 ACE-2005: an agreement study

In this section we investigate some problems with the ACE annotation scheme via a study of annotator agreement. The data was first labeled by two annotators independently, then adjudicated by a senior annotator. To our knowledge, agreement numbers on this task have not been published to date. In order to assess both the quality of the data and the difficulty of the task, we compute inter-annotator agreement as follows. Using the 533 documents from the adjudicated data set that were marked by two annotators in the first step, we compute Cohen's κ (Cohen, 1960) for entity class annotations over the four labels SPC, GEN, USP and NEG.

Intuitions about NP genericity are most reliable for subject position as other argument positions involve additional difficulties (Link, 1995). To get a better sense of the difficulty of annotating subjects compared to that for other argument positions, we compute agreement over mentions whose (manually marked) head is the grammatical subject of some other node in a dependency graph (including any dependency type containing `subj`). We obtain dependency graphs using the Stanford parser (Klein and Manning, 2002).

An additional complication in entity mention annotation is determining the mention span. Because spans are not pre-marked in the ACE corpora but identified independently by each annotator, we compute κ only over all exactly-matching entity mention spans for the two annotators. For all mentions, annotators mark about 90% of spans marked by the other annotator. For subject mentions, this number is even higher, at about 95%. The spans of the remaining mentions overlap for the two annotators. We exclude them from this study as we cannot be sure that the two mention spans refer to the same entity.

Discussion. Table 2 shows the confusion matrices of labels for the all-mentions-case and the subjects-only case. In both cases, confusion between SPC and GEN is acceptable, but confusion between USP and both SPC and GEN is rather high. For example, in the case of subjects, annotator 1 tags 652 mentions as GEN that annotator 2 marks USP, but the two of them only agree on 597 mentions to be GEN. Although it may be useful to create a separate category for unclear or underspecified cases, the definition of USP is not yet clear-cut and compounded with lack of *specificity*, which refers to whether the speaker presumably knows the referent's identity or not. Even if the identity of a referent may be 'difficult to locate' (as in *Officials reported...*). The clause certainly does not make a statement about the *kind* 'official'; instead, it expresses an existential statement (*There are officials who reported...*). The definition of SPC states that the reader does not necessarily have to know the identity of the entity, possibly making the distinction hard for annotators.

Another difficult case are noun modifiers in compounds (e.g. *a <u>subway</u> system*); these are marked as GEN in the corpus. Using the automatic parses,

all mentions		*annotator 2*			
		SPC	USP	GEN	NEG
annotator 1	SPC	28168	1575	684	3
	USP	1142	1954	963	2
	GEN	757	1261	1707	10
	NEG	8	5	7	71

subjects only		*annotator 2*			
		SPC	USP	GEN	NEG
annotator 1	SPC	9830	830	234	1
	USP	634	1091	476	1
	GEN	272	652	597	4
	NEG	4	1	2	46

Table 2: **Confusion matrices** of entity class tags for ACE 2005 for mentions where annotators agree on spans.

we find that 9.5% of all mentions marked GEN in the adjudicated corpus are one-token mentions modifying another noun via an *nn* dependency relation. Genericity as reference to kinds is a discourse phenomenon and thus defined as an attribute of referring expressions. Because nominal modifiers do *not* introduce discourse referents, they should not be treated on the genericity annotation layer.

The data shows moderate agreement for the first two passes of entity class annotation ($\kappa = 0.53$ for all mentions and $\kappa = 0.50$ for subject mentions). Note that κ scores are not directly comparable across different annotation projects (see also Section 5), we give the above scores for the sake of completeness. Observed and expected agreement are 0.83 and 0.65 for the all-mentions case and 0.79 and 0.58 for subject mentions. This indicates that the all-mentions case may contain some trivial cases, one of which is the case of nominal modifiers described above.

In summary, the ACE scheme problematically fails to treat subject NPs differently from NPs in other syntactic positions, and 'fuzzy' points in the guidelines, particularly concerning the USP label, contribute to disagreements between annotators.

4 Annotating genericity as reference to kinds on NP- and clause-level

We next present an annotation scheme for marking both clauses and their subject NPs with regard to whether they are generic. Our scheme is primarily motivated by the contributions of clauses to the discourse (Friedrich and Palmer, 2014): do they report on a particular event or state, or do they report on some regularity? These different types of clauses have different entailment properties, and differ in how they contribute to the temporal structure of the discourse. In this work, we focus on separating generic clauses from other types of clauses. We approach the problem from a linguistic perspective rather than focusing on any particular content extraction task, arguing that any generally applicable annotation scheme must be based on solid theoretical foundations. We believe our annotation scheme is a step toward solving the problems of marking genericity in natural text. We apply our annotation scheme to two text corpora[4], reaching substantial agreement on Wikipedia texts.

4.1 Annotation scheme

The definition of our annotation scheme is guided by the following questions: (a) does a clause's subject refer to a kind rather than a particular individual; (b) if so, does the clause make a characterizing statement about the kind or its members, or does it report a particular episode related to the kind?

Task NP: genericity of subject. In this step, annotators decide whether the subject of the clause refers to a kind (**generic**) or to a particular individual (**non-generic**) as in (5d). In English, definite singular NPs (5a) or bare plural NPs (5b) can reference kinds. Indefinite singular NPs (5c) can refer to arbitrary members of a kind; these are also marked **generic**.

(5) *(a) The lion is a predatory cat.* ***(generic)***
(b) Lions have manes. ***(generic)***
(c) A lion may eat up to 30kg in one sitting. ***(generic)***
(d) Simba the lion flees into exile. ***(non-generic)***

The label **non-generic** also includes cases of non-specific reference if the reader can infer that the clause makes a statement about some particular individual (or group of individuals), even if the identity is unknown, as (6a). This is precisely where the ACE guidelines are somewhat unclear, mixing annotation of genericity and specificity. We aim to convey and mark this difference clearly. In (6b), the determiner 'some' could be added without changing the meaning significantly, showing that the bare plural here is existential, not generic (Carlson, 1977).

(6) *(a) A lion must have eaten the rabbit.* ***(non-specific, non-generic)***
(b) Lions are in this cage. ***(non-generic)***
(c) Dinosaurs are extinct. ***(generic)***

Task Cl: genericity of clause. We define **generic** clauses as making characterizing statements about kinds. This includes both clauses predicating something directly of the 'kind individual' itself (6c) and clauses that predicate something of the members of a kind, such as (5b) and (5c). According to our definition, **generic** sentences may be lexically characterizing, as in (5a) or (5b), or they may describe something that members of the kind do regularly, as in (5c). The latter type of sentences are called *habituals*. The subject of a **generic** clause must necessarily be **generic**. In addition, episodic events, classified as **non-generic** clauses, can have a **generic** NP as their subject, as in example (7). Note that we mark any clause about particular individuals as **non-generic**, including habituals making a statement about particular individuals (8). The question of whether a clause with a **non-generic** subject is habitual or not is another interesting related question, but for the moment, we leave this to future work and concentrate on the distinction of whether a clause relates to kinds.

(7) *In September 2013 the blobfish was voted the "World's Ugliest Animal".* ***(generic** subject,* ***non-generic** clause)*

(8) *John cycles to work.* ***(non-generic)***

Task Cl+NP. Using the information from Tasks NP and Cl, we automatically derive a combination label from the following set for each *clause*:

- **GEN_gen**: a **generic** clause, subject is **generic** by definition;
- **NON-GEN_non-gen**: a **non-generic** clause with a **non-generic** subject;
- or **NON-GEN_gen**: an episodic (**non-generic**) clause with a **generic** subject, see example (7).

The combination **GEN_non-gen** is not possible, by definition.

[4]The annotated corpora are freely available from http://sitent.coli.uni-saarland.de

	# documents	# clauses	Task NP	Task Cl	Task Cl+NP	% generic
botany	6	592	0.68	0.70	0.69	77.8
games	5	567	0.61	0.63	0.59	77.4
animals	13	1924	0.66	0.70	0.67	65.6
music	12	861	0.76	0.75	0.74	61.3
medicine	7	561	0.72	0.78	0.73	59.8
science	8	711	0.62	0.66	0.60	47.0
sports	8	1242	0.70	0.72	0.67	43.1
politics	16	1466	0.62	0.65	0.61	40.9
ethnic groups	8	582	0.57	0.60	0.57	40.0
religion	8	622	0.57	0.62	0.58	35.7
crime	4	588	0.50	0.60	0.52	26.3
biographies	7	563	0.63	0.69	0.63	8.9
all	102	10279	0.69	0.72	0.68	50.1

Table 3: **IAA on WikiGenerics. Fleiss'** κ for three annotators that marked the entire data set. % generic = percentage of clauses marked as generic in Task Cl according to the majority vote gold standard.

4.2 Corpus data: MASC/WikiGenerics

We apply the annotation scheme explained above to two corpora comprising texts of a wide range of genres and domains. We annotate several sections of the Manually Annotated SubCorpus (MASC) of the Open American National Corpus (Ide et al., 2010). In addition, we collect 102 texts from Wikipedia (**WikiGenerics** corpus) from a variety of categories (see Table 3). Our aim is to create a corpus that is balanced in the sense that it contains many generic and non-generic sentences, and also many different varieties of generic sentences. The corpus contains (among others) sentences about animals (9a), rule-like knowledge about sports and games (9b), and clauses describing abstract concepts (9c).

(9) *(a) Blobfish are typically shorter than 30 cm.*
(b) The offensive team must line up in a legal formation before they can snap the ball.
(c) A dictatorship is a type of authoritarianism.

Note that we mark complete texts: the genericity of some sentences clearly depends on their context. For example, (9b) is **generic** as the text describes the rules of a game rather than a specific instance of the game.

We use the discourse parser SPADE (Soricut and Marcu, 2003) to segment the first 70 sentences of each Wikipedia article into clauses, which are the basis for annotation. Subjects are not pre-marked and do not necessarily have to have their mention spans in the same segment, as illustrated in (10).

(10) *(a) Blobfish look funny (**GEN_gen**)*
*(b) and were voted the most ugly animal. (**NON-GEN_gen**)*

Annotators were allowed to skip clauses that do not contain a finite verb, which constitute about 5% of all pre-marked clauses. These clauses are mostly headlines consisting only of an NP.

4.3 Inter-annotator agreement

Our aim is to create a gold standard via majority voting. Annotators were given a written manual and a short training on documents not included in the corpus. The WikiGenerics corpus was marked completely by three paid annotators (students of computational linguistics), and agreement is given in Table 3 in terms of Fleiss' κ (Fleiss, 1971). We observe substantial agreement in almost all categories, and moderate agreement in only three categories: games, ethnic groups and organized crime. The categories ethnic groups and organized crime were especially hard to annotate because they contain many cases where it is not clear whether a mention refers to a very large particular group or whether this group rather counts as reference to a kind, as in (11).

(11) *The Bari also known as the Karo ethnic groups in South Sudan occupy the Savanna lands of the White Nile Valley.*

For MASC, two annotators mark each section; we report agreement as Cohen's κ for these two annotators in Table 4. Then, a third annotator marks all

section	# clauses	Task NP (subject)	Task Cl (clause)	Task Cl+NP (clause)	% generics
essays‡	1590	0.55	0.56	0.54	27.9
travel†	1922	0.38	0.45	0.41	19.0
letters†	1944	0.33	0.41	0.40	14.2
journal†	1927	0.42	0.52	0.48	13.0
jokes†	3376	0.56	0.63	0.58	11.6
blog†	2723	0.09	0.13	0.14	10.4
news‡	2557	0.25	0.33	0.29	3.4
fiction†*	4124	0.50	0.59	0.54	2.5

Table 4: **IAA for MASC.** The sections were marked by different pairings of annotators: †Cohen's κ for 2 annotators; ‡Fleiss' κ for 3 annotators. *fiction: agreement for 70% of data that was marked by the same two annotators. % generic = percentage of clauses marked as generic in Task Cl according to the majority vote gold standard.

clauses on which the two annotators of the first step disagreed, without seeing the annotations of the first step. Hence, this does not constitute an adjudication step. Two sections, essays and news, were marked completely by three annotators. Five paid annotators, all students of computational linguistics, participated in the annotation of MASC. The various MASC sections show a larger variation both in the percentage of generic clauses and in the agreement numbers. News and fiction contain almost no generics, while essays, travel, and letters contain notable numbers. Agreement on the blog section is surprisingly low. One annotator rarely used the category **generic** here, while the other annotator did. Manual inspection showed that this section contains many intrinsically ambigous instances of 'you' and 'one'. The third annotator agrees well with the annotator who marked more clauses as generic.

Discussion. In general, κ numbers are difficult to compare, as the expected agreement depends on the distribution of labels (Di Eugenio and Glass, 2004). If the distribution is skewed, the expected agreement is high and it is thus harder to reach a high κ score. We give the percentage of clauses labeled as generic in Task Cl. A small percentage but a relatively high κ score (as in the jokes section) means that in this category, it was apparently easier for the annotators to agree. For example, in the fiction genre, there are very few generics, but a high agreement was reached nonetheless. In the narratives of this subcorpus, the generics apparently 'stand out' clearly.

In this study, substantial agreement was reached on Wikipedia texts using our annotation scheme. The lower agreement reached on some MASC sections indicates that the annotation task is harder for some text types, and this difficulty is only partially explained by the skewedness of the label distribution: some genres simply contain more borderline cases than others.

5 Discussion and future work

We have proposed an annotation scheme for labeling clauses with regard to whether they make a characterizing statement about kinds, and NPs with regard to whether they refer to kinds or not. Our scheme aims at a linguistically motivated annotation in order to advance our understanding of generics and to see to what extent existing linguistic theories can be applied to natural text of various genres and domains.

Across all of the surveyed annotation studies and also in our own experience, agreement on the task of annotating genericity was moderate to substantial, however, κ-scores need to be interpreted in relation to the distribution of labels and are not directly comparable across different annotation projects. Annotating genericity is not an easy task even for trained annotators, as there are many borderline cases, which occur frequently in some texts and very infrequently in others. As future work, we want to investigate whether it is possible to reliably label such 'underspecified' cases, redefining ACE's USP class in a way that disentangles the annotation of genericity and specificity.

The present survey focuses on resources in English, and our new annotation scheme has only been worked out for English. We plan to extend the annotation scheme and corpus to other languages including German and Chinese.

Acknowledgments. We thank Andrea Horbach for helpful comments, and our annotators Fernando Ardente, Christine Bocionek, Ambika Kirkland, Ruth Kühn and Kleo Mavridou. This research was supported in part by the MMCI Cluster of Excellence, and the first author is supported by an IBM PhD Fellowship.

References

Cosmin Adrian Bejan and Sanda Harabagiu. 2010. Unsupervised event coreference resolution with rich linguistic features. In *Proceedings of ACL.*

Archna Bhatia, Chu-Cheng Lin, Nathan Schneider, Yulia Tsvetkov, Fatima Talib Al-Raisi, Laleh Roostapour, Jordan Bender, Abhimanu Kumar, Lori Levin, Mandy Simons, et al. 2014a. Automatic classification of communicative functions of definiteness. *Proceedings of COLING*, pages 1059–1070.

Archna Bhatia, Mandy Simons, Lori Levin, Yulia Tsvetkov, Chris Dyer, and Jordan Bender. 2014b. A unified annotation scheme for the semantic/pragmatic components of definiteness. In *Proceedings of LREC.*

Anders Björkelund, Kerstin Eckart, Arndt Riester, Nadja Schauffler, and Katrin Schweitzer. 2014. The extended DIRNDL corpus as a resource for coreference and bridging resolution. In *Proceedings of the Ninth International Conference on Language Resources and Evaluation (LREC'14).*

Kristina Nilsson Björkenstam and Emil Byström. 2012. SUC-CORE: SUC 2.0 Annotated with NP Coreference. *Proceedings of SLTC.*

Alena Böhmová, Jan Hajič, Eva Hajičová, and Barbora Hladká. 2003. The prague dependency treebank. In *Treebanks*, pages 103–127. Springer.

Gregory Norman Carlson. 1977. *Reference to kinds in English.* Ph.D. thesis.

Gennaro Chierchia. 1998. Reference to kinds across language. *Natural language semantics*, 6(4):339–405.

Jacob Cohen. 1960. A coefficient of agreement for nominal scales. *Educational and Psychological Measurement*, pages 37–46.

Agata Cybulska and Piek Vossen. 2014. Using a sledgehammer to crack a nut? lexical diversity and event coreference resolution. In *Proceedings of LREC.*

Barbara Di Eugenio and Michael Glass. 2004. The kappa statistic: A second look. *Computational Linguistics*, 30(1):95–101.

George R Doddington, Alexis Mitchell, Mark A Przybocki, Lance A Ramshaw, Stephanie Strassel, and Ralph M Weischedel. 2004. The Automatic Content Extraction (ACE) Program-Tasks, Data, and Evaluation. In *Proceedings of LREC.*

Joseph L Fleiss. 1971. Measuring nominal scale agreement among many raters. *Psychological Bulletin*, 76(5):378.

Annemarie Friedrich and Alexis Palmer. 2014. Situation entity annotation. In *Proceedings of the 8th Linguistic Annotation Workshop (LAW VIII)*, page 149.

Susan A Gelman and Twila Tardif. 1998. A cross-linguistic comparison of generic noun phrases in English and Mandarin. *Cognition*, 66(3):215–248.

Aurelie Herbelot and Ann Copestake. 2010. Annotating underquantification. In *Proceedings of the Fourth Linguistic Annotation Workshop.*

Aurelie Herbelot and Ann Copestake. 2011. Formalising and specifying underquantification. In *Proceedings of the International Conference on Computational Semantics.*

Erhard Hinrichs, Sandra Kübler, Karin Naumann, Heike Telljohann, and Julia Trushkina. 2004. Recent developments in linguistic annotations of the TüBa-D/Z treebank. In *Proceedings of the Third Workshop on Treebanks and Linguistic Theories*, pages 51–62.

Eduard Hovy, Mitchell Marcus, Martha Palmer, Lance Ramshaw, and Ralph Weischedel. 2006. Ontonotes: the 90% solution. In *Proceedings of HLT-NAACL: Short Papers*, pages 57–60.

Nancy Ide, Christiane Fellbaum, Collin Baker, and Rebecca Passonneau. 2010. The manually annotated sub-corpus: A community resource for and by the people. In *Proceedings of ACL: Short papers*, pages 68–73.

Dan Klein and Christopher D Manning. 2002. Fast exact inference with a factored model for natural language parsing. In *Advances in neural information processing systems*, pages 3–10.

Manfred Krifka, Francis Jeffrey Pelletier, Gregory N. Carlson, Alice ter Meulen, Godehard Link, and Gennaro Chierchia. 1995. Genericity: An Introduction. *The Generic Book*, pages 1–124.

Linguistic Data Consortium. 2000. Entity Detection and Tracking - Phase 1, ACE Pilot Study Task Definition. https://www.ldc.upenn.edu/collaborations/past-projects/ace/annotation-tasks-and-specifications.

Godehard Link. 1995. Generic information and dependent generics. *The Generic Book*, pages 358–382.

Annie Louis and Ani Nenkova. 2011. Automatic identification of general and specific sentences by leveraging discourse annotations. In *Proceedings of IJCNLP.*

Thomas A. Mathew and E. Graham Katz. 2009. Supervised categorization of habitual and episodic sentences. In *Sixth Midwest Computational Linguistics Colloquium*, Bloomington, Indiana: Indiana University.

Alexis Mitchell, Stephanie Strassel, Mark Przybocki, JK Davis, George Doddington, Ralph Grishman, Adam Meyers, Ada Brunstein, Lisa Ferro, and Beth Sundheim. 2003. ACE-2 Version 1.0 LDC2003T11. Philadelphia: Linguistic Data Consortium.

Anna Nedoluzhko. 2013. Generic noun phrases and annotation of coreference and bridging relations in the Prague Dependency Treebank. In *Proceedings of the 7th Linguistic Annotation Workshop and Interoperability with Discourse*, pages 103–111.

Massimo Poesio. 2004. Discourse annotation and semantic annotation in the GNOME corpus. In *Proceedings of the ACL Workshop on Discourse Annotation*, pages 72–79. Association for Computational Linguistics.

Sandeep Prasada. 2000. Acquiring generic knowledge. *Trends in cognitive sciences*, 4(2):66–72.

Nils Reiter and Anette Frank. 2010. Identifying generic noun phrases. In *Proceedings of ACL*, pages 40–49, Uppsala, Sweden.

Radu Soricut and Daniel Marcu. 2003. Sentence level discourse parsing using syntactic and lexical information. In *Proceedings of NAACL-HLT*, pages 149–156.

Christopher Walker, Stephanie Strassel, Julie Medero, and Kazuaki Maeda. 2006. ACE 2005 Multilingual Training Corpus LDC2006T06. Philadelphia: Linguistic Data Consortium.

Design and Annotation of the First Italian Corpus for Text Simplification

Dominique Brunato, Felice Dell'Orletta, Giulia Venturi, Simonetta Montemagni
Istituto di Linguistica Computazionale "Antonio Zampolli" (ILC–CNR)
ItaliaNLP Lab - *www.italianlp.it*
{name.surname}@ilc.cnr.it

Abstract

In this paper, we present design and construction of the first Italian corpus for automatic and semi–automatic text simplification. In line with current approaches, we propose a new annotation scheme specifically conceived to identify the typology of changes an original sentence undergoes when it is manually simplified. Such a scheme has been applied to two aligned Italian corpora, containing original texts with corresponding simplified versions, selected as representative of two different manual simplification strategies and addressing different target reader populations. Each corpus was annotated with the operations foreseen in the annotation scheme, covering different levels of linguistic description. Annotation results were analysed with the final aim of capturing peculiarities and differences of the different simplification strategies pursued in the two corpora.

1 Introduction and Background

Automatic Text Simplification (ATS) is receiving growing attention over the last few years due to the implications it has for both machine– and human–oriented tasks. ATS has been employed as a preprocessing step to improve the efficiency of e.g. parsing, machine translation and information extraction. Recently, ATS has been used in educational scenarios and assistive technologies; e.g. for the adaptation of texts to particular readers, like children (De Belder et al., 2010), L2 learners (Petersen and Ostendorf, 2007), people with low literacy skills (Aluísio et al., 2008), cognitive disabilities (Bott and Saggion, 2014) or language impairments, e.g. aphasia (Carroll et al., 1998) or deafness (Inui et al., 2003).

The purpose of ATS, within both perspectives, is to reduce lexical and syntactic complexity while preserving the original meaning of the text. To this aim, three main approaches have been followed. The more traditional one relies on the use of hand-crafted rules (Chandrasekar et al., 1996; Siddharthan, 2002; Siddharthan, 2010; Siddharthan, 2011), which typically cover specific phenomena that are symptoms of linguistic complexity, especially at the syntactic level (e.g. passives, relative clauses, appositions). Recently, the availability of larger parallel corpora, i.e. sentence-aligned corpora consisting of both the original and the simplified version of the same text (e.g. English and Simple English Wikipedia, in short EW and SEW), has allowed a consistent use of machine learning techniques for automatically acquiring simplification rules. This is the approach followed by e.g. Woodsend and Lapata (2011), who based their ATS system on a quasi-synchronous grammar, Zhu et al. (2010), who adapted a Statistical Machine Translation (SMT) algorithm to implement simplification operations on the parse tree, and Narayan and Gardent (2014), who similarly adopted SMT techniques but also combined a deep semantic representation of the sentence. Both hand-written and automatically acquired rules have advantages and shortcomings. While the former can potentially account for the maximum linguistic information, they are extremely costly to develop and tend to cover only a few lexical and syntactic constructs; on the other side, data-driven approaches require the least linguistic knowledge but they are not feasible

Proceedings of LAW IX - The 9th Linguistic Annotation Workshop, pages 31–41,
Denver, Colorado, June 5, 2015.

without a large quantity of aligned data. Hybrid approaches seem to offer a good alternative; as shown by Siddharthan and Angrosh (2014), a system that combines automatically harvested lexical rules with hand-crafted syntactic rules outperformed the state of the art. Besides, all these systems exploit the EW/SEW dataset as a training corpus. Such resources are lacking for languages other than English, making it rather impossible to approach ATS as pure machine learning task. For some of these languages, parallel monolingual corpora are annotated with simplification rules corresponding to transformations to perform on a complex sentence. This is the approach followed by Brouwers et al. (2014) for French; Bott and Saggion (2014) for Spanish; Caseli et al. (2009) for Brazilian Portuguese. A different approach is advanced by Specia (2010) for Brazilian Portuguese, who adopted phrase-based machine learning from a parallel corpus. For Basque, Aranzabe et al. (2013) used the output of a readability assessment system for detecting complex sentences, which are simplified by a large set of hand-crafted rules.

Typically, ATS approaches rely on the output of a syntactic parser although the main cause of errors for an ATS system is due to erroneous parses also when state–of–the–art parsers are used (De Belder et al., 2010; Siddharthan, 2011; Drndarević et al., 2013; Brouwers et al., 2014; Siddharthan and Angrosh, 2014). In particular, this concerns relative clause attachments and clause boundary identification (Siddharthan and Angrosh, 2014). According to Drndarević et al. (2013), one third of ATS errors depends on previous parsing errors and Brouwers et al. (2014) revealed that 89% of text simplification (TS) errors are due to preprocessing errors.

ATS is largely underinvestigated for what concerns Italian. The only exception is (Barlacchi and Tonelli, 2013), who devised a rule–based architecture focusing on a limited set of linguistic structures, but no previous study has addressed ATS by using parallel corpora.

2 Our Contribution

We present the first Italian resource for automatic and semi-automatic text simplification. We collected and hand–aligned two monolingual corpora representative of two different strategies of manual simplification and addressing different target readers. The corpora were annotated with a set of rules designed to capture simplification operations at diverse levels of linguistic description. There are several motivations underlying the proposed approach. As a universal *native simplified–language speaker* does not exist (Siddharthan, 2014), it follows that ATS systems are typically specialized with respect to a specific target user. Hence, we introduce a new annotation scheme able to handle different simplification strategies, at the level of both method and target users.

This is the starting point to develop a flexible automatic or semi–automatic TS system.The proposed resource can be used to train a supervised classifier aimed at carrying out a semi–automatic TS task. In the semi–automatic scenario, the system will be able to identify the areas of linguistic complexity within a sentence and suggest the authors the most appropriate simplification rule for the intended audience and domain. This classifier, using the information extracted from the syntactic tree as one of the features exploited to predict the rules to be applied, is expected to be more robust to syntactic parsing errors than TS systems based on hand–crafted or automatically acquired rules heavily relying on parses transformations. To give an idea of how wrong parses can affect a TS system, let's consider that the accuracy of the state-of-the-art dependency parser for Italian is 87.89% in terms of Labeled Attachment Score corresponding to 293 erroneously parsed sentences out of the total of 376, i.e. 78% of the test sentences contain at least one parsing error.[1]. Moreover, it should be noted that in a TS scenario the parsers are typically tested on domains outside of the data from which they were trained or developed on (i.e. out–domain scenario) and it is widely acknowledged that state–of–the–art statistical parsers have a dramatic drop of accuracy when tested in a out–domain scenario (Gildea, 2001).

In this paper, we also carried out a comparative analysis between different TS strategies addressing different target users: this was possible thanks to

[1]These data are reported in the Evalita evaluation campaign and were obtained by combining four state–of–the–art parsers using a test set with gold (i.e. manually revised) part–of–speech tags (Bosco et al., 2014)

the internal composition of the developed resource, which allowed us to investigate the effects of simplification rules on the linguistic peculiarities of abridged texts with respect to their original versions.

3 Corpora

The annotated resource[2] presented here is made up of two sub–corpora that can be considered representative of two different TS strategies: the "structural" and the "intuitive" strategy, following Allen (2009)'s definition, who addressed TS in the context of L2 learning. The former uses predefined graded lists (covering both word and structural levels) or traditional readability formulas. The latter is dependent on the author's teaching experience and personal judgments about the comprehension ability of learners. Although with main distinctions, this classification can be applied for our purpose.

The first sub–corpus (*Terence*) contains 32 short novels for children and their manually simplified version.[3] The simplification was carried out in a cumulative fashion with the aim of improving the comprehension of the original text at three different levels: global coherence, local cohesion and lexicon/syntax. To align the corpus, we selected the last two levels of simplification (i.e. local cohesion and lexicon/syntax) which were considered respectively as the original and the simplified version. This was motivated by the need of tackling only those textual simplification aspects with a counterpart at the morpho–syntactic and syntactic level. We hand-aligned the resulting 1036 original sentences to the 1060 simplified ones. The results (Table 1) provide some insights into the typology of human editing operations. In 90% of the cases a 1:1 alignment is reported; 39 original sentences (3.75%) have a correspondence 1:2, thus suggesting an occurred split; 2 original sentences underwent a three–fold split (0.19%), i.e. they correspond to three sentences in the simplified version; 15 pairs of original sentences were merged into a single one (2.88%). Finally, the percentage of unaligned sentences is 1%.

The second sub–corpus (*Teacher*) is composed by 24 pairs of original/simplified texts, which were collected by surfing specialized educational websites providing free resources for teachers. They cover different textual genres, such as literature (e.g. extracts from famous Italian novels) and handbooks for high school on diverse subjects (e.g. history, geography), and they are addressed to different targets. Unlike *Terence*, the simplification was performed independently by a teacher, with the aim of adapting the text to the need of audience, typically L2 students with at least a B2 level in Italian. Thus, *Teacher* can be considered as an instance of "intuitive" simplification: while the target is usually the same (i.e. L2 learners), each text was produced by a different author and the interventions made on the text span over different linguistic levels without any predefined distinction or hierarchy. On the contrary, *Terence* exemplifies a "structural" simplification, since: i) it was produced by a pool of experts; ii) it addressed a well–defined target; iii) it was consistent with a predefined guideline tackling the simplification at three separate textual dimensions. This can also explain the higher percentage of texts which were perfectly aligned at sentence level (92.1% see Table 1) with respect to *Teacher* (68.32%).

	1:1	1:2	1:3	2:1	1:0	0:1
Terence	92.1	3.75	0.19	2.88	0.67	0.38
Teacher	68.32	11.45	0.76	13.74	1.15	0.0

Table 1: Percentage of sentence alignments.

To compare the two different simplification strategies with respect to the effect of the simplification process, we evaluated the two corpora with the readability index existing for the Italian language, i.e. READ–IT (Dell'Orletta et al., 2011). For both the corpora, we calculated the Spearman's correlation between the scores obtained by different READ–IT models (i.e. using different types of linguistic features) on the original and the simplified version. As reported in Table 2, the two simplified corpora are significantly correlated with all READ–IT models. In particular, *Teacher* is especially correlated with the model using a combination of *raw text* and *lexical* features (*READ–IT lexical* model in Table 2). This possibly follows from the "intuitive" simplification process of *Teacher* that mostly concerns lexical substitution operations.

[2]http://www.italianlp.it/software-data/

[3]This corpus was produced within the EU project Terence targeting "poor comprehenders": http://www.terenceproject.eu

Readability index	Terence	Teacher
READ–IT global	**0.77**∗	**0.47**
READ–IT base	**0.80**∗	**0.50**
READ–IT lexical	**0.65**∗	**0.72**∗
READ–IT syntax	**0.54**∗	**0.46**

Table 2: Spearman's correlation between different READ-IT models and the simplified corpora. Significant correlations ($p < 0.05$) are bolded; those with $p < 0.001$ are also marked with ∗.

The two corpora were annotated by two undergraduate students in computational linguistics, who received preliminary training lessons on the simplification rules covered by the annotation tagset. Each student annotated a different corpus and all their annotations were verified by a trained linguist.

4 Simplification Annotation Scheme

We defined an annotation scheme covering six macro–categories: *split*, *merge*, *reordering*, *insert*, *delete* and *transformation*. Following Bott and Saggion (2014), we used a two–level structure, i.e. for some categories more specific subclassed have been introduced. In Table 3, we show the tagset of the annotation scheme. In the following examples extracted from the annotated corpus, we bolded the text span marked in the original sentence by each rule-tag and we highlighted in italics the corresponding text span in the simplified version.[4]

Split: it is the most investigated operation in ATS, for both human– and machine–oriented applications. Typically, a split affects coordinate clauses (introduced by coordinate conjunctions, colons or semicolons), subordinate clauses (e.g. non–restrictive relative clauses), appositive and adverbial phrases. Nevertheless, we do not expect that each of these sentences undergoes a split, as the human expert may prefer not to detach two clauses, for instance when a subordinate clause provides the necessary background information to understand the matrix clause.

O: Mamma Gorilla sembrava completamente distrutta per le cure che dava al suo vivace cucciolotto Tito, **che stava giocando vicino alle grosse sbarre di acciaio che circondavano il recinto**. [Mummy Gorilla looked completely worn out from looking after her lively baby, Tod, **who was playing by the thick steel bars that surrounded the enclosure.**]

S: Mamma Gorilla sembrava proprio distrutta per le cure che dava al suo vivace cucciolotto Tito. *Tito stava giocando vicino alle grosse sbarre di acciaio che erano intorno alla loro area.* [Mummy Gorilla looked completely worn out from looking after her lively baby Tod. *Tod was playing by the thick steel bars that surrounded the enclosure.*]

Merge: it is to be taken as the reverse of split, i.e. the operation by which two (or more) original sentences are joined into a unique simplified sentence. This transformation is less likely to be adopted, as it creates semantically denser sentences, more difficult to process (Kintsh and Keenan, 1973). Yet, to some extent (see the alignment results), this is a choice the expert can make and it can be interesting to verify whether the sentences susceptible to be merged display any regular pattern of linguistic features that can be automatically captured.

O: **Clara pensò che fosse uno dei cigni. Ma poi si rese conto che stava urlando! [Clara thought it was one of the swans. But then she realised it was shouting!**]

S: *In un primo momento, Clara pensò che fosse uno dei cigni, ma poi sentì urlare!* [*At first, Clara thought it was one of the swans, but then she heard it shouting.*]

Reordering: this tag marks word order changes between the original sentence and its simplified counterpart. Clearly, altering the position of the elements in a sentence depends, in turn, upon modifications at lexicon or syntax; e.g. replacing an object clitic pronoun (which is preverbal with finite verbs in Italian) with its full lexical antecedent yields the unmarked order SVO, associated with easier comprehension and earlier acquisition (Slobin and Bever, 1982). Conversely, the author of the simplified text may sometimes prefer a non–canonical order, when she believes e.g. that it allows the reader to keep the focus stable over two or more sentences.

O: Il passante gli spiegò che, per arrivare al bidone,**doveva contare ben 5 bidoni a partire dal semaforo**. [The passer-by explained him that, to get to the dustbin, **he had to count exactly 5 dustbins starting from the traffic light.**]

[4]In all the examples of aligned sentences, O stands for original and S for simplified.

Simplification Annotation Scheme					
Classes	Subclasses	Terence		Teacher	
Split		1.71	(43)	2.06	(35)
Merge		0.81	(20)	1.30	(22)
Reordering		8.65	(212)	7.89	(134)
Insert	Verb	4.92	(121)	2.53	(43)
	Subject	1.79	(44)	1.94	(33)
	Other	12.01	(295)	11.19	(190)
Delete	Verb	2.04	(50)	1.88	(32)
	Subject	0.49	(12)	0.24	(4)
	Other	19.41	(477)	23.20	(394)
Transformation	Lexical Substitution (word level)	26.50	(651)	20.73	(352)
	Lexical Substitution (phrase level)	13.39	(329)	11.60	(197)
	Anaphoric replacement	0.61	(15)	3.53	(60)
	Noun_to_Verb	1.59	(39)	0.88	(15)
	Verb_to_Noun (nominalization)	0.61	(15)	0.47	(8)
	Verbal Voice	0.53	(13)	0.77	(13)
	Verbal Features	4.92	(121)	9.78	(166)

Table 3: Simplification tagset and the percentage distribution (with its absolute value) for each rule-tag.

S: Il signore spiegò a Ugolino che *doveva contare 5 bidoni a partire dal semaforo*, per arrivare al bidone della carta. [The man explained Little Hugh that *he had to count 5 dustbins starting from the traffic light* to get to the wastepaper dustbin.]

Insert: the process of simplification may even result in a longer sentence, because of the insertion of words or phrases that provide supportive information to the original sentence. Despite the cognitive literature suggests reducing the inference load of a text, especially with less skilled or low–knowledge readers (Ozuru et al., 2009), it is difficult to predict what an author will actually add to the original sentence to make it clearer. It can happen that the sentence is elliptical, i.e. syntactically compressed, and the difficulty depends on the ability to retrieve the missing arguments, which are then made explicit as a result of the simplification. Our annotation scheme has introduced two more specific tags to mark insertions: one for verbs and one for subject. The latter signals the transformation of a covert subject into a lexical noun phrase[5].

O: Essendo da poco andata in pensione dal suo lavoro, disse che le mancavano i suoi studenti [...] [Having just retired from her job, she said that she missed her students]

[5]The covert/overt subject realization is an option available in null–subject languages like Italian.

S: Essendo da poco andata in pensione dal suo lavoro *come insegnante*, disse che le mancavano i suoi studenti [...] [Having just retired from her job *as a school teacher*, she said that she missed her students]

Delete: dropping redundant information is also a strategy for simplifying a text. As for the *insert* tag, also deletion is largely unpredictable, although we can imagine that simplified sentences would contain less adjunct phrases (e.g. adverbs or adjectives). Such occurrences have been marked with the underspecified *delete* rule; two more restricted tags, *delete_verb* and *delete_subj*, have been introduced to signal, respectively, the deletion of a verb and of an overt subject (made implicit and recoverable through verb agreement morphology).

O: **Sembrò veramente che** il fiume stesse per straripare. [**It really seemed that** the river was going to burst.]

S: Il fiume stava per straripare. [The river was going to burst.]

Transformation: this label covers six typologies of transformations that a sentence may undergo to become more comprehensible for the intended reader. Such modifications can affect the sentence at the lexical, morpho–syntactic and syntactic level, also giving rise to overlapping phenomena. Our annotation scheme has intended to cover the following phenomena.

– *Lexical substitution (word level)*: when a single word is replaced by another word (or more than one), which is usually a more common synonym or a less specific term.

O: Il **passante** gli spiegò che, per arrivare al bidone, doveva contare ben 5 bidoni a partire dal semaforo. [The **passer-by** explained him that, to get to the dustbin, he had to count exactly 5 dustbins starting from the traffic light.]

S: Il *signore* spiegò a Ugolino che doveva contare 5 bidoni a partire dal semaforo, per arrivare al bidone della carta. [The *man* explained to Little Hug that he had to count 5 dustbins starting from the traffic light, to get to the dustbin.]

Given the relevance of lexical changes in TS, which is also confirmed by our results, previous works have proposed feasible ways to automatize lexical simplification, e.g. by relying on electronic resources, such as WordNet (De Belder et al., 2010) or word frequency lists (Drndarevic et al., 2012). However, synonyms or hypernyms replacements do not cover all the editing options, since we observed that an author might also restate the meaning of the complex word with a multi-word pharaphrase.

O: Tutti si **precipitarono** verso il tendone. [Everyone **rashed** outside the tent.]

S: Tutti si *misero a correre* verso la tenda. [Everyone *came running* outside the tent.]

– *Lexical substitution (phrase level)*: it differs from the previous rule with respect to the "size" of the original unit involved in the substitution, which in this case consists of a phrase. But, similarly to the previous one, the simplified unit can be either a single word or a phrase itself.

O: Persino il tempo era **di buon umore**. [Even the weather was **in a party mood**.]

S: Persino il tempo era *buono*. [Even the weather was *good*.]

– *Anaphoric replacement*: the substitution of a referent pronoun with its full lexical antecedent (a definite noun phrase or a proper noun).

O: Il passante **gli** spiegò che, per arrivare al bidone, doveva contare ben 5 bidoni [...] [The passer-by explained **him** that, to get to the dustbin, he had to count exactly 5 dustbins]

S: Il signore spiegò *a Ugolino* che doveva contare 5 bidoni a partire dal semaforo [...] [The man explained *to Little Hug* that he had to count 5 dustbins starting from the traffic light]

– *Noun_to_Verb*: when a nominalization or a support verb construction is replaced by a simple verb. In this case, the correspondence between the noun and the verb involved in the transformation had to be suggested by the presence of a similar morphological root.

O: Il giorno **della partenza**, i bambini salutarono i loro genitori durante la colazione. [On the day of their **parents' departure**, the children said their goodbyes to their parents over breakfast.]

S: Il giorno *in cui i genitori partirono*, i bambini li salutarono durante la colazione. [The day *that their parents left*, the children said them goodbye over breakfast.]

– *Verb_to_Noun*: to mark the presence of a nominalization or of a support verb construction instead of an original simple verb.

O: Benedetto era molto arrabbiato e voleva **vendicare** sua sorella. [Ben was very angry and he wanted **to avenge** his sister.]

S: Benedetto era molto arrabbiato e voleva *ottenere vendetta* per sua sorella. [Ben was very angry and he wanted *to get revenge* for his sister.]

– *Verbal voice*: to signal the transformation of a passive sentence into an active or vice versa. Within both the corpora very few examples of the latter were found; this result was expected since passive sentences represent an instance of non-canonical order: they are acquired later by typically developing children (Maratsos, 1974; Bever, 1970) (for Italian, (Cipriani et al., 1993; Ciccarelli, 1998)) and have been reported as problematic for atypical populations, e.g. deaf children (Volpato, 2010). Yet, the "passivization" rule may still be productive in other textual typologies, where it can happen that the author of the simplification prefers not only to keep, but even to insert, a passive, in order to avoid more unusual syntactic constructs in Italian (such as impersonal sentences). This is also in line with what Bott and Saggion (2014) observed for passives.

O: Solo il papà di Luisa, "Crispino mangia cracker" era dispiaciuto, perché **era stato battuto da Tonio Battaglia**. [Only Louise's Dad, "Cream

Cracker Craig", was disappointed, because **he'd been beaten by Tod Baxter**.]

S: Solo il papà di Luisa era triste, perché *Tonio Battaglia lo aveva battuto*. [Only Louise's Dad was sad, because *Tod Baxter had beaten him*.]

– *Verbal features*: Italian is a language with a rich inflectional paradigm and changes affecting verbal features (mood, tense) have proven useful in discriminating between easy– and difficult–to–read texts in readability assessment task (Dell'Orletta et al., 2011). Poor comprehenders also find it difficult to properly master verb inflectional morphology; the same holds for other categories of atypical readers, e.g. dyslexics (Fiorin, 2009), but also for L2 learners (Sorace, 1993); thus, the simplification, according to the intended target, will probably alter the distribution of verbal features.

O: Non capisco e non **potrei** parlare con nessuno. [I can't understand and I **could** not talk to anybody.]

S: Non capisco e non *posso* parlare di queste cose con nessuno. [I can't understand and I *can* not speak of such things to anybody.]

5 Simplification Rules and Linguistic Features

The analysis of the frequency distribution of each rule within the two annotated corpora (Table 3) allows us capturing similarities and variations across corpora representing two different TS strategies and addressed to diverse categories of readers. The majority of rules are similarly distributed across the two corpora showing that a number of simplification choices are shared by a team of experts and independent teachers. This is an interesting finding as it might suggest the existence of an "independent" simplification process shared by approaches targeting different audience and based on different simplification methods. Exceptions are represented by some rules involving verbs (i.e. transformation of verbal features and insert verb) and anaphoric replacements. For what concerns the latter, it should be noted that the *Terence* original version here adopted inherits previous sentence transformations covering, among others, anaphoric replacements. The different distribution of rules involving verbs might reflect both the different simplification choices related to the *structural* and *intuitive* simplification strategies and the different textual genres included in *Teacher* and *Terence*.

For a more in-depth analysis of the impact and the significance of each simplification rule, we focused on the most frequently applied rules and we chose a set of features which are typically involved in automatic readability assessment and also express language–specific peculiarities. For each linguistic feature, we calculated the Spearman's correlation between the feature values extracted from the original text and from the simplified version with respect to the selected rules.

5.1 Linguistic Features

The set of linguistic features spans across different levels of linguistic analysis and are broadly classifiable into four main classes: raw text, lexical, morpho–syntactic and syntactic features, shortly described below. They were extracted from the corpora automatically tagged by the part–of–speech tagger described in Dell'Orletta (2009) and dependency–parsed by the DeSR parser (Attardi, 2006).

Raw text features (Features [1–2] in Table 4) are typically used within traditional readability metrics and include *sentence length* (average number of words per sentence), and *word length* (average number of characters per words).

Feature [3] refers to the percentage of all unique words (types) on the *Basic Italian Vocabulary* (*BIV*) by De Mauro (2000) in the sentence. The *BIV* includes a list of 7,000 words highly familiar to Italian native speakers.

The set of morpho–syntactic features [4–19] ranges from the probability distribution of part–of–speech types, to the lexical density of the text, calculated as the ratio of content words (verbs, nouns, adjectives and adverbs) to the total number of lexical tokens in a text. It also includes verbal mood and tense distributions, a language–specific feature related to Italian rich verbal morphology.

The set of syntactic features [20–35] captures different aspects of the syntactic structure, such as:
– **parse tree depth features**, going from the *depth of the whole parse tree* [26], calculated in terms of the longest path from the root of the dependency tree to some leaf, to a more specific feature referring to the *average depth of embedded complement 'chains'* [23] governed by a nominal head and including ei-

ther prepositional complements or nominal and adjectival modifiers;
– **verbal predicate features**, going from the *arity of verbs* [27], meant as the number of instantiated dependency links sharing the same verbal head (covering both arguments and modifiers), to the *distribution of verbal roots with explicit subject* [28] with respect to all sentence roots occurring in a text and the *relative ordering of subject and object with respect to the verbal head* [29–32].
– **subordination features** include the *distribution of subordinate vs. main clauses* [20–21]; for subordinates, their *relative ordering with respect to the main clause* [33–34] and the *average depth of 'chains' of embedded subordinate clauses* [22];
– the **length of dependency links** is calculated in terms of the words occurring between the syntactic head and the dependent: the feature includes the *length of all dependency links* [24] and the *maximum dependency links* [25];
– **clause length** [35] is measured as the number of tokens occurring within a clause.

5.2 Correlation

Table 4 illustrates the correlations between the linguistic features and the most frequently applied simplification rules. It can be noted that all the rules are strongly correlated with the linguistic features. This reveals that these rules have a great impact on the linguistic structure of the simplified text. It also shows the effectiveness of such features to capture simplification operations at varying degrees of linguistic description. Interestingly, if we examine more in-depth the significance value, we can observe a distinction between the two corpora. *Terence* reports a higher number of stronger correlations (i.e. $p < 0.001$) with respect to *Teacher*. These results seem to provide an evidence to the existence of different simplification strategies, which vary according to the person (i.e. expert vs. non-expert), textual genres and intended target. Specifically, the teachers prefer a more vocabulary-oriented simplification approach, as testified by *a)* the highest significant correlations reported by the rules dealing with lexical replacements (i.e. *LexSub_word* and *LexSub_phrase*) and *b)* the fact that the majority of significant correlations at > 0.5 affects linguistic features from [1] to [19], i.e. features not dealing with the syntactic structure. This might suggest that, independently from the simplification rule adopted, the resulting sentence has not undergone a strong modification in its grammatical structure. This is not the case of the "structural" simplification, in which all the rules significantly correlate with both lexical/morpho–syntactic features (set [1-19]) and syntactic features (set [20-35]). On the other side, the correlation results reported by the *Delete*, *LexSub_word* and *LexSub_phrase* rules reveal the existence of a common approach to simplification. In the two corpora these rules are correlated with mainly the same linguistic features.

For what concerns the evaluation of the overall significance of each rule, we observe that a wide number of correlations at ≥ 0.6 occurs especially when *Split* and *LexSub_word* were applied. Both these simplification operations are expected to greatly redefine the structure of the sentence; a split e.g. not only correlates with sentence length, but it also reduces prepositional chains [23]. Split might be triggered by long noun phrases with a deverbal noun; to simplify them the author could have chosen to turn them into an autonomous sentence, by also adding a verb (see the high correlation between [23] and *InsertVerb*).

6 Conclusion

We have presented the first Italian corpus for text simplification. This annotated resource is composed by two monolingual parallel corpora, representing two different strategies of simplification: "structural" and "intuitive". We have defined an annotation scheme able to capture manual simplifications at different levels of linguistic structure as well as to handle the different strategies of simplification. We have carried out an in-depth analysis of the impact of each simplification rule with respect to a set of linguistic features related to text complexity. This study has highlighted the existence of an "independent" simplification process shared by the two considered simplification approaches targeting different audience. We are currently using this finding in the development of a semi–automatic supervised TS system trained on the two corpora able to handle these shared simplification phenomena. Current developments are also devoted to refining the anno-

Feature	Insert		Delete		Reord		LexSub_word		LexSub_phrase		Split		InsertVerb	
[1] Sentence length	**.796∗**	**.342**	**.772∗**	**.345∗**	**.820∗**	**.451∗**	**.818∗**	**.463∗**	**.787∗**	**.433∗**	**.799∗**	**.501**	**.714∗**	**.573∗**
[2] Word length	**.595∗**	**.431∗**	**.593∗**	**.518∗**	**.627∗**	**.637∗**	**.636∗**	**.559∗**	**.512∗**	**.449∗**	**.700∗**	**.581**	**.612∗**	**.375**
[3] Word types in the *BIV*	**.663∗**	**.315**	**.707∗**	**.382∗**	**.699∗**	**.456∗**	**.735∗**	**.580∗**	**.654∗**	**.472∗**	**.630∗**	**.865∗**	**.690∗**	**.413**
[4] Lexical density	**.639∗**	**.246**	**.685∗**	**.416∗**	**.704∗**	**.410∗**	**.757∗**	**.400∗**	**.617∗**	**.402∗**	**.646∗**	**.696∗**	**.566∗**	.082
[5] Adjective	**.693∗**	**.450∗**	**.689∗**	**.406∗**	**.752∗**	**.564∗**	**.724∗**	**.585∗**	**.726∗**	**.527∗**	**.779∗**	**.662**	**.787∗**	.245
[6] Adverb	**.546∗**	**.324**	**.652∗**	**.424∗**	**.667∗**	**.311**	**.729∗**	**.445∗**	**.581∗**	**.245**	**.670∗**	.292	**.716∗**	**.351**
[7] Coord Conjunction	**.609∗**	**.345**	**.707∗**	**.454∗**	**.735∗**	**.588∗**	**.765∗**	**.554∗**	**.746∗**	**.494∗**	**.474**	**.662**	**.667∗**	.306
[8] Subord Conjunction	**.510∗**	**.532∗**	**.611∗**	**.478∗**	**.564∗**	**.606∗**	**.700∗**	**.483∗**	**.716∗**	**.414∗**	**.726∗**	**.554**	**.641∗**	**.441**
[9] Preposition	**.687∗**	**.492∗**	**.678∗**	**.404∗**	**.690∗**	**.354**	**.794∗**	**.498∗**	**.680∗**	**.447∗**	**.688∗**	**.491**	**.743∗**	**.480**
[10] Pronoun	**.619∗**	.179	**.629∗**	**.277**	**.550∗**	**.304**	**.716∗**	**.317∗**	**.594∗**	**.338∗**	**.552∗**	**.578**	**.368∗**	-.030
[11] Noun	**.707∗**	**.566∗**	**.702∗**	**.586∗**	**.708∗**	**.474∗**	**.761∗**	**.601∗**	**.721∗**	**.548∗**	**.666∗**	**.544**	**.728∗**	**.490**
[12] Verb	**.703∗**	**.401∗**	**.634∗**	**.464∗**	**.655∗**	**.435∗**	**.722∗**	**.506∗**	**.653∗**	**.468∗**	**.743∗**	**.679**	**.656∗**	.268
[13] Verb infinitive mood	**.718∗**	**.488∗**	**.644∗**	**.481∗**	**.649∗**	**.440∗**	**.752∗**	**.528∗**	**.720∗**	**.459∗**	**.554∗**	**.753∗**	**.395∗**	**.405**
[14] Verb gerundive mood	**.574∗**	nan	**.585∗**	nan	**.554∗**	nan	**.691∗**	-.038	**.677∗**	nan	**.499∗**	nan	**.519∗**	**.558∗**
[15] Verb participle mood	**.530∗**	.210	**.439∗**	**.395∗**	**.380∗**	**.323**	**.554∗**	**.335∗**	**.349∗**	**.368∗**	**.527∗**	.204	**.371∗**	.148
[16] Verb indicative mood	**.584∗**	.223	**.630∗**	**.422∗**	**.581∗**	.100	**.697∗**	**.344∗**	**.675∗**	**.323**	**.686∗**	**.495**	**.491∗**	.156
[17] Verb present tense	**.573∗**	**.254**	**.622∗**	**.307**	**.574∗**	**.275**	**.683∗**	**.394∗**	**.558∗**	**.296**	**.599∗**	**.568**	**.727∗**	**.527**
[18] Verb imperfect tense	**.741∗**	**.638∗**	**.786∗**	**.533∗**	**.768∗**	**.635∗**	**.849∗**	**.542∗**	**.771∗**	**.479∗**	**.813∗**	**.884∗**	**.777∗**	**.432**
[19] Verb past tense	**.703∗**	.214	**.832∗**	.088	**.787∗**	.080	**.840∗**	**.260∗**	**.811∗**	.187	**.902∗**	nan	**.801∗**	**.504**
[20] Main clauses	**.492∗**	.215	**.395∗**	**.198**	**.495∗**	.046	**.520∗**	**.215**	**.518∗**	.191	**.337**	.000	**.277**	.097
[21] Subord clauses	**.492∗**	.215	**.395∗**	**.204**	**.495∗**	.151	**.520∗**	**.209**	**.518∗**	**.254**	**.337**	.145	**.277**	.238
[22] Embedded subord clauses	**.356∗**	**.303**	**.478∗**	**.351∗**	**.369∗**	**.323**	**.529∗**	**.415∗**	**.463∗**	**.404∗**	**.422**	**.472**	**.499∗**	.173
[23] Prepositional 'chains'	**.647∗**	**.352**	**.547∗**	**.305**	**.679∗**	.225	**.740∗**	**.424∗**	**.627∗**	**.514∗**	**.724∗**	**.712∗**	**.664∗**	**.507**
[24] Length of dependency links	**.608∗**	**.403∗**	**.567∗**	**.431∗**	**.457∗**	**.278**	**.619∗**	**.433∗**	**.571∗**	**.468∗**	**.498∗**	.215	**.512∗**	**.562∗**
[25] Longest dependency links	**.643∗**	**.321**	**.582∗**	**.345∗**	**.523∗**	**.307**	**.621∗**	**.428∗**	**.599∗**	**.493∗**	**.514∗**	.160	**.578∗**	**.596∗**
[26] Parse tree depth	**.559∗**	.166	**.586∗**	**.275**	**.506∗**	**.280**	**.671∗**	**.379∗**	**.602∗**	**.405∗**	**.509∗**	.376	**.499∗**	.294
[27] Verb arity	**.630∗**	.231	**.518∗**	**.236**	**.417∗**	.191	**.588∗**	**.365∗**	**.548∗**	**.321**	**.494**	.019	**.511∗**	.003
[28] Verbal roots with subj	**.469∗**	.182	**.583∗**	**.324∗**	**.438∗**	**.331**	**.585∗**	**.347∗**	**.473∗**	**.365∗**	.017	.439	**.614∗**	.216
[29] Post-verbal obj	**.566∗**	.224	**.570∗**	.178	**.471∗**	**.288**	**.634∗**	**.389∗**	**.575∗**	**.228**	**.573∗**	.162	**.511∗**	.082
[30] Pre-verbal obj	**.416∗**	**.340**	**.524∗**	**.227**	**.380∗**	**.605∗**	**.616∗**	**.307∗**	**.519∗**	**.315**	**.670∗**	-.076	**.619∗**	-.065
[31] Post-verbal subj	**.363∗**	.204	**.381∗**	**.294**	**.207**	**.500∗**	**.521∗**	**.349∗**	**.266∗**	**.228**	**.615∗**	**.570**	**.344∗**	.343
[32] Pre-verbal subj	**.476∗**	.141	**.498∗**	.163	**.220**	.076	**.568∗**	**.326∗**	**.328∗**	**.324**	**.441**	.089	**.572∗**	-.024
[33] Post-verbal subord clauses	**.552∗**	**.337**	**.534∗**	**.336∗**	**.488∗**	**.260**	**.647∗**	**.469∗**	**.528∗**	**.388∗**	**.505∗**	**.556**	**.385∗**	.052
[34] Pre-verbal subord clauses	**.299∗**	.155	**.378∗**	**.233**	**.445∗**	.105	**.495∗**	**.159**	**.308∗**	.085	**.315**	**.444**	**.424∗**	-.100
[35] Clause length	**.707∗**	**.485∗**	**.592∗**	**.481∗**	**.635∗**	**.388**	**.711∗**	**.513∗**	**.659∗**	**.450∗**	**.637∗**	**.514**	**.622∗**	**.462**

Table 4: Spearman's correlation between the most frequent rules and a subset of linguistic features. Significant correlations ($p < 0.05$) are bolded; those with $p < 0.001$ are also marked with $*$. For each column, the left value refers to *Terence*, the right value to *Teacher*.

tation scheme, also by testing the suitability of this scheme for other corpora.

References

D. Allen. 2009. A study of the role of relative clauses in the simplification of news texts for learners of English. *System*, 37(4): 585–599.

S. M. Aluísio, L. Specia, T. A. Pardo, E. G. Maziero and R. P. de Mattos Fortes. 2008. Towards Brazilian Portoguese automatic text simplification systems. *Proceedings of the eighth ACM symposium on Document engineering*, 240–248.

M. J. Aranzabe, A. D. De Ilarraza, I. Gonzalez-Dios 2013. Transforming complex sentences using dependency trees for automatic text simplification in Basque. *Procesamiento del lenguaje natural*, 50, 61–68.

G. Attardi. 2006. Experiments with a multilanguage non-projective dependency parser. *Proceedings of the Tenth Conference on Computational Natural Language Learning (CoNLL-X '06)*, 166–170.

G. Barlacchi and S. Tonelli. 2013. ERNESTA: A Sentence Simplification Tool for Children's Stories in Italian. *Proceedings of the 14th Conference on Intelligent Text Processing and Computational Linguistics (CICLing-2013)*, 476–487.

T. G. Bever. 1970. The cognitive basis for linguistic structures. J. R. Hayes (ed.), *Cognition and the development of Language*. New York, Wiley.

C. Bosco, F. Dell'Orletta, S. Montemagni, M. Sanguinetti and M. Simi. 2014. The Evalita 2014 Dependency Parsing Task. *Proceedings of Evalita'14, Evaluation of NLP and Speech Tools for Italian*, Pisa, December.

S. Bott and H. Saggion. 2014. Text simplification resources for Spanish. *Language Resources and Evaluation*, 48(1): 93–120.

L. Brouwers, D. Bernhard, A.-L. Ligozat and T. François. 2014. Syntactic Sentence Simplification for French. *Proceedings of the 3rd Workshop on Predicting and Improving Text Readability for Target Reader Populations (PITR)*, 47–56.

J. Carroll, G. Minnen, Y. Canning, S. Devlin, and J. Tait. 1998. Practical Simplification of English Newspaper Text to Assist Aphasic Readers. *Proceedings of the AAAI-98 Workshop on Integrating Artificial Intelligence and Assistive Technology, Association for the Advancement of Artificial Intelligence (AAAI)*

H. Caseli, T. Pereira, L. Specia, T. Pardo, C. Gasperin, and S. Aluísio. 2009. *Building a Brazilian Portuguese parallel corpus of original and simplified texts*. Proceedings of the 10th Conference on Intelligent Text Processing and Computational Linguistics.

R. Chandrasekar, C. Doran, and B. Srinivas. 1996. Motivations and methods for text simplification. *Proceedings of the international conference on computational Linguistics*, 1041–1044.

L. Ciccarelli. 1998. *Comprensione del linguaggio, dei processi di elaborazione e memoria di lavoro: uno studio in età prescolare*. PhD dissertation, University of Padua.

P. Cipriani, A. M. Chilosi, P. Bottari, and L. Pfanner. 1993. *L'acquisizione della morfosintassi in italiano: fasi e processi*. Padova: Unipress.

J. De Belder and M-F Moens. 2010. Text Simplification for Children. *Proceedings of the SIGIR 2010 Workshop on Accessible Search Systems.*

J. De Belder, K. Deschacht, and M-F Moens. 2010. Lexical simplification. *Proceedings of Itec2010: 1st International Conference on Interdisciplinary Research on Technology, Education and Communication.*

T. De Mauro. 2000. *Il dizionario della lingua italiana*. Torino, Paravia.

F. Dell'Orletta, S. Montemagni, and G. Venturi. 2011. READ-IT: assessing readability of Italian texts with a view to text simplificatio. *Proceedings of the Second Workshop on Speech and Language Processing for Assistive Technologies (SLPAT 2011)*, 73–83.

F. Dell'Orletta. 2009. Ensemble system for Part-of-Speech tagging. *Proceedings of Evalita'09, Evaluation of NLP and Speech Tools for Italian*, Reggio Emilia, December.

B. Drndarević, S. Štajner, S. Bott, S. Bautista and H. Saggion. 2013. Automatic Text Simplification in Spanish: A Comparative Evaluation of Complementing Modules. A. Gelbukh (ed.) *14th Conference on Computational Linguistics and Natural Language Processing (CICLing'14)*, LNCS 7817 (2):488–500.

B. Drndarevic, S. Stajner, and H. Saggion. 2012. Reporting Simply: A Lexical Simplification Strategy for Enhancing Text Accessibility. *Proceedings of "Easy to read on the web"*, online symposium.

G. Fiorin. 2009. The Interpretation of Imperfective Aspect in Developmental Dyslexia. *Proceedings of the 2nd International Clinical Linguistics Conference*, Universidad Autónoma de Madrid, Universidad Nacional de Educación a Distancia, and Euphonia Eds.

D. Gildea. 2001. Corpus variation and parser performance. *Proceedings of Empirical Methods in Natural Language Processing (EMNLP 2001)*, Pittsburgh, PA.

K. Inui, A. Fujita, T. Takahashi, R. Iida, and T. Iwakura. 2003. . Text Simplification for Reading Assistance: A Project Note. *Proceedings of the Second International Workshop on Paraphrasing, ACL.*

W. Kintsch and J. Keenan. 1973. Reading rate and retention as a function of the number of prepositions in the base structure of sentences. *Cognitive Psychology*, 5: 257–274.

M. Maratsos. 1974. Children who get worse at understanding the passive: A replication to Bever. *Journal of Psycholinguistic Research*, 3:65–74.

S. Narayan and C. Gardent. 2014. Hybrid Simplification using Deep Semantics and Machine Translation. *Proceedings of the 52nd Annual Meeting of the Association for Computational Linguistics*, 435–445.

Y. Ozuru, K. Dempsey, and D. McNamara. 2009. Prior knowledge, reading skill, and text cohesion in the comprehension of science texts. *Learning and Instruction*, 19): 228–242.

S. E. Petersen and M. Ostendorf. 2007. Text Simplification for Language Learners: A Corpus Analysis. *Speech and Language Technology for Education.*

A. Siddharthan. 2014. A survey of research on text simplification. *International Journal of Applied Linguistics*, 165(2): 259–298.

A. Siddharthan. 2002. An Architecture for a Text Simplification System. *Proceedings of the Language Engineering Conference (LEC 2002)*

A. Siddharthan and M.A. Angrosh. 2014. Hybrid text simplification using synchronous dependency grammars with hand-written and automatically harvested rules. *Proceedings of the 14th Conference of the European Chapter of the Association for Computational Linguistics (EACL 2014).*

A. Siddharthan. 2010. Complex lexico-syntactic reformulation of sentences using typed dependency representations. *Proceedings of the 6th International Natural Language Generation Conference*, 125-133.

A. Siddharthan. 2011. Text Simplification Using Typed Dependencies: A Comparison of the Robustness of Different Generation Strategies. *Proceedings of the 13th European Workshop on Natural Language Generation (ENLG'11)*, Nancy, France: 2–11.

D. I. Slobin and R. G. Bever. 1982. Children use canonical sentence schemas. A cross-linguistic study of word order and inflections. *Cognition*, 12(3): 229–265.

A. Sorace. 1993. Incomplete vs. divergent representations of unaccusativity in non native grammars of Italian. *Second Language Research*, 9(1), 22–47.

L. Specia. *Translating from complex to simplified sentences.* Computational Processing of the Portoguese Language, 6001:30–39.

F. Volpato. 2010. *The acquisition of relative clauses and phi-features: evidence from hearing and hearing-impaired populations*. PhD dissertation, Ca' Foscari University of Venice.

K.Woodsend and M. Lapata. 2011. Learning to simplify sentences with quasi-synchronous grammar and integer programming. *Proceedings of the Conference on Empirical Methods in Natural Language Processing*, 409–420.

Z. Zhu, D. Bernhard, and I. Gurevych. 2010. A monolingual tree-based translation model for sentence simplification. *Proceedings of the 23rd international conference on computational linguistics*, 1353–1361.

On the Discoursive Structure of Computer Graphics Research Papers

Beatriz Fisas, Francesco Ronzano and Horacio Saggion
Natural Language Processing Group, Pompeu Fabra University, Barcelona, Spain
{beatriz.fisas,francesco.ronzano,horacio.saggion}@upf.edu

Abstract

Understanding the structure of scientific discourse is of paramount importance for the development of appropriate Natural Language Processing tools able to extract and summarize information from research articles. In this paper we present an annotated corpus of scientific discourse in the domain of Computer Graphics. We describe the way we built our corpus by designing an annotation schema and relying on three annotators for manually classifying all sentences into the defined categories. Our corpus constitutes a semantically rich resource for scientific text mining. In this respect, we also present the results of our initial experiments of automatic classification of sentences into the 5 main categories in our corpus.

1 Introduction

Understanding the internal organization of text documents is important for many content assessment tasks such as summarization or information extraction. Several studies have investigated the structure and peculiarities of scientific discourse across distinct domains, such as biology (Mizuta and Collier, 2004), chemistry and computational linguistics (Teufel et al., 2009), or astrophysics (Grover et al., 2004). The coherence of the argumentative flow that authors adopt to expose scientific contents is essential to properly contextualize these contents, to characterize their connections with related pieces of research as well as to discover relevant aspects, novelties and future directions.

Because of both the huge, growing amount of scientific literature that is accessible online and the complexity that often characterizes scientific discourse, currently researchers and professionals are experimenting more and more difficulties when trying to keep themselves up to date.

The analysis of the internal organization of the scientific discourse and the identification of which role each piece of text plays in the scientific argument contribute to structure and thus ease the interpretation of scientific information flow. In addition, the explicit characterization of scientific discourse provides useful meta-information to support tasks like targeted information extraction, content retrieval and summarization.

Although several studies have characterized scientific domains, the area of Computer Graphics, a sub-field of Computer Science, has not been studied in previous work. We have developed an annotation scheme and produced an annotated corpus of scientific discourse in this domain.

The rest of the paper is structured as follows: After a review of previous work in the next section, we present and motivate the annotation scheme in section 3, describing the corpus dataset in section 4. We provide details of annotation process in section 5, followed by the values of the attained inter-annotator agreement and an analysis of the structure of the resulting corpus in section 6. Finally, before closing the paper with conclusions and future work, we explain our first experiments in automatic sentence classification in section 7.

2 Scientific discourse characterization: related work

The analysis and annotation of scientific discourse has been approached from different points of view in previous works.

Although the focus of the analysis is manifold and spans along different linguistic concepts, the scientific discourse annotation schema we propose in this paper builds upon the proposals of Teufel (1999; 2009; 2010) and Liakata (2010) hence the following subsections describe in more detail their contributions.

Simone Teufel's model (Teufel, 1999; Teufel and Moens, 2002; Teufel et al., 2009), which was named Argumentative Zoning, focuses on knowledge claims and is based on previous schemes for

Proceedings of LAW IX - The 9th Linguistic Annotation Workshop, pages 42–51,
Denver, Colorado, June 5, 2015.

classifying the citation functions (Garfield, 1965; Melvin Weinstock, 1971; Spiegel-Rösing, 1977).

Liakata (2010) analyses the content and conceptual structure of scientific articles with an ontology-based annotation scheme, the Core Scientific Concepts scheme (CoreSc). Closely related to this approach is the multidimensional scheme of Nawaz (2010), tailored to bioevents, and the works of De Waard (2009) in classifying sentences in 5 epistemic types and White (2011), who concentrates on identifying hypothesis, explanations and evidence in the biomedical domain.

In terms of scope, abstracts, considered to be a brief summary of the whole article, have been the object of research in the works of Guo (2010), Lin (2006), Ruch (2007), Hirohata (2008) and Thompson (2009).

Among researchers who explore full articles, Lin (2006) and Hirohata (2008) have based their analysis on section names, offering a coarse-grained annotation, while Liakata (2010; 2012), Teufel (2009) and Shatkay (2008) adopt a finer-grained approach.

The annotation unit is also a controversial matter. While most researchers agree to classify sentences into categories (Liakata and Soldatova, 2008; Liakata et al., 2010; Teufel and Moens, 2002; Teufel et al., 2009; Lin et al., 2006; Hirohata et al., 2008), others segment sentences into smaller discourse units (Shatkay et al., 2008; DeWaard, 2009).

Bioscience is by far the most studied domain and acts as a motor for research in information extraction from scientific publications (Mizuta et al., 2006; Wilbur et al., 2006; Liakata et al., 2010). Nevertheless, some work has also been done in the Computational Linguistics and Chemistry domains, where Teufel (2009) has implemented her AZ-II extended annotation scheme.

2.1 Argumentative Zoning - AZ

Teufel's main assumptions are that scientific discourse contains descriptions of positive and negative states, refers to other's contributions, and is the result of a rhetorical game intended to promote the authors contribution to the scientific field. In fact, Teufel argues that scientific texts should make clear what the new contribution is, as opposed to previous work and background material.

From a theoretical point of view she develops the Knowledge Claim Discourse Model (KCDM) which she adapts into three annotation schemes: Knowledge Claim Attribution (KCA), Citation Function Classification (CFC) and Argumentative Zoning (AZ).

Teufel annotates a corpus of Computational Linguistics papers with the first version of Argumentative Zoning (AZ) (Teufel and Moens, 2002). She later extends the AZ scheme for annotating chemistry papers, thus creating a new version, the AZ-II, with 15 categories (Teufel et al., 2009) instead of the first 7 in AZ.

The AZ-II annotated corpus consists of 61 articles from the Royal Society of Chemistry.

2.2 Core Scientific Concepts - CoreSc

Liakata (2010) believes that a scientific paper is a human-readable representation of a scientific investigation and she therefore seeks to identify how and where the components of a scientific research are expressed in the text.

As Teufel, Liakata also proposes a sentence-based annotation for scientific papers, but unlike Teufel, who proposes a domain independent annotation scheme based on argumentative steps, Liakata's scheme supports ontology motivated categories representing the core information about a scientific paper.

It was constructed with 11 general scientific concepts based on the EXPO ontology (Soldatova and King, 2006), which constitute the first layer of the annotation. The second layer allows the annotation of properties (New/Old, Advantage/Disadvantage) of certain sentences labeled in the first layer. Finally, in the third layer, several instances of a concept can be identified.

With the CoreSC annotation scheme and guidelines, Liakata's team produced the CoreSC corpus, constituted by 265 annotated papers from the domains of physical chemistry and biochemistry.

Liakata (2010) compares her approach to Teufel's and concludes that they are complementary and that combining the two schemes would be beneficial. They are both computational-oriented as the annotated corpora are intended to serve as a basis for linguistic innovative technologies such as summarisation, information extraction and sentiment analysis. CoreSC is more fine-grained in content-related categories while AZ-II covers aspects of knowledge claims that permeate across several CoreSC concepts.

Corpora annotated with Argumentative Zoning-II (Teufel et al., 2009) and Core Scientific Concepts (Liakata et al., 2010) have been exploited to build automatic rhetorical sentence classifiers.

3 Scientific Discourse Annotation Scheme

3.1 The domain: Computer Graphics

Computer Graphics is a vast field which includes almost anything related to the generation, manipulation and use of visual content in the computer. It is a relatively young discipline which has not been yet described in terms of its discourse, which differs mainly from the Bioscience's discourse in its much more mathematical content.

Research in Computer Graphics is based on multiple technical backgrounds, (mainly Physics, Mechanics, Fluid Dynamics, Geometry, Mathematics) and its results are the development of practical applications for their exploitation in several industries.

Scientific publications in Computer Graphics reflect the characteristics of this domain. It is expected that they include a section where a theoretical model is presented in detail - with algorithms, equations, algebra and mathematical reasoning - and a section where a computational experiment demonstrates an application that contributes to the knowledge in the area or to enhance techniques already in use in the mentioned industries. Experiments in computational sciences are basically algorithmical and do not include materials nor physical processes in laboratories.

3.2 The annotation scheme design

We defined our Scientific Discourse Annotation Schema by relying on both Teufel's and Liakata's annotation schemas and contributions. In particular, we extended and enriched Liakata's CoreSc scheme at this first stage, leaving the knowledge claim approach for a second stage.

A thorough review of the previous work in annotation of scientific publications as well as the analysis of the contents of papers in our domain, lead us to select 9 categories from Liakata's annotation scheme and the Discourse Elements Ontology (DEO), which

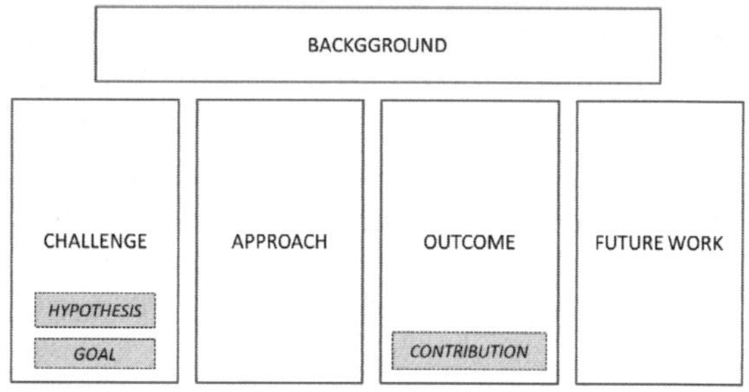

Figure 1: Simplified Annotation Scheme: 5 categories and 3 subcategories

were later increased to a total of 16, in order to cover the scientific concepts that might appear in an article.

However, this first scheme proved to be too complex, and we agreed to follow an annotation workflow characterized by subsequent steps with different levels of granularity. Thus, the corpus annotation process should go through a first coarse-grained phase and later increase the level of details with a finer-grained annotation scheme.

The 16 categories of the extended scheme were grouped into 5 main categories (Fig. 2).

Nevertheless and in order to provide the annotated corpus with more detailed information, we decided to leave annotators the possibility to specify three especially significant sub-categories: Hypothesis, Goal and Contribution.

Fig.1 shows the final version of our scientific discourse simplified annotation scheme.

4 Corpus Dataset for annotation: Data collection and Annotation unit

To populate our corpus we randomly selected a set of 40 documents, available in PDF format, among a bigger collection provided by experts in the domain, who pre-selected a representative sample of articles in Computer Graphics. Articles were classified into four important subjects in this area: Skinning, Motion Capture, Fluid Simulation and Cloth Simulation. We included in the corpus 10 highly representative articles for each subject.

The annotation is sentence based as we have considered sentences to be the most meaningful minimal unit for the analysis of scientific discourse, in agreement with earlier work.

CHALLENGE: The current situation faced by the researcher: it will normally include a Problem Statement, the Motivation, a Hypothesis and/or a Goal.
BACKGROUND:This section presents all the information which is helpful for understanding the situation or problem that is the subject of the publication. It will include sentences that state widely accepted knowledge in the domain (Common Ground) as well as previous related work (Related Work).
APPROACH: In this section the author explains HOW he intends to carry out the investigation. He may refer to a theoretical model or framework (Model), give some or many details of the experimental setup (Experiment), point to some data/phenomena observed during the experimentation (Observations) or comment on his decisions for choosing this methodology (Method).
OUTCOME: Here the author offers the study findings: measurable data without discussion (Results), an interpretation or analysis of the results in support of the conclusion (Discussion), how the research will contribute to the current knowledge in the field (Contribution) and an overall conclusion that should reject or support the research hypothesis (Conclusion). Any comments on the limitations of the authors work will also be included in the OUTCOME section.
FUTURE WORK: In most articles, the author will suggest or recommend further research to improve or extend his own work.

Figure 2: Description of the 5 categories of our Simplified Discourse Annotation Scheme

5 The Annotation Process

5.1 Annotators

The annotators are not domain experts. Two of them are computationally oriented linguists and the third is both a linguist and the developer of the annotation scheme. Each of them has annotated the whole set of documents. Therefore, the annotation outcome is a collection of 40 papers whose sentences have been annotated by the three annotators. The categories associated to each sentence by each annotator are then merged to create the Gold Standard version of the corpus.

5.2 Annotation Task

The 40 documents selected for our corpus were provided to each annotator so as to start the sentence annotation process. All the annotators use GATE v.7.1 as annotation tool, with a customized view where they have a window with the ready-to-annotate documents, segmented into sentences. Their task is to select a sentence and choose the appropriate category from a pop-up list.

Each sentence of each document of the Corpus is classified as belonging to a category among: *Approach*, *Background*, *Challenge*, *Challenge_Goal*, *Challenge_Hypothesis*, *FutureWork*, *Outcome* or *Outcome_Contribution*. Sentences were classified as *Unspecified* when the identification of the category was not possible (for example, metadiscourse or acknowledgements) or as *Sentence* when the selected text was characterized by segmentation or character encoding problems (for example, when a footnote appears incorrectly in the text flow).

5.3 Annotation Support

In order to ensure the quality of the annotation, the annotators were provided with the following support: an introductory training session, a visual schema of the proposed discourse structure, guidelines for the annotation, a series of conflict resolution criteria and recommendations. Moreover, two follow-up conflict-resolution meetings were scheduled to perform inter-annotator agreement checks along the first stages of the annotation process.

5.4 Annotation Workflow

After the training session, the annotators were encouraged to test the tool, and try the schema with a couple of documents before the annotation task really started. Once the process was triggered, two conflict resolution meetings were scheduled after the annotation of the first 5 papers, and after the subsequent 10 papers. Agreement was measured in these two milestones in order to detect deviations in an early stage. The articles were sorted by subject, to facilitate the better comprehension of the text for the annotators, as articles concerning the same subject

Category	Annotated Sent.	%
Approach	5,038	46.70
Background	1,760	16.32
Challenge	351	3.25
Challenge_Goal	91	0.84
Challenge_Hypotesis	7	0.06
FutureWork	136	1.26
Outcome	1,175	10.89
Outcome_Contribution	219	2.03
Unspecified	759	7.04
Sentence	1253	11.61
Total	10,789	100

Table 1: Number/Percentage of sentences per category

deal with similar concepts and terminology.

6 Annotation Results

6.1 Annotated corpus description

The Corpus includes 10,789 sentences, with an average of 269.7 sentences per document.

We are currently defining the best approach to make Corpus annotations available to the research community, since most of its 40 documents are protected by copyright.

The Gold Standard was built with the following criteria for each sentence: If all annotators or two of them assigned the same category to the sentence, it was included in the Gold Standard version with such category; otherwise, the category selected by the annotator who designed the scheme was preferred and used in the Gold Standard. Table 1 details the number of sentences of each category in the Gold Standard version of the annotated corpus and its percentage in reference to the total number of annotated sentences in the whole corpus.

6.2 Inter-annotator Agreement Values

We used Cohen κ (Cohen et al., 1960) to measure the inter-annotator agreement. Cohen κ is an extensively adopted measure to quantify the inter-annotator agreement, previously exploited in several other annotation efforts, including the corpora created by Liakata and Teufel, previously introduced.

Depending on how documents are combined, there are several options for calculating the agreement measures over a corpus. Micro averaging essentially treats the corpus as one large document, whereas macro averaging calculates on a per document basis, and then averages the results. Macro averaging tends to increase the importance of shorter documents.

	κ	N	n	k	domain
Liakata	0.57	255	11	9	Biochem.
Liakata	0.50	5022	11	9	Biochem.
Teufel	0.71	3745	15	3	Chemistry
Teufel	0.65	1629	15	3	Comp.Ling.
Teufel	0.71	3420	7	3	Comp.Ling.

Table 2: Summary of κ values in previous works: N=#sentences, n=#categories, k=#annotators

In our corpus, the κ value of inter-annotator agreement (Cohen's κ), averaged among all annotators' pairs, considering the 5 categories and the 3 subcategories of our Simplified Annotation Schema (see Figure 1) is equal to 0.6567 for the macro average and 0.6667 if the micro average is computed. If we consider only the 5 top categories of our Simplified Annotation Schema the inter-annotator agreement grows: the macro average becomes 0.674 and the micro average 0.6823. In both cases, the micro average is slightly greater than the macro average since there are documents with a number of sentences below the mean (269.7 sentences per document) that are characterized by low κ values, thus negatively affecting the macro-averaged computation of κ.

These κ values are comparable to those achieved by Teufel for 1,629 sentences in the domain of Computational Linguistics, with an annotation scheme of 15 categories and 3 annotators (see Table 2). The micro average κ achieves the cut-off point of 0.67, over which agreement is considered difficult to reach in linguistic annotation tasks (Teufel, 2010).

The agreement measures in the 2 milestones, showed evolution of the inter-annotator agreement throughout the annotation process: Cohen's κ is substantially stable between two of the annotators, while the third annotator sensibly improves his agreement with the other two very quickly in the first 5 documents and remains stable after the second milestone. In particular, the annotator with the lowest agreement in the initial stage increased his agreement with the other two annotators respecively from 0.59 for the first 5 documents to 0.68 for the last 25 documents and from 0.56 for the first 5 documents to 0.66 for the last 25 documents.

An analysis of the sentence distribution according to their agreement degree results in the following values: totally agreed sentences (65.09%), partially agreed sentences (31.24%) and totally disagreed sentences (3.66%).

Not all the categories are equally distributed, as each one of them has its own characteristics in terms of number of sentences, ambiguity or conflicts with other categories.

Background and *Approach*, the most highly represented categories, are highly reliable. In fact, more than 45% of the sentences of the corpus were tagged with agreement by the three annotators pairs as *Approach* or *Background*. If we also take into account the sentences with partial agreement (2 annotators agreed), then sentences classified as *Approach* and *Background* are more than 60% in the Gold Standard version of our annotated corpus.

FutureWork and *Outcome* are quite reliable, although the difference between them is that the ratio of totally agreed/partially agreed is considerably higher in *FutureWork* compared to the same ratio in *Outcome* (3.3 vs 0.9). This is due to the fact that although *FutureWork* sentences (1.3%) are much fewer than *Outcome* sentences (10.9%), those are much more easily recognized, as they include specific lexical clues (*for further research, in future investigation, more research is needed in, it could be interesting to, a better understanding,etc.*).

Clearly, *Challenge* is the category where the proportion of total disagreement is higher. This category which tends to appear at the beginning of a scientific paper shows more than any other the author's skills in writing, synthesis and ability to communicate the scope of the challenge they are presenting. Authors must be able to provide a context and outline the situation in order to attract the attention of the reader, who must understand the goal and complexity of the research.

When studying the relation between the number of sentences of a category and the annotation match between annotators, data reveal that the observed agreement among annotator pairs varies considerably according to the relative frequency of the an-

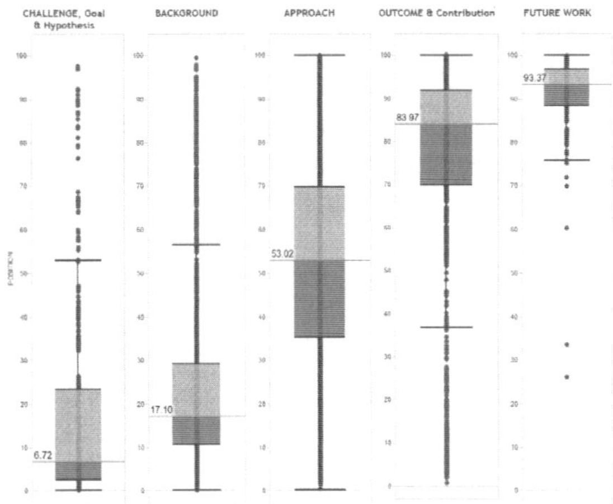

Figure 3: Box plots that show the distribution of the sentences of the 5 main categories of the Scientific Discourse Annotated Corpus

notation classes in the Corpus.

Agreement improves as the number of sentences of the category increases, getting close to 0.80 for the most frequent categories.

6.3 Discoursive Structure Analysis

The box plots of the 5 main categories (Fig. 3) give a clear picture of the discoursive structure of an average scientific paper in the Computer Graphics domain. In fact, the 5 main categories show a neat layout of the main zones (inside the box) in the argumentative structure distributed along the article. Even if one can find all types of sentences along the whole document, the central 50% of each category seems clearly limited to a zone with little overlapping of one another. When searching for information about one of these categories, a reader or researcher will find the central 50% of the sentences of each category in the following article length ranges: *Challenge* in between the 3% and 23%, *Background* in between the 11% and 29%, *Approach* in between the 35% and 70%, *Outcome* in between the 70% and 92%, *FutureWork* in between the 88% and 97%.

The identification of these ranges will allow readers, scientists, search engines, etc. to focus the exploring effort in a specific area of the article.

7 Automatic sentence classification: initial experiments

Recently several approaches to the automatic classification of the discursive function of textual excerpts from research papers have been proposed (Merity et al., 2009; Liakata et al., 2012; Guo et al., 2013). We present our initial experiments of automatic sentence classification with our Corpus. We describe the set of features we use to model and thus to characterize the contents of each sentence in order to enable the execution of proper classification algorithms. In particular, by relying on these features, we compare the performances of two classifiers: Logistic Regression (Wright, 1995) and Support Vector Machine (Suykens and Joos, 1999).

7.1 Description of sentence features

In order to support the extraction of the features that should characterize each sentence, we mine its contents by means of a pipeline of natural language processing tools, properly customized so as to deal with several peculiarities of scientific texts. As a consequence we are able to automatically extract from each sentence:

- **inline citation markers** - like *(AuthorA et al., 2010)* or *[11]*;
- **inline citation spans** that are text spans made of one or more contiguous inline citation markers. Examples of inline citation spans including one incline citation marker are: *(ALL2011)* or *[11]*. Examples of text spans including more than one inline citation marker are: *[10, 12]* or *(AuthorA. and AuthorB, 2010; AuthorC, 2014)*;
- for each inline citation span, if it has or not a **syntactic role**. For instance, in the sentence *[11, 12] demonstrate the theorem*, the inline citation span *[11, 12]* has a syntactic role since it is the subject of the sentence. In the sentence *We exploited the ABA method [14]*, the inline citation span *[14]* has no syntactic role.

We process each sentence by a MATE dependency parser (Bohnet, 2010) to determine its syntactic structure. A customized version of the parser is exploited to properly deal with the presence of inline citations. In particular, inline citations spans are excluded from the dependency tree if they have no syntactic functions in the sentence where they are present. After dependency parsing is performed, it is possible to identify the token of each sentence together with their Part-Of-Speech and syntactic relations.

- **unigrams**, **bigrams** and **trigrams** built from the lemmas of each sentence, lowercased and without considering stop-words. We included only unigram, bigrams and trigrams with corpus-frequency equal or greater than 4;
- **depth** and **number of edges by edge type** of the dependency tree;
- **dependency tree tokens** with corpus-frequency equal or greater than 4. Each dependency tree token is the result of the concatenation of three parts: kind of dependency relation, lowercased lemma of the source and lowercased lemma of the target of the dependency relation. For instance, one of the dependency tree tokens of the sentence *We demonstrate the theorem* is: *SBJ_we_demonstrate*, because "we" is the subject (SBJ) of the verb "demonstrate";
- **number of inline citation markers**;
- **number of inline citation spans that include two or more contiguous inline citation markers**;
- **number of citations with a syntactic role**;
- **position of the sentence in the document**, by dividing the document in 10 unequal segments (referred to as Loc. feature in (Teufel, 1999));
- **position of the sentence in the section**, by dividing the section into 7 unequal slices (referred to as Struct-1 feature in (Teufel, 1999));
- **category of the previous sentence**. We use gold standard previous sentence categories in our experiments.

7.2 Classification experiments

By relying on the features just described, we compare the sentence classification performances of two

Category	**Logistic Regression**	**SVM**
Approach	0.876	0.851
Background	0.778	0.735
Challenge	0.466	0.430
Future Work	0.675	0.496
Outcome	0.679	0.623
Avg. F1:	**0.801**	**0.764**

Table 3: F1 score of 10-fold cross validation of Logistic Regression and SVM - 10 fold cross validation over 8,777 manually classified sentences.

classifiers: Logistic Regression and Support Vector Machine with linear kernel. From our corpus we consider the set of 8,777 sentences that have been manually associated to one of the 5 high level classes of our scientific discourse annotation schema (see Figure 1): *Background*, *Challenge*, *Approach*, *Outcome*, and *Future Work*. We collapse the subcategories *Hypothesis* and *Goal* into the parent category *Challenge* and the sub-category *Contribution* into the parent category *Outcome*. We perform a 10-fold cross validation of the two classification algorithms, over the collection of 8,777 sentences. The results are shown in the Table 3.

The Logistic Regression classifier outperforms the SVM one both globally and by considering each single category. We can note that in general the F1 score obtained in each category decreases as the number of training instances does. This trend is not confirmed by the category *Future Work*. The corpus includes 136 sentences that belong to the category *Future Work*. This number is considerably lower than the 449 examples of *Challenge* sentences and the 1,175 examples of *Outcome* sentences. Anyway, the Logistic Regression F1 score of the category *Future Work* (0.675) is almost equal to the one of the category *Outcome* (0.679) and considerably higher than the F1 score of the category *Challenge* (0.446). This happens because some linguistic features that characterize *Future Work* sentences are strongly distinctive with respect to the elements of this class. For instance, the use of the future as verb tense as well words like *plan*, *future*, *venue*, etc. consistently contribute to automatically distinguish *Future Work* sentences, even if we have few training examples in our corpus.

8 Conclusions and Future Work

We have developed an annotation scheme for scientific discourse, adapted to a non-explored domain, Computer Graphics. We relied on the 5 categories and 3 subcategories of our annotation schema to manually annotate the sentences of a scientific discourse corpus made of 40 papers.

We have observed that the larger categories (in terms of number of sentences) - *Approach*, *Background* and *Outcome* - are highly predictable, while *Challenge*, which corresponds mainly with the introductory part of the scientific discourse is more heterogeneous and highly dependable of the author's style. Sentences classified as *FutureWork* have special lexical characteristics as confirmed by the results of our automatic classification experiments. We have also characterized specific zones for each of the 5 categories, thus contributing to a deeper knowledge of the internal structure of the scientific discourse in Computer Graphics.

In future we plan to focus on the characterization of other peculiarities of scientific text, including citations, thus properly extending our annotation schema. We are also confident that our Simplified Annotation Scheme will be suitable in other domains, and are therefore planning to verify it. A two-layered annotation scheme could then be applicable to most domains, the first layer being coarse-grained and general, and a second layer being finer-grained and domain-dependent for certain categories.

As future venues of research concerning automatic sentence classification, we are planning to carry out more extensive experiments and evaluations by increasing the set of features that describe each sentence, evaluating the contributions of single features and considering new classification algorithms.

Acknowledgments

The research leading to these results has received funding from the European Project Dr. Inventor (FP7-ICT-2013.8.1 - grant agreement no 611383).

References

Bernd Bohnet. 1999. *Very high accuracy and fast dependency parsing is not a contradiction.* Proceedings of the 23rd International Conference on Computational Linguistics. Association for Computational Linguistics, 2010.

Paolo Ciccarese, Elizabeth Wu, Gwen Wong, Marco Ocana, June Kinoshita, Alan Ruttenberg, and Tim Clark. 2008. *The SWAN biomedical discourse ontology.* Journal of Biomedical Informatics, 41, (5):739–751.

J. Cohen. 1960. *A Coefficient of Agreement for Nominal Scales.* Educational and Psychological Measurement, 20(1):(37).

Anita de Waard, Paul Buitelaar and Thomas Eigner 2009 *Identifying the Epistemic Value of Discourse Segments in Biology Texts* Proceedings of the Eighth International Conference on Computational Semantics, IWCS-8 '09, 351–354,Stroudsburg,PA, USA, Association for Computational Linguistics.

Eugene Garfield 1965. *Can Citation Indexing Be Automated?*, Statistical Association Methods for Mechanized Documentation, Symposium Proceedings, National Bureau of Standards Miscellaneous Publication volume 269, 189–192 Prentice-Hall, Englewood Cliffs, NJ.

Claire Grover, Ben Hachey, and Ian Hughson. 2004. *The HOLJ Corpus: supporting summarisation of legal texts.*. Proceedings of the 5th International Workshop on Linguistically Interpreted Corpora (LINC-04) Geneva, Switzerland.

Yufan Guo, Anna Korhonen, Maria Liakata, Ilona Silins, Lin Sun and Ulla Stenius. 2010. *Identifying the Information Structure of Scientific Abstracts: An Investigation of Three Different Schemes.* Proceedings of the 2010 Workshop on Biomedical Natural Language Processing:99–107, Uppsala, Sweden. Association for Computational Linguistics.

Yufan Guo, Ilona Silins, Ulla Stenius, and Anna Korhonen 2013. *Active learning-based information structure analysis of full scientific articles and two applications for biomedical literature review.* (Bioinformatics 29.11): 1440-1447

Kenji Hirohata, Naoaki Okazaki, Sophia Ananiadou, and Mitsuru Ishizuka. 2008. *Identifying sections in scientific abstracts using conditional random fields.* In Proceedings of the IJCNLP 2008, p.381–388.

Maria Liakata, Shyamasree Saha, Simon Dobnik, Colin Batchelor, and Dietrich Rebholz-Schuhmann. 2012. *Automatic recognition of conceptualization zones in scientific articles and two life science applications.* Bioinformatics, 28,(7):991–1000.

Maria Liakata and Larisa Soldatova. 2008. *Guidelines for the annotation of general scientific concepts.* Aberystwyth University, JISC Project Report, http://ie-repository. jisc. ac. uk/88.

Maria Liakata, Simone Teufel, Advaith Siddharthan and Colin Batchelor. 2010. *Corpora for the Conceptualisation and Zoning of Scientific Papers.* Proceedings of the Seventh conference on International Language Resources and Evaluation (LREC'10). Valletta, Malta, may 2010 Nicoletta Calzolari et al., European Language Resources Association (ELRA).

Jimmy Lin, Damianos Karakos, Dina Demner-Fushman, and Sanjeev Khudanpur. 2006. *Generative Content Models for Structural Analysis of Medical Abstracts.* In Proceedings of the Workshop on Linking Natural Language Processing and Biology: Towards Deeper Biological Literature Analysis, BioNLP '06, p.65–72, Stroudsburg, PA, USA. Association for Computational Linguistics.

Stephen Merity, Tara Murphy, and James R. Curran 2009. *Accurate argumentative zoning with maximum entropy models.* Proceedings of the 2009 Workshop on Text and Citation Analysis for Scholarly Digital Libraries Association for Computational Linguistics

Yoko Mizuta and Nigel Collier. 2004. *Annotation scheme for a rhetorical analysis of biology articles.* Proceedings of the Fourth International Conference on Language and Evaluation (LREC2004),1737–1740 , Lisbon, Portugal. European Language Resources Association (ELRA).

Yoko Mizuta, Anna Korhonen, Tony Mullen and Nigel Collier. 2006. *Zone analysis in biology articles as a basis for information extraction.* International Journal of Medical Informatics, 75(6):468–487.

Raheel Nawaz, Paul Thompson, John McNaught, and Sophia Ananiadou 2010 *Meta-Knowledge Annotation of Bio-Events*, Proceedings of the Seventh International Conference on Language Resources and Evaluation (LREC'10), Valletta, Malta, May, 2010. European Language Resources Association (ELRA).

Patrick Ruch, Celia Boyer, Christine Chichester, Imad Tbahriti, Antoine Geissbhler, Paul Fabry, Julien Gobeill, Violaine Pillet, Dietrich Rebholz-Schuhmann, Christian Lovis and Anne-Lise Veuthey. 2007. *Using argumentation to extract key sentences from biomedical abstracts.* International Journal of Medical Informatics,76,(2-3):195–200.

Hagit Shatkay, Fengxia Pan, and Andrey Rzhetsky, and W. John Wilbur. 2008. *Multi-dimensional classification of biomedical text: Toward automated, practical provision of high-utility text to diverse users.* Bioinformatics, 24, 18:2086–2093.

Larisa N. Soldatova and Ross King. 2006. *An ontology*

of scientific experiments. Journal of the Royal Society Interface, 3 (11):795–803.

Ina Spiegel-Rösing. 1977. *Science Studies: Bibliometric and Content Analysis*, 7 (1). Social Studies of Science, 97–113.

Johan AK Suykens and Vandewalle Joos. 1999. *Least squares support vector machine classifiers*. Neural processing letters 9.3 (1999): 293-300.

Simone Teufel 1999. *Argumentative Zoning: Information Extraction from Scientific Text*, School of Cognitive Science, University of Edinburgh, UK.

Simone Teufel, 2010 *The Structure of Scientific Articles: Applications to Citation Indexing and Summarization, CSLI Publications (CSLI Studies in Computational Linguistics), Stanford, CA.*

Simone Teufel and Marc Moens 2002 *Summarizing Scientific Articles: Experiments with Relevance and Rhetorical Status*. Computational Linguistics, 28, (4), 409–445.

Simone Teufel, Advaith Siddharthan, and Colin Batchelor. 2009. *Towards Discipline-independent Argumentative Zoning: Evidence from Chemistry and Computational Linguistics*, Proceedings of the 2009 Conference on Empirical Methods in Natural Language Processing: Volume 3,EMNLP '09, Singapore, 1493–1502, Association for Computational Linguistics, Stroudsburg, PA, USA.

Paul Thompson, Syed A. Iqbal, John McNaught, and Sophia Ananiadou. 2009. *Construction of an annotated corpus to support biomedical information extraction*. BMC Bioinformatics, 10:349.

Melvin Weinstock 1971. *Citation indexes*, Encyclopedia of Library and Information Science, 5,16–40. Marcel Dekker, Inc., New York.

Elizabeth White, K. Bretonnel Cohen, and Larry Hunter. 2011. *Hypothesis and Evidence Extraction from Full-Text Scientific Journal Articles*. Proceedings of BioNLP 2011 Workshop:134–135, Portland, Oregon, USA, Association for Computational Linguistics.

W.John Wilbur, Andrey Rzhetsky, and Hagit Shatkay. 2006. *New directions in biomedical text annotation: definitions, guidelines and corpus construction*. BMC Bioinformatics, 7:356.

Raymond E. Wright, 1995. *Logistic regression*.

Semantic Annotation of Japanese Functional Expressions and its Impact on Factuality Analysis

Yudai Kamioka[1] **Kazuya Narita**[1] **Junta Mizuno**[2] **Miwa Kanno**[1] **Kentaro Inui**[1,3]
[1] Graduate School of Information Sciences, Tohoku University / Miyagi, Japan
[2] Resilient ICT Research Center, NICT / Miyagi, Japan [3] JST, RISTEX
{yudai.k, narita}@ecei.tohoku.ac.jp junta-m@nict.go.jp {meihe, inui}@ecei.tohoku.ac.jp

Abstract

Recognizing the meaning of functional expressions is essential for natural language understanding. This is a difficult task, owing to the lack of a sufficient corpus for machine learning and evaluation. In this study, we design a new annotation scheme and construct a corpus containing 2,327 Japanese sentences and 8,775 functional expressions. Our scheme achieves high inter-annotator agreement with kappa score of 0.85. In the experiments, we confirmed that machine learning-based functional expression analysis contributes to factuality analysis.

1 Introduction

In natural language, many expressions are used to convey information beyond the propositional content of the sentence, such as modality and polarity. Understanding such information is essential for natural language understanding.

The extra-propositional aspects of meaning are often expressed by function words and their combinations. For example, consider the following sentence:

(1) パソコンが壊れてしまったかもしれない。
(*My computer may have been broken.*)

Three expressions are used to add extra information to the propositional content 壊れ (*break*): function words てしまっ (means it is unintentional), た (*have been*) and かもしれない (*may*) mean UNINTENTIONAL, COMPLETION, and UNCERTAIN, respectively.

Some function words such as た are used alone, and others are combined to express their meaning, such as てしまっ and かもしれない. We call the former a "function word," and the latter a "compound functional expression (CFE)." These are collectively called "functional expressions" (FEs) in this paper. Recognizing the meaning of FEs is useful for various natural language processing tasks, such as factuality analysis, machine translation, and question answering. However, two main issues cause difficulties in FE analysis. First, because FEs are usually expressed with multiple tokens, we must resolve the chunking problem. Second, FEs indicating different meanings can have the same surface form. For example, ている is used to indicate CONTINUOUS in 食べているところです (*now eating*) and used to indicate HABIT in いつも歌っている (*always sing*).

In Japanese, there is no corpus large enough for machine learning and evaluation. Matsuyoshi et al. (2006) first built a dictionary of Japanese FEs named *Tsutsuji*. Imamura et al. (2011) reported that this dictionary lacks many expressions. Therefore, we designed a new scheme for annotating FE meanings, and constructed a corpus containing 2,327 sentences and 8,775 FEs. In this scheme, we reorganize a dictionary of FEs on the basis of *Tsutsuji*. Our scheme and corpus are especially compatible with factuality analysis. We selected factuality analysis as our application, because it provides verifiable evidence to confirm the importance of FEs. Using the annotations of actual text, we investigate the problems associated with FE annotation. We also verified the effect of our corpus and FE analysis on factuality analysis. Our contributions are three fold:

(1) we introduce a new annotation scheme for Japanese FEs;

(2) we build a Japanese FE corpus with high inter-

Proceedings of LAW IX - The 9th Linguistic Annotation Workshop, pages 52–61,
Denver, Colorado, June 5, 2015.

annotator agreement;

(3) we demonstrate that improvements in FE analysis contribute to factuality analysis.

2 Related Work

Previous research efforts have addressed the problem of disambiguating functional and content usage. Tsuchiya et al. (2005) reported that more than 50% of the most frequent 180 CFEs contain ambiguities between functional and content usage. Tsuchiya et al. (2006) and Utsuro et al. (2007) used support vector machines (SVMs) for chunking, and showed that a machine learning model had advantages over a rule-based model. Suzuki et al. (2012) disambiguated functional and content usage using an example-based system.

Surprisingly, NLP research has paid insufficient attention to recognizing the meaning of FEs. Tsuchiya et al. (2005) constructed a Japanese CFE corpus. However the corpus focused only on a restricted range of expressions and is insufficient for machine learning. Matsuyoshi et al. (2006) organized a hierarchical Japanese FE dictionary, named *Tsutsuji*. *Tsutsuji* contains more than 16,000 FEs, which are categorized into 89 classes based on linguistic dictionaries. While *Tsutsuji* covers a wide range of FEs and their derivations, Imamura et al. (2011) reported that some expressions are not included. Some CFEs are contained in a dictionary of multiword expressions (Shudo et al., 2011). For example, とはいえ is included as "however."

In English, some research efforts have addressed the problem of modality and factuality. Saurí and Pustejovsky (2012) defined a list of modal words such as *perhaps* and *probably* for the factuality analysis. Szarvas et al. (2008) produced the BioScope corpus, which consists of biomedical texts annotated with negation and uncertainty, and their scopes. Diab et al. (2009) classified the writer's belief into three categories (committed belief, non committed belief, or not applicable). Diab et al. manually annotated the 10,000 words covering different domains and genres, and achieved high inter-annotator agreement of 95%. de Marneffe et al. (2012) used list of modal words and linguistic markers of negative contexts such as *no* and *any*, to automatically distribute event veridicality. Incorporating information about modality and negation has been shown to be useful for a wide range of applications. For example, Harabagiu et al. (2006) used negative markers such as *n't* as classifier features to recognize contradictions between two texts. Baker et al. (2010) showed the structure-based modality tagger improved the machine translation.

3 Annotation Scheme Design

3.1 Aims of Annotation

With the aim of creating a corpus for FE analysis, we designed an annotation scheme. The goal was to annotate its meanings to Japanese FEs. Because we are planning to use annotated labels in application tasks such as factuality analysis and FE analysis, the annotation scheme should be compatible with many applications.

3.2 Design Procedure

In the linguistics field, the meanings of FEs have been extensively researched. For example, Morita and Matsuki (1989) collected and categorized CFEs and provided explanations using an abundance of examples. As for the field of NLP, Matsuyoshi et al. (2006) provided an electronically-processable dictionary of Japanese FEs named *Tsutsuji*. *Tsutsuji* was composed according to linguistic dictionaries. There are many expressions that *Tsutsuji* lacks, because it has not been annotated for any actual texts.

We designed our annotation scheme by beginning with the semantic type categories defined in *Tsutsuji* and improving each category and entry where necessary. To be more precise, we added FEs that were not included in *Tsutsuji* but should have been. We also added and segmentalized some categories that were not appropriate for the application tasks. We used 1,627 sentences as development data, and alternated designing our scheme and annotating the corpus. A series of process was repeated several times while we carefully analyzed the feedback from the factuality analyzer described in Section 6. The following sections describe the problems encountered during the scheme's design phases, and how they were addressed.

3.3 Functional Expressions

Because different research efforts have adopted slightly different definitions of the term functional expression, we now clarify our definition. In this research, we define FEs as functional words and their combinations. Function words are non-content words; in terms of parts-of-speech (POS), they are categorized as particles and auxiliary verbs in the Japanese POS Tagset[1]. In the phrase 読みたい (*want to read*), for example, たい is categorized as an auxiliary verb and means WISH. These are the counterparts of the modal verbs (i.e., *might, will*) and verbs in English. Treating these words as FEs is common in linguistics research.

We define some FEs as compound functional expressions (CFEs), which are expressions whose meaning cannot be derived from their components. For example, かもしれない contains three words and means UNCERTAIN. The meaning of UNCERTAIN comes only after three words are combined; however none of the three words have the meaning of UNCERTAIN. We define such multiword expressions whose meanings are clear only after their components are combined, as CFEs.

Some CFEs are composed only of function words, and some contain content words. For example, ではない is composed from three function words で, は and ない. This expression means NEGATION when its components are combined. In another case, かもしれない is composed of function words かも and ない, and contentive しれ (*know*). However, the verb しれ (*know*) in かもしれない has no meaning as a verb, and the complete expression means UNCERTAIN. We consider these expressions to be a type of FE, even if some of the components are categorized in contentive. Function words and CFEs are collectively called functional expressions (FEs) in this paper.

3.4 Category Redesign

We categorized the meanings of FEs by referring to *Tsutsuji*. Because some categories were not compatible with application tasks, we added and segmentalized some of them. For example, かもしれない (*possibly*) and だろう (*probably*) are categorized as SPECULATION in *Tsutsuji*. However, these are actually different in the following aspects: 食べるだろう (*probably eat*) has more certainty than 食べるかもしれない (*possibly eat*). This fact is useful when determining the author's degree of conviction. Thus, we segmentalized these categories into different categories.

In another example, ている is categorized only as CONTINUOUS in *Tsutsuji*. This expression actually means continuation, however it sometimes means past experience: 歩いている (*be walking*) means continuation of 歩い (*to walk*), 指摘している (*pointed out*) means past experience. This fact will have an effect on the task of temporal relation analysis. Therefore, we introduced some new categories such as EXPERIENCE to annotate appropriate labels to these expressions. As a result, meanings of Japanese FEs are classified into 72 categories in our annotation scheme. Note that the number of categories is less than that of *Tsutsuji* because we left some FEs in *Tsutsuji* out of consideration in our scheme. Some FEs, such as が and を, have no information that is useful to us, as they are related more closely to predicate-argument structure.

4 Corpus Annotated with FE

We constructed a Japanese corpus annotated with the semantic labels of FEs based on the annotation scheme we developed. All labels were annotated using the Balanced Corpus of Contemporary Written Japanese (BCCWJ)[2]. We selected texts categorized in Yahoo! Answers in terms of usefulness, and because they were annotated with Extended Modality Tags (Matsuyoshi et al., 2010). The Extended Modality Tags contain *Actuality*, which can be used as a gold standard for factuality analysis. At this time, 2,327 out of 6,323 sentences in BCCWJ have been annotated. The guideline and corpus are available on `http://tinyurl.com/ja-fe-corpus`.

4.1 Labels

Labels are annotated at the token level. To annotate CFEs, we employed the IOB2 format (Sang, 2000) to express the range of FEs, and we used the label P for predicates. An example is shown in Table 1.

Label	Description
P	Predicates
B	Head of FE
I	Inner of FE
O	Otherwise

Token	Label
壊れ	P
て	B-UNINTENTIONAL
しまっ	I-UNINTENTIONAL
た	B-COMPLETION
かも	B-UNCERTAIN
しれ	I-UNCERTAIN
ない	I-UNCERTAIN

Table 1: Labels used in the corpus. (Chunk labels (left) and an example of actual labels (right))

4.2 Annotation

Our corpus is composed of a development set and test set. The development set contains 1,627 sen-

[1] `http://sourceforge.jp/projects/ipadic/docs/ipadic-2.7.0-manual-en.pdf/en/1/`

[2] `http://www.ninjal.ac.jp/corpus_center/bccwj/`

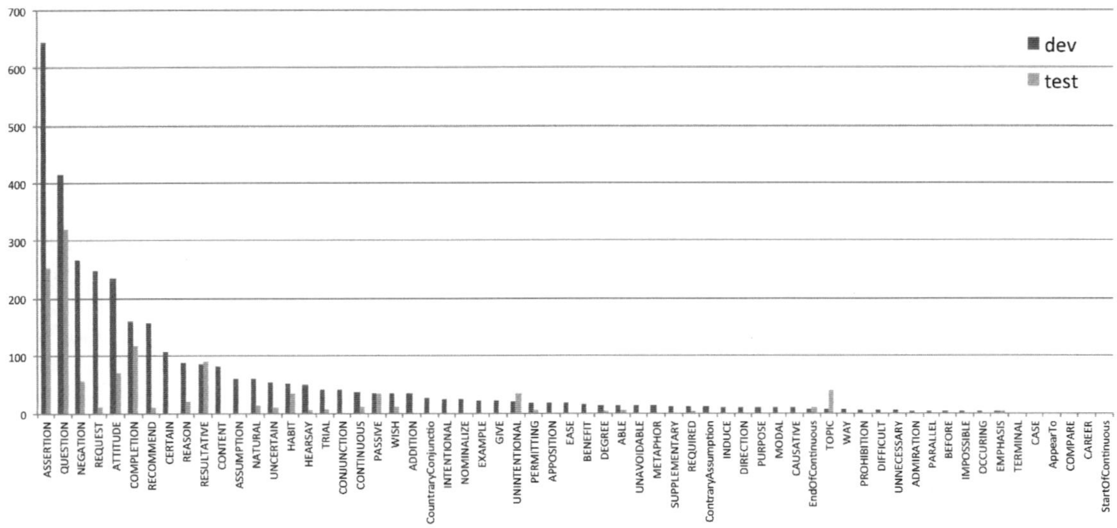

Figure 1: Distribution of semantic labels in the head clauses of the development set and the test set. (The development set contains all FEs in the sentence, while the test set contains FEs only in the head clauses. Only the labels agreed between two annotators were counted in the test set.)

tences randomly sampled from 6,323 sentences. We then labeled the 4,696 sentences using the development set as training data, and then sampled 700 sentences that contained more than three FE tokens in the head clause. We use these 700 sentences as a test set, in order to evaluate our annotation scheme and to conduct an open test.

The development set was annotated by a native Japanese speaker. For the development set, the annotator encountered issues with the original guidelines; after discussing the problems, we updated our guidelines accordingly and used the resulting guidelines for our development set. We outsourced the annotation of our test set to two other annotators, who were provided with our latest annotation guidelines and the list of FEs from the development set. To reduce time and cost, only the expressions in the head clauses were annotated in the test set, while all expressions in the development set were annotated.

The annotation procedure is as follows: i) The annotator is given the token sequence of a sentence. ii) The annotator selects a predicate that precedes an FE and annotates it with the predicate label (P). iii) On each FE, chunking labels are annotated for both head and inner chunks. iv) The most appropriate semantic label in the annotation scheme is annotated. Note that the annotator used only predicates and FEs to determine the semantic label. If the annotator could not locate an appropriate label in our scheme, the closest label was annotated and a comment was provided. The entire procedure was conducted using a spreadsheet, and we constructed a corpus from the resulting data.

4.3 Corpus Statistics

Statistical information of the constructed corpus is shown in Table 2. The results show that the percentage of CFEs in the development set was 74%, and 67% in both test sets. These percentages were significantly higher than our expectations; and extracting CFEs correctly is a crucial problem that we must resolve. Note that the number of FEs is much lower than that of *Tsutsuji*; this is because some of the FEs listed in *Tsutsuji* are infrequent and thus not found in the corpus.

	dev		test	test
	all	head	by worker1	by worker2
Sent.	1,627		700	700
FE	5,993 (584)	3,407 (317)	1,378 (179)	1,404 (187)
CFE	1,861 (437)	577 (216)	697 (121)	710 (126)
Label	67	62	37	34

Table 2: Corpus Statistics. (FEs and CFEs are noted in brackets)

As for the labels that appeared in the corpus, the development set contained 62 labels in the head clauses, and the test set contained roughly half of that. This is because the development set contained infrequent semantic labels which did not appear in the test set. Fig. 1 shows the distribution of FE semantic labels in the head clauses of development and test set. Some labels, such as TOPIC and UNINTENTIONAL, were frequent only in the test set. This was caused by the difference of annotator between the development set and the test set. More precise guidelines will reduce these differences. Conversely, labels such as NEGATION and REQUEST were infrequent in the test set although they appeared frequently in the development set. This is because we sampled sentences for the test set, depending on the number of FE tokens in the head clauses. Some FEs consist of less than three FE tokens did not appear in the test set.

In the development set, 106 of 584 FEs contain semantic ambiguity. These expressions are likely to be labeled with more than two types of labels, and they should be disambiguated during FE analysis. The number of newly added FEs is 485. Because we only added FEs which appeared in the corpus, some FEs and their derivations must still be added.

4.4 Reported Issues

The development set was annotated according to the conditions in Section 4.2, and all FEs were annotated completely. However, the test set annotators reported some issues with annotation. The following section describes two of them.

4.4.1 Variation of functional expressions

One of the biggest problems is that many FEs have a variety of derivations. During the annotation of the development set, we treated these derived expressions the same as base forms, and we indicated this to the test set annotators. While we thought it would be easy for native Japanese speakers to identify the derivations, the annotator reported some confusion when attempting to determine whether two expressions were the same. For example, one annotator reported that he was confused when attempting to determine whether ばよろしい had the same meaning as ばよい. In reality, these were slightly different in their degree of politeness; however, the proposed scheme could not identify the difference. It was confusing because the scheme indicated that they were the same; however, ばよろしい is not in the known lists. To resolve this problem, we should complement the list or create more precise guidelines with additional derivation pattern definitions.

4.4.2 Difference between contentives and functional expressions

The second problem involves difficulties in deciding whether a token is a predicate. As we mentioned previously, some contentives lose their original meaning and can be components of compounds. For example, in したら良いのでしょうか, there are two content words: し and 良い. Our annotation scheme defines たら良い as one of the FEs; therefore, し should be annotated as a predicate and 良い is the inner FE. However, it was difficult for our annotator because 良い slightly maintains its meaning as a contentive. This example shows that our definition of the differences between contentives and FEs was not specific enough.

4.5 Annotator Agreement

To evaluate our annotation scheme, we tested two types of inter annotator agreements using the data in the test set; two outsourced annotators were employed for the evaluation. Note that the annotations in the test set were only performed on the head clauses. To evaluate the inter-annotator agreements, we employed kappa statistics and calculated three different agreements: predicate agreement, chunk agreement, and semantic label agreement. Predicate agreement shows whether two different annotators agree on the location of a head clause. Chunk agreement shows whether they agree on the beginning and ending locations of the expressions, and is calculated according to the predicate location agreed upon by both annotators. If the predicate and chunk locations are agreed to by both annotators, we then calculate the semantic label agreement according to the choice of FE semantic type. Table 4 lists the kappa results, which show very high values for all three agreements. While detecting predicate position is a difficult problem, we achieved very high agreement because of the restricted annotation range. Because we are planning to create a corpus in which all predicates and FEs are annotated, predicate agreement should be calculated once again after all instances are annotated. Table 4 also shows a kappa score of .97 for chunking. This suggests extremely high agreement. Once predicate positions are given, it should be relatively easy for a human annotator to detect the beginnings and ends of FEs.

Label	Precision	Recall	F
QUESTION	93.67(296/316)	94.59(297/314)	94.13
ASSERTION	92.86(247/266)	95.37(247/259)	94.10
COMPLETION	80.85(114/141)	93.44(114/122)	86.69
RESULTATIVE	54.32(88/162)	74.79(89/119)	62.93
HABIT	89.47(34/ 38)	40.00(34/ 85)	55.38
ATTITUDE	90.79(69/ 76)	88.46(69/ 78)	89.61
NEGATION	80.00(52/ 65)	70.27(52/ 74)	74.82
PASSIVE	94.87(37/ 39)	92.86(39/ 42)	93.85
CONTINUOUS	71.43(10/ 14)	25.64(10/ 39)	37.74
TOPIC	100.00(38/ 38)	97.44(38/ 39)	98.70
UNINTENTIONAL	82.93(34/ 41)	100.00(34/ 34)	90.67
RECOMMEND	76.92(10/ 13)	34.48(10/ 29)	47.62
REASON	100.00(21/ 21)	91.30(21/ 23)	95.45
WISH	100.00(12/ 12)	85.71(12/ 14)	92.31
NATURAL	92.31(12/ 13)	78.57(11/ 14)	84.89
REQUEST	66.67(10/ 15)	100.00(11/ 11)	80.00

Label	Precision	Recall	F
UNCERTAIN	100.00(10/ 10)	100.00(10/ 10)	100.0
EndOfContinuous	36.84(7/ 19)	100.00(9/ 9)	53.85
PERMITTING	100.00(5/ 5)	83.33(5/ 6)	90.91
TRIAL	100.00(6/ 6)	100.00(6/ 6)	100.0
ABLE	71.43(5/ 7)	100.00(5/ 5)	83.33
HEARSAY	100.00(5/ 5)	100.00(5/ 5)	100.0
REQUIRED	60.00(3/ 5)	75.00(3/ 4)	66.67
MANNER	100.00(4/ 4)	100.00(4/ 4)	100.00
AppearTo	50.00(2/ 4)	100.00(2/ 2)	66.67
NOMINALIZE	0.00(0/ 2)	0.00(0/ 2)	0.00
INTENTIONAL	100.00(2/ 2)	100.00(2/ 2)	100.00
CONTENT	0.00(0/ 1)	0.00(0/ 2)	0.00
PURPOSE	100.00(1/ 1)	50.00(1/ 2)	66.67
EXAMPLE	100.00(1/ 1)	100.00(1/ 1)	100.00
EASE	100.00(1/ 1)	100.00(1/ 1)	100.00
All labels	84.66(1142/1349)	83.31(1148/1378)	83.98

Table 3: Label-specific Inter Annotator Agreement. (Precision, Recall, and F-measure assuming worker 1 produces "gold data" and worker 2 produces system output. More details on each semantic label can be found in the annotation guidelines on the web site.)

	kappa
Predicate agreement	0.8508
Chunk agreement	0.9708
Semantic label agreement	0.8514

Table 4: Inter-Annotator Agreement (kappa)

To evaluate the semantic label agreements, we calculated the inter-annotator agreement in more detail; we treated one annotator's annotation results as "gold data," and the other annotator's results as system estimation, and evaluated F-measure. Table 3 shows the results of precision, recall, and F-measure calculations. Note that each annotator annotates different semantic label sets, and the resulting agreements differ depending on which annotator we treat as "gold." Because the differences between these two result sets are relatively miner, Table 3 shows only one of them. Semantic label-specific agreement shows that the label of CONTINUOUS and HABIT labels achieved the lowest scores. These labels contain ambiguity: each label was annotated to the same functional expression ている. These results show that determining such ambiguous labels is still difficult for native Japanese speakers.

5 FE Analysis

We evaluated our FE analysis system and verified how useful our scheme will be for actual tasks. We consider FE analysis as a sequence labeling problem. In our evaluation, we used the conditional random fields (CRF) method (Lafferty et al., 2001) because it is commonly applied to solve sequence labeling problems. We used CRFSuite (Okazaki, 2007) to implement the CRF model.

Dataset The closed test experiments were performed using 10-fold cross validation on the development set; the open tests were performed using the test set, with development set as training data.

Features The unigram and bigram features that were used included tokens, POS, and base forms. Note that POS is subdivided into four stages: we used each of them for unigrams, and only the first two stages for bigrams.

We used the longest match principle as a baseline when using the dictionary. The baseline uses the constraints for the preceding token's POS. Dictionary entries and constraints were collected from the development set. Furthermore, the system outputs the most frequent label in the development set if the expression takes more than one label.

We employed the standard evaluation metrics of precision, recall, and F-measures. Each metric was calculated by considering FEs as a unit. In other words, we accepted only the expressions in which a chunking labels (B and I) sequence matched correctly. Furthermore, we only evaluated BI sequences, because recognizing the compounds is one of the main problems in FE analysis. The entire experiment focused on only FEs, while contentives were disregarded.

The results are shown in Table 5. Every result indicates that the CRF model provides better results than the baseline. The table also shows that

Table 5: Results of FE analysis evaluation

		Method	Precision	Recall	F
Closed	Chunk	Baseline	94.91 (5257/5539)	86.50 (5184/5993)	90.51
		CRF	95.39 (5851/6134)	95.93 (5749/5993)	95.66
	Semanti label	Baseline	76.44(4234/5539)	70.43(4221/5993)	73.31
		CRF	79.83 (4897/6134)	81.18 (4865/5993)	80.50
	Chunk (only head clause)	Baseline	95.00 (2339/2462)	82.85 (2299/2775)	88.51
		CRF	93.96 (2689/2862)	94.77 (2630/2775)	94.36
	Semantic label (only head clause)	Baseline	79.37 (1954/2462)	70.09 (1945/2775)	74.44
		CRF	80.61 (2307/2862)	82.05 (2277/2775)	81.32
Open	Chunk	Baseline	83.42 (815/ 977)	58.49 (672/1149)	68.76
		CRF	91.49 (1053/1151)	92.08 (1058/1149)	91.78
	SemLabel	Baseline	53.33(521/ 977)	45.52(523/1149)	49.11
		CRF	77.32 (890/1151)	79.11 (909/1149)	**78.21**

CRF achieved a high score on chunking F-measure. These results show that it is easier than expected to detect compounds from an FE sequence. Conversely, the F-measure of semantic label estimation exceeded 80%. We analyzed outputs from the closed test to determine why the F-score was low.

(2) いつも読んでいる雑誌でもかまわない。
(*Magazines that you read all the time is okay.*)
(Gold: HABIT System: RESULTATIVE)

(3) 両親とも働いているのが条件です。
(*Working of both parents is required.*)
(Gold:CONTINUOUS, System:RESULTATIVE)

(4) 感情の高ぶりがよく描かれている。
(*The novel portrayed heightened emotion well.*)
(Gold, System: RESULTATIVE)

In (2) and (3), RESULTATIVE was labeled incorrectly; the answer shold have been HABIT and CONTINUOUS. (4) shows an example of FE correctly labeled as RESULTATIVE. These examples were ambiguous, and caused lower inter-annotator agreement. Therefore, we should improve our corpus to include more precise guidelines.

6 Factuality Analysis

To verify the practical effectiveness of our corpus for factuality analysis, we used a rule-based factuality analyzer based on FE semantic labels. We applied our factuality analyzer to 1,475 events to which FEs were attached in the head clauses of 1,627 sentences for the closed test, and to 650 events in the head clauses of 700 sentences for the open test[3]. We only selected events in head clauses because the factuality in subordinate clauses is determined not only by FEs, but also by other factors such as predicates.

In our corpus, extended modality is also annotated for each event mentioned by Matsuyoshi et al. (2010). The *actuality* of extended modality denotes the author's degree of certainty and corresponds to factuality. In this paper, by comparing the results of factuality analysis based on each of the four FE types, we show that annotating events with both FEs and factuality leads to some quantitative investigations such as i) how much effect our FE redesign has on factuality analysis, ii) how much does FE disambiguation contribute to factuality analysis, and iii) for how many events can we analyze factuality based on FEs.

FE I and II are the results of the longest matches using POS-attachment rules by *Tsutsuji* (Matsuyoshi et al., 2006) and using our dictionary. We investigate the effect of our label redesign by comparing the results based on FE I and II. In our corpus, FEs and their semantic labels are added to the dictionary *Tsutsuji*. We make comparisons based on gold data from *Tsutsuji* and our dictionary to investigate the strict effects of our label redesign. However, *Tsutsuji* does not provide gold data; therefore, we approximate the results of the longest matches. FE I and II cannot determine one semantic label for ambiguous FEs. Therefore, FE I and II allow ambiguous FEs for multiple semantic label such as "HEARSAY, UNCERTAIN, METAPHOR;" in the factuality analysis step, all effects of semantic labels are applied.

FE III is the result of the CRF shown in section 5. We investigate the contribution of FE disambiguation by comparing the results based on FE II and III.

[3]FE annotation and extended modality annotation have different criteria for judging events. 650 of 700 events in head clauses were judged as events in extended modality corpus, so we use 650 events for factuality analysis.

Table 6: The distribution of factuality values

	CT+	PR+	PR−	CT−	U	Total
Closed	476	215	51	107	626	1,475
Open	283	18	0	50	299	650

FE IV is gold annotation data. We investigate incorrect events based only on the FEs of the results based on FE IV. For the open test set, we conducted experiments using the gold data from two annotators.

6.1 Model

We use factuality values generated by combining certainty and polarity, as per Narita et al. (2013). They classify events into five factuality classes: CT+ (fact), PR+ (probable), PR− (not probable), CT− (counterfact), U (unknown or uncommitted), with reference to Saurí and Pustejovsky (2012). Table 6 shows the distribution of factuality values in our experiment. In the extended modality corpus, CT+ constitutes 68% of the total events (Matsuyoshi et al., 2010); however, in our experiment, U has the highest rate because events with FEs are selected.

Our analyzer determines event factuality by attaching FEs. For example, a NEGATION FE switches factuality to negative if it is positive, and vice versa. We constructed the following update rules and corresponding FE semantic labels for each rule:

A. polarity: +→ −, − →+
(NEGATION, IMPOSSIBLE, POINTLESS, UNNECESSARY, DIFFICULTY)

B. certainty: CT→PR
(UNCERTAIN, HEARSAY, INTENTIONAL, EASE, MODAL)

C. certainty: CT→U, PR→U
(QUESTION, REQUEST, WISH, RECOMMEND, INDUCE)

First, the factuality is set to CT+ as an initial value. Then, the analyzer identifies the attached FEs. If FEs that have update rules are found, the factuality is updated according to the rule. Rules of all attached FEs determine the factuality of the event.

Figure 2 shows the example of our model. The factuality of the event 進め (*work out*) is classified as PR− by the NEGATION FE ない and the UNCERTAIN FE みたい.

6.2 Discussion

Table 7 shows the evaluation results on different FE analysis. The open test shows higher performance

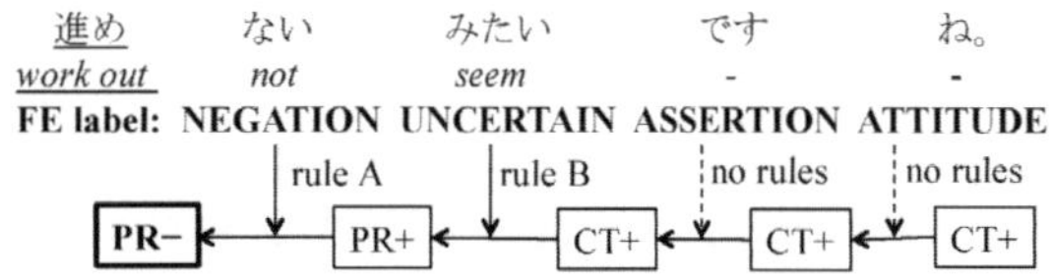

Figure 2: Applying our model to the sentence 進めないみたいですね (*It does not seem that you work out.*)

than the closed test because the open test set contains simpler events, as the frequency of PR− shows. We investigated the effect of our label redesign by comparing i) the longest-match results produced by our dictionary and *Tsutsuji*, ii) the contribution of FE disambiguation, which is obtained by comparing the CRF-based results and our dictionary, and iii) the incorrect events based only on FEs resulting from the gold data.

First, to investigate the effects of our label redesign, we compared the results of FE I and II. Table 7 shows that our label redesign improves factuality analysis.

(5) その方がより <u>分かり</u>[やすい]です。
(It is easier to <u>understand</u>.)
(FE I: CT+, FE II: PR+, Gold factuality: PR+)

(5) is an improved example from our dictionary. No items for やすい are in *Tsutsuji*; therefore, adding EASE as the semantic label of the FE やすい provides an improvement.

Second, to investigate the contribution of FE disambiguation, we compared the results of FE II and III. Table 7 shows that FE disambiguation improves factuality analysis.

(6) 5階から落ちて <u>助かっ</u>たんでした[よね]。
(He <u>survived</u> a fall from the 5th floor.)
(FE II: U, FE III: CT+, Gold factuality: CT+)

(6) is an improved example produced by CRF. The factuality of the event 助かっ (*survive*) is misclassified as U by our dictionary, because the FE よね is labeled as QUESTION. In contrast, CRF labels the FE よね as ATTITUDE based on context such as the COMPLETION FE た and period; therefore, so the factuality of the event 助かっ (*survive*) is correctly classified as CT+.

Finally, to investigate incorrect events based only on FEs, we evaluate the results based on FE IV. In the closed test set, approximately 40% of the events are incorrect despite the use of gold FEs. It shows that improvements in FE analysis are necessary, but

Table 7: Results of factuality analysis evaluation

	FE		Accuracy	Macro-Average		
				Precision	Recall	F_1
Closed	FE I:	longest match by *Tsutsuji*	44.00 (649/1,475)	36.46	33.53	32.13
	FE II:	longest match by our dictionary	54.51 (804/1,475)	50.70	44.28	46.56
	FE III:	CRF	57.90 (854/1,475)	55.70	48.38	50.42
	FE IV:	Gold data	61.90 (913/1,475)	56.71	54.58	54.59
Open	FE I:	longest match by *Tsutsuji*	52.00 (338/650)	38.04	54.89	29.57
	FE II:	longest match by our dictionary	66.46 (432/650)	50.34	61.96	50.86
	FE III:	CRF	92.62 (602/650)	94.93	86.29	89.54
	FE IV:	Gold data by annotator 1	94.62 (615/650)	97.14	92.83	94.76
		Gold data by annotator 2	94.46 (614/650)	97.02	93.57	95.15

Table 8: Error type distribution

		output	
		CT+	others
FE	granularity of semantic labels	10	21
	annotation error of FEs	6	4
factuality	update rule of FEs: insufficient/misapply	9	2
	equivalent predicate of FEs	9	2
	preceding adverb/particle	4	5
	ellipse of FEs	5	0
	annotation error of factuality	3	14
Other (morphological analysis error, etc.)		4	2

not sufficient for factuality analysis. We conducted an error analysis to investigate other factors aside from FEs. Out of 562 errors, 149 events were misclassified as CT+; 413 events were misclassified into other classes. Table 8 shows the error type distribution in 50 events. Other contributing factors included predicates equivalent to FEs, adverbs, and particles. Update rules also remain controversial.

Furthermore, errors caused by the granularity of semantic labels were found.

(7) どうやって色を判別してる[んでしょうか]?
(*How does it discriminate between colors?*)
(FE IV: U, Gold factuality: CT+)

For example in (7), んでしょうか is the QUESTION FE; therefore, the factuality of the event 判別し (*discriminate*) is misclassified as U. However, this sentence presupposes that the event 判別し (*discriminate*) is fact, because the author asks how to *discriminate*. There are two methods to resolve the problem: One is to subcategorize semantics labels such as QUESTION into QUESTION-HOW; however, this might lead to a proliferation of labels. Another is to improve the factuality analyzer by considering the scope of FEs or other elements in the sentence.

Annotating events with both FEs and factuality led us to these quantitative investigations for factuality analysis. We showed that our corpus contributes to factuality analysis.

7 Conclusion

In this paper, we designed an annotation scheme for Japanese FEs and constructed a corpus annotated with FE semantic labels based on the scheme. The corpus achieved very high inter-annotator agreement. Our guidelines and the corpus are publicly available. Statistical analysis based on our corpus clarified ambiguous FEs and the distribution of semantic labels. We identified the issues regarding the ambiguity of FE analysis. For factuality analysis, annotating events with both FEs and factuality provided us with some quantitative investigations. We also experienced challenges in applying our corpus to wider areas.

In future work, we will consolidate annotation guidelines by referencing linguistic studies that forcus on ambiguous FEs. Futhermore, to obtain better training data, we will redesign the scheme to combine some of the infrequently used labels.

Acknowledgement

This work was supported by MEXT KAKENHI Grant Number 23240018 and by RISTEX, JST.

References

Kathrin Baker, Michael Bloodgood, Bonnie Dorr, Nathaniel W. Filardo, Lori Levin, and Christine Piatko. 2010. A modality lexicon and its use in automatic tagging. In *Proceedings of the Seventh International Conference on Language Resources and Evaluation (LREC'10)*, pages 1402–1407.

Marie-Catherine de Marneffe, Christopher D. Manning, and Christopher Potts. 2012. Did It Happen? The Pragmatic Complexity of Veridicality Assessment. *Computational Linguistics*, 38(2):301–333.

Mona T. Diab, Lori S. Levin, Teruko Mitamura, Owen Rambow, Vinodkumar Prabhakaran, and Weiwei Guo. 2009. Committed belief annotation and tagging. In *Linguistic Annotation Workshop*, pages 68–73.

Sanda Harabagiu, Andrew Hickl, and Finley Lacatusu. 2006. Negation, contrast and contradiction in text processing. In *Proceedings of the 21st national conference on Artificial intelligence*, pages 755–762.

Kenji Imamura, Tomoko Izumi, Genichiro Kikui, and Satoshi Sato. 2011. Jutsubu kinouhyougen-no imiraberu tagaa {Semantic label tagging to functional expressions in predicate phrases}. In *Proceedings of the 17th Annual Meeting of the Association for Natural Language Processing*, pages 308–311. (in Japanese).

John Lafferty, Andrew K. McCallum, , and Fernando Pereira. 2001. Conditional random fields: probabilistic models for segmenting and labeling sequence data. In *ICML*, pages 282–289.

Suguru Matsuyoshi, Satoshi Sato, and Takehito Utsuro. 2006. Compilation of a Dictionary of Japanese Functional Expressions with Hierarchical Organization. In *Proceedings of the 21st International Conference on Computer Processing of Oriental Languages (ICCPOL)*, pages 395–402.

Suguru Matsuyoshi, Megumi Eguchi, Chitose Sao, Koji Murakami, Kentaro Inui, and Yuji Matsumoto. 2010. Annotating event mentions in text with modality, focus, and source information. In *Proceedings of the Seventh International Conference on Language Resources and Evaluation (LREC'10)*, pages 1456–1463.

Yoshiyuki Morita and Masae Matsuki. 1989. *Nihongo Hyougen Bunkei*. ALC Press Inc. (in Japanese).

Kazuya Narita, Junta Mizuno, and Kentaro Inui. 2013. A lexicon-based investigation of research issues in japanese factuality analysis. In *Proceedings of the Sixth International Joint Conference on Natural Language Processing*, pages 587–595.

Naoaki Okazaki. 2007. CRFsuite: a fast implementation of conditional random fields (CRFs).

Erik F. Tjong Kim Sang. 2000. Noun phrase recognition by system combination. In *Proceedings of the Language technology Joint Conference ANLP-NAACL2000*, pages 50–55.

Roser Saurí and James Pustejovsky. 2012. Are you sure that this happened? assessing the factuality degree of events in text. *Computational Linguistics*, 38(2):261–299.

Kosho Shudo, Akira Kurahone, and Toshifumi Tanabe. 2011. A comprehensive dictionary of multiword expressions. In *Proceedings of the 49th Annual Meeting of the Association for Computational Linguistics: Human Language Technologies - Volume 1*, pages 161–170.

Takafumi Suzuki, Yusuke Abe, Itsuki Toyota, Takehito Utsuro, Suguru Matsuyoshi, and Masatoshi Tsuchiya. 2012. Detecting Japanese Compound Functional Expressions using Canonical/Derivational Relation. In *Proceedings of the 8th International Language Resources and Evaluation.*

György Szarvas, Veronika Vincze, Richárd Farkas, and János Csirik. 2008. The bioscope corpus: annotation for negation, uncertainty and their scope in biomedical texts. In *Proceedings of the Workshop on Current Trends in Biomedical Natural Language Processing*, pages 38–45.

Masatoshi Tsuchiya, Takehito Utsuro, Suguru Matsuyoshi, Satoshi Sato, and Seiichi Nakagawa. 2005. A Corpus for Classifying Usages of Japanese Compound Functional Expressions. In *Proceedings of the Conference Pacific Association for Computational Linguistics*, pages 345–350.

Masatoshi Tsuchiya, Takao Shime, Toshihiro Takagi, Takehito Utsuro, Kiyotaka Uchimoto, Suguru Matsuyoshi, Satoshi Sato, and Seiichi Nakagawa. 2006. Chunking Japanese Compound Functional Expressions by Machine Learning. In *Proceedings of the Workshop on Multi-word-expressions in a Multilingual Context*, pages 25–32.

Takehito Utsuro, Takao Shime, Masatoshi Tsuchiya, Suguru Matsuyoshi, and Satoshi Sato. 2007. Chunking and Dependency Analysis of Japanese Compound Functional Expressions by Machine Learning. In *Proceedings of the 7th China Japan Natural Language Processing Joint Research Promotion Conference.*

A Qualitative Analysis of a Corpus of Opinion Summaries based on Aspects

Roque E. López[1], Lucas V. Avanço[1], Pedro P. B. Filho[1], Alessandro Y. Bokan[1], Paula C. F. Cardoso[1], Márcio S. Dias[1], Fernando A. A. Nóbrega[1], Marco A. S. Cabezudo[1], Jackson W. C. Souza[2], Andressa C. I. Zacarias[2], Eloize M. R. Seno[3], Ariani Di Felippo[2], Thiago A. S. Pardo[1]

Interinstitutional Center for Computational Linguistics (NILC)

Institute of Mathematical and Computer Sciences, University of São Paulo[1]
Av. Trabalhador São-Carlense, 400 - Centro, São Carlos, Brazil

Federal University of São Carlos[2]
Rodovia Washington Luís, Km 235, P.O.Box 676, São Carlos, Brazil

Federal Institute of São Paulo[3]
Rodovia Washington Luís, Km 235, AT-6, Room 119, São Carlos, Brazil

Abstract

Aspect-based opinion summarization is the task of automatically generating a summary for some aspects of a specific topic from a set of opinions. In most cases, to evaluate the quality of the automatic summaries, it is necessary to have a reference corpus of human summaries to analyze how similar they are. The scarcity of corpora in that task has been a limiting factor for many research works. In this paper, we introduce OpiSums-PT, a corpus of extractive and abstractive summaries of opinions written in Brazilian Portuguese. We use this corpus to analyze how similar human summaries are and how people take into account the issues of aspect coverage and sentiment orientation to generate manual summaries. The results of these analyses show that human summaries are diversified and people generate summaries only for some aspects, keeping the overall sentiment orientation with little variation.

1 Introduction

Opinion summarization, also known as sentiment summarization, is the task of automatically generating summaries for a set of opinions about a specific target (Conrad et al., 2009). According to Liu (2012), there are three main approaches to generate summaries of opinions: traditional summarization, contrastive view summarization and aspect-based summarization. Most of the works in opinion summarization follows the aspect-based approach, because it produces summaries with more information (Hu and Liu, 2004).

Aspect-based opinion summarization generates summaries of opinions for the main aspects of an object or entity. Objects could be products, services, organizations (e.g., a smartphone), and aspects are attributes or components of them (such as the battery or the screen for a smartphone). An automatic system of aspect-based opinion summarization receives as input a set of opinions about an object and produces a summary that expresses the sentiment for some relevant aspects.

Opinion summaries could be extractive or abstractive. Most automatic methods in opinion summarization produces extractive summaries, which are created selecting the most representative text segments (usually sentences) from the original opinions (Mani, 1999) (Radev et al., 2004). An opinion summary could also be abstractive, in which the content of the summary is rewritten using new text segments (Radev and McKeown, 1998) (Lin and Hovy, 2000). There are few works that produce abstractive summaries, because they require some complex Natural Language Processing tasks such as text generation or sentence fusion.

In both cases, to evaluate the performance of au-

Proceedings of LAW IX - The 9th Linguistic Annotation Workshop, pages 62–71,
Denver, Colorado, June 5, 2015.

tomatic methods, it is usually necessary to have a reference corpus of human summaries. With a corpus, automatic and human summaries could be compared to know how similar they are. Through that comparison, we could identify the errors of these automatic methods and, consequently, improve their performance. Moreover, a corpus of opinion summaries could be used in machine learning methods as training data to learn patterns for extracting important information from opinions.

Unfortunately, there are few available corpora for aspect-based opinion summarization (Ganesan et al., 2010) (Zhu et al., 2013) (Kim and Zhai, 2009), which difficults the progress of this task. Most of these corpora have focused on English. For Brazilian Portuguese language, to the best of our knowledge, there is no available corpus of opinion summaries.

In this paper, we present OpiSums-PT (**Opi**nion **Sum**maries in **Port**uguese), a corpus of opinion summaries based on aspects, written in Brazilian Portuguese. OpiSums-PT contains multiple human summaries, in which each summary comes from the analysis of 10 opinions. The building of this corpus was motivated by two main reasons: (i) to address the absence of a corpus of opinion summaries in Brazilian Portuguese and (ii) to evaluate how people generate summaries of opinions. Particularly, we analyze how similar human summaries are (for the same set of opinions) and how important the information of aspect coverage and sentiment orientation are.

The results of these analyses indicate that agreement for human summaries, in terms of Kappa coefficient (Carletta, 1996) and ROUGE-1 measure (Lin, 2004), is low. The results also show that people generate summaries only for some aspects and they keep the overall sentiment orientation, with little variation, in the summaries.

The remaining of the paper is organized as follows: in Section 2, we introduce the main related works; in Section 3, we describe the resources used in this research; in Section 4, we explain how the corpus of summaries was created; the experiments and results of annotator agreement, aspect coverage and sentiment orientation are presented in Section 5; finally, in Section 6, we conclude this work.

2 Related Work

Many research works in aspect-based opinion summarization have created their own dataset crawling review websites or social networks. Of these resources, few could be considered as standard datasets. The dataset proposed in Hu and Liu (2004) is the most used resource in aspect-based opinion summarization. However, that corpus did not contain manual summaries, but aspects annotated and their associated sentiment. To evaluate automatic summaries in those works, the authors have used survey questions to select the best summaries.

In previous works in which opinion summaries were manually created, the annotation of the corpus has not been described in detail because it was not the main focus of these studies.

In Tadano et al. (2010), three participants annotated 25 reviews (approximately with 450 sentences) of opinions about a videogame. From the 25 reviews, 50 sentences were selected to the summary. In the experiments, ROUGE-1 measure between the annotator's summaries was 0.480, which shows that it is difficult to generate the same summary for opinions, even among humans.

Xu et al. (2011) crawled 32,007 reviews for three aspects (food, service and ambience) from 173 restaurants. From these reviews, 10 restaurants were chosen for evaluations and 7 restaurants to configure some parameters of the automatic method proposed by Xu et al. For each aspect of a restaurant, the authors created an extractive summary selecting several sentences with representative and diverse opinions. Each summary was composed by 100 words in average.

In Carenini et al. (2006), 28 annotators created abstractive summaries for a corpus of reviews about a digital camera and a DVD player. Each participant in the annotation received 20 reviews randomly selected from the corpus and generated a summary of 100 words. As instructions, the participants assumed that they worked for a manufacturer of products (either digital camera or DVD player). The purpose of these instructions was to motivate the user to look for the most important information worthy of summarization.

Ganesan et al. (2010) created a corpus of manual abstractive summaries using reviews of hotels, cars and various electronic products. To collect the reviews, the authors used 51 "topic queries" (e.g., Ipod:sound and Toyota:comfort). Each "topic query" had 100 redundant sentences related to the query. Ganesan et al. used a crowdsourcing marketplace to get 5 human workers to create 5 different summaries for each "topic query". After the creation of the summaries, the authors reviewed each set of summaries and dropped summaries that had little or no correlation with the majority of them. Finally, each "topic query" had approximately 4 reference summaries.

Unlike these works, we performed a qualitative analysis of opinion summaries based on aspects. Besides that, we also compare extractive and abstractive summaries in terms of annotators agreement, aspect coverage and sentiment orientation. To the best of our knowledge, there are no similar works, most likely due to the difficulty of generating human-written summaries for opinions.

3 Corpora

To create the corpus of opinion summaries, we used reviews from two domains: books and electronic products. For the first one, we used the opinions of ReLi corpus (Freitas et al., 2013), a collection of opinions about 13 books. For the second domain, we collected reviews of 4 electronic products from Buscapé[1] website. The purpose of using these two domains is to have a corpus with different characteristics in the opinions. In the following sections, these two resources are explained in more detail.

3.1 Books

For book opinions, we used the ReLi corpus (Freitas et al., 2013). This corpus is composed of 1,600 reviews with 12,000 sentences about 13 books written by 7 famous authors of classical and contemporary literature. The opinions of ReLi were freely written by different users in specialized review websites.

The annotated opinions in ReLi are directly related to the books and their aspects (e.g., characters, chapters and story). Opinions about other books or movies of the books were not considered. In ReLi, reviews were annotated at the segment and sentence levels in three phases: (i) identification and annotation of the sentence polarity, (ii) identification of objects in sentences and (iii) identification of polarity in segments that contain sentiment. E.g., for the sentence *"The book is very interesting but its chapters are too long"*, the polarity sentence is positive, the identified objects are *book* and *chapters*, and the polarities for the segments *very interesting* and *too long* are positive and negative, respectively.

The annotation of ReLi was conducted by linguists who attended a training process to be familiar with the task and instructions. According to Freitas et al. (2013), the agreement was calculate in a sample of 170 reviews and the obtained results were satisfactory. In the polarity identification of sentences, identification of objects and polarity identification in segments that contain sentiment, the agreement values were 98.3%, 72.6% and 99.8% in average, respectively.

For the annotation of our corpus, we randomly selected 10 reviews for each book of ReLi, taking as example other related works ((Carenini et al., 2006), (Tadano et al., 2010)) that have used a similar number of opinions as data source. In the selection of reviews, we determined that they contain at most 300 words. We used this filter because people prefer to read concise opinions instead of reviews with too many words. This criterion was also used in the selection of electronic product opinions.

3.2 Electronic Products

We collected opinions about electronic products from Buscapé, a website where users comment about different products (e.g. smartphones, clothes, videogames, etc.). These comments are written in a free format within a template with three sections: Pros, Cons, and Opinion.

To create the corpus of summaries, we collected a set of reviews about 4 electronic products: 2 smartphones (Samsung Galaxy S III and Iphone 5) and 2 televisions (LG Smart TV and Samsung Smart TV). For each product, we randomly selected 10 reviews.

This set of reviews was annotated by one person with strong knowledge in Sentiment Analysis. The annotation consisted in the identification of product aspects, e.g., battery and photo for smartphones, and sound and price for televisions. The identification of the polarity of segments that contain sentiment about the aspects was also annotated.

[1]http://www.buscape.com.br/

4 Corpus Annotation

According to Ulrich et al. (2008), abstractive summarization is the main goal of many research works, since it is what people naturally do, but extractive summarization has been more explored and effective since it is easier to compute. In this annotation, we generated both, extractive and abstractive summaries, to assistant different researches and to analyze how they are generated in opinions.

In OpiSums-PT, we created multiple reference summaries in order to reduce the overall subjectivity and any possible bias. For each book and electronic product, we generated 5 extractive and 5 abstractive summaries. In total, 170 summaries were manually created. Table 1 shows the content of OpiSums-PT in relation to the number of sentences, tokens, types and their average by summary.

Table 1: Content of OpiSums-PT

Features	Extractive Summaries	Abstractive Summaries
Summaries	85	85
Sentences	534	430
Tokens	8435	8611
Types	1702	1833
Average sentences by summary	6.3	5.1
Average tokens by summary	99.2	101.3
Average types by summary	71.1	72.4

This annotation was carried out by 14 participants with strong knowledge in Computational Linguistics and Natural Language Processing. Each participant created 12 summaries approximately during the annotation process. Each set of 5 summaries (extractive or abstractive) was generated by 5 different annotators.

To generate a summary, either extractive or abstractive, each annotator read 10 opinions about books or electronic products. This number of opinions was chosen because we believe that, when people look for opinions, they do not read large amounts of opinions, but a small sample of them.

The task of annotation was daily performed during 13 days, approximately. In the first meeting, the annotators received a training session together with the annotation manual document to be familiar with the task. In that document, we presented all instructions as well as the aspects identified in the opinions of ReLi and Buscapé. These aspects were taken from the annotation of these two data sources and were shown to the participants with the sole intention that annotators know them. Table 2 shows the objects and aspects presented to the participants in the annotation of OpiSums-PT.

Table 2: Objects and aspects identified in opinions

Objects	Aspects
Books	characters, story, chapters, dialogues, phrases, author's style, titles, images, vocabulary, text
Smartphones	battery, design, processor, screen, price, camera, weight, operating system, internet, photo, video, wi-fi, sound, size, headphones, speed, chip
TVs	design, price, camera, image quality, brightness, wi-fi, sound, durability, internet

In the other days of annotation, the annotators created summaries at home and sent them by email, as it was conducted in (Dias et al., 2014). Each day, an annotator generated only one summary (extractive or abstractive). We opted for this scheme in order to simplify the task for annotators and, consequently, to get good summaries.

Another instruction in the annotation was related to the summary length. Both extractive and abstractive summaries should be composed by 100 words with a tolerance of ± 10 words, approximately. We choose the same number of words for these types of summaries to evaluate how they are generated under similar restrictions. A compression ratio in percentage (e.g., 25%) was not used because the vast majority of the works in aspect-based opinion summarization do not use this scheme (Carenini et al., 2006) (Ganesan et al., 2010) (Tadano et al., 2010).

4.1 Extractive Summaries

To create extractive summaries in our annotation, we asked the annotators to select the most important sentences from the original opinions. We did not establish a criterion to determine the importance of a sentence, it was a decision of each annotator. Likewise, we did not oblige to exclude sentences with dangling anaphora. We opted for this autonomy with the purpose that the creation of summaries to be as natural as possible. The number of aspects included in the final summary was chosen by each annotator.

The final summary was composed by complete

sentences. It was not allowed to rewrite the sentences of the original opinions. If a sentence presented misspellings and/or grammatical mistakes, they should not be corrected.

Each sentence of the source opinions had an identifier in the end part. This identifier allowed linking the summary sentence with the source opinion. Thus, for example, the identifier "<D20_S3>" indicates the third sentence of the opinion (document) 20. Figure 1 shows an example of an extractive summary (in bold, the identifiers of the sentences).

Um Smartphone quase Perfeito! **<D3_S1>**
O que gostei: Hoje é o melhor no mercado em relação ao seu processamento. **<D2_S3>**
A bateria dura bastante e os aplicativos ja instalados sao otimos. **<D7_S5>**
A camera é maravilhosa. **<D7_S4>**
O que não gostei: Ele esquenta um Pouco na parte de baixo mas não chega a incomodar, na cor branca ele parece ser muito frágil e o S Voice ainda não funciona em português. **<D3_S5>**
Esperava muito mais do Galaxy SIII pelo suspense que a Samsung promoveu. **<D2_S1>**
Depois dessa, quem tem coragem de investir em média R$ 1.700,00 no Galaxy SIII ou tentar a sorte com o Galaxy S4? **<D6_S9>**

[Translation]

A Smartphone almost perfect! **<D3_S1>**
What I liked: Today is the best on the market in relation to its processing. **<D2_S3>**
The battery lasts a lot and its installed applications are great. **<D7_S5>**
The camera is wonderful. **<D7_S4>**
What I did not like: It heats a little at the bottom but not enough to bother, in white color it seems very fragile and the S Voice does not work yet in Portuguese. **<D3_S5>**
I expected more of Galaxy SIII due to the suspense that Samsung promoted. **<D2_S1>**
After that, who has the courage to invest around R$ 1,700.00 in Galaxy SIII or try luck with the Galaxy S4? **<D6_S9>**

Figure 1: Example of Extractive Summary

As we can see in Figure 1, the extractive summary is composed by seven sentences from different opinions (D2, D3, D6 and D7). This happened frequently in our extractive summaries, indicating that relevant sentences for annotators were written by different web users. As consequence of this, the lack of cohesion between summary sentences was notorious.

4.2 Abstractive Summaries

To create abstractive summaries is more difficult than extractive summaries, since it implies generating new text. In our annotation, we asked the annotators to generate summaries as rewritten as possible in order to get more differentiated summaries in relation to the extractive summaries.

Abstractive summaries should indicate the actual scenario of source opinions (general predominant sentiment). Similar to the extractive summaries, the number of aspects to be included in abstractive summaries and the structure of the text were decisions of each annotator.

In Figure 2, we show an example of abstractive summary about Twilight book. In the first part of the text, the author's summary gives the overall sentiment for this book, and, then, describes the web user's sentiment for some book aspects. This structure was adopted by the majority of annotators.

A grande maioria dos leitores avaliaram negativamente o livro Crepúsculo, pois em geral, eles argumentaram que o livro tem um romance exagerado. Entre as principais desvantagens do livro, os leitores mencionaram que os personagens são superficiais, a escrita é péssima e a história é chata. Muitos dos usuários não conseguiram terminar de ler o livro e não recomendariam ele para outras pessoas. Por outro lado, outra pequena parte dos leitores acharam que o livro Crepúsculo é bom, pois consideraram que ele é intenso, romântico, cheio de mistérios e brilhante. Estes leitores afirmaram que, embora Crepúsculo seja um livro fictício, ele mostra a importância de um verdadeiro amor.

[Translation]

The vast majority of readers evaluated negatively Twilight book, because, in general, they argued that it has an exaggerated romance. Among the main disadvantages of this book, readers mentioned that characters are superficial, the writing is bad and the story is boring. Many users were not able to finish the reading of the book and they would not recommend it to other people. On the other hand, another small part of readers think that Twilight book is good, because they considered it intense, romantic, full of mysteries and amazing. These readers said that, although Twilight is a fictional book, it shows the importance of the true love.

Figure 2: Example of Abstractive Summary

In comparison with extractive summaries, these ones did not present the problem of lack of cohesion and show explicitly what was the predominant sentiment in the source opinions.

5 Experiments

After the annotation, we performed some experiments over OpiSums-PT. First, we calculated the annotators agreement to know how difficult this task is. Second, we analyzed the aspect coverage to estimate the proportion of aspects that is preserved in the summaries. Finally, the sentiment orientation in the summaries was computed to verify if it is proportional to the general sentiment in source opinions.

In this paper, we focused on these three issues. It is believed that (i) people generate not very similar opinion summaries, (ii) not all aspects are consid-

Table 3: Annotators agreement results

Books/ Electronic Products	Extractive Summary					Abstractive Summary
	Total Agreement	Majority Agreement	Minority Agreement	No Agreement	ROUGE-1	ROUGE-1
Capitães da Areia	0.000	0.267	0.200	0.533	0.405	0.218
Crepúsculo	0.000	0.286	0.357	0.357	0.414	0.239
Ensaio sobre a Cegueira	0.000	0.043	0.217	0.739	0.250	0.251
Fala sério. amiga!	0.077	0.154	0.154	0.615	0.606	0.299
Fala sério. amor!	0.118	0.118	0.294	0.471	0.600	0.287
Fala sério. mãe!	0.000	0.222	0.167	0.611	0.325	0.308
Fala sério. pai!	0.000	0.143	0.143	0.714	0.418	0.352
Fala sério. professor!	0.000	0.235	0.353	0.412	0.344	0.345
O Apanhador nos Campos de Centeio	0.000	0.091	0.409	0.500	0.360	0.253
O Outro lado da meia noite	0.000	0.136	0.182	0.682	0.392	0.232
O Reverso da Medalha	0.000	0.100	0.250	0.650	0.339	0.305
Se houver Amanhã	0.000	0.200	0.200	0.600	0.471	0.309
1984	0.000	0.263	0.316	0.421	0.366	0.238
Iphone 5	0.000	0.308	0.154	0.538	0.342	0.230
Samsung Galaxy S III	0.000	0.100	0.200	0.700	0.235	0.276
LG Smart TV	0.000	0.040	0.240	0.720	0.274	0.270
Samsung Smart TV	0.000	0.238	0.333	0.429	0.451	0.270
Average	**0.011**	**0.173**	**0.245**	**0.570**	**0.388**	**0.275**

ered in the final summary and (iii) humans consider the sentiment orientation to create an opinion summary. However, as far as we know, there are no previous works that proved these hypotheses. In this study, we explore these three hypotheses.

5.1 Inter-Annotator Agreement

We calculated the inter-annotator agreement for extractive and abstractive summaries. For both, we used the ROUGE score (Lin, 2004). For extractive summaries, Kappa coefficient (Carletta, 1996) was also calculated, as well as the percentage of common sentences in the summaries.

In extractive summaries, we calculated Kappa agreement for each book and electronic product, taking the sentences of source opinions and verifying which of them were included in the human summaries. In average, the Kappa value obtained in the experiments was 0.185. According to Liu and Liu (2008), the Kappa values reported for text and meeting summarization were 0.38 and 0.28 in average, respectively. Compared to these values, the Kappa agreement obtained by us in aspect-based opinion summarization is lower. This is likely due to the fact that in opinion summarization there are many different sentences that express the same meaning. Thus, different annotators could have chosen different sentences with similar content.

To compensate this problem of Kappa, we also used the ROUGE-N score. The ROUGE measure computes the n-gram overlap between summaries and, thus, could help to identify sentences that are similar in content. In our experiments, we used the ROUGE-1 score (unigram overlap).

For each annotator, we computed ROUGE-1 scores using other annotators' summaries as references, and then we calculated the average between them. Table 3 shows the values of ROUGE-1 obtained for each book and electronic product in extractive and abstractive summaries. These results are better than Kappa results and may indicate that annotators choose different sentences that have similar content. The results for extractive summaries are better than abstractive summaries, because in abstracts annotators have independence to use different words, possibly synonyms and paraphrases.

For extractive summaries, we also computed the percentage of common sentences among the summaries created by annotators. In Table 3, we show the results. Total Agreement indicates the proportion of common sentences selected by five annotators; Majority Agreement, by four or three annotators; and Minority Agreement, by two annotators. No agreement indicates that annotators did not agree in the selection of sentences.

On one hand, the results for these metrics indicate that annotators choose the same sentences in few cases. In average, only 1.1% (0.011) of sentences was selected by all annotators, and only 17.3% (0.173) of them by the majority of annotators. We believe that this is mainly due to the large number of sentences that annotators have to read to generate the summary (in average, 40 sentences). On the other hand, in many cases, annotators choose different sentences (see columns Minority and No Agreement), because, as it is reported in (Rath et al., 1961), in the summarization task, there is no single set of representative sentences chosen by humans. In addition, we believe that some especial linguistic characteristics of opinions, such as irony or usage of slangs, make this task more challenging.

In general, all results reported in Table 3 show that it is difficult to generate similar opinion summaries based on aspects (extractive or abstractive) even among humans. Although these results are low, they could be used as a topline performance to evaluate other automatic methods.

5.2 Aspect Coverage

An important issue in aspect-based opinion summarization is the aspect coverage. Aspect coverage is an indicator of how many aspects of the source opinions are preserved in the generated summary. Most research works have been focused on producing a summary for each aspect (Blair-Goldensohn et al., 2008) (Tadano et al., 2010) (Xu et al., 2011). However, if we want an overall summary, that approach could be not ideal.

In our work, we produced overall summaries based on aspects, i.e., a summary contains the most important aspects, according to the annotators, for a set of source opinions. In the experiments, to calculate the aspect coverage, we considered the objects or entities as aspects, similar to Gerani et al. (2014).

To estimate the aspect coverage for extractive summaries, we get the aspects annotated in the opinions of ReLi and Buscapé, and then it was verified how many of them are preserved in the summaries. In abstractive summaries, we used a semi-automatic search. We look for aspects using a list with their names. After that, we manually reviewed the summaries in order to add possible synonyms to the aspect list. For example, the word *"narrative"* was considered a synonym of the *"story"* aspect. Finally, we determined how many aspects were in the summaries. For each book and electronic product, we calculated the proportion of aspects preserved in the five summaries, and then we computed the average.

Table 4 shows the percentage of aspect coverage for extractive and abstractive summaries. As we can see, abstractive summaries have wider coverage than extractive summaries because annotators have less restriction to write an abstractive summary and, thus, they can include more aspects. On the other hand, in extractive summaries, annotators are limited to the content of the source opinion's sentences.

Table 4: Coverage of aspects in summaries

Books/ Electronic Products	**Extractive Summary**	**Abstractive Summary**
Capitães da Areia	0.450	0.700
Crepúsculo	0.467	0.567
Ensaio sobre a Cegueira	0.300	0.600
Fala sério, amiga!	1.000	1.000
Fala sério, amor!	0.550	0.550
Fala sério, mãe!	0.400	0.767
Fala sério, pai!	0.800	0.900
Fala sério, professor!	0.700	1.000
O Apanhador nos Campos de Centeio	0.550	0.800
O Outro lado da meia noite	0.800	0.760
O Reverso da Medalha	0.650	0.800
Se houver Amanhã	0.640	0.680
1984	0.600	0.760
Iphone 5	0.444	0.578
Samsung Galaxy S III	0.333	0.400
LG Smart TV	0.514	0.714
Samsung Smart TV	0.720	0.760
Average	**0.583**	**0.726**

There are few cases where all aspects are included in the summaries (books "Fala sério, amiga!" and "Fala sério, professor!"). In these cases, less than three aspects were presented in source opinions. By contrast, when the number of aspects in the source opinions was high, few of them were included in the summary (e.g., product Samsung Galaxy S III). It was most notorious in electronic products because they have more technical opinions that include many aspects.

Results in Table 4 indicate that, for an overall aspect-based summary, humans consider only some aspects in the text. We did not find other works

Table 5: Sentiment orientation of summaries

Books/ Electronic Products	Actual Polarity		Extractive Summary		Abstractive Summary	
	Positive	Negative	Positive	Negative	Positive	Negative
Capitães da Areia	0.784	0.216	0.978	0.022	**0.370**	**0.630**
Crepúsculo	0.391	0.609	0.075	0.925	**0.510**	**0.490**
Ensaio sobre a Cegueira	0.812	0.188	0.880	0.120	**0.471**	**0.529**
Fala sério, amiga!	0.895	0.105	0.960	0.040	0.723	0.277
Fala sério, amor!	0.968	0.032	0.980	0.020	0.967	0.033
Fala sério, mãe!	0.510	0.490	0.680	0.320	0.569	0.431
Fala sério, pai!	0.842	0.158	0.877	0.123	0.950	0.050
Fala sério, professor!	0.621	0.379	0.791	0.209	0.686	0.314
O Apanhador nos Campos de Centeio	0.300	0.700	0.204	0.796	0.283	0.717
O Outro lado da meia noite	0.705	0.295	0.667	0.333	0.633	0.367
O Reverso da Medalha	0.667	0.333	0.521	0.479	0.558	0.442
Se houver Amanhã	0.867	0.133	0.952	0.048	0.716	0.284
1984	0.757	0.243	0.877	0.123	0.627	0.573
Iphone 5	0.975	0.025	0.971	0.029	0.810	0.190
Samsung Galaxy S III	0.584	0.416	**0.272**	**0.728**	**0.460**	**0.540**
LG Smart TV	0.622	0.378	0.674	0.326	0.753	0.247
Samsung Smart TV	0.556	0.444	0.502	0.498	0.536	0.464

to compare the results of aspect coverage, but we believe that our results show an approximation of how many aspects humans consider in a summary. Thus, automatic opinion summarization methods could use these results as indicator of how many aspects could be included in the summaries.

5.3 Sentiment Orientation

To communicate to summary's readers what is the sentiment in the opinions about the entity and its aspects is not simply a matter of classifying the summary as positive or negative. Summary's readers want to know if all opinions that evaluate the entity made it in a similar way or if they were varied. Thus, opinion summaries must preserve the polarity distribution as much as possible to reflect the overall sentiment about the entity and its aspects.

In our experiments, we evaluated how much humans (annotators) maintain the sentiment orientation in the manual summaries. To estimate the general sentiment presented in the source opinions, we extract the segments that contain sentiment with its polarities from the annotations of ReLi and Buscapé. We calculated the percentage of positive and negative segments. Table 5 shows the percentage of positive and negative sentiments presented in the source opinions (column "Actual Polarity") for each book and electronic product.

To calculate the sentiment in extractive summaries, we estimate the sentiment for positive and negative classes using the annotations of ReLi and Buscapé. For abstractive summaries, we calculated the sentiment with the automatic lexicon-based method proposed in Taboada et al. (2011) using the SentiLex lexicon (Silva et al., 2012), because, according to Balage Filho et al. (2013), it gets better results in comparison with other Brazilian Portuguese dictionaries.

Table 5 shows the results of the sentiment orientation for each book and electronic product. In general, annotators reflected the sentiment distribution of source opinions in the summaries. The proportions between positive and negative sentiments were not exactly the same, but were very similar. This shows that humans (annotators) take into account the sentiment to create the summary and consider both classes, positive and negative, according to how they appeared in the source opinions.

There are few cases where the sentiment orientation of summaries is opposite of the source opinions (marked in bold). This indicates that annotators focused only in one part of the source opinions ignoring the overall sentiment.

Extractive summaries got better correlations than abstractive summaries because the sentences of extractive summaries are the same of the source opinions and also because the sentiment in abstractive summaries was automatically calculated.

6 Conclusion

In this paper, we presented OpiSums-PT, a corpus of opinion summaries, extractive and abstractive, based on aspects written in Brazilian Portuguese. We also made a qualitative analysis about how people generate these types of summaries. As was previously showed, human summaries are diversified and people generate summaries only for some aspects keeping the overall sentiment orientation with little variation.

This work has been motivated, mainly, by the importance that a corpus has in this task and to assist future researches in the opinion summarization field.

The complete version of OpiSums-PT is available for download through the Sucinto project webpage[2] under a Creative Commons license.

Future work includes extending OpiSums-PT with other type of annotations, such as sentence alignment between summaries and identification of elementary discourse units.

Acknowledgments

Part of the results presented in this paper were obtained through research on a project titled "Semantic Processing of Texts in Brazilian Portuguese", sponsored by Samsung Eletrônica da Amazônia Ltda. under the terms of Brazilian federal law No. 8.248/91. We would like to thank professor Lucia Rino and the other annotators for their valuable help in the building of the corpus.

References

Pedro Balage Filho, Thiago Pardo, and Sandra Aluísio. 2013. An Evaluation of the Brazilian Portuguese LIWC Dictionary for Sentiment Analysis. In *Proceedings of the 9th Brazilian Symposium in Information and Human Language Technology (STIL)*, pages 215–219. Sociedade Brasileira de Computação.

Sasha Blair-Goldensohn, Kerry Hannan, Ryan McDonald, Tyler Neylon, George A Reis, and Jeff Reynar. 2008. Building a Sentiment Summarizer for Local Service Reviews. In *WWW Workshop on NLP in the Information Explosion Era*.

Giuseppe Carenini, Raymond Ng, and Adam Pauls. 2006. Multi-document Summarization of Evaluative Text. In *Proceedings of the European Chapter of the Association for Computational Linguistics (EACL)*, pages 305–312.

Jean Carletta. 1996. Assessing Agreement on Classification Tasks: The Kappa Statistic. *Computational Linguistics*, 22(2):249–254.

Jack G. Conrad, Jochen L. Leidner, Frank Schilder, and Ravi Kondadadi. 2009. Query-based Opinion Summarization for Legal Blog Entries. In *Proceedings of the 12th International Conference on Artificial Intelligence and Law*, pages 167–176. ACM.

Márcio Dias, Alessandro Bokan, Carla Chuman, Cláudia Barros, Erick Maziero, Fernando Nobrega, Jackson Souza, Marco Sobrevilla, Marina Delege, Lucía Castro, Naira Silva, Paula Figueira, Pedro Balage, Roque López, Ariani Di Felippo, Maria das Graças Volpe, and Thiago Pardo. 2014. Enriquecendo o Córpus CSTNews - a Criação de Novos Sumários Multi-documento. In *Proceedings of the 1st Workshop on Tools and Resources for Automatically Processing Portuguese and Spanish - ToRPorEsp*, pages 1–8.

Cláudia Freitas, Eduardo Motta, Ruy Milidiú, and Juliana Cesar. 2013. Sparkle Vampire LoL! Annotating Opinions in a Book Review Corpus. In *11th Corpus Linguistics Conference*.

Kavita Ganesan, ChengXiang Zhai, and Jiawei Han. 2010. Opinosis: A Graph-Based Approach to Abstractive Summarization of Highly Redundant Opinions. In *Proceedings of the 23rd International Conference on Computational Linguistics*, pages 340–348. Association for Computational Linguistics.

Shima Gerani, Yashar Mehdad, Giuseppe Carenini, Raymond T. Ng, and Bita Nejat. 2014. Abstractive Summarization of Product Reviews Using Discourse Structure. In *Proceedings of the 2014 Conference on Empirical Methods in Natural Language Processing (EMNLP)*, pages 1602–1613. Association for Computational Linguistics.

Minqing Hu and Bing Liu. 2004. Mining and Summarizing Customer Reviews. In *Proceedings of the Tenth ACM SIGKDD International Conference on Knowledge Discovery and Data Mining*, pages 168–177. ACM.

Hyun Duk Kim and ChengXiang Zhai. 2009. Generating Comparative Summaries of Contradictory Opinions in Text. In *Proceedings of the 18th ACM Conference on Information and Knowledge Management*, pages 385–394. ACM.

Chin-Yew Lin and Eduard Hovy. 2000. The Automated Acquisition of Topic Signatures for Text Summarization. In *Proceedings of the 18th Conference on Computational Linguistics*, pages 495–501. Association for Computational Linguistics.

Chin-Yew Lin. 2004. Looking for a Few Good Metrics: Automatic Summarization Evaluation-How

[2]http://www.icmc.usp.br/pessoas/taspardo/sucinto/

many Samples are Enough? In *Proceedings of the NTCIR Workshop*, pages 1–10.

Fei Liu and Yang Liu. 2008. What Are Meeting Summaries?: An Analysis of Human Extractive Summaries in Meeting Corpus. In *Proceedings of the 9th SIGdial Workshop on Discourse and Dialogue*, pages 80–83. Association for Computational Linguistics.

Bing Liu. 2012. Sentiment Analysis and Opinion Mining. *Synthesis Lectures on Human Language Technologies*, 5(1):1–167.

Inderjeet Mani. 1999. *Advances in Automatic Text Summarization*. MIT Press.

Dragomir R. Radev and Kathleen R. McKeown. 1998. Generating Natural Language Summaries from Multiple On-line Sources. *Computational Linguistics*, 24(3):470–500.

Dragomir R. Radev, Timothy Allison, Sasha Blair-Goldensohn, John Blitzer, Arda Çelebi, Stanko Dimitrov, Elliott Drábek, Ali Hakim, Wai Lam, Danyu Liu, Jahna Otterbacher, Hong Qi, Horacio Saggion, Simone Teufel, Michael Topper, Adam Winkel, and Zhu Zhang. 2004. MEAD - A Platform for Multidocument Multilingual Text Summarization. In *Proceedings of the 4th International Conference on Language Resources and Evaluation (LREC)*.

G.J. Rath, A. Resnick, and T.R. Savage. 1961. The Formation of Abstracts by the Selection of Sentences. *American Documentation*, 12(2):139–141.

Mário J. Silva, Paula Carvalho, and Luís Sarmento. 2012. Building a Sentiment Lexicon for Social Judgement Mining. In *Proceedings of the 10th International Conference on Computational Processing of the Portuguese Language*, pages 218–228. Springer-Verlag.

Maite Taboada, Julian Brooke, Milan Tofiloski, Kimberly Voll, and Manfred Stede. 2011. Lexicon-based Methods for Sentiment Analysis. *Computational Linguistics*, 37(2):267–307.

Ryosuke Tadano, Kazutaka Shimada, and Tsutomu Endo. 2010. Multi-aspects Review Summarization Based on Identification of Important Opinions and their Similarity. In *Proceedings of the 24th Pacific Asia Conference on Language, Information and Computation*, pages 685–692.

Jan Ulrich, Gabriel Murray, and Giuseppe Carenini. 2008. A Publicly Available Annotated Corpus for Supervised Email Summarization. In *Proceedings of AAAI EMAIL Workshop*, pages 77–87.

Xueke Xu, Tao Meng, and Xueqi Cheng. 2011. Aspect-based Extractive Summarization of Online Reviews. In *Proceedings of the 2011 ACM Symposium on Applied Computing*, pages 968–975. ACM.

Linhong Zhu, Sheng Gao, Sinno Jialin Pan, Haizhou Li, Dingxiong Deng, and Cyrus Shahabi. 2013. Graph-Based Informative-Sentence Selection for Opinion Summarization. In *Advances in Social Networks Analysis and Mining (ASONAM)*, pages 408–412. IEEE.

Developing Language-tagged Corpora for Code-switching Tweets

Suraj Maharjan[1] and **Elizabeth Blair**[2] and **Steven Bethard**[2] and **Thamar Solorio**[1]
[1]Department of Computer Science
University of Houston
Houston, TX, 77004
smahajan2@uh.edu solorio@cs.uh.edu
[2]Department of Computer and Information Sciences
University of Alabama at Birmingham
Birmingham, AL, 35294
{eablair, bethard}uab.edu

Abstract

Code-switching, where a speaker switches between languages mid-utterance, is frequently used by multilingual populations worldwide. Despite its prevalence, limited effort has been devoted to develop computational approaches or even basic linguistic resources to support research into the processing of such mixed-language data. We present a user-centric approach to collecting code-switched utterances from social media posts, and develop language universal guidelines for the annotation of code-switched data. We also present results for several baseline language identification models on our corpora and demonstrate that language identification in code-switched text is a difficult task that calls for deeper investigation.

1 Introduction

A common phenomenon among multilingual speakers is *code-switching*, that is, switching between languages within a single context (Lipski, 1978). Code-switching can occur on a sentence-by-sentence basis, known as intersentential code-switching, as well as between words within a single sentence, known as intrasentential code-switching (Poplack, 1980).

Developing technology that can process this kind of mixed language data is important for a number of different sectors. In the fight against organized crime, human and drug trafficking smugglers travel between Mexico and the United States, and processing the mixed Spanish-English data that accompanies this trafficking could yield more actionable intelligence for law enforcement. In the service industry, companies like LENA[1] analyze child language to provide parents with a variety of metrics on child development, and their language processing tools must be taught to handle the language mixing common to bilingual children. And in data mining applications, companies like Dataminr[2] want to transform Twitter into actionable signals, and ignoring the multilingual portion of the world's population represents significant lost business opportunities.

In this paper, we describe our efforts in the development and annotation of corpora containing code-switched data in written form for two language pairs: Spanish-English and Nepali-English. These two language combinations are well suited for research in code switching: Spanish-English as an example of a large multilingual minority population (in the United States), and Nepali-English is an example of a population that is almost entirely multilingual. In both cases the two languages are written using the same Latin script. This is true for Nepali, even though Devanagari is its official script, because the education system in Nepal teaches typing only for English, so for digital content like social media it is common for Nepalese speakers to type using English characters.

We chose Twitter as the source of our data as the informal nature of tweets makes them a more natural source for code-switching phenomena. Many researchers have turned to Twitter as a source of data for research (i.e. (Roberts et al., 2012; Reyes et al., 2013; Tomlinson et al., 2014; Kong et al., 2014; Temnikova et al., 2014; Williams and Katz, 2012)). Typically, collecting Twitter data is a straightforward

[1]http://www.lenafoundation.org/
[2]https://www.dataminr.com/

Proceedings of LAW IX - The 9th Linguistic Annotation Workshop, pages 72–84,
Denver, Colorado, June 5, 2015.

process involving the Twitter API, specifying the desired language, and a set of keywords or hash tags. For example, in the research on user intentions some of the hash tags used include: #mygoal, #iwon, #madskills, #imapro, #dowhatisay, #kissmyfeet, #proud. A similar process was followed by all of the previous work listed above. However, Twitter allows only one desired language to be specified, and no simple keywords exist for finding code-switched tweets. Searching for the words "code-switching" or "Spanglish" would have resulted in unnatural data, where the users were aware of the linguistic phenomenon, rather than the spontaneous use of more than one language that we seek. This is akin to research in cyberbullying, where data collection on Twitter using hash tags or keywords like #bully or #cyberbullying does not result in the actual bullying tweets (Dinakar et al., 2011). We present here a strategy to locate the right data in Twitter. We hope other researchers whose data needs cannot be met by simple keyword search can benefit from our lessons learned.

After collecting a sufficient amount of data with code-switching, we set out on the task of annotating the data using a combination of in-lab and crowdsourcing annotations. We develop a set of annotation guidelines that can be used for Twitter data and any language combination. The design of these annotation standards reflects the unique needs of mixed language data and the goal of supporting research in linguistic and sociolinguistic aspects of code-switching, as well as research in statistical methods for the automated processing of code-switching. Therefore, the annotations are theory agnostic, and follow a pragmatic definition of code-switching.

Finally, to show that the processing of code-switching text requires further advancement of our NLP technology, we present a case study in language identification with our corpora. Language identification of monolingual text has been considered a solved problem for some time now (McNamee, 2005) and even in Twitter the problem has been shown to be tractable when annotated data is available (Bergsma et al., 2012). However, as we demonstrate in this paper, when code-switching is present, the performance of state-of-the-art systems is not on par with that of monolingual sources. We predict that the difficulty increases for deeper and higher-level NLP tasks. In fact, Solorio and Liu (2008b) have shown already that part-of-speech tagging performance in code-switching data is also lagging behind that observed in monolingual sources.

2 Related Work

Although code-switching has not been investigated as deeply as monolingual text in the natural language processing field, there has been some work on the topic. An earlier example is the work by Joshi (Joshi, 1982), where he proposes a system that can help to parse and generate code-switching sentences. His approach is based on the matrix language-embedded language formalism and although the paper has a good justification it lacks an empirical evaluation supporting the proposed model. A few more recent examples of work in NLP and code-switching are the methods examined by Solorio and Liu that include developing a better part of speech tagging approach for code-switching text (Solorio and Liu, 2008b) and identifying potential code-switching points within text (Solorio and Liu, 2008a). In each of these projects, however, code-switching data was scarce, coming primarily from conversations. Because of complications with traditional evaluation measures, the code-switching point detection project used a new evaluation method, in which artificial code-switched content was generated and compared with genuine content (Solorio and Liu, 2008a).

In the past, most language identification research has been done at the document level. Some researchers, however, have developed methods to identify languages within multilingual documents (Singh and Gorla, 2007; Nguyen and Doğruöz, 2013; King and Abney, 2013). Their test data comes from a variety of sources, including web pages, bilingual forum posts, and jumbled data from monolingual sources, but none of them are trained on code-switched data, opting instead for a monolingual training set per language. This could prove to be a problem when working on code-switched data, particularly in shorter samples such as social media data, as the code-switching context is not present in training material.

One system tackled both the problems of code-switching and social media in language and code-switched status identification (Lignos and Marcus, 2013). Lignos and Marcus gathered millions of monolingual tweets in both English and Spanish in order to model the two languages and used crowdsourcing to annotate tens of thousands of Spanish tweets, approximately 11% of which contained code-switched content. This system was able to achieve 96.9% word-level accuracy and a 0.936 F-measure in identifying code-switched tweets.

The issue still stands that relatively little code-switching data, such as that used in Lignos and Marcus' research, is readily available. Even in their data, the percentage of code-switched tweets was barely over a tenth of the total test data. There have been other corpora built, particularly for other language pairs such as Mandarin-English (Li et al., 2012; Lyu et al., 2010), but the amount of data available and the percentage of code-switching present are not up to the standards of other areas of the natural language processing field. With this in mind, we sought to provide corpora for multiple language pairs, each with a better distribution of code-switching. In this paper we discuss the process we followed for two language pairs and our current efforts are targeted to grow the number of language pairs collected and annotated.

3 Corpus Creation

Developing the corpus involved two steps: locating code-switching tweets and using crowdsourcing to annotate them for language and an assortment of other tags. A small portion of these annotations were reviewed by in-lab annotators to measure agreement and gauge the quality of the crowdsourced data.

All token-level annotations were done according to a set of guidelines provided to all annotators and presented in this paper as Appendix A. There we show the guidelines specific for Spanish-English. For Nepali-English only a small customization of examples was needed. The tags they could select from were Lang1 (English), Lang2 (Spanish or Nepali), Named Entity, Ambiguous, Mixed, or Other. Words that exist in both languages, such as 'me' or 'no', were disambiguated using context if possible; if not, they were assigned the Ambiguous tag. The Mixed tag was reserved for words that contained portions of multiple languages, such as 'snap*chateame*' which contains both English and Spanish content. Anything that did not fall into these categories, such as other languages, gibberish, Twitter user handles, URLs, emoticons, symbols, and punctuation, were given the label Other. Hashtags were annotated according to the text following the # symbol. Slang, misspellings, and abbreviations were labeled according to the word(s) they represented.

3.1 Locating Code-Switched Data

Although locating code-switched tweets was not initially one of the bigger concerns of this project, it developed into quite an interesting problem. To refrain from biasing the data set towards particular words or phrases, we did not wish to use keyword-based search in order to obtain tweets. Our method of gathering data therefore became finding users who code-switched often and pulling their tweet histories. For Nepali, we searched for users that constantly switched between Nepali and English. An initial set of users was easily found via a collaborator from Nepal who has ties with many Nepali-English bilingual users on Twitter. We then looked for users mentioned in their tweets and checked to see if they too, were frequently code-switching. Eventually, we identified 42 frequent code-switchers and collected nearly 2000 tweets each from them. We filtered out all the retweets and tweets with urls.

For Spanish-English, however, locating code-switching users was difficult as we had no Spanish speaking collaborators with ties to a code-switching Twitter community. We first used Twitter's recent tweet search API to find tweets using English terms (taken from the most frequent English words in the Bangor Miami Corpus[3]) and restricted to tweets that Twitter's language detection identified as Spanish and that were sent from areas close to California and Texas. Results from this search were passed to in-lab annotators for token-level annotations according to the annotation guidelines. Code-switching ratios were low in this data set, so we ran a new search for tweets from the same geographical regions that Twitter identified as English containing the Spanish words that were most frequent in the results of the first search (ignoring ambiguous and stop words). Results from both searches were filtered to remove extremely similar tweets, spam tweets such as news and automatic posts from other social media sources, retweets, and tweets containing URLs (which were

[3]http://www.language-archives.org/item/oai:talkbank.org:BilingBank-Bangor-Miami

particularly prone to spam). We then pulled the first 50 tweets of each of the 135 most frequent users from the combined search results. These were annotated in-lab at the tweet level for code-switched content. Any users with fewer than three code-switching tweets were discarded, resulting in 44 users.

A small portion of this data, 1163 tweets distributed evenly among the 44 users, was two-way annotated in-lab at the token level, and used as quality control data for CrowdFlower annotation (see section 3.2). We used the resulting annotations to identify the frequency of code-switching for each user. All available tweets were pulled from the nine users with the highest code-switching frequency, and tweets from the next thirteen users were used to fill in up to 14,000 tweets.

We tried to extract some demographic characteristics of the users in our corpora. As the Twitter API does not give the gender information of users, we manually checked their profiles and used their names and profile pictures to identify their gender. Even with this method, we could not determine the gender for two Spanish-English and two Nepali-English users. The rest of the users were split almost evenly for Spanish-English (9 male and 11 females), while in the Nepali-English data we have 15 males and 6 females. Twitter also provides information about geographical location of the users. Our Spanish-English users came from Eastern, Central, Pacific, Mountain (US & Canada) timezones whereas all users for Nepali-English came from Kathmandu as per the Twitter API.

For the purpose of system development, testing and benchmarking, we divided the corpora into train and test sets. For Spanish-English the training set has 11,400 and the test set has 3,014 tweets. The Nepali-English corpus was split into 9,993 tweets for training and 2,874 tweets for testing. Table 1 shows the distribution of the six different tags across the training and test datasets for both Nepali-English and Spanish-English. As can be inferred from the table, the concentration of Lang1, Lang2 and Other tags is much higher than NE, Ambiguous and Mixed tags for both language pairs.

The Twitter users in each set (training vs. test) are disjoint to ensure that systems would not be overfitting to the idiosyncrasies of particular users. The split was designed to maintain the same balanced distribution of tweet content in both sets.

Table 1: Distribution of tags across training and test datasets.

	Nep-En (%)		**Es-En(%)**	
Tag	**Training**	**Test**	**Training**	**Test**
Lang1	31.14	19.76	54.78	43.28
Lang2	41.56	49.1	23.52	30.34
Mixed	0.08	0.60	0.04	0.03
NE	2.73	4.19	2.07	2.22
Ambiguous	0.09	-	0.24	0.12
Other	24.41	26.35	19.34	24.02

3.2 Crowdsourcing Annotations

In order to efficiently annotate the large amount of tweets needed for the corpus, we used the crowdsourcing platform CrowdFlower. This platform, similar to the Amazon Mechanical Turk (AMT) service, provides access to a community of crowdsourced workers who are willing to complete small tasks for relatively low pay. CrowdFlower differs from AMT in offering additional quality control services.

To gather the annotations, we created CrowdFlower tasks at the word level for each tweet. One task in the CrowdFlower interface consisted of the selected word designated within the full tweet in order to provide context. Following the recommendations in (Callison-Burch and Dredze, 2010), the tweet was made into an image displaying the text with the selected token highlighted by a yellow box. This was done in order to prevent users from simply copying the text into a language detection program. Underneath the image was a question asking them to select the correct annotation for the word using radio buttons listing each annotation category. There was also an optional comments section where they could leave a note about the question. To speed up the process and save money, words in the Other category that could be automatically detected (Twitter user handles, URLs, emoticons, symbols and punctuation) were excluded from CrowdFlower annotation.

Instructions for the job were provided to the workers at the beginning of each page of tasks. We provided a basic description of the job and how to interpret each portion of the task. After that, we gave a link to a PDF of a slightly modified, CrowdFlower-friendly version of the annotation guidelines provided to the in-lab annotators. The guidelines gave a description of the overall job and of each label, along with examples. There was also a section in the job's instructions containing a few key notes, such as how to handle named entities and slang.

We gave 15 tasks at a time to each crowdsourced worker. They were paid $0.03 for each fifteen-task page they completed. Payment was only given if the users met the strict quality controls built into the platform. CrowdFlower takes gold-annotated tasks along with the blank tasks and uses that gold to test workers as the job runs, removing the burden from the job organizers. To begin the job, workers must obtain at least 70% accuracy on an eight-question quiz made of the gold tasks. If they pass the quiz, they begin work on the task proper, but gold is continuously woven into their work. If they fall below the 70% threshold, their work is removed from the total data to avoid contamination and they are not paid for the low-quality annotations. Following the suggestions of (Zhai et al., 2013), we added gold equal to 20% of the job's tasks. To avoid additional negative results, we also limited workers to those from the United States, Argentina, Chile, Colombia, Mexico, and Peru for the Spanish-English corpus and Nepal and Bhutan for the Nepali-English corpus.

A few pilot jobs were run for each language pair on 100-tweet samples, using tweets that had already been annotated in-lab – three-way for Spanish-English and two-way for Nepali-English – to judge the accuracy of CrowdFlower workers' results. Analysis of the agreement allowed for improvement of the guidelines, particularly in the named entity and ambiguous categories, as well as confirmation that three-way CrowdFlower annotation provided acceptable results at the current payment scheme. The pilots also showed that CrowdFlower's aggregated results outperformed majority and trust-weighted voting schemes, so they were used in the final work.

The 14,000 Spanish-English tweets collected in section 3.1 were run through CrowdFlower in batches of 2000 tweets. All batches used the same set of gold tasks, which consisted of the 1163 tweets annotated two-way in the lab. Because we were unsure whether workers were reading the PDF instructions, we changed the instruction scheme for one of these jobs. The new scheme moved the label descriptions inline, where the workers could read them without clicking away. The PDF link was still provided to give them access to the examples.

The Nepali data, which was found to have a higher concentration of code-switching tweets during the in-lab annotations, was simply run in two 5,000 tweet batches and one 3,000 tweet batch. The gold data for quality control of this task contained 1,000 tweets that were annotated by two in-lab annotators.

3.3 Review and Agreement

To judge the validity of the CrowdFlower annotations, one-way in-lab review was performed on small segments of the crowdsourced results. 1,000 tweets were reviewed from jobs using the PDF instruction scheme and another 500 were reviewed from the job using the inline instruction scheme. Inter-annotator agreement measures were calculated between the original and reviewed annotations for each scheme. The measures used were observed agreement, Fleiss multi-π, and Cohen multi-κ (Artstein and Poesio, 2008) calculated for the full data set, as well as observed agreement per annotation category.

The CrowdFlower annotation results' agreement with the in-lab review was above expectations. All three overall agreement measures were at or above 0.9. At the category level, agreement was high for the simpler categories, such as Lang1, Lang2, and Other, but dipped considerably for the more complicated ones such as named entities. This is consistent with the error analysis done by King and Abney (2013), where the most frequent source of error was named entities. Ambiguous and Mixed made up only approximately one tenth of a percent each of the total annotations given, so the agreements on these are unreliable. Named entities, at three to five percent of the data, show a more reliable result.

There was little difference, at most 0.01, in the annotation agreement between the jobs using PDF and inline instruction schemes. It is unlikely that this small difference in agreement is indicative of a useful difference in annotation quality. Optional customer experience surveys provided to workers by CrowdFlower after task completion showed slightly more happiness with pay and test questions when using the inline instructions, even though neither of these factors changed between jobs. It is possible that although performance is unchanged, worker satisfaction may be higher when using inline instructions instead of linking to an external PDF.

4 Benchmark Systems

To show the shortcomings of state-of-the-art systems on code-switched social media text, two benchmark systems for language identification were run on the annotated corpora. The first was a simple dictionary approach, while the second was a state-of-the-art word-level language identification system designed for multilingual documents (King and Abney, 2013).

The two systems were evaluated on their performance in language identification at the word level and identifying code-switching at the tweet level. Performance was measured using accuracy, precision, recall, and F-measure. A tweet was marked as code-switching only if it contained at least one label for each language.

4.1 Language Identification with Dictionaries

The dictionary approach was designed as the simplest possible system for language identification using the collected training data. The lowercase form of all of the words in the training data were split into separate lexicons based on their tag. Hashtags had the # removed and the text was included as a word.

The system only assigned language tags (Lang1, or Lang2) and Other. If the lowercase form of a word appeared in one lexicon but not the other, it assigned that lexicon's language. If the word was a Twitter user handle, URL, emoticon, symbol or punctuation, it assigned the Other category. Otherwise, if the word existed in both or neither lexicons, it assigned the majority language from the training data.

4.2 Language Identification with CRFs

The state-of-the-art language identification system of King and Abney (2013) was designed for word-level annotation on multilingual documents, and was thus a suitable choice for our task. This weakly supervised system uses Conditional Random Fields (CRF) with Generalized Expectation (GE) criteria (Mann and McCallum, 2008). The system itself was provided by the authors, so no reimplementation was necessary.

The CRF GE language id system requires samples of monolingual text from each language as training data. The English and Spanish training sets were pulled from Twitter searches in the Texas and California areas for consistency, using Twitter's language

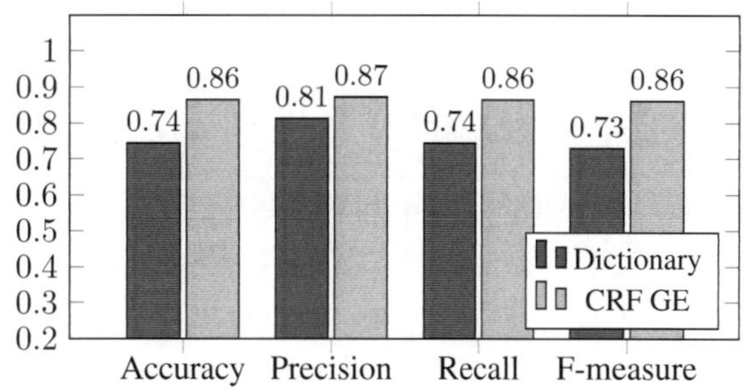

Figure 1: Benchmark system performance at the word level on Spanish-English language tags.

identification along with the language's stop words as queries in order to get reliable results. Equal amounts, approximately 10MB each, of data were collected for each language. Monolingual Nepali tweets in Roman script were harder to find. The Twitter API only allows to search for tweets using Devanagari. So, we looked for other sources of Romanized Nepali text, such as song lyrics websites, news websites etc. We crawled nearly 1.2MB of song lyrics from song lyrics websites. However, this was not enough. Hence we returned to Twitter to identify users who tweet in Nepali by using Devanagari script. We collected the remaining 9MB of data (117,806 tweets) from these users and then transliterated them to Roman Script by using our Devanagari to Roman transliteration script[4].

The training data was gathered into a single file per language and fed into the CRF GE system. Then each test tweet was input to the system for prediction. We removed from the tweet tokens with a hash tag, emoticons and tokens of the type @username.

5 Benchmark Results

To provide a fair comparison of the benchmark systems we only evaluate prediction performance for the words labeled with Lang1 or Lang2 in the gold data, as the benchmark systems were not designed for named entities, ambiguous words or mixed words. We report results using the familiar metrics accuracy, precision, recall, and F-measure. The results are shown in Figures 1 and 2. For Spanish-English, both systems performed well under the state of the art from Lignos and Marcus who obtained 96.9% word-level

[4]The script can be downloaded from http://www2.cs.uh.edu/~suraj/scripts/devnagari2roman.py

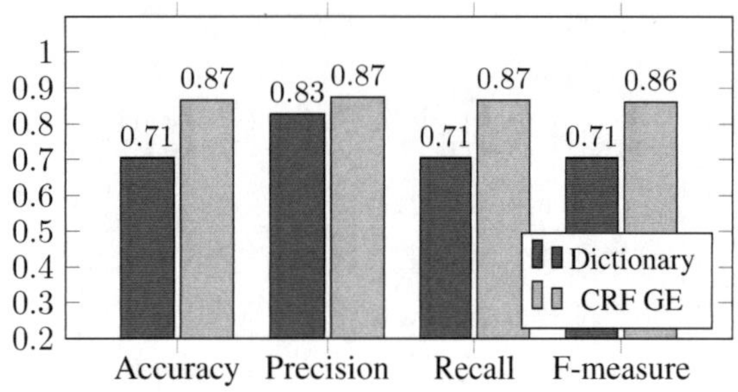

Figure 2: Benchmark system performance at the word level on Nepali-English language tags.

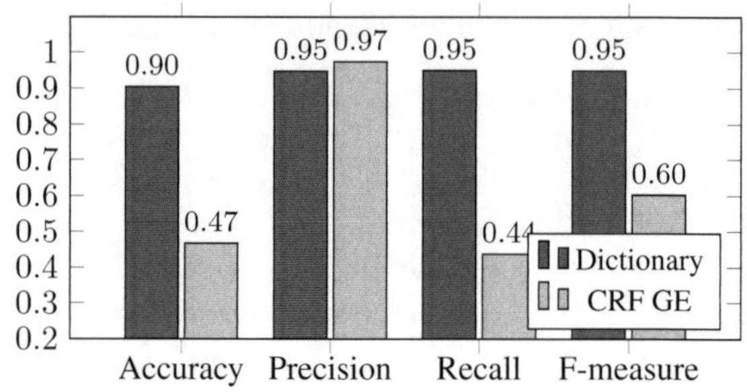

Figure 4: Performance at the tweet level on Nepali-English code-switching detection.

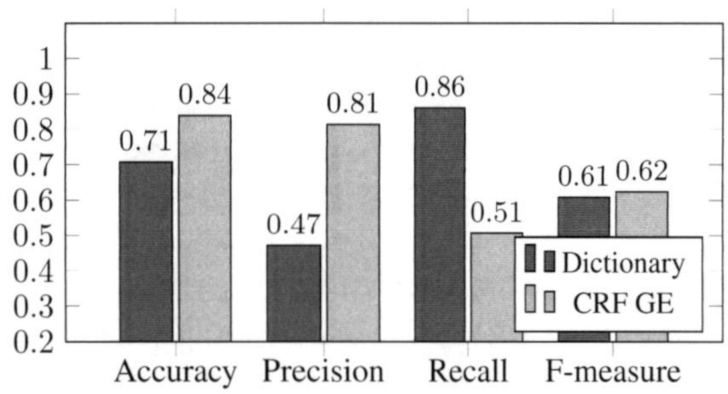

Figure 3: Performance at the tweet level on Spanish-English code-switching detection.

accuracy and a 0.936 F-measure in identifying code-switched tweets for multilingual documents, with the dictionary at 74% accuracy and the CRF GE at 86%. We observe a similar result for Nepali-English, with the dictionary at 70% and the CRF GE at 87%. These unsurprising results show that even systems designed to receive more than one language as input assume longer monolingual contexts. But spontaneous code switching does not obey these patterns.

The tweet level analysis seen in Figures 3 and 4 show that for Spanish-English, performance is on par with the token-level results, while for Nepali-English the dictionary system outperforms the CRF GE model with an accuracy of 90%. The strength of the dictionary system for Nepali-English may be due to the smaller word and character overlap between these languages.

6 Analysis

Since the Dictionary Approach considers only the tokens and ignores the context, tokens that are spelled the same way in both English and another language are often mislabeled. This is the case for words like *man* , *gate* and *din* that in Nepali mean like, date and day, respectively, and words like *me*, *red*. Also, as expected, language identification fails in the case of infrequent, unseen and misspelled tokens, such as *comrade*, *yuss*(yes), *b-lated*, and *vokamanchey*(hungry men). Another source of error for Nepali-English is that there is no standard Romanized spelling for Nepali words. People just use whatever sounds phonetically similar. For example, in Nepali the word for pain may be written as *pidaa*, *peeda*, or *pida*.

The CRF GE failed to detect small code-switched content embedded inside large monolingual segments. We observed many cases of single English words in Nepali context classified as Nepali. We believe that these misclassifications might be occurring due to the underlying sequential model of the CRF GE that relies on larger contexts.

In another analysis, we computed the overlap of words and n-grams (2-5) between each pair of languages, Nepali-English and Spanish-English, in the training datasets. Our goal was to quantify the overlap of lexical items in each code-switching language pair. Our assumption is that higher overlap represents a more challenging task for the language identification task. Table 2 shows percentages of common tokens between languages. Bigrams show similar overlap in each language pair, but as the n-grams become larger, the overlap between Spanish-English is considerably larger than that for Nepali-English.

A natural question from our data is if both bilingual communities have similar linguistic behaviors. This study requires a deeper syntactic analysis of the samples and we leave this for future research. But a simple exploratory analysis can consider the most frequent items used in English, their common lan-

Table 2: N-gram overlap across language pairs.

Tokens	Nep-Eng (%)	Span-Eng (%)
words	1.39	3.54
char -2	52.01	52.21
char -3	33.36	40.36
char -4	12.66	21.31
char -5	3.43	9.00

guage. We looked at the most frequent English words and found that both communities use similar English words while code-switching. These words mainly include function words (*the*, *to*, *yo*, *he*, *she*, *and*) and abbreviations used in social media (*lol*, *lmao*, *idk*). Stop words are the most commonly occurring words even in monolingual texts, so it is no surprise that they appear here too. In the case of abbreviations, some of them such as *lol* and *lmao* have become social media lingo rather than abbreviations of English words and thus cross language barriers.

Figure 5 shows the learning curve for Spanish-English and Nepali-English training dataset using the Dictionary Approach. For this experiment, we divided the training data into 80:20 ratio. The 20% of the training data was used for cross validation. We gradually increased the training data and computed error on training as well as cross validation dataset. The graphs show that adding more data is likely to improve the performance as cross validation error seems to be decreasing with addition of more lexicons. This experiment justifies our investment on annotating more data using Crowdflower.

7 Discussion

Upon reviewing the size and content distribution of the corpora, we believe our attempt to generate sets of code-switching social media content was successful. Although code-switching does not make up the majority of the data, there is a strong balance between it and other types of data, such as the named entities, ambiguous and mixed words, and monolingual tweets of both languages. This blend provides additional data for the development of research systems and gives a more realistic sample of how Twitter users approach code-switching.

Finding code-switching tweets for Spanish-English required significant effort, but our approach led to a selection of data with an acceptable amount of code-switched content. Because we wanted to avoid the kind of bias caused by searching for particular words, heuristically filtering the data, or working with a single user, the process was difficult; it was, however, worth the effort to make sure that a system could not gain an unfair advantage by training on a particular user or set of repeated words.

If possible, as it was with the Nepali data set, finding a community that uses code-switching often appears to be the easiest method to obtain the data in bulk. If that is not available, however, searching for tweets in one language while querying for terms in another appears to be an effective way to locate such users. The small batch of in-lab work was enough to identify some users, but a larger set such as the first CrowdFlower job was much more effective at identifying the most useful users.

When developing more corpora, it would be ideal to find a way to identify users with higher code-switching concentrations in their timelines. One potential approach that could be addressed in future work is to look into the Twitter users that a code-switching user is following, as they may have a high probability of code-switching as well. If the percentage of code-switching tweets can be increased, it would allow for more flexibility when selecting data to include in the set, as well as potentially lowering annotation costs if a particular percentage of code-switching content is required.

In total, the CrowdFlower jobs cost $1,541.62 for Spanish-English and $1,636.81 for Nepali-English. The token-level costs come out to $0.0088 per token for Spanish-English and $0.0087 per token for Nepali-English. This is far less expensive than the same three-way annotations would have cost if done in-lab, and without these low rates, a data set of this size would not have been possible for the project. When combined with the exceptional inter-annotator agreement observed between the CrowdFlower results and the lab, it is evident that CrowdFlower's customization and quality control measures can provide inexpensive, high-quality annotations.

8 Conclusion

Code-switching is a prevalent, complex, and growing aspect of communication – particularly in social media – which will not disappear any time soon. To keep up with this trend, natural language processing research must consider code-switched text, not just monolingual sources. We have detailed the methods and issues behind the development of multiple code-switching corpora of Twitter data, providing a point from which more of this research can branch forth.

The corpora themselves can be useful to those seeking samples of data containing code-switched text, along with all of the noise that comes with social media data. The corpora contain a balance of code-switched text with monolingual and other types of data which have been tagged not only for the primary languages, but also for named entities, ambiguous and mixed words, and irrelevant characters. These annotations were primarily generated through crowd-sourcing, but their quality has been verified through high agreement with conventional, in-lab annotators.

We believe a major benefit of our research is the method of gathering and annotating the data, which we have described in detail, from the first steps of collection to the final review. Hopefully, these methods of searching for tweets and locating code-switching users can be helpful in the creation of data sets in broader scopes and additional language pairs. The approach to crowdsourcing via CrowdFlower that we have used has also provided us with good results and may be of use in further expansion. Potential improvements on these methods, such as gathering chains of followers for code-switching users on Twitter or attempting different instruction schemes on CrowdFlower, could provide even better results.

The datasets can be downloaded from the site: `http://emnlp2014.org/workshops/CodeSwitch/call.html`

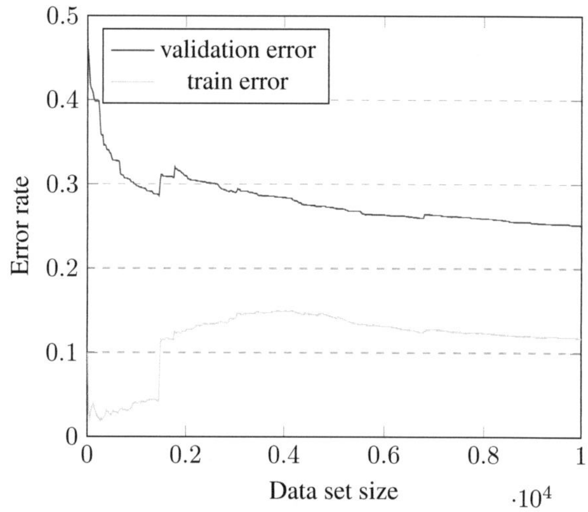

(a) Nepali-English Lexicon Learning Curve

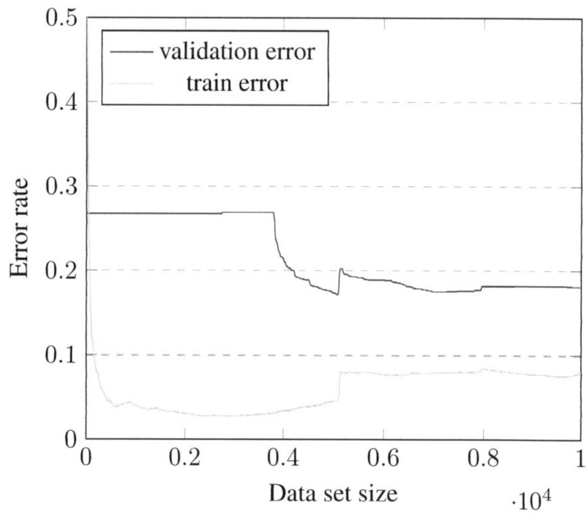

(b) Spanish-English Lexicon Learning Curve

Figure 5: Learning curve for Nepali-English and Spanish-English

Acknowledgments

We thank our collaborators Mona Diab and Julia Hirschberg for their contributions to the general annotation guidelines as well as the in lab annotators and CrowdFlower contributors for their labelling efforts. This research was partially funded by the National Science Foundation under award No. 1462142.

Appendix A. Spanish-English Code-switching Annotations for Twitter

1. WORD-LEVEL ANOTATIONS

Tokens that **start with a @ character**, **urls**, **emoticons** or any token that does not contain any letters such as **punctuation marks** and **numbers** (examples: ♥, ! , -_-, , •• >, @____)), and the **{symbol}** tokens should all be labeled as '**None of the above**'.

If a number represents a word in the sentence it should be labeled as the language of that word instead of 'None of the above'. An example is 'I like 2 party.', but not 'Meet me in 2 hours.'

For tokens beginning with a # tag consider them as a single token and label them according to the regular word level guidelines.

1.1. Language

For each word in the Source, identify whether it is **Spanish**, **English**, **Mixed**, **Other**, **Ambiguous**, or **NE** (for named entities, which are proper names that represent names of people, places, organizations, locations, movie titles, and song titles). Below is an example showing the correct tags (labels) for each token in the source.

Source	**Language**
i	English
always	English
tell	English
him	English
to	English
sing	English
to	English
me	English
pero	Spanish
nunca	Spanish
quiere	Spanish

Source	**Language**
Tuesdays	English
Around	English
6	None of the above
pero	Spanish
it	English
's	English
not	English
worth	English
it	English

Ambiguous words

Ambiguous words are words that, in context, could belong to either language. This can happen because words such as `red`, `a`, `doctor`, `me`, and `can` are valid words in both languages. However, every instance of such a word is not ambiguous – only those instances where there is not enough context to decide whether the word is being used as English or Spanish. The fragment on the left shows an example where a potentially ambiguous word, `me`, is not ambiguous because the context helps identify the language, while the example on the right shows a truly ambiguous word, `NO`, which could be in either English or Spanish. Note that typos and misspellings should be labeled with the corresponding language.

Source	**Language**
i	English
always	English
tell	English
him	English
to	English
sing	English
to	English
me	**English**
pero	Spanish
nunca	Spanish
quiere	Spanish

Source	**Language**
Johnny	NE
Depp	NE
para	Spanish
Dr.	NE
Strange	NE
?..	None of the above
NO	**Ambiguous**

Mixed words

Mixed words are words that are partially in one language and partially in another. This can occur when the first part of a word is in English and the second part is in Spanish, or vice versa. The mixed category should only be used if the word clearly has a portion in one language and another portion in a different language. It is not for words that could exist entirely in either language (see Ambiguous).

Source	**Language**
@Sof_1D17	None of the above
Ayy	Spanish
que	Spanish
pepe	NE
snapchateame	**Mixed**
el	Spanish
arreglo	Spanish

Named Entities (NE)

This is a difficult section. Please read carefully. NEs are proper names. Examples of NEs are names that refer to people, places, organizations, locations, movie titles, and song titles. Named entities are usually, **but not always**, capitalized, so capitalization can't be the only criterion to distinguish them. **Named entities can be multiple words, including articles (see the examples).** Examples of NEs and their tags are shown below.

Source	**Language**	**Source**	**Language**	**Source**	**Language**
Mejor	Spanish	and	English	@username	None of the above
Vente	Spanish	I	English	it	English
para	Spanish	told	English	's	English
el	Spanish	her	English	on	English
West	**NE**	to	English	**telemundo**	**NE**
Coast	**NE**	record	English	**el**	**NE**
and	English	**La**	**NE**	**señor**	**NE**
visit	English	**Reina**	**NE**	**de**	**NE**
me	English	**del**	**NE**	**los**	**NE**
lol	English	**Sur**	**NE**	**cielos**	**NE**

Abbreviations

Abbreviations should be labeled according to the full word(s) they represent. Some examples are shown below.

Source	**Language**	**Source**	**Language**	**Source**	**Language**
Mr.	**English**	**lol**	**English**	jajaja	Spanish
Smith	NE	yeah	English	**ntc**	**Spanish**
was	Spanish	I	English	gracias	Spanish
quejandose	Spanish	hear	English	por	Spanish
como	Spanish	you	English	todo	Spanish
siempre	Spanish	wey	Spanish		

Other

Languages other than Spanish or English should be labeled as Other. This category includes gibberish and unintelligible words. The example on the left shows some content that is not in English or Spanish (it is in Portuguese). The example on the right is an example of gibberish.

Source	**Language**	**Source**	**Language**
eu	**Other**	**Zaaas**	**Other**
voto	**Other**	viejas	Spanish
por	**Other**	zorras	Spanish
um	**Other**		
mundo	**Other**		
onde	**Other**		

References

Ron Artstein and Massimo Poesio. 2008. Inter-coder agreement for computational linguistics. *Computational Linguistics*, 34(4):555–596, December.

Shane Bergsma, Paul McNamee, Mossaab Bagdouri, Clayton Fink, and Theresa Wilson. 2012. Language identification for creating language-specific twitter collections. In *Proceedings of the Second Workshop on Language in Social Media*, pages 65–74, Montréal, Canada, June. Association for Computational Linguistics.

Chris Callison-Burch and Mark Dredze. 2010. Creating speech and language data with amazon's mechanical turk. In *Proceedings of the NAACL HLT 2010 Workshop on Creating Speech and Language Data with Amazon's Mechanical Turk*, pages 1–12, Los Angeles, June. Association for Computational Linguistics.

Karthik Dinakar, Roi Reichart, and Henry Lieberman. 2011. Modeling the detection of textual cyberbullying. In *Workshop on the Social Mobile Web*.

A. Joshi. 1982. Processing of sentences with intrasentential code-switching. In Ján Horecký, editor, *COLING-82*, pages 145–150, Prague, July.

Ben King and Steven Abney. 2013. Labeling the languages of words in mixed-language documents using weakly supervised methods. In *Proceedings of the 2013 Conference of the North American Chapter of the Association for Computational Linguistics: Human Language Technologies*, pages 1110–1119, Atlanta, Georgia, June. Association for Computational Linguistics.

Lingpeng Kong, Nathan Schneider, Swabha Swayamdipta, Archna Bhatia, Chris Dyer, and Noah A. Smith. 2014. A dependency parser for tweets. In *Proceedings of the 2014 Conference on Empirical Methods in Natural Language Processing (EMNLP)*, pages 1001–1012, Doha, Qatar, October. Association for Computational Linguistics.

Ying Li, Yue Yu, and Pascale Fung. 2012. A mandarin-english code-switching corpus. In Nicoletta Calzolari, Khalid Choukri, Thierry Declerck, Mehmet Uğur Doğan, Bente Maegaard, Joseph Mariani, Jan Odijk, and Stelios Piperidis, editors, *Proceedings of the Eighth International Conference on Language Resources and Evaluation (LREC-2012)*, pages 2515–2519, Istanbul, Turkey, May. European Language Resources Association (ELRA). ACL Anthology Identifier: L12-1573.

Constantine Lignos and Mitch Marcus. 2013. Toward web-scale analysis of codeswitching. In *87th Annual Meeting of the Linguistic Society of America*.

J. Lipski. 1978. Code-switching and the problem of bilingual competence. In M. Paradis, editor, *Aspects of bilingualism*, pages 250–264. Hornbeam.

D.C. Lyu, T.P. Tan, E. Chng, and H. Li. 2010. Seame: a mandarin-english code-switching speech corpus in south-east asia. In *INTERSPEECH*, volume 10, pages 1986–1989.

S. Gideon Mann and Andrew McCallum. 2008. Generalized expectation criteria for semi-supervised learning of conditional random fields. In *Proceedings of ACL-08: HLT*, pages 870–878. Association for Computational Linguistics.

Paul McNamee. 2005. Language identification: A solved problem suitable for undergraduate instruction. *J. Comput. Sci. Coll.*, 20(3):94–101, February.

Dong Nguyen and A. Seza Doğruöz. 2013. Word level language identification in online multilingual communication. In *Proceedings of the 2013 Conference on Empirical Methods in Natural Language Processing*, pages 857–862, Seattle, Washington, USA, October. Association for Computational Linguistics.

S. Poplack. 1980. Sometimes I'll start a sentence in Spanish y termino en español: toward a typology of code-switching. *Linguistics*, 18(7/8):581–618.

Antonio Reyes, Paolo Rosso, and Tony Veale. 2013. A multidimensional approach for detecting irony in twitter. *Language Resources and Evaluation*, 47(1):239–268.

Kirk Roberts, Michael A. Roach, Joseph Johnson, Josh Guthrie, and Sanda M. Harabagiu. 2012. Empatweet: Annotating and detecting emotions on twitter. In *Proceedings of the Eighth International Conference on Language Resources and Evaluation (LREC-2012)*. European Language Resources Association (ELRA).

Anil Kumar Singh and Jagadeesh Gorla. 2007. Identification of languages and encodings in a multilingual document. In *Proceedings of ACL-SIGWAC's Web As Corpus3*, Belgium.

Thamar Solorio and Yang Liu. 2008a. Learning to predict code-switching points. In *Empirical Methods on Natural Language Processing, EMNLP-2008*, pages 973–981, Honolulu, Hawaii, October. Association for Computational Linguistics.

Thamar Solorio and Yang Liu. 2008b. Part-of-speech tagging for English-Spanish code-switched text. In *Empirical Methods on Natural Language Processing, EMNLP-2008*, pages 1051–1060, Honolulu, Hawaii, October. Association for Computational Linguistics.

Irina Temnikova, Andrea Varga, and Dogan Biyikli. 2014. Building a crisis management term resource for social media: The case of floods and protests. In Nicoletta Calzolari (Conference Chair), Khalid Choukri, Thierry Declerck, Hrafn Loftsson, Bente Maegaard, Joseph Mariani, Asuncion Moreno, Jan Odijk, and Stelios Piperidis, editors, *Proceedings of the Ninth International Conference on Language Resources and Evalu-*

ation (LREC'14), Reykjavik, Iceland, may. European Language Resources Association (ELRA).

Marc Tomlinson, David Bracewell, Wayne Krug, and David Hinote. 2014. #mygoal: Finding motivations on twitter. In *Proceedings of the Ninth International Conference on Language Resources and Evaluation (LREC-2014)*. European Language Resources Association (ELRA).

Jennifer Williams and Graham Katz. 2012. A new twitter verb lexicon for natural language processing. In Nicoletta Calzolari (Conference Chair), Khalid Choukri, Thierry Declerck, Mehmet Uur Doan, Bente Maegaard, Joseph Mariani, Asuncion Moreno, Jan Odijk, and Stelios Piperidis, editors, *Proceedings of the Eight International Conference on Language Resources and Evaluation (LREC'12)*, Istanbul, Turkey, may. European Language Resources Association (ELRA).

H. Zhai, T. Lingren, L. Deleger, Q. Li, M. Kaiser, L. Stoutenborough, and I. Solti. 2013. Web 2.0-based crowdsourcing for high-quality gold standard development in clinical natural processing. *Journal of Medical Internet Research*, 15(4). Retrieved May 15, 2014 from `http://www.ncbi.nlm.nih.gov/pmc/articles/PMC3636329/`.

Annotating Geographical Entities on Microblog Text

Koji Matsuda[1], **Akira Sasaki**[1], **Naoaki Okazaki**[1,2], and **Kentaro Inui**[1]

[1]Graduate School of Information Sciences, Tohoku University
6-6-05 Aramakiaza-Aoba, Aoba-ku, Sendai, 980-8579, Japan
[2]Japan Science and Technology Agency (JST)
[1]{matsuda, aki-s, okazaki, inui}@ecei.tohoku.ac.jp

Abstract

This paper presents a discussion of the problems surrounding the task of annotating geographical entities on microblogs and reports the preliminary results of our efforts to annotate Japanese microblog texts. Unlike prior work, we not only annotate geographical location entities but also facility entities, such as stations, restaurants, shopping stores, hospitals and schools. We discuss ways in which to build a gazetteer, the types of ambiguities that need to be considered, reasons why the annotator tends to disagree, and the problems that need to be solved to automate the task of annotating the geographical entities. All the annotation data and the annotation guidelines are publicly available for research purposes from our web site.

1 Introduction

The ability to analyze microblog texts according to a spatial or temporal axis has become increasingly important in recent years. For example, with Twitter, users can share knowledge of situations and sightings of events at a low cost, with much of the information being integrated in the form of natural language. If it were possible to anchor these posts (known as "tweets") to specific locations in the real world, this would benefit a wide variety of applications such as marketing, social surveys (Li et al., 2014), disease monitoring (Signorini et al., 2011; Collier, 2012), and disaster response (Middleton et al., 2014; Ohtake et al., 2013; Varga et al., 2013).

For example, with respect to natural disasters, such as the 2011 Tohoku earthquake, large amounts of information were posted on social networking services (SNS), and some of these posts offered information that could aid rescue operations.

In this paper, we discuss the language expressions that are used, in particular those representing a "specific location". For example, expressions that refer to a location (henceforth referred to as "location reference expressions", **LRE**) are often mentioned in such SNS posts, and if it were possible to associate a specific set of coordinates with an area (grounding), this text information could be transferred to a map. By mapping tweets posted during disasters on time and spatial axes, it would possible to gain an improved understanding of a disaster situation.

In this case, it seems that it would be possible to use GPS information that has been attached as metadata to tweets. However, whether GPS information is included in tweets is controlled by the user, in their client settings. It was reported in a recent study (Middleton et al., 2014) that less than 1% of tweets have GPS information appended to them. LREs are expressed in natural languages in the tweet, and an analysis would make it possible to map the actual spatial entity. As explained above, even though there is a large demand for this kind of application, a corpus that annotates geographical entities to LREs in microblog texts does not currently exist.

In this paper, we report the results of the trial that was conducted with the aim of creating a corpus that annotates specific entity information with the coordinate information to LREs appearing in Japanese texts sampled from microblogs. We provide details as to how we made the decisions on the various de-

Proceedings of LAW IX - The 9th Linguistic Annotation Workshop, pages 85–94,
Denver, Colorado, June 5, 2015.

Figure 1: Overview of the corpus

sign aspects, how we built the entity gazetteer, and how we defined the representation of the annotated target. In addition, we describe how the validity of the proposed schema was verified by having it annotated by multiple people and we describe the problems identified from the results of this verification.

As will be discussed later in this paper, not only location names, but also facility names often appear in microblog texts. We compiled a large (more than 5 million entries) gazetteer of locations and facility entities from data obtained from the Web, and managed to annotate about 40% of these entities (an eightfold increase on previous work) with facility names for which the writer assumes a specific location.

Finally, we analyzed part of our corpus to enable us to discuss the technical problems that would need to be resolved to perform the grounding of LREs. The resulting corpus, documentation, and annotation guidelines are available on our web site [1].

2 Related Work

Studies that automatically annotate location information according to text are basically divided into the following types: The first is **Document Geolocation**, that is, inferring the location information for the whole of the given text. A typical example of this form of research is the automatic annotation of location information in Wikipedia articles, or inferring the residency of a Twitter user. This approach is mainly used for supervised learning, with text converted to feature representation. However, it has been reported that this method does not work well on short documents such as tweets (Schulz et al., 2013).

A contrasting approach assigns specific geographical entities by automatically analyzing LREs to identify information such as a toponym that appears in the text (**Geoparsing, Toponym Resolution**) (Leidner, 2007). Speriosu and Baldridge (2013) proposed a supervised learning method by using an indirect supervision technique. DeLozier et al. (2015) proposed a gazetteer independent method by using density estimation techniques.

These studies were evaluated by using a reference corpus such as the TR-CoNLL (Leidner, 2007) or LGL(Local-Global Lexicon) (Lieberman et al., 2010) corpus. However, these corpora are annotated only by location entities, and not by facility entities. In addition, existing corpora have mainly been compiled from the newspaper domain.

Our main aim is the analysis and mapping of social media text; therefore, we need to investigate the behavior of different toponym resolution methods on social media text. This prompted us to annotate text sampled from SNSs.

Mani et al. (2010) annotated location information to text, by annotating both the location and facility entities, but their corpus is sampled from the ACE corpus, which is drawn mainly from broadcast conversations and news magazines. However, in our investigation of their corpus, out of all the LREs in the expressions that were annotated, only 5% were tagged as "Facility", and these were only very popular entities such as "the Pentagon" and "the White House".

In contrast, as our corpus study reveals below, real-life microblog texts include as many mentions referring to facilities whose location can be uniquely identified as are mentions referring to location entities. The annotation of these facility-referring mentions poses interesting research challenges, which motived our corpus study reported in this paper.

Recently, Zhang and Gelernter (2014) annotated Twitter messages, but their annotation focus is limited to toponyms, and facility names are not annotated. Examples of geoparsing for Japanese text,

[1] http://www.cl.ecei.tohoku.ac.jp/~matsuda/LRE_corpus/

GeoNLP (Kitamoto and Sagara, 2012) exist, but there are no reports of quantitative evaluations of the performance, because there is no corpus for evaluation.

3 Challenges in Annotating LREs on Microblog Text

In this section, we describe the new research challenges associated with annotating geographical entities in Microblog text and our policies for addressing these issues.

3.1 Systematic Polysemy of LREs

One prominent issue in annotating facility entities is the so-called *systematic polysemy* inherent in mentions referring to facilities (see, for example, Peters and Peters (2000)). For example, the mention "the Ministry of the Environment" in the sentence (1) below refers to a specific location while the mention "the Ministry of the Environment" in (2) should be interpreted as an organization and does not refer to the location of the organization.

(1) 午後は 環境省 にいます / I'll be at the Ministry of the Environment this afternoon.

(2) これから 環境省 の職員に会ってきます / I will go to meet a staff member of the Ministry of the Environment.

This distinction can be crucial in potential applications of annotated geographical entities. In our annotation guidelines, ambiguities of this nature need to be resolved.

3.2 Analysis of not annotated examples

Another issue in annotating facilities in microblogs is how to manage cases in which a mention refers to a certain (unique) facility entity, but the reader (annotator) cannot resolve it to any specific entry in the gazetteer by only using the information from the local context. For example, the mention "the park" refers to a certain unique location but the local context provides insufficient information for identifying it.

(3) 公園 でスケボーしてる人達眺めてる / I'm looking at the people skateboarding in the park.

According to our corpus study, roughly 50% of facility-referring mentions in our microblog text samples cannot be resolved to a specific entry in the gazetteer. One straightforward way to manage these type of mentions is to discard all common noun phrases from the targets of our annotation. However, since one can also quite often find common nouns that can be resolved to a specific gazetteer entry as in Figure 1, it is intriguing to see the distribution of such cases through a large corpus study and consider the task of building a computational model for analyzing them. Motivated by this consideration, we incorporate the following two tags in our annotation specifications:

Underspecified (UNSP) indicates that the tagged segment refers to a certain unique geographical entity but is not identifiable (i.e. cannot be resolved to any entry from the gazetteer).

Out of Gazetteer (OOG) indicates that the referent of the tagged segment is a geographical entity and can be identified, but is not included in the gazetteer.

3.3 Building a Gazetteer of Facility Entities

Another problem we faced was to decide how to build a gazetteer. For location entities (toponyms), it tends to be easier to find a comprehensive list from public databases such as GeoNames (Leidner, 2007; Middleton et al., 2014). For facilities, on the other hand, since the referents of LREs in microblogs include a broad variety of facilities, including stations, restaurants, shopping stores, hospitals, and schools, it is not a trivial job to build a comprehensive list of those facilities with a sufficient coverage even if the targets are limited to a single country.

For our corpus study, we were fortunate to be able to use the data collection from the Location Based Social Networking Service (LBSNS) as reported in Section 4.2. However, our corpus study suggests that our gazetteer still needs to be extended to ensure improved coverage. In addition, we also had to determine ways in which to share the database with other research sites.

4 Annotation Specifications

In this section, we provide an overview of the specifications of our annotation schema based on the is-

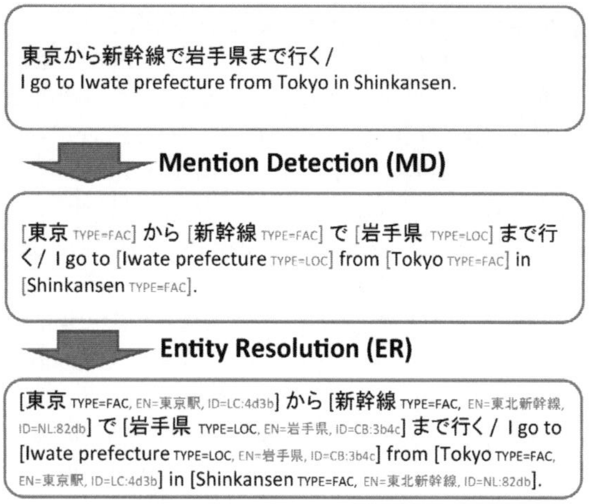

Figure 2: Flow of our annotation scheme

sues discussed in Section 3.

4.1 Annotation

In the existing named entity tagged corpora in Japanese, expressions are annotated with a named entity class and its boundaries. However, the corpora does not contain annotations as to whether each of the expressions actually relates to an entity. Partly following the annotation guidelines in TAC KBP (Ji et al., 2014)[2], the extended named entity tag set (Sekine et al., 2002) and the Japanese extended Named Entity-tagged corpus, we followed the approach illustrated in Figure 2 to annotate microblog texts. The annotation task consists of the following two subtasks:

Mention Detection (MD) Given a microblog text (i.e., a tweet), an annotator annotates all the mentions which refer to specific geographic entities with a predefined set of tags given in Table 1.

Entity Resolution (ER) For each detected mention, an annotator searches the gazetteer for its referred entity and annotates the linking. We allow a mention to be linked to multiple gazetteer entries. If the referent cannot be found in the gazetteer, annotate the mention as **OOG**, and if the referent is not identifiable, annotate the mention as **UNSP**.

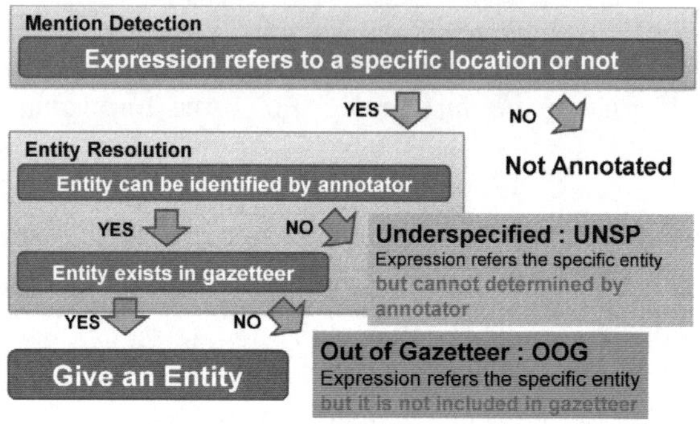

Figure 3: Description of OOG and UNSP tag

In our annotation, all potential LREs in the text are annotated. Following (Mani et al., 2010), non-referring expressions,such as "town" and "city" in "It is better to live in a small town than in a big city", are not annotated. Deictic references such as "there" and pronouns are not annotated. The annotators are allowed to use the information from the writer's profile for reference purposes.

4.2 Gazetteer

In Japan, under open data initiatives, government agencies have released data with the specific latitude and longitude for the name to be used as a postal address, such as the prefecture and city (City-block level location reference information[3]). Therefore, this can be used as the location name gazetteer. However, for facility entities, there is no existing comprehensive database. We used data crawled from Yahoo! Loco[4], which is one of the Location Based Social Networking Services (LBSNSs). This is a large, but noisy, amount of data, which contains many duplicate records of the entity and surface variations. Therefore, we cleaned up entries that were ambiguous or those of which the name was either too short or too long by using several handwritten rules. In addition, we used entities downloaded from "National Land Numerical Information" for railroad data. Table 2 presents an overview of the resulting entity gazetteer. The Location entity gazetteer includes prefectures, cities, and other administrative areas such as "oaza" (sections) and villages. The Facility entity gazetteer includes a

[2]http://nlp.cs.rpi.edu/kbp/2014/elquery.pdf

[3]http://nlftp.mlit.go.jp/isj/

[4]http://loco.yahoo.co.jp/

Table 1: Definition of the tags used in our annotation

Tag	Example	Description
LOC(Location)	埼玉県 / Saitama-prefecture, 仙台市 / Sendai-city	Specific geographical area
FAC(Facility)	仙台駅 / Sendai-station, 九州大学 / Kyusyuu University, 南武線 / Nanbu-line, 東北道 / Tohoku-expressway	Facility/Road/Railroad entity that has a specific location

Table 2: Overview of entity gazetteer used in our annotation

Gazetteer Type	Source	Number of Entries
Locations	City-block level location reference information	147774
Facilities	Yahoo! Loco, National Land Numerical Information	4990239

broad variety of facilities including stations, restaurants, shopping stores, hospitals, and schools. As a result, we compiled a large (more than 5 million entries) gazetteer of location and facility entities in Japan.

Each entity is formatted as GeoJSON Feature object [5], as this format is easy to use with other GIS applications.

4.3 Two Sub-corpora for Annotation

We performed annotations for 10,000 randomly sampled tweets that were tweeted during a specific time period (**RANDOM**), but this proved problematic for refining the annotation scheme rapidly. Because randomly sampled tweets very rarely contain an LRE, the yield ratio of entities is low and inefficient. Therefore, we performed annotations for another 1,000 tweets (**FIL**), which were filtered according to the following rules: (1) Tweets must include two or more potential location names that can be verified by peforming a simple string matching to the location entity gazetteer. (2) One of the location names of rule (1) must be the location name of a prefecture in which the annotator resides. These filters increase the LRE density, and enable us to rapidly advance the discussion to the annotation guideline. In a later section, we discuss the inter-annotator agreement in the FIL sub-corpus.

4.4 Tool for Corpus Annotation

Compared with mention detection, entity resolution tends to be considerably more expensive particularly when the gazetteer at hand has a large coverage. For a given geographical mention, the gazetteer may have dozens of candidate entries, from which the annotator would have to select the correct one. The tasks of searching for the candidate entries and choosing the most appropriate one from among them can be substantially supported with an adequate computational environment. For this purpose, we created an annotation support tool especially designed for our annotation schema. Unlike tools devised in prior work (Leidner, 2007), our tool stores the entire data of our gazetteer (including, for example, the postal address, ontological category, etc., for each facility entity) on a standard full-text search engine and allows the use to search for candidate entries with an arbitrary query string, as illustrated in Figure 5.

This tool works as a Web application, and is capable of working with more than one person at the same time. Figure 4 shows an example of the annotated data, in which the annotated entities are represented by the list of GeoJSON objects, and each object has an ID that uniquely corresponds to an entity in the gazetteer.

5 Corpus Annotation and Evaluation

Using the annotation tools mentioned in the section 4, we annotated 10,000 tweets randomly selected from tweets sent during 2014. Table 3 shows the number of tagged expressions in the annotated corpus.

In addition, as an evaluation of the coverage extent of the gazetteer, we calculated those location and facility names which are annotated with entities in the gazetteer. This result shows that 519 out of

[5] http://geojson.org/

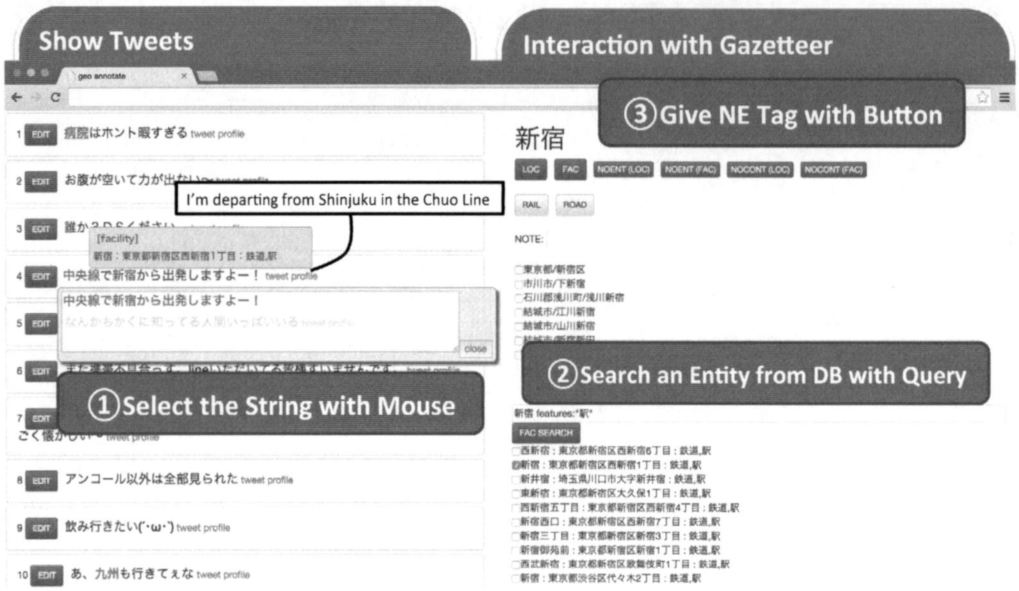

Figure 5: Screenshot of annotation tool

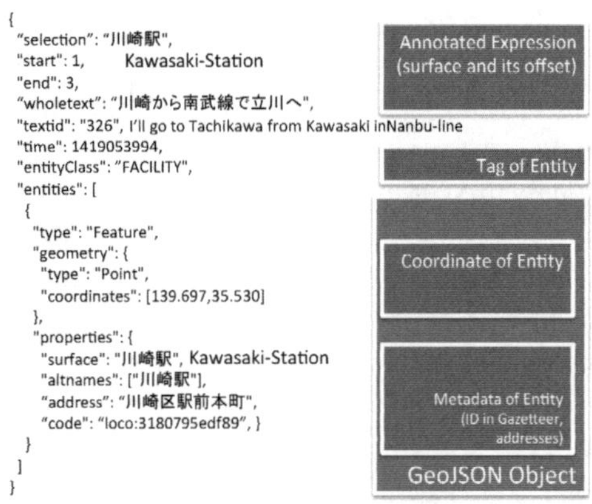

Figure 4: Example of annotated data

951 (54.6%) LREs were annotated with entities. As we analyzed instances without entities, we made the following observations.

Location These instances mainly suffer from an absence of foreign location names, consisting of surrounding areas such as "Higashi Mikawa", and tourist resorts such as "Mount Zao".

Facility In most cases, highly ambiguous instances, such as "house", "McDonald's", and "workplace", were difficult to annotate with an entity. As these instances are dependent on the context of the writer, a third person would be unable to guess the specific entity despite considering the whole text.

5.1 Quality of Annotation: Mention Detection

To discuss the annotation specification, two annotators independently annotated 200 tweets.

First, two annotations were converted into IOB2 codings at the character level, and assuming that the annotation on one side is correct, we then calculated the precision, recall, and the F1-Score of the annotation on the other side. For reference, comparing two annotations at the character level, Cohen's Kappa was 0.892. Table 4 shows the evaluation results of the inter-annotator agreement. This indicated that the annotation is generally successful, but the annotation quality of the FAC tag is slightly lower. As mentioned above, in this annotation, annotators need to interpret the intent of the writer of a text (irrespective of whether a specific location is assumed).

(4) これでもう 大学図書館 から取り寄せてもらわなくていいのね… / I don't need to order from university library anymore.

Table 3: Number of tagged expressions in annotated corpus

Tag	#tagged expression	#tagged with entity	**OOG**	**UNSP**
LOC	406	298 (73.4%)	14 (3.4%)	94 (23.2%)
FAC	545	221 (40.6%)	43 (7.9%)	281 (51.6%)
TOTAL	951	519 (54.6%)	57 (6.0%)	375 (39.4%)
#Tweet		10000		
#Character		332739		

Table 4: Evaluation results of inter-annotator agreement (assuming the annotation on one side is correct)

Tag	Precision	Recall	$F_{\beta=1}$
LOC	87.68% (178/203)	97.27% (178/183)	92.23
FAC	89.25% (83/ 93)	72.81% (83/114)	80.19
Overall	88.18% (261/296)	87.88% (261/297)	88.03

In this example, one annotator judged "university library" as a facility name, on the other hand, the other judged it as an organization and did not annotate it as an LRE. This arrangement probably makes annotation harder; hence, we would have to re-examine this guideline for future work.

5.2 Quality of Annotation: Entity Resolution

To evaluate our entity resolution annotation scheme quantitatively, we compare the coordinate pair of the entity that was annotated by two annotators, as described in the section 5.1. As error metrics, we use the Average Error Distance (AED) and Median Error Distance (MED) to ensure comparability with related work. Each of the two annotators annotated 243 expressions, and the AED was determined as 1648 meters, whereas the MED was found to be 0 meters. Of these 243 instances, 199 (81.9%) show an error distance of 0 meters. In other words, two annotators annotated exactly the same entity for these instances. The following example shows instances with large errors in the distance. This instance indicates that the two annotators made different interpretations, and thus the annotations differed. We denote the annotators as A and B.

(5) (Error Distance: 70.8 km) 江坂周辺、[淡路 A:LOC/兵庫県淡路市 B:FAC/淡路駅 (大阪市東淀川区)] 周辺、西中島南方周辺、新大阪周辺でバイト見つけたい / I want to work in a part-time job near Esaka, [Awaji A:LOC/Awaji-shi, Hyogo B:FAC/Awaji Station(Yodogawa-ku, Osaka-shi)], Nishi-Nakajima, or Shin-Osaka.

According to the two annotators, one annotator interpreted each location name in this example literally and confirmed that these location names belong to "Kansai region", then annotated "Awaji-shi", which has the largest population. The other annotator perceived that these location names are station names in a specific region, then interpreted "Awaji" as a station name in "Osaka-shi". We plan to discuss how much reasoning or background knowledge should be used for annotation.

5.3 Required Clues for Entity Resolution

As we show below, although some LREs need complex reasoning and annotations for them disagree, on the other hand, there are also LREs which are easily annotated by a simple clue. We investigated the annotated entities of 10,000 tweets in **RANDOM**, judged what types of clues are required for manual entity resolution, and examined the distribution. When we performed manual judgement, we assumed that the LRE tag (location or facility name) and the boundary is given, and then we focused on the types of clues required for entity resolution, which can require multiple clues. In addition, LREs annotated with a single entity are subject to investigation. Therefore, 267 location names and 169 facility names were investigated. Table 5 shows the result. This table enables us to make the following observations.

Nearly 30% of location names presented no ambiguity, and more than half of these were annotated with the candidate entity with the largest population. Therefore, as for location names, population seems to be a good baseline for entity resolution. This

Table 5: Required Clues for entity resolution

Clue	LOC	FAC	TOTAL
(1) No ambiguity (There was only one candidate entity in the gazetteer, and it was the correct entity)	85(31.8%)	48(28.4%)	133(30.5%)
(2) Candidate entity which has the largest population is the correct entity	151(56.6%)	0(0.0%)	151(34.6%)
(3) Need to deal with abbreviations or variations of surface form	5(1.9%)	74(43.8%)	79(18.1%)
(4) Resolved by considering other LREs in the text	25(9.4%)	17(10.1%)	42(9.6%)
(5) Resolved by considering contextual information in the text	0(0.0%)	34(20.1%)	34(7.8%)
(6) Resolved by considering global context (profile data, URL, photo, and so on)	1(0.4%)	11(6.5%)	12(2.8%)

result is consistent with those of (Leidner, 2007), which targeted the newspaper domain.

However, in the case of facility names, entity resolution was more complicated. Although the proportion considered to be unambiguous is virtually the same as that of the location names, there are no existing metrics, such as population, for facility entities. Therefore, defining metrics, such as population, is desirable. For that purpose, we would prefer to consider a term such as "popularity". To calculate these metrics, the check-in counts of a Location Based Social Network Service (LBSNSs), such as Foursquare[6] or Loctouch[7], appear to be useful.

In addition, 40% of facility names require the ability to process abbreviations and variations of surface forms. For example, "Hama-sta" in the following text seems to refer to "Yokohama Stadium"; however, it is not possible to look this up directly in the facility entity gazetteer.

(6) ハマスタ で試合観戦なう / I'm watching a game at Hama-sta.

To address this, we would have to consult the gazetteer flexibly, by using methods such as approximate string matching (Okazaki and Tsujii, 2010). As this is a widespread problem with facility names, it would have to be addressed to enable grounding to be performed.

Moreover, 20% of facility names required local context in the text (other than LRE). The following is an example.

(7) 山手線で 東京 から品川に向かっています / I'm going toward Shinagawa From Tokyo.

In this example, "Tokyo" seems to refer to "Tokyo Station", considering the local context in the text. As far as we searched, most of the entities requiring local context were station names such as "Tokyo Station".

6 Conclusion

This paper discusses the problems associated with the task of annotating geographical entities on Japanese microblog texts and reports the preliminary results of the actual annotation. All the annotation data and the annotation guidelines are publicly available for research purposes from our web site.

The annotation task consisted of two subtasks: mention detection and entity resolution. Our corpus study showed that our annotation scheme could achieve a reasonably high inter-annotator agreement.

The scope of the annotation was extended to facility entities by introducing the **OOG** and **UNSP** tags. The distributions of these tags obtained through our corpus study will provide useful implications for our future work for an improved annotation setting.

We also investigated the types of clues that are considered useful for entity resolution and found

[6] https://foursquare.com/

[7] http://tou.ch/

that the task of identifying facility entities poses interesting research issues including abbreviations, variations of surface forms, and the popularity of each facility. In particular, the popularity appears to be important in resolving facility entities. The automatic estimation of the popularity over a broad range of facilities may present an interesting research issue.

Acknowledgments

This research was supported by the program *Research and Development on Real World Big Data Integration and Analysis* of the Ministry of Education, Culture, Sports, Science and Technology, Japan and by the Precursory Research for Embryonic Science and Technology (PRESTO), Japan Science and Technology Agency (JST).

References

Nigel Collier. 2012. Uncovering text mining: A survey of current work on web-based epidemic intelligence. *Global Public Health*, 7(7):731–749. PMID: 22783909.

Grant DeLozier, Jason Baldridge, and Loretta London. 2015. Gazetteer-independent toponym resolution using geographic word profiles. In *Proceedings of AAAI 2015*. The AAAI Press.

Heng Ji, HT Dang, J Nothman, and B Hachey. 2014. Overview of tac-kbp2014 entity discovery and linking tasks. *Proc. Text Analysis Conference (TAC2014)*.

Asanobu Kitamoto and Takeshi Sagara. 2012. Toponym-based geotagging for observing precipitation from social and scientific data streams. In Gerald Friedland Liangliang Cao, editor, *Proceedings of the 2012 ACM Workshop on Geotagging and Its Applications in Multimedia, GeoMM'12 (co-located with ACM Multimedia 2012)*, pages 23–26. ACM, 11.

Jochen L. Leidner. 2007. Toponym resolution in text: Annotation, evaluation and applications of spatial grounding. *SIGIR Forum*, 41(2):124–126, December.

Jiwei Li, Alan Ritter, and Eduard Hovy. 2014. Weakly supervised user profile extraction from twitter. In *Proceedings of the 52nd Annual Meeting of the Association for Computational Linguistics (Volume 1: Long Papers)*, pages 165–174. Association for Computational Linguistics.

Michael D. Lieberman, Hanan Samet, and Jagan Sankaranarayanan. 2010. Geotagging with local lexicons to build indexes for textually-specified spatial data. In Feifei Li, Mirella M. Moro, Shahram Ghandeharizadeh, Jayant R. Haritsa, Gerhard Weikum, Michael J. Carey, Fabio Casati, Edward Y. Chang, Ioana Manolescu, Sharad Mehrotra, Umeshwar Dayal, and Vassilis J. Tsotras, editors, *ICDE*, pages 201–212. IEEE.

Inderjeet Mani, Christy Doran, Dave Harris, Janet Hitzeman, Rob Quimby, Justin Richer, Ben Wellner, Scott Mardis, and Seamus Clancy. 2010. Spatialml: annotation scheme, resources, and evaluation. *Language Resources and Evaluation*, 44(3):263–280.

S.E. Middleton, L. Middleton, and S. Modafferi. 2014. Real-time crisis mapping of natural disasters using social media. *Intelligent Systems, IEEE*, 29(2):9–17, Mar.

Kiyonori Ohtake, Jun Goto, Stijn De Saeger, Kentaro Torisawa, Junta Mizuno, and Kentaro Inui. 2013. Nict disaster information analysis system. In *The Companion Volume of the Proceedings of IJCNLP 2013: System Demonstrations*, pages 29–32. Asian Federation of Natural Language Processing.

Naoaki Okazaki and Jun'ichi Tsujii. 2010. Simple and efficient algorithm for approximate dictionary matching. In *Proceedings of the 23rd International Conference on Computational Linguistics*, COLING '10, pages 851–859, Stroudsburg, PA, USA. Association for Computational Linguistics.

Wim Peters and Ivonne Peters. 2000. Lexicalised systematic polysemy in wordnet. In *Proceedings of the Second International Conference on Language Resources and Evaluation (LREC'00)*. European Language Resources Association (ELRA).

Axel Schulz, Aristotelis Hadjakos, Heiko Paulheim, Johannes Nachtwey, and Max Mhlhuser. 2013. A multi-indicator approach for geolocalization of tweets. In Emre Kiciman, Nicole B. Ellison, Bernie Hogan, Paul Resnick, and Ian Soboroff, editors, *ICWSM*. The AAAI Press.

Satoshi Sekine, Kiyoshi Sudo, and Chikashi Nobata. 2002. Extended named entity hierarchy. In *Proceedings of the Third International Conference on Language Resources and Evaluation (LREC-2002)*, Las Palmas, Canary Islands - Spain, May. European Language Resources Association (ELRA).

Alessio Signorini, Alberto Maria Segre, and Philip M. Polgreen. 2011. The use of twitter to track levels of disease activity and public concern in the u.s. during the influenza a h1n1 pandemic. *PLoS ONE*, 6(5):e19467, 05.

Michael Speriosu and Jason Baldridge. 2013. Text-driven toponym resolution using indirect supervision. In *Proceedings of the 51st Annual Meeting of the Association for Computational Linguistics (Volume 1: Long Papers)*, pages 1466–1476. Association for Computational Linguistics.

István Varga, Motoki Sano, Kentaro Torisawa, Chikara Hashimoto, Kiyonori Ohtake, Takao Kawai, Jong-Hoon Oh, and Stijn De Saeger. 2013. Aid is out there: Looking for help from tweets during a large scale disaster. In *Proceedings of the 51st Annual Meeting of the Association for Computational Linguistics (Volume 1: Long Papers)*, pages 1619–1629. Association for Computational Linguistics.

Wei Zhang and Judith Gelernter. 2014. Geocoding location expressions in twitter messages: A preference learning method. *J. Spatial Information Science*, 9(1):37–70.

The Annotation Process of the ITU Web Treebank

Tuğba Pamay, Umut Sulubacak, Dilara Torunoğlu-Selamet, Gülşen Eryiğit
Department of Computer Engineering
Istanbul Technical University
Istanbul, 34469, Turkey
{pamay,sulubacak,torunoglud,gulsen.cebiroglu}@itu.edu.tr

Abstract

The potential of processing user-generated texts freely available on the web is widely recognized, but due to the non-canonical nature of the language used in the web, it is not possible to process these data using conventional methodologies designed for well-edited formal texts. Procedures for properly annotating raw web data have not been as extensively researched as those for annotating well-edited texts, as also evident from the viewpoint of Turkish language processing. Moreover, there is a considerable shortage of human-annotated corpora derived from Turkish web data. The ITU Web Treebank is the first attempt for a diverse corpus compiled from Turkish texts found on the web. In this paper, we first present our survey of the non-canonical aspects of the language used in the Turkish web. Next, we discuss in detail the annotation procedure followed in the ITU Web Treebank, revised for compatibility with the language of the web. Finally, we describe the web-based annotation tool following this procedure, on which the treebank was annotated.

1 Introduction

As researchers grow more conscious of the potential of applications on user-generated web data, developing methodologies for processing the language of the web becomes increasingly important. The amount of raw data freely available on the web is not only massive, but also it is constantly being expanded and renewed. As such, if web data were to be processed as accurately as edited texts which have been in the spotlight for a long time, they would constitute a data source substantially larger than any human-annotated corpus to date, bolstering up research on unsupervised and semi-supervised learning.

Despite the potential, processing web data is a challenge for any system designed for or trained on edited texts, due to radical differences in the languages employed in the domains. The Internet has its own idiosyncratic language that is very loose and colloquial compared to the formal language standard. Web users are often not concerned with grammar and directly transcribe their spontaneous speech to their writing. The language of the Internet is also highly memetic and dominated by various sub-cultures. Often, users experiment with their own house rules instead of canonical grammar, omitting letters or replacing them with foreign characters, deliberately making spelling mistakes and putting words in inappropriate letter cases. Such practices render the language of the Internet highly non-canonical and complicate the processing of web data.

The ITU Web Treebank is a data set containing sentences collected from various domains on the Internet, inspired by recent efforts on other languages (Seddah et al., 2012; Bies et al., 2012). In the absence of Turkish language resources originating from the web, the ITU Web Treebank aimed to establish the first manually annotated web language resource for Turkish. Sulubacak and Eryiğit (2014) described the annotation procedure of the ITU Web Treebank in detail, outlining the treebank composition, the annotation setting and the syntactic framework. Another aim of the ITU Web Treebank was to put forward and demonstrate an approach for annotating the non-canonical language found in the web. This paper goes into detail and thoroughly describes

Proceedings of LAW IX - The 9th Linguistic Annotation Workshop, pages 95–101,
Denver, Colorado, June 5, 2015.

this approach, along with the motivations for any changes proposed over the previous de facto annotation standard for Turkish.

Section 2 discusses the non-canonical elements commonly found in the language of the web. Section 3 goes into detail about our annotation procedure and the layered structure of the ITU Web Treebank. Finally, Section 4 introduces the updated annotation tool we used in annotating the ITU Web Treebank.

2 Non-Canonical Forms in Web

The language of the web is not entirely arbitrary, and it is still possible to work out the ways in which it differs from canonical language. The colloquial expressions and peculiar grammatical conventions still reveal a pattern, and word usages can be likened to an elaborate jargon. We present our analysis of the non-canonical aspects of the language of the Turkish web below, in an exclusive category for each aspect.

Punctuation: Punctuation is very often omitted by users on the web, especially in daily conversations. Especially abundant in social media, where posts are usually directed to each user's own limited network rather than the public, this phenomenon is not limited to terminal periods and also often affects punctuation like commas, semicolons and apostrophes that serve as constituent or morpheme boundaries. The omission of terminal punctuation overly complicate the task of splitting sentences that are semantically independent but syntactically appear as a single sentence. Moreover, syntactically similar constituents pose a challenge for syntactic annotation and parsing when they are not properly disjoined by punctuation.

Abbreviated Writing: Whether forced by websites such as microblogs that impose a character limit on messages or motivated by a need to respond quickly to the dynamics of a social medium, there is a widespread trend of using abbreviations and shorthand on the web. As abbreviated writing is manifested in a variety of ways, it is a major challenge to handle such expressions.

Exaggerated Writing: Another spelling anomaly is manifested in excessively repeated letters, usually vowels, in order to emphasize an expression or convey frustration, excitement or exclamation. These expressions often correspond to interjections and other vocatives.

Spelling Mistakes: Mistakes in spelling are among the most commonly occurring aspects in informal language, and they can be encountered in virtually any platform on the web. While some spelling errors can be made deliberately as part of a jargon, they most commonly stem from overlooked typing mistakes, as it is not common practice to double-check typing.

Foreign Characters: Internet users may prefer not to use the letters in the original spelling a word for a variety of reasons. For instance, non-letter characters may be substituted for regular letters with similar shapes, in order to adapt to experimental spelling trends. Also, because some platforms restricting character encoding do not support certain Turkish letters such as 'ç', 'ğ', 'ş', 'ı', 'İ', 'ö' and 'ü', users may be forced to use the closest ASCII versions 'c', 'g', 's', 'i', 'I', 'o' and 'u'. Moreover, certain input methods may not provide a convenient means to type non-English letters, further encouraging users to make the ASCII substitution.

Letter Case: A significant portion of the users on the web do not attach importance to letter cases. Capitalizing the initial letters of proper nouns and the first words of sentences is often disregarded, abbreviations in uppercase are occasionally typed out in lowercase, and stylizing certain proper nouns in mixed case is also frequently neglected.

Web Entities: It has become fairly common for web users to share URLs and e-mail addresses with other users from their private networks. Additionally, with the advent of Twitter, microblogging services call for the active usage of mentions, hashtags and other metadata tags. The usage of emoticons to express feelings in plain text has also become extremely popular. As such web-specific entities may exhibit irregular morphology and syntax, it is necessary to detect and handle them.

3 Annotation Procedure

In order to attain a more proper and lenient framework for annotating non-canonical language, we revised the entire annotation procedure since Atalay et al. (2003) and made several extensions and modifications. Going by the common convention, we processed our raw data through consecutive steps, each establishing a separate aspect of the data. Before any morphological or syntactic tagging, we applied an extensive normalization routine in order to facilitate the processing of the data by the later modules. We also updated our morphological and syntactic annotation schemes and designated particular morphological tags and dependency labels in an attempt to formalize various morphosyntactic phenomena common in the language of the web.

The ITU Web Treebank is organized in three cascading layers: 1) The normalization layer, 2) The morphology layer and 3) The syntax layer. Annotating data involves firstly the manual normalization, and then the consecutive morphological and dependency tagging of the data. Starting from the raw data, the result of each annotation phase contributes to the next layer of the treebank.

The cascading nature of the layers on the raw data makes it possible to compare each successive layer and extract training and validation corpora from the data. As such, the ITU Web Treebank comprises major resources for both training and validating systems aiming to automatize tasks corresponding to each annotation phase, such as automatic normalizers, morphological disambiguators and dependency parsers, each naturally attuned to non-canonical web data.

The subsections below provide a description of our annotation phases and the changes made on each phase in adapting to the non-canonical language of the Internet.

3.1 Normalization

Our manual normalization phase acts as a preprocessing routine before morphological annotation. Because morphological and syntactic taggers are typically designed to process formal language and would require a radical redesign to handle non-canonical language on their own, normalization is called for as an initial step also in automatically processing non-canonical language. In this phase, we manually tokenize raw sentences and process each token in order to eliminate any errors in spelling and word cases, expand non-standard abbreviations and contractions, and mark web entities such as URLs for later phases, as established in Eryiğit and Torunoğlu-Selamet (2015).

We investigate the following issues during manual normalization.

Abbreviations: We replace informal abbreviations such as ***kib*** for ***kendine iyi bak*** (*"take care of yourself"*) with their full forms. Institutionalized and formal abbreviations used for entire classes of words such as titles like ***dr*** for ***doktor*** (*"doctor"*) and units of measurement like ***kg*** for ***kilogram*** are left as they are, to be handled later in the morphology layer.

Shorthand: We fully type out shorthand that omits or replaces certain characters and leaves out a fragment from which it is still possible to guess the full form. Such usages may omit any non-initial vowel as in ***anldm*** for ***anladım*** (*"I get it"*), the postvocalic 'ğ' as in ***saol*** for ***sağ ol*** (*"thanks"*), and other elided consonants such as a postconsonantal 'h' as in ***mrb*** for ***merhaba*** (*"hello"*). Shorthand may also involve contractions such as ***naber*** for ***ne haber*** (*"what's up"*), as well as heavily assimilated or broken verb suffixes typed out as though they were pronounced with a nonstandard accent as in ***-yon*** for ***-yorsun*** (the present progessive tense, 2nd person suffix).

Web Entities: We enclose all URLs, e-mail addresses, mentions, hashtags and emoticons in corresponding tags for each class, respectively `@url[...]`, `@email[...]`, `@mention[...]`, `@hashtag[...]` and `@smiley[...]`. These classes of web-specific tokens are often found to deviate from regular punctuation (for emoticons) and nouns (for the rest of the classes) in their participation in syntax. By applying these tags, we provide clues to the morphological analyzer so that it would generate special morphological features for these semantic classes of tokens, which in turn provide clues to the syntactic parser.

Letter Case: We investigate the letter cases of each token and make corrections as necessary. This is among the most demanded tasks, since the capitalization of sentence-initial tokens and proper nouns are very commonly omitted in the language of the web. The task is however not limited to capitalization, as it is sometimes proper to put tokens in uppercase (e.g. in *"NAACL"*) or even mixed case (e.g. in *"LaTeX"*), as well as decapitalize tokens that should have been in lowercase. This task is also quite important, since morphological analyzers are often case-sensitive and may not work properly with inputs in wrong letter cases.

Character Repetition: We eliminate excessive character repetitions, excluding punctuation, often used for exclamation or emphasis as in ***lütfeeeeen*** (*"pleeeeease"*).

Improper Glyphs: We restore the appropriate Turkish letters whenever they are replaced by a non-Turkish letter or a non-letter character as in ***$aqa*** instead of ***şaka*** (*"joke"*). This is roughly equivalent to the *Leetspeak* of the English web, practiced to add some humorous flair to the language, though rather uncommonly. A more common practice is to use the closest ASCII versions of non-English letters in the Turkish alphabet as in ***cus*** for ***çüş*** (*"whoa"*), and replacing such letters is also part of this task.

Spelling Mistakes: As should be intuitive, we also correct any remaining spelling mistakes after all the aforementioned checks are completed.

3.2 Morphology

The next phase after normalization is the morphological tagging phase. Since morphological analyzers would be able to automatically process the data after normalization, the phase usually amounts to manually disambiguating between automatically generated morphological analyses for each token. We use a version of the morphological framework described in Şahin et al. (2013), with some additional fine POS categories integrated in order to properly annotate certain elements of non-canonical language. For such, it is also occasionally required to manually provide morphological analyses when a token is not analyzed properly by the base analyzer due to its non-canonical aspects.

One of our significant additions to the framework is the support for formally acceptable abbreviations, which are automatically assigned their full forms as their lemmata and treated as nouns with the newly introduced fine POS `+Abbr`, such as units of measurement. Not only does this increase the expressiveness of the framework for formal texts, but also it takes a significant burden from the normalization phase by removing the need to replace most abbreviations commonly used on the web with their full forms. However, as discussed before in Section 3.1, certain abbreviations representing multiple words and other non-standard abbreviations do not fall under this scope.

Our other major revision involves the morphological annotation of web entities, as outlined previously in Section 3.1. Such entities often have idiosyncratic usages deviating from those of regular tokens with the same assigned POS, and parsers therefore require an alternative cue in order to distinguish these entities and learn the exclusive syntax applying to them. In our framework, emoticons are unambiguously treated like punctuation, and this is reflected in their morphological features by tagging them as punctuation with the fine POS `+Smiley`. Other web entities are treated as nouns in the same manner, with the fine POS `+URL`, `+Email`, `+Mention` and `+Hashtag`. For a different viewpoint, Foster et al. (2011) automatically assign generic surface forms like *Username* and *Hashtag* to such web entities, letting the parser discern them by their lexical features. However, we find that encoding this information in morphology as in Gimpel et al. (2011) allows our data-driven parsers to successfully distinguish these entities without obscuring their original lexical features. We facilitate the morphological tagging of web entities with the help of a pre-tagger processing the lexical tags assigned in the normalization phase, as explained previously in Section 3.1.

3.3 Syntax

The third and last phase of annotation is the dependency parsing of the normalized and morphologically tagged tokens. We follow the revised, web-compatible dependency annotation framework described in Sulubacak and Eryiğit (2014), which also introduced the ITU Web Treebank for the first time. This framework considers many aspects of the non-canonical language of the web and offers comprehensive and convenient annotation schemes to express them.

Our updated annotation scheme takes care not to make any assumptions about the syntactic structures of sentences outside of the most fundamental elements. Dependencies to tokens that may be left out in sentences found on the web are eliminated whenever possible. The annotation schemes of coordination and relativizer structures, sentence predicates and punctuation are all revised as part of this effort. Additionally, certain restrictions on the root node are relaxed, so that multiple constituents can now depend on the root node, even though the root node itself is not allowed to have a head. Constituents depending on the root node can also be assigned any permissible dependency relation rather than the single dummy relation **ROOT**, allowing for more semantically appropriate annotation schemes for constituents like predicates and vocatives that essentially modify the sentence. The full set of changes on the dependency grammar are described in Sulubacak and Eryiğit (2014).

4 Annotation Tool

In this study, we introduce an updated version of the ITU Treebank Annotation Tool (Eryiğit, 2007) to annotate the ITU Web Treebank. The new version is a web-based application supporting annotation for the normalization layer in addition to the morphology and syntax layers, allowing concurrent operation by multiple annotators on the same data.

The new version of the annotation tool comes with a set of changes in the annotation interfaces in compliance with the changes in the annotation methodologies for web data compatibility. The tool can now automatically generate morphological analyses for certain orthographically tagged tokens such as web entities in addition to the output fetched from a morphological analyzer, to be later disambiguated by hand. The dependency annotation interface now supports the specification of multiple head tokens for a given constituent, allowing the annotation of deep dependencies on the tool while still enforcing at least one head for each dependent. The interface also displays the root node as a separate token and allows regular dependencies to the root node.

In addition to the annotation of the ITU Web Treebank, our updated annotation tool is used in the creation of the revised IVS (Eryiğit and Pamay, 2007 2014) Corpus and the IMST (Sulubacak and Eryiğit, 2014) Corpus, as well as the validation corpus for the Turkish mobile assistant developed by Çelikkaya and Eryiğit (2014).

The annotation interfaces of our new tool are shown in Figures 1 and 2. Figure 1 displays the normalization and morphological tagging interfaces on a unified window, whereas Figure 2 shows the syntactic tagging interface along with the dependency relation table for the sentence being processed.

5 Conclusion

In this paper, we presented the web-compatible revision of our annotation procedure, which we used to annotate the ITU Web Treebank, the first manually annotated web treebank for Turkish organized in three layers, namely normalization, morphology and syntax. We provided a survey of new expressions common in the non-canonical language of the web, and detailed the measures we took in order to handle them during normalization, morphological tagging and dependency annotation. We described the new version of our treebank annotation tool updated in accordance with these measures. We believe the layered annotation framework we outlined in this work would serve as an effective baseline for any study involving the annotation of non-canonical web data.

Acknowledgments

We would like to acknowledge that this work is part of a research project entitled "Parsing Web 2.0 Sentences" subsidized by the TÜBİTAK (Turkish Scientific and Technological Research Council) 1001 program (grant number 112E276) and part of the ICT COST Action IC1207. We would hereby like to offer our sincere gratitude to our colleagues Ayşenur Genç, Can Özbey, Kübra Adalı and Gözde Gül Şahin who offered additional help during the annotation phase.

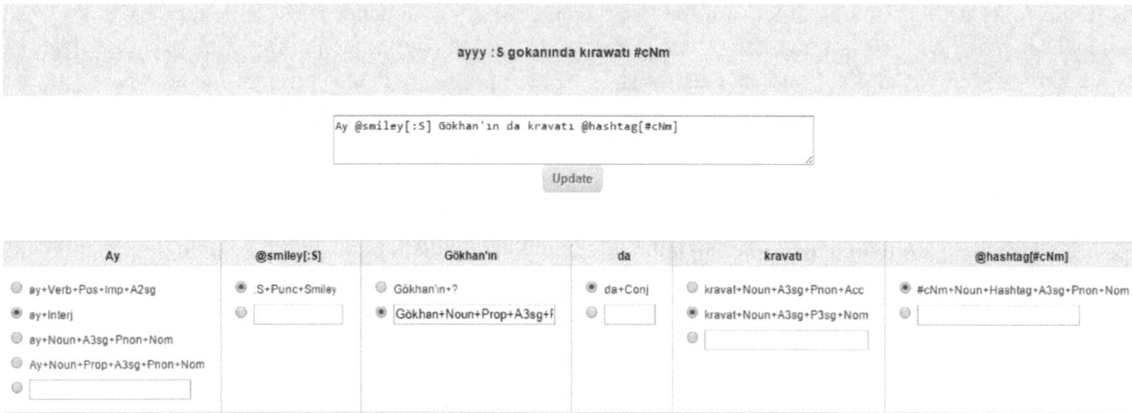

Figure 1: **The Normalization and Morphological Tagging Phases**
A snapshot from the unified normalization and morphological tagging screen from the new annotation tool. The example shows the hypothetical Turkish tweet "***ayyy :S gokanında kırawatı #cNm***", roughly translated to English as "*ohhh :S gokans tie too #aWw*", normalized as "***Ay @smiley[:S] Gökhan'ın da kravatı @hashtag[#cNm]***". The morphology window displays three different cases for tokens where the annotator 1) manually disambiguates between generated morphological analyses, 2) verifies a morphological analysis automatically derived from orthographic tags, or 3) has to manually type in an analysis.

Figure 2: **The Syntactic Annotation Phases**
A snapshot showing the syntactic annotation screen of the new annotation tool. The example shows the normalized and morphologically tagged sentence marked for dependencies. Each row of the relation table corresponds to a dependency arc, where the columns respectively denote the dependent token, the head token, the dependency relation, and the inflectional group index of the head token.

References

Nart B Atalay, Kemal Oflazer, Bilge Say, et al. 2003. The annotation process in the Turkish treebank. In *Proceedings of the 4th International Workshop on Linguistically Interpreteted Corpora (LINC)*.

Ann Bies, Justin Mott, Colin Warner, and Seth Kulick. 2012. English Web Treebank. *Linguistic Data Consortium*.

Gökhan Çelikkaya and Gülşen Eryiğit. 2014. A mobile assistant for Turkish. In *Proceedings of the 2nd International Conference on Turkic Language Processing (TURKLANG)*, Istanbul, 06-07 November.

Gülşen Eryiğit and Tuğba Pamay. 2007-2014. ITU Validation Set for Metu-Sabancı Turkish treebank. In *Proceedings of the 2nd International Conference on Turkic Language Processing (TURKLANG)*, Istanbul, 06-07 November.

Gülşen Eryiğit and Dilara Torunoğlu-Selamet. 2015. Social media text normalization for Turkish. (Under review).

Gülşen Eryiğit. 2007. ITU treebank annotation tool. In *Proceedings of the 1st Linguistic Annotation Workshop (LAW)*, pages 117–120. Association for Computational Linguistics.

Jennifer Foster, Özlem Çetinoglu, Joachim Wagner, Joseph Le Roux, Stephen Hogan, Joakim Nivre, Deirdre Hogan, and Josef van Genabith. 2011. #hardtoparse: POS tagging and parsing the Twitterverse. In *AAAI 2011 Workshop on Analyzing Microtext*, pages 20–25.

Kevin Gimpel, Nathan Schneider, Brendan O'Connor, Dipanjan Das, Daniel Mills, Jacob Eisenstein, Michael Heilman, Dani Yogatama, Jeffrey Flanigan, and Noah A Smith. 2011. Part-of-speech tagging for twitter: Annotation, features, and experiments. In *Proceedings of the 49th Annual Meeting of the Association for Computational Linguistics: Human Language Technologies*, pages 42–47. Association for Computational Linguistics.

Muhammet Şahin, Umut Sulubacak, and Gülşen Eryiğit. 2013. Redefinition of Turkish morphology using flag diacritics. In *Proceedings of The 10th Symposium on Natural Language Processing (SNLP-2013), Phuket, Thailand, October*.

Djamé Seddah, Benoit Sagot, Marie Candito, Virginie Mouilleron, and Vanessa Combet. 2012. The French Social Media Bank: a treebank of noisy user generated content. In *Proceedings of the 24th International Conference on Computational Linguistics (COLING)*.

Umut Sulubacak and Gülşen Eryiğit. 2014. A redefined Turkish dependency grammar and its implementations: A new Turkish web treebank & the revised Turkish treebank. (Under review).

Part of Speech Annotation of Intermediate Versions in the Keystroke Logged Translation Corpus

Tatiana Serbina
RWTH Aachen University
Kármánstraße 17-19
52062 Aachen, Germany
serbina@anglistik.rwth-aachen.de

Paula Niemietz
RWTH Aachen University
Kármánstraße 17-19
52062 Aachen, Germany
niemietz@anglistik.rwth-aachen.de

Matthias Fricke
RWTH Aachen University
Dennewartstraße 27
52068 Aachen, Germany
matthias.fricke@ima-zlw-ifu.rwth-aachen.de

Philipp Meisen
RWTH Aachen Universtiy
Dennewartstraße 27
52068 Aachen, Germany
philipp.meisen@ima-zlw-ifu.rwth-aachen.de

Stella Neumann
RWTH Aachen University
Kármánstraße 17-19
52062 Aachen, Germany
neumann@anglistik.rwth-aachen.de

Abstract

Translation process data contains non-canonical features such as incomplete word tokens, non-sequential string modifications and syntactically deficient structures. While these features are often removed for the final translation product, they are present in the unfolding text (i.e. intermediate translation versions). This paper describes tools developed to semi-automatically process intermediate versions of translation data to facilitate quantitative analysis of linguistic means employed in translation strategies. We examine the data from a translation experiment with the help of these tools.

1 Introduction

Within the area of translation studies, there is a growing interest in the investigation of the process-related aspects of translation (see e.g. Göpferich, 2008 for an overview). Insights into the ongoing translation process can be gained by conducting psycholinguistic experiments, often characterized through a combination of eye-tracking and keystroke logging methods (e.g. Alves et al., 2010; Jakobsen, 2011). The resulting process data is typically analyzed in terms of behavioral measures, such as pauses during text production and gaze patterns within the texts, linked to the more abstract level of cognitive processing during a translation task. We adopt a corpus perspective on the keystroke logs (Alves and Magalhães, 2004; Alves and Vale, 2009, 2011), which contain rich information on key presses and mouse clicks during a translation session. This perspective entails that the data present in the logs can be queried, enabling us to perform quantitative, linguistically informed analyses of the translations. We take into account not only originals and the corresponding final versions of translated texts – which are also present in the traditional parallel corpora used in translation studies and contrastive linguistics, e.g. the CroCo corpus (Hansen-Schirra et al., 2012) – but also the intermediate versions of translations. We define the intermediate versions as variants of the unfolding texts produced at certain points in time during the translation process. The explicit linguistic annotation of text versions proposed here is not found in existing data collections containing keystroke logs: for instance, the TPR database (Carl, 2012a) involves part of speech (POS) annotation of source and target language tokens but does not analyze the intermediate versions. Investigation of these text versions allows us to identify potential translation problems and strategies, contributing to our understanding of cognitive processing, and also to provide best practice solutions for problems encountered in machine translation.

Proceedings of LAW IX - The 9th Linguistic Annotation Workshop, pages 102–111,
Denver, Colorado, June 5, 2015.

However, in order to study specific research questions from the field of translation studies with the help of such a corpus, we first need a transformation of sequences of production, deletion and separation keystrokes (see section 3.1) into word tokens, their annotation with linguistic information and also alignment between originals and the corresponding translations. The present paper concentrates on completed work involving the tokenization and (semi-)automatic POS annotation of the intermediate versions identified in the unfolding translations.

The corpus presents a type of non-canonical language, which is to some extent comparable to spoken data, as it also contains online repairs of the ongoing text production (cf. Heeman and Allen, 1999). Online repair can take place when a word or a grammatical structure present in one of the intermediate versions is replaced by another variant, either immediately before the participant moves to the translation of the subsequent parts or at a later stage of the translation process. This can be shown using Example 1 taken from the keystroke logged translation corpus (KLTC). It contains the source text (ST), two intermediate versions of the unfolding translation (IT_1 and IT_2) and the target text (TT).

ST Crumpling a sheet of paper seems
IT_1 Ein Blatt Papier zu knüllen *scheint*
'a leaf paper to crumple seems'
IT_2 Ein Blatt Papier zu knüllen
'a leaf paper to crumple'
TT Ein Blatt Papier zu knüllen *erscheint*
'a leaf paper to crumple appears'

Example 1. KLTC, translator A11.

From the intermediate versions of the text we know that the translator typed *scheint* 'seems', deleted it, and at a later point typed *erscheint* 'appears'. In other words, this experiment participant replaced one verb with another nearly synonymous one, filling the same slot in the produced sentence. Apart from such cases, the corpus also contains several versions of the same word tokens along with incomplete tokens and structures. Taking into account these non-canonical features, traditional NLP tools have to be modified to some extent, in order to make the automatic processing of the process data feasible.

The type of data included in the current version of the keystroke logged translation corpus is described in section 2. Section 3 presents how our Tokenizer processes the intermediate translation versions and discusses alternative methods of POS annotation. In section 4 we show how these pre- and post-processing steps can help us in the analysis of translation studies phenomena. Finally, section 5 provides an outlook on the next steps.

2 Keystroke logged translation corpus

The data used for this study was collected using the keystroke logging software Translog II (Carl, 2012b) and the remote eyetracker Tobii TX 300. It comprises two source texts (two variants[1] of a popular-scientific text originally published in the journal *Scientific American*[2]), nine translations and the matching set of nine key logs. All translation participants are German L1 students of English linguistics with little or no experience in translation. During the translation task from English into German, they were allowed to consult the bilingual online dictionary *leo*.

The source and target texts considered in this paper contain a total of 2,188 words. This calculation does not include word tokens identified in the intermediate versions. At the present stage of the project, we have concentrated on this small data set to test the automatic annotation procedures that have been developed. Once the gold standard is established, we intend to apply these methods to annotate further data available within the corpus.

3 Processing intermediate versions

3.1 Tokenizer

The Tokenizer automatically searches for words and word tokens in a selected set of keystroke events identifying the intermediate versions of the target text. The initial data, created by Translog II,

[1] We used two variants of the source text in order to counterbalance grammatically simple and complex stimuli. This will allow us to investigate the link between grammatical complexity and cognition in future work.

[2] Scientific American Online, February 5, 2002, Sarah Graham: A New Report Explains the Physics of Crumpled Paper. http://www.scientificamerican.com/article.cfm?id=a-new-report-explains-the

consists of the source text (ST) and the final target text (TT) along with a list of all keystrokes, i.e. the keys pressed, and the timestamp of each keystroke during the translation process. In order to transform series of connected keystroke events into word tokens, each file is processed in a number of steps, as illustrated in (1).

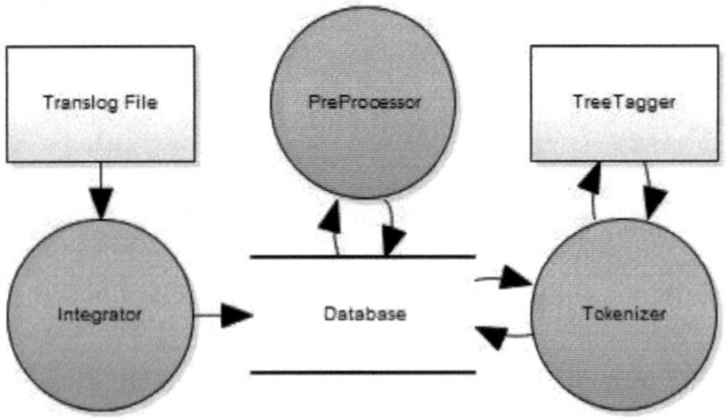

Figure 1. From a file to the annotated data.

In the first step (Integrator), the events as well as the ST and the TT, are loaded from the original XML files generated by Translog II into our corpus in which data is saved in the form of a database. This ensures easy and fast data access for future modification and annotation. In addition, the data quality is monitored through integrity checks. In the second step (PreProcessor), a type is assigned to each event based on the action performed. The types we used to categorize the events are *production* (letter keys or numbers), *deletion* (delete or backspace), *separation* (space, return or punctuation), *navigation* (use of the arrow keys or mouse to change the cursor position), *system* (for application specific messages like 'start' or 'stop logging') and *clipboard* (copy, paste and cut). This ensures the usage of normalized labels for all events across different Translog versions and applications. The third and last step (Tokenizer) replays the logged recording and creates different tokens and intermediate text versions. Each result is written into the database. Thus, the results are easily searchable, can be exported into a .tsv or other file for further analysis, or visualized by a GUI.

A token consists of the token string, a list of keystroke logging events that belong to the token, a list of parent tokens, a list of child tokens, and a list of POS tags (cf. section 3.2). If an existing token is modified in some way, it receives the label 'parent' and the modified version is referred to as its 'child' token. The Tokenizer also generates a version of the currently replayed text at each time an event caused a modification in the text. Figure 2 illustrates the data structure and an example for the token *Test*. As shown, the token *Test* was created by four events (*T*, *e*, *s* and *t*) and is classified as 'production' type. The target text (e.g. the character sequence *TextVersions*) is available after each event and refers to the token it belongs to. In addition, the created token is linked with its POS information.

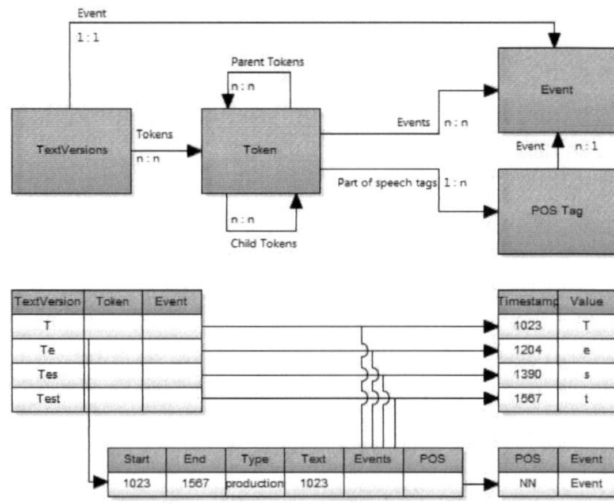

Figure 2. An example of a token and its data structure.

At each text modifying event (i.e. production, deletion, separation, or clipboard[3]) there are two possible actions, namely to extend an already existing token or create a new one. A token is extended if and only if the modifying event is not identical to that of the current token. For example, a word that is written in one production burst without an intervening deletion or navigation is always saved as one token (cf. Figure 3.I for production of the word token *ein* 'a'). In contrast, a new token is created each time the type of the event differs. For example, if a word is separated into two words by typing a space, three new tokens are created (two word tokens of the type 'production' and one separation token), all having the same parent token. Figure 3.II shows this process for production of the two word tokens *Blatt* 'sheet' and *Papier* 'paper' from the sequence *BlattPapier*. If an existing token is shortened by an event of type 'deletion', a new token is generated which has the former production or separation token as its parent. Tokens that are

[3] The copy-clipboard event does not modify the text and is, therefore, ignored here. Nevertheless, the cut- or paste-events are handled as text modification.

deleted stay in the list of tokens and can be found in the keystroke logs exactly at the place where they have been deleted. A token present in the intermediate version can be deleted completely, so that it is not present in the final target text (cf. 3.III for deletion of the token *er*). Moreover, a deleted separation token can lead to a unification token that joins two separate tokens together into a new one (cf. 3.IV for the production of the word token *zerknüllen* 'scrunch' with an intermediate stage of the token *zerknüll* that is created by deleting the space within formerly separated tokens *zer* and *knüll*). The Tokenizer returns a list of tokens that were found in the recording as well as a list of text versions which represent every intermediate version of the target text at any given point in time.

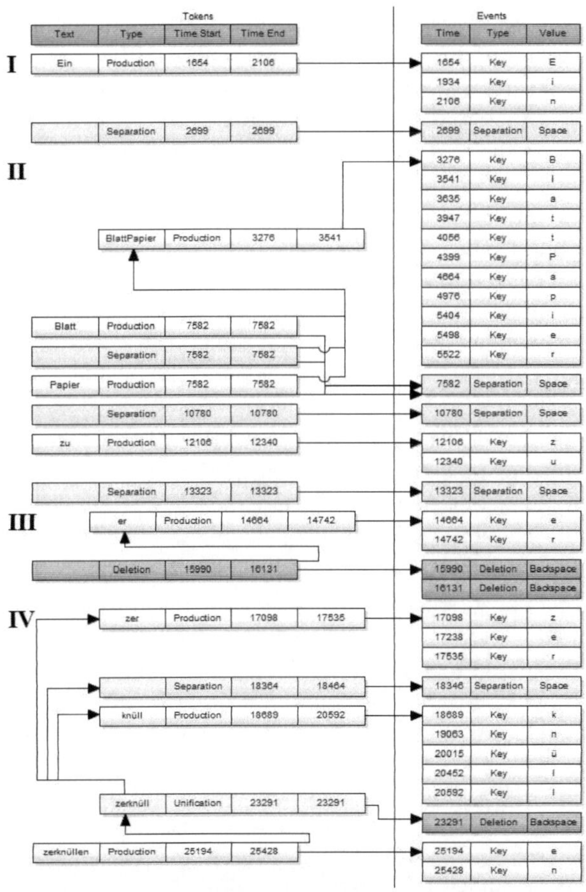

Figure 3. A result of the application of the Tokenizer.

3.2 Part of Speech annotation

As mentioned above, intermediate versions encountered in the keystroke logged translation corpus exhibit features typically associated with non-canonical data. As such, they can be compared to other types of non-standard language, including computer-mediated communication or learner texts. Previous studies in this area have noted the challenges of applying the existing NLP tools and tagsets, which are often trained on the basis of newspaper language, to the data that deviates from this standard (Neunerdt et al., 2013; Zinsmeister et al., 2014). This issue is addressed by development of modified taggers as well as adaptations of the tagsets, for instance to include tags that are unique to a certain type of data (cf. e.g. Neunerdt et al., 2013 for annotation of social media texts or Westpfahl and Schmidt, 2013 for enrichment of spoken German).

The POS annotation of our data is created by the Tokenizer, using the latest version of the TreeTagger (Schmid, 1994) working with the Stuttgart-Tübingen TagSet (STTS: Schiller et al., 1999). At the moment the annotation can be called in two different modes: either post mode or direct mode.

In post mode, all tokens occurring in all final versions of the TTs are first annotated, creating an experiment-specific list of possible tokens along with their corresponding POS tags. Then, after the Tokenizer has emulated the entire Translog recording, the tokens found in the intermediate versions are matched against this experiment-specific list. If an intermediate version token can be found in this list, then a reference to the corresponding POS tag is saved with the token, as shown in Figure 4.I for the tokens *Ein* 'a' and *Blatt* 'sheet'. If no match is found, the Tokenizer searches for a POS tag that poses the closest match to the token string by using the Levenshtein distance (Levenshtein, 1966) with a set maximum distance.

In the direct mode the TreeTagger is called each time the text is modified (i.e. if a modifying event is detected). The Tokenizer creates an array containing all words in the current text adjusted to match the requirements of the TreeTagger, which does not allow spaces or any of several other special characters like “, / or line feeds. The data returned by the TreeTagger is modified in a way that allows it to match the provided tags to the tokens that formed the current text version, cf. Figures 2 and 5. Thus, each token has a list of POS tags and each POS tag has a reference to the event that led to its existence. A new POS tag is only added to the list if it differs from the previous element in the list. Figure 4 illustrates this process as the word classes (e.g. Noun [NN] → Separated verb particle [PTKVZ] → Article [ART]) of the tokens change over the course of their creation.

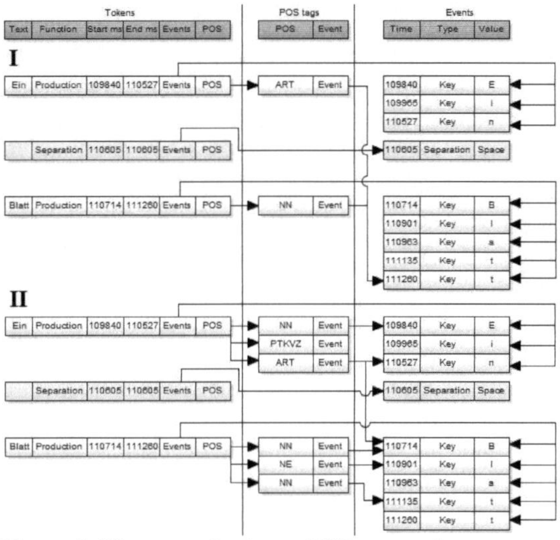

Figure 4. The created tokens, POS tags and events.

Figure 5 shows the events used to create the data presented in 4.II after time-stamp 111260. The tokens *Ein* 'a' and *Blatt* 'sheet' both have a list of POS tags that expanded during the creation of the TT. The additional reference to the creating event inside the POS tag makes it possible for the user to search in both directions: from the POS tag to the event which led to its creation, as well as from an event to all the POS tags created by this event. For example, the production event 'B' with the timestamp 110714 is referenced in multiple POS tags and marks the change of *Ein* from a separated verb particle [PTKVZ] into an article [ART] and the creation of *Blatt* as a noun [NN].

Timestamp	**Text**
109840	E[NN]
109965	Ei[NN]
110527	Ein[PTKVZ]
110605	Ein [PTKVZ]
110714	Ein[ART] B[NN]
110901	Ein[ART] Bl[NE]
110963	Ein[ART] Bla[NE]
111135	Ein[ART] Blat[NN]
111260	Ein[ART] Blatt[NN]

Figure 5. Change of POS tags in the creation of the TT.

Each of these POS modes has advantages over the other. The post mode successfully eliminates false positive matches that occur in the direct mode like *Ei* 'egg' [NN] at 109965 as seen in Figure 5, which does not make any sense in the given text. This disadvantage of the direct mode is connected to lower reliability in assignment of certain POS tags. For instance, in Figure 5 the intermediate token *Ein* is tagged as a separated verb particle, even though the [ART] tag is more plausible taking into account the general frequency of the relevant elements. At the same time, the direct mode has the advantage of preserving the references to the point in time at which a POS tag was matching the token. The major disadvantage of the post mode is that it is limited to words that appeared in a TT – but not every word does. For example, if a word like *Papierblatt* 'paper sheet' is created in an intermediate version but is always changed to *Blatt Papier* 'sheet of paper' there will be no matching tag for *Papierblatt* in the precompiled TT corpus. The direct mode, on the other hand, can assign a [NN] tag to the token *Papierblatt.*

As the first step in evaluating the accuracy of the POS enrichment we looked at the post mode annotation of the data from six participants. A participant produced on average 297 tokens (whereby all token modifying events except for spaces were counted). An average of 73% of these tokens were exact POS matches; an additional 18% were assigned using Levenshtein distance (a considerable amount of tokens in this group consisted of punctuation marks). The remaining 9% of the tokens did not receive any POS tag (about half of these tokens consisted of a single letter). In terms of using the Levenshtein distance for annotation, we found that, on average, 70% of string matches and their POS tags could be considered contextually correct. Next steps will include evaluation of the direct mode and, where necessary, manual correction of tag assignments.

The open design of the Tokenizer and the data structure ensure that files from other keystroking logging systems can be easily added and compared with each other, independent of the origin. Furthermore, additional POS or grammatical tagging tools can be integrated easily within the process.

4 Initial analysis of annotated translation revisions

The keystroke logged translation corpus enriched with information on intermediate word tokens and parts of speech can be used to investigate translation strategies employed during the translation process. These strategies are reflected through revisions of the unfolding target text which exhibit, for instance, alternative lexical choices for the same slot in a sentence, or the choice of different syntactic structures. Such types of revisions can be performed to correct or further refine the target texts (Malkiel, 2009a). Previous research has suggested that revisions of the target text can be considered as one of the indicators of difficulties encountered during the translation process (Dragsted, 2012: 86). In other words, the place and type of corrections, among other measures, can be used to operationalize the difficulty, i.e. the amount of cognitive effort, involved in a translation of certain linguistic features.

In this study we adopt a bottom-up perspective and look at cases where multiple attempts at translating the same source text word have been identified. Previous investigations of such self-corrections have typically relied on time-consuming manual analyses of the keystroke logs[4] using either the replay function (Malkiel, 2009a) or visualization of the data (Dragsted, 2012) illustrated in Figure 6, where the symbol '•' represents the space key and '◀' stands for backspace. Our pre-processing of the data (cf. section 3) helps us to identify multiple attempts belonging to the same translation event automatically, which will facilitate subsequent quantitative analysis.

erhöte•i◀◀◀◀hte•e◀Energiespeicherung

Figure 6. Linear representation in Translog II.

An explorative examination of our data shows various types of revision. One of these is lexical substitution, illustrated through Example 1 above. Malkiel (2009a: 158) observes that more than half of the revisions (excluding changes in spelling) in her data can be attributed to the category of replacing a word or expression with a synonym[5].

[4] See, however, Carl et al. (2010) for an example of an automatic analysis.

[5] It should be, however, noted that in the study by Malkiel (2009a) this group of revisions is rather broad, comprising clarifications (*impossible deadlines* changed into *impossible deadlines to meet*) and modifications in the order of elements (*We once used to* change into *Once, we used to*).

Our data sample contains only a few revisions that are very straightforward examples of lexical substitutions where a complete word is typed and then replaced with a different one. In another group of cases, intermediate versions contain incomplete tokens which are deleted and replaced by an alternative, or simply a change in grammatical gender of an article, as is the case in Example 2:

ST Yet the fact that the ball is able…
IT Doch die Tatsache, dass *der*
'yet the fact that the:masc'
TT Doch die Tatsache, dass *die* *Kugel*
'yet the fact that the:fem ball'

Example 2. KLTC, Translator A6.

It is difficult to disentangle alternative text production versions of a string from a simple correction of typing or grammatical errors. Whereas in some cases we could safely assume that the spelling changes were made to correct a typing error (e.g. the string *Pape* changed to *Pap* and then completed to form the word token *Papier* 'paper'), other intermediate versions (as in Example 2) are more ambiguous. Rather than excluding these instances from further analysis, we adopt the notion of target hypotheses. In the context of translation data, target hypotheses refer to several potential plans of the translator for the unfolding target text (Serbina et al., forthc.). This method was originally developed to account for non-standard structures in learner language (Lüdeling, 2008; Reznicek et al., 2013): instead of establishing one of the canonical structures potentially intended by the learner, researchers can formulate several hypotheses that can function in the respective context. During the development of the corpus, the formulation of alternative target hypotheses motivated through the linguistic context of intermediate versions and final target texts allows us to consider possible intentions of the translator, leaving further interpretation of the data to the analysis stage.

Coming back to Example 2, the change from the word token *der* 'the:masc' to the token *die* 'the:fem' can be considered a typing error. This would mean that the translator's plan was to type *die Kugel* 'ball', which appears in the final version, and s/he accidentally typed first the wrong article. However, we can also suggest an alternative target hypothesis, according to which the change from masculine to feminine article form is deliberate. As the source text contains *ball,* we might hypothesize that the translator originally planned to use the cognate *Ball* 'ball' (requiring the masculine article *der*) but at some point changed to the synonym *Kugel*. The formulation of this hypothesis is additionally motivated by the final target versions of all participants: this instance of the noun *ball* was translated by *Ball* by five out of nine participants. Assuming this target hypothesis, the change of plan could be potentially explained through the wish to avoid cognates, which are more readily accessible than other synonyms but can result in non-idiomatic target language expressions (Malkiel, 2009b).

The POS annotation of the word tokens in the intermediate translation versions can be used to systematically extract all such cases in which one article, or alternatively, an attributive pronoun or adjective is replaced with another. In German, all of these word classes reflect grammatical gender. Therefore, a change in the morphological ending of such an element can hint at a change in translator's plan (similar to Example 2 discussed above). To identify such cases, we analyzed text parts, where one of the elements mentioned above was altered creating another form of the same word. In these cases, two or more subsequent word tokens tagged as article [ART], a type of an attributive pronoun [PIAT], [PDAT], [PPOSAT], [PRELAT], [PWAT] or an attributive adjective [ADJA] appear in the data, only one of which is preserved in the final version of the translation.

In this step, 49 sequences of tokens meeting the formulated requirements have been extracted. The quantification of examples involving revisions that lead to a production of longer sequences, such as *der weiteren Kompression des Blattes* 'the further compression of the sheet' considers the number of nominal slots with which the preceding elements have to agree. In other words, in this particular example, revisions of the initial definite article, the following adjective, both of which agree with the noun *Kompression* 'compression', and the second definite article, which agrees with the noun *Blatt* 'sheet', are counted as two distinct cases. On the basis of changes in suffixes that were most likely performed to change grammatical gender rather than case or number, 39% (19/49) of the examples distributed across eight keystroke logs were classified as involving several target hypotheses on the level of lexical choices (even though it was not always possible to determine what a potential alternative version was). In one additional case, the experiment participant deleted a part of the produced noun phrase only to retype it. Here it is even less clear whether there was a change of plan or perhaps general uncertainty. The noun *Kugel* 'ball' was involved in the revisions most frequently, namely in 32% (6/19) of cases in the data from four different participants. At least in some cases there is good reason to believe that the original plan was to produce its synonym *Ball* (cf. Example 2 above).

While previous studies dismissed all instances of revisions aimed at correcting the spelling of a word (Malkiel, 2009a) and the so-called short-distance revisions, i.e. immediate modifications of the words (Carl et al., 2010), as typing errors, the discussion above shows that there might be more to these types of revisions. We consider the cases described above as examples that can give us additional insights into (possible) translation strategies, which are within reach because of the linguistic annotation of the keystroke logging data.

Until now we have discussed revisions characterized by a mere lexical replacement. In addition, the small data sample examined here contains a few changes of syntactic structures. For instance, one revision has been interpreted as an example of explicitation, named among the properties of translated texts (Baker, 1996). As seen in Example 3, the intermediate translation version is characterized by ellipsis of the head noun within the subject function of the second clause. However, the reference to *Kanten* 'edges' is made more explicit later, when the translator inserts the second instance of the noun.

ST these ridges collapse and smaller ones form
IT kollabieren die Kanten und kleinere werden
'collapse the edges and smaller are'
gebildet
'formed'
TT kollabieren die Kanten und kleinere *Kanten*
'collapse the edges and smaller edges'
werden gebildet.
'are formed'

Example 3. KLTC, Translator A2.

A small number of revisions involving the level of syntactic structures could be explained taking into account the participant group in question. Previous studies indicated that, in contrast to professional translators, (translation) students tend to concentrate on the level of individual words (Lörscher, 1996: 30; Malkiel, 2009a: 161), trying primarily to solve problems connected to lexical choices (Lörscher, 1996: 30-31). Therefore, once the analysis of intermediate versions is extended to include experiments with professional translators, we expect to find more complex revisions related to larger stretches of text.

This initial investigation of our sample data has indicated the benefits of the available enrichment of intermediate translation versions. Using this annotation, we are now able to systematically extract a specific group of cases which potentially reflect a change in translation plan. Formulation of several alternative target hypotheses enables us to stay objective by indicating a range of possibilities that exist during the translation process. If we adopt the hypotheses according to which the changes in suffixes observed in the data reflect modifications in translators' plans, the translation of the nouns following the revised premodifiers likely pose additional cognitive effort for the participants of the experiment. It is certainly necessary to keep in mind that not all of changes in plan are visible as "traces in the typing data in the form of corrections" (Dragsted, 2012: 95). However, automatic identification of changes during the translation process that result in different parts of speech may give us additional clues as to the intentions of the translators.

5 Outlook

Further development of the Tokenizer will address special cases in which the tool identifies a large number of children tokens in the intermediate versions that do not represent additional value to the researcher. These production tokens are generated when the translator types a larger chunk of text without using a separation character (e.g. space) to separate the new word from an existing word token. In the current version of the Tokenizer, the token immediately preceding the inserted material functions as a parent token for all of the inserted characters that are immediately attached to it. A solution can be an automatic identification of these cases that would facilitate their resolution, i.e. chunking into more meaningful word tokens.

Until now the target hypotheses have been generated based on a manual inspection of the data. But to effectively manage larger volumes of data, it is possible to partly automatize the annotation procedure by taking into account the range of translations available for any given source text item in the final translations of all experiment participants (cf. Koehn, 2009 for a similar approach in machine translation). This step requires alignment on different linguistic levels created between originals and the corresponding translations, both final and intermediate versions. Once the alignment links are available, automatic generation of a list of likely target units is planned.

Moreover, as mentioned above, we intend to apply the pipeline of pre- and post-processing steps described in this paper to larger collections of data, in particular to study the revision strategies of professional translators. Based on larger samples of revisions involving changes in syntactic structures, it will be possible to develop queries similar to the one discussed above for further types of modifications using the POS annotation available for intermediate translation versions. This, in turn, is a prerequisite for a quantitative study across several participants. The results on revisions could then be linked to the available eye-tracking data to get further insights into the cognitive processing during the process of translation.

The annotation procedures discussed in the present paper are not limited to the analysis of translation data. Since translation logs involve non-canonical features, the described methods can be generalized to other types of non-standard language found, for instance, in computer-mediated communication or spoken data. Moreover, a quantitative analysis of features present in the intermediate translation versions contributes to identification of effective translation strategies that can be applied in machine translation.

Acknowledgments

The work on the Tokenizer was performed within the HumTec Boostfund project *e-cosmos*, funded by the Excellence Initiative of the German State and Federal Governments.
The data used for analysis was generated within the German Research Foundation (DFG) project *TRICKLET* (Translation Research in Corpora,

Keystroke Logging and Eye Tracking), research grant no. NE1822/2-1.

References

Alves, Fabio and Célia Magalhaes. 2004. Using small corpora to tap and map the process-product interface in translation. *TradTerm,* 10: 179–211.

Alves, Fabio and Daniel Couto Vale. 2009. Probing the unit of translation in time: Aspects of the design and development of a web application for storing, annotating, and querying translation process data. *Across Languages and Cultures,* 10(2): 251–273.

Alves, Fabio, Adriana Pagano, and Igor da Silva. 2010. A new window on translators' cognitive activity: Methodological issues in the combined use of eye tracking, key logging and retrospective protocols. In Methodology, technology and innovation in translation process research: A tribute to Arnt Lykke Jakobsen, Inger M. Mees, Fabio Alves, and Susanne Göpferich, editors. Frederiksberg, Copenhagen, pages 267–91.

Alves, Fabio and Daniel Couto Vale. 2011. On drafting and revision in translation: A corpus linguistics oriented analysis of translation process data. *Translation: Computation, Corpora, Cognition,* 1: 105–122.

Baker, Mona. 1996. Corpus-based translation studies: The challenges that lie ahead. In *Terminology, LSP and translation: Studies in language engineering in honour of Juan C. Sager*, Harold Somers, editor. Benjamins, Amsterdam, pages 175–186.

Carl, Michael. 2012a. The CRITT TPR-DB 1.0: A database for empirical human translation process research." In *Proceedings of the AMTA 2012 Workshop on Post-Editing Technology and Practice*: 9–18.

Carl, Michael. 2012b. Translog - II: A program for recording user activity data for empirical reading and writing research. In *Proceedings of the Eight International Conference on Language Resources and Evaluation*: 4108–4112.

Carl, Michael, Martin Kay, and Kristian T.H. Jensen. 2010. Long-distance revisions in drafting and post-editing. *Proceedings of CiCling*: 193-204.

Dragsted, Barbara. 2012. Indicators of difficulty in translation: Correlating product and process. *Across Languages and Cultures,* 13(1): 81-98.

Göpferich, Susanne. 2008. *Translationsprozessforschung: Stand - Methoden - Perspektiven.* Narr, Tübingen.

Hansen-Schirra, Silvia, Stella Neumann, and Erich Steiner. 2012. *Cross linguistic corpora for the study of translations: Insights from the language pair English-German.* de Gruyter, Berlin.

Heeman, Peter A. and James F. Allen. 1999. Speech repairs, intonational phrases, and discourse markers: Modeling speakers' utterances in spoken dialogue. *Computational Linguistics*, 25(4): 527–571.

Jakobsen, Arnt Lykke. 2011. Tracking translators' keystrokes and eye movements with Translog. In *Methods and strategies of process research: Integrative approaches in translation studies*, Cecilia Alvstad, Adelina Hild, and Elisabet Tiselius, editors. Benjamins, Amsterdam, pages 37–55.

Koehn, Philipp. 2009. A process study of computer-aided translation. *Machine Translation Journal*, 23(4): 241-263.

Levenshtein, Vladimir. 1966. Binary codes capable of correcting deletions, insertions, and reversals. *Soviet Physics-Doklady,* 10(8): 707–710.

Lörscher, Wolfgang. 1996. A psycholinguistic analysis of translation processes. *Meta,* 41(1): 26-32.

Lüdeling, Anke. 2008. Mehrdeutigkeiten und Kategorisierung: Probleme bei der Annotation von Lernerkorpora. In: Patrick Grommes and Maik Walter, *Fortgeschrittene Lernervarietäten.* Niemeyer, Tübingen, pages 119–140.

Malkiel, Brenda. 2009a. From Ántonia to My Ántonia. Tracking self-corrections with Translog. In *Behind the mind. Methods, models and results in translation process research.* Susanne Göpferich, Arnt Lykke Jakobsen und Inger M. Mees, editors. Frederiksberg, Samfundslitteratur, pages 149–166.

Malkiel, Brenda. 2009b. When idioti (idiotic) becomes "fluffy". Translation students and the avoidance of target language cognates. *Meta,* 54(2): 309–325.

Neunerdt, Melanie, Michael Reyer, and Rudolf Mathar. 2013. A POS tagger for social media texts trained on web comments. *Polibits*, 48: 61-68.

Reznicek, Marc, Anke Lüdeling, and Hagen Hirschmann. 2013. Competing target hypotheses in the Falko corpus: A flexible multi-layer corpus architecture. In *Automatic treatment and analysis of learner corpus data,* Ana Díaz-Negrillo, editor. Benjamins, Amsterdam, pages 101–123.

Schiller, Anne, Simone Teufel, Christine Stöckert, and Christine Thielen. 1999. Guidelines für das Tagging deutscher Textcorpora mit STTS. Technical report, University of Stuttgart.

Schmid, Helmut. 1994. Probabilistic part-of-speech tagging using decision trees. *Proceedings. International Conference on New Methods in Language Processing,* Manchester, UK.

Serbina, Tatiana, Paula Niemietz, and Stella Neumann. Forthcoming. Development of a keystroke logged translation corpus. In *New directions in corpus-based translation studies*, Claudio Fantinuoli and Federico Zanettin, editors. Berlin: Language Science Press.

Vinay, Jean-Paul, and Jean Darbelnet. 1995 (1958). *Comparative stylistics of French and English: A methodology for translation,* Juan C. Sager and M.-J.

Hamel, editors and translators. Benjamins, Amsterdam.

Westpfahl, Swantje, and Thomas Schmidt. 2013. POS für(s) FOLK: Part of Speech Tagging des Forschungs- und Lehrkorpus Gesprochenes Deutsch. *Journal for Language Technology and Computational Linguistics*, 1: 139-153.

Zinsmeister, Heike, Ulrich Heid, and Kathrin Beck. 2014. Adapting a part-of-speech tagset to non-standard text: The case of STTS. *Proceedings of the Ninth International Conference on Language Resources and Evaluation (LREC'14)*: 4097-4104.

A Hierarchy with, of, and for Preposition Supersenses

Nathan Schneider
University of Edinburgh
nschneid@inf.ed.ac.uk

Vivek Srikumar
University of Utah
svivek@cs.utah.edu

Jena D. Hwang **Martha Palmer**
University of Colorado at Boulder
{hwangd,martha.palmer}@colorado.edu

Abstract

English prepositions are extremely frequent and extraordinarily polysemous. In some usages they contribute information about spatial, temporal, or causal roles/relations; in other cases they are institutionalized, somewhat arbitrarily, as case markers licensed by a particular governing verb, verb class, or syntactic construction. To facilitate automatic disambiguation, we propose a general-purpose, broad-coverage taxonomy of preposition functions that we call **supersenses**: these are coarse and unlexicalized so as to be tractable for efficient manual annotation, yet capture crucial semantic distinctions. Our resource, including extensive documentation of the supersenses, many example sentences, and mappings to other lexical resources, will be publicly released.

Prepositions are perhaps the most beguiling yet pervasive lexicosyntactic class in English. They are everywhere; their functional versatility is dizzying and largely idiosyncratic (1). They are nearly invisible, yet indispensable for situating the where, when, why, and how of events. In a way, prepositions are the bastard children of lexicon and grammar, rising to the occasion almost whenever a noun-noun or verb-noun relation is needed and neither subject nor object is appropriate. Consider the many uses of the word *to*, just a few of which are illustrated in (1):[1]

(1) a. My cake is **to** die for.
b. If you want I can treat you **to** some.
c. How about this: you go **to** the store
d. **to** buy ingredients.
e. Then if you give the recipe **to** me
f. I'm happy **to** make the batter
g. and put it in the oven for 30 **to** 40 minutes
h. so you'll arrive **to** the sweet smell of chocolate.
i. That sounds good **to** me.
j. That's all there is **to** it.

Sometimes a preposition specifies a relationship between two entities or quantities, as in (1g). In other scenarios it serves a case-marking sort of function, marking a complement or adjunct—principally to a verb (1b–1e, 1h, 1i), but also to an argument-taking noun or adjective (1f). Further, it is not always possible to separate the semantic contribution of the preposition from that of other words in the sentence. As amply demonstrated in the literature, prepositions play a key role in multiword expressions (Baldwin and Kim, 2010), as in (1a, 1b, 1j).

An adequate descriptive annotation scheme for prepositions must deal with these messy facts. Following a brief discussion of existing approaches to preposition semantics (§1), this paper offers a new approach to characterizing their functions at a coarse-grained level. Our scheme is intended to apply to almost all preposition tokens, though some are excluded on the grounds that they belong to a larger multiword expression or are purely syntactic (§2). The rest of the paper is devoted to our coarse semantic categories, **supersenses** (§3).[2] Many of these categories are based on previous proposals—primarily, Srikumar and Roth (2013a) (so-called *preposition relations*) and VerbNet (*thematic roles*; Bonial et al., 2011; Hwang, 2014, appendix C)—but we organize them into a hierarchy and motivate a number of new or altered categories that make the scheme more robust. Because prepositions are so frequent, so polysemous, and so crucial in establishing relations, we believe that a wide variety of NLP applications (including knowledge base construction, reasoning about events, summarization, paraphrasing, and translation) stand to benefit from automatic disambiguation of preposition supersenses.

[1] Though infinitival *to* is traditionally not considered a preposition, we allow it to be labeled with a supersense if the infinitival clause serves as a PURPOSE (as in (1d)) or FUNCTION. See §2.

[2] Supersense inventories have also been described for nouns and verbs (Ciaramita and Altun, 2006; Schneider et al., 2012; Schneider and Smith, 2015) and adjectives (Tsvetkov et al., 2014). Other inventories characterize semantic functions expressed via morphosyntax: e.g., tense/aspect (Reichart and Rappoport, 2010), definiteness (Bhatia et al., 2014, also hierarchical).

Proceedings of LAW IX - The 9th Linguistic Annotation Workshop, pages 112–123,
Denver, Colorado, June 5, 2015.

A wiki documenting our scheme in detail can be accessed at `http://tiny.cc/prepwiki`. It maps fine-grained preposition senses to our supersenses, along with numerous examples. The wiki is conducive to browsing and to exporting the structure and examples for use elsewhere (e.g., in an annotation tool). From our experience with pilot annotations, we believe that the scheme is fairly stable and broadly applicable.

1 Background

The descriptive challenges raised by prepositions have not gone unnoticed in the literature; see, e.g., Saint-Dizier (2006a) for an assortment of syntactic and semantic issues. Here we touch on some of the lines of inquiry, resources, and NLP approaches to preposition semantics found in previous work.

1.1 Linguistic Approaches

Most studies of preposition semantics are limited to so-called "lexical" (essentially, spatiotemporal) usages. The lexical-vs.-functional dimension and, relatedly, the degree of association between prepositions and other words (especially verbs) used in combination has received some theoretical attention (e.g., Bolinger, 1971; Vestergaard, 1977; Jolly, 1993; Rauh, 1993; O'Dowd, 1998; Tseng, 2000). We draw on insights from this literature where possible, but find that many of the proposed diagnostics are insufficiently clear and robust for a general-purpose preposition annotation scheme.

The structured polysemy analysis of *over* put forward by Brugman (1981) and elaborated by Lakoff (1987, pp. 416–461), Dewell (1994), Tyler and Evans (2003, ch. 4), and others has been influential within cognitive linguistics. Working in this tradition, Lindstromberg (2010) examines over 90 English prepositions, considering the schematic spatial situations that can be expressed as well as their non-spatial extensions. Chapter 21 gives an inventory of about 75 "non-spatial notions"—these are not unlike the categories we will adopt below, though some are quite fine-grained: e.g., BEING RESOLVED, FIXED as in *pin him* ***down*** vs. BEING UNRESOLVED, UNDECIDED as in *everything's still* ***up*** *in the air*. How well annotators could be trained to agree on Lindstromberg's detailed categorization is unknown.

Crosslinguistic variation in adpositions and spatial categorization systems has received considerable attention from theorists (Bowerman and Choi, 2001; Hagège, 2009; Regier, 1996; Xu and Kemp, 2010; Zelinsky-Wibbelt, 1993) but is of practical interest as well, especially when it comes to machine translation and second language acquisition. A corpus creation project for German preposition senses (Müller et al., 2010, 2011) is similar in spirit to the supersense approach taken below. Finally, the PrepNet resource (Saint-Dizier, 2006b) aimed to describe the semantics of prepositions across several languages; however, it seems not to have progressed beyond the preliminary stages. Thus far, our approach has focused on English, but aims to define supersense categories semantically rather than by language-specific criteria (e.g., syntactic tests) so as to encourage its adaptation to other languages in the future.

1.2 Preposition Resources

The following corpus resources contain semantic categorizations that apply to English prepositions:

The Penn Treebank. As detailed by O'Hara and Wiebe (2009), the PTB since version II (Marcus et al., 1994) has included a handful of coarse function tags (such as LOCATION and TIME) that apply to constituents, including PPs.

FrameNet. Semantic relationships in FrameNet (Baker et al., 1998) are organized according to scenes, known as **frames**, that can be evoked by predicates in a sentence. Each frame defines roles, or **frame elements**, for components of the scene that can be elaborated with **arguments** in the sentence. Many roles are highly specific to a single frame, while others are quite generic. Arguments are often realized as PPs, thus the frame element labels can be interpreted as disambiguating the function of the preposition.

The Preposition Project (TPP). This is an English preposition lexicon and corpus project (Litkowski and Hargraves, 2005) that adapts sense definitions from the *Oxford Dictionary of English* and applies them to prepositions in sentences from corpora. A dataset for the SemEval-2007 shared task on preposition WSD (Litkowski and Hargraves, 2007) was created by collecting FrameNet-annotated sentences (originally from the BNC) and annotating 34 frequent preposition types (listed in (2) below) with a total of 332 attested senses. (The SemEval-2007 sentences—of which there are over 25,000, each with a single preposition token annotated—were handpicked by FrameNet lexicographers and so are not a statistically representative corpus sample.) TPP now incorporates additional prepositions and resources, with new annotated corpora under development (Litkowski, 2013, 2014).

Dahlmeier et al. To learn and evaluate their joint model of semantic roles and preposition senses, Dahlmeier et al. (2009) annotated TPP senses in the PropBank WSJ corpus for 7 high-frequency prepositions (*of*, *in*, *for*, *to*, *with*, *on*, and *at*). This amounted to 3,854 statistically representative instances in the news domain. The inter-annotator agreement rate was estimated at 86%, which suggests that clearly applicable TPP senses are available for the preponderance of tokens, but gives little insight into TPP's suitability for rare or borderline usages.

Tratz. Tratz (2011, ch. 4) refined the TPP sense inventory for the SemEval-2007 corpus with the goal of improving its descriptive adequacy and measuring inter-annotator agreement for all 34 prepositions. The total number of senses was reduced from 332 to 278, though a few prepositions gained additional senses.

Srikumar and Roth (S&R). Srikumar and Roth (2013b) modeled preposition token *relations*, i.e., the preposition's governor, object, and semantic label. For their experiments, Srikumar and Roth coarsen the original TPP SemEval-2007 sense annotations into 32 categories determined semi-automatically (the fine-grained senses were clustered automatically, then the clusters were manually refined and given names). Detailed in Srikumar and Roth (2013a), those categories cut across preposition types to combine related TPP senses for better data-driven generalization. Cohen's κ for inter-annotator agreement was 0.75, which is encouraging, though it is unclear whether the disagreements were due to systematic differences in interpretation of the scheme or to difficulty with rare preposition usages. We shall return to this scheme in §3 below.

1.3 Prepositions in NLP

Despite a steady trickle of papers over the years (see Baldwin et al., 2009 for a review), there is no apparent consensus approach to the treatment of preposition semantics in NLP. Studies have examined preposition semantics within multiword expressions (Cook and Stevenson, 2006), in spatial relations (Hying, 2007), across languages (Saint-Dizier, 2006b), in nonnative writing (Chodorow et al., 2007), in semantic role labeling (Dahlmeier et al., 2009), in vector space models (Zwarts and Winter, 2000), and in discourse (Denand and Rolbert, 2004).

Preposition sense disambiguation systems have been evaluated against one or more of the resources described in §1.2 (O'Hara and Wiebe, 2003, 2009; Ye and Baldwin, 2007; Dahlmeier et al., 2009; Tratz and Hovy, 2009; Hovy et al., 2010, 2011; Srikumar and Roth, 2013b). Unfortunately, all of these resources are problematic. Neither the PTB function tags nor the FrameNet roles were designed with prepositions in mind: the former set is probably not comprehensive enough to be a general-purpose account of prepositions, and the latter representation only makes sense in the broader analytical framework of frame semantics, which we believe should be treated as a separate task (Das et al., 2014). The Preposition Project data, though extensive, were selected and annotated from a lexicographic, *type-driven* perspective—i.e. with the goal of describing and documenting the uses of individual prepositions in a lexical resource rather than labeling a corpus with free-text preposition annotations. We hope that the latter, *token-driven* approach will be taken for annotating text with preposition supersenses so that those annotations will be suitable for training statistical NLP systems.

2 Our Approach

With the end of free-text semantic annotation in mind, we develop and document a preposition supersense tagset. Notably, we seek to include in our resource example sentences for each known preposition–supersense pairing; these examples should be particularly useful for assisting human annotators.

Before discussing the supersense tagset, it is necessary to establish the scope of the phenomenon that our scheme aims to address.

Preposition types. For brevity, we will sidestep the controversial aspects of defining "preposition", and defer to Pullum and Huddleston's (2002) broad definition of a lexical class including words such as *to*, *for*, *of*, and *up*, whether they take an object (forming a transitive PP) or act as a non-idiomatic adverbial particle (e.g., *lift the book **up***).

In documenting the supersense categories thus far,

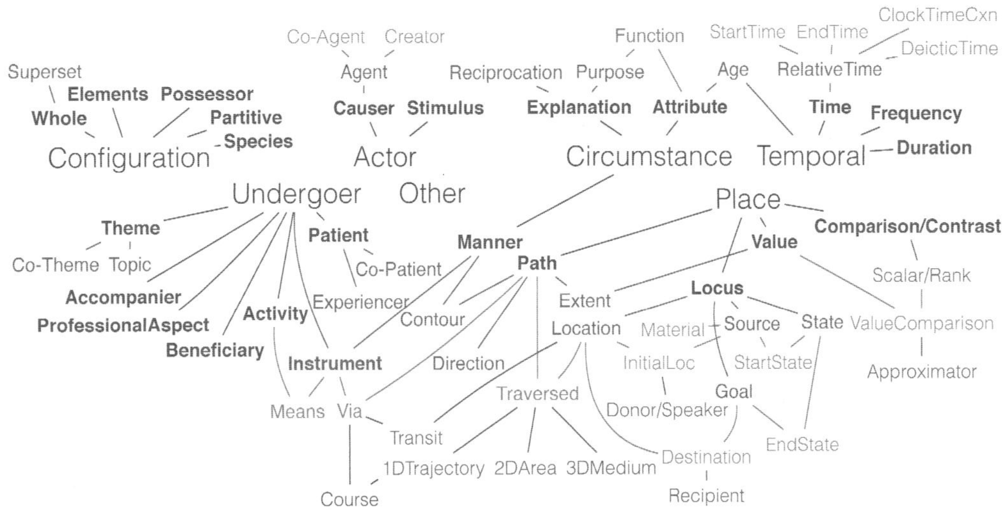

Figure 1: The full supersense hierarchy: categories in large font (CONFIGURATION, ACTOR, UNDERGOER, etc.) are top-level categories, and their subcategories extend outward. Colors emphasize the different levels of the hierarchy.

our attention has been focused on the 34 preposition types annotated in the SemEval-2007 data (§1.2):

(2) about, above, across, after, against, along, among, around, as, at, before, behind, beneath, beside, between, by, down, during, for, from, in, inside, into, like, of, off, on, onto, over, round, through, to, towards, with

Of the 332 fine-grained TPP senses for these 34 prepositions, 285 have been mapped to one or more supersense categories; preliminary annotation suggests that these account for the vast majority of preposition tokens in corpora (the remaining senses are generally infrequent). Our resource further includes the full set of TPP sense definitions, bringing it to a total of 309 preposition types[3] and 797 senses, though most senses for these new prepositions have not yet been assigned to a supersense.

Multiword expressions. Multiword expressions functioning as prepositions (e.g., *out of*, *except for*) receive a supersense as a unit, as do PP multiword expressions (*on fire*, *on the run*, *out of one's mind*). However, in other cases where a preposition belongs to a multiword expression, it is generally excluded from receiving a preposition supersense label. Verbal expressions like *make up* 'invent', *come to* 'regain consciousness', and *take someone for something* 'regard as' (as in *take him for a fool*) are assumed to receive a *verb* supersense—not a preposition supersense—in a separate annotation pass. Prepositions belonging to discourse and other connectives are assigned to a separate category, e.g.: *apart from that*, *in other words*, *of course*.

Special syntactic functions. Tokens with a subordinating function are included: e.g., *Unity is not possible* ***with*** *John sitting on the throne* is labeled CIRCUMSTANCE. Infinitival *to* is considered only for the PURPOSE and FUNCTION supersenses. All other uses are excluded.

3 Preposition Tags

In developing our preposition supersense hierarchy, we took Srikumar and Roth's (2013a) inventory (hereafter, S&R) as a starting point: as noted in §1.2, it clusters fine-grained dictionary senses of the prepositions in (2) into 32 labeled classes. Many of the classes resemble semantic roles (e.g., TEMPORAL, LOCATION, AGENT) or spatial relations (PHYSICALSUPPORT, SEPARATION). We revise and extend S&R to improve its descriptive power so it can be deployed directly as an annotation scheme. The main areas of improvement are highlighted below; full details and many more examples can be found in the resource itself.

Two other semantic annotation schemes offer similarly sized inventories of roles/relations: VerbNet (Kipper et al., 2008) and AMR (Banarescu et al.,

[3] A majority of TPP types are multiword prepositions (e.g., *all over*). Many of the single-word prepositions are archaic, orthographically nonstandard, or rare beyond specialized domains.

Supersense	S&R	VerbNet	AMR
Actor		V	
– Stimulus		V	
– Causer	S	V	≈:cause
– – Agent	S	V	
– – – Co-Agent		V	
– – – Creator			
Undergoer +1		V	
– Accompanier			A
– Activity +1	S		
– Beneficiary	S	V	A
– Theme		V	
– – Co-Theme		V	
– – Topic	S	V	A
– Patient		V	
– – Co-Patient		V	
– – Experiencer		V	
– ProfessionalAspect	S		:employed-by/:role
Place		V	
– Locus			
– – Location	S	V	A
– – – InitialLocation (^Source)		V	
– – – – Donor/Speaker			
– – – Destination (^Goal)	S	V	A
– – – – Recipient	S	V	≈:beneficiary
– – – Traversed (^Path)			
– – – – 1DTrajectory			
– – – – – Course (^Via)			
– – – – 2DArea			
– – – – 3DMedium			≈:medium
– – – Transit (^Via)			
– – State +2			
– – Source +1	S	V	A
– – – Material		V	
– – – StartState (^State)	S		
– – Goal +1		V	
– – – EndState (^State)	S	≈Result	
– Path +3			:path
– – Direction	S		A
– – Contour (^Manner)			
– Value +1		V/Asset	A/:cost
– – Extent (^Path)		V	A
– Comparison/Contrast			:compared-to
– – Scalar/Rank			
– – – ValueComparison (^Value)			
– – – – Approximator			
Temporal	S	Time	
– Frequency		V	A
– Duration		V	A
– Age (^Attribute)			A
– Time			A
– – RelativeTime			
– – – StartTime		Initial_Time	
– – – EndTime		Final_Time	
– – – DeicticTime			
– – – ClockTimeCxn			
Circumstance		V	
– Explanation			≈:cause
– – Reciprocation			
– – Purpose	S		A
– – – Function (^Attribute)			≈:meaning
– Attribute +2	S	V	≈:mod/:part
– Manner +1	S	V	A
– – Instrument (^Undergoer)	S	V	A
– – – Means (^Activity)			
– – – Via (^Path) +2			≈:medium
Configuration			
– Elements			:ex/:subset
– Partitive			≈:consist-of
– Possessor	S		:poss
– Species	S		
– Whole			:part-of
– – Superset			:superset
Other	S		

Table 1: The supersense hierarchy and its mappings to the S&R inventory, VerbNet thematic role hierarchy, and AMR non-core roles. Supersenses with multiple parents appear with one of them in parentheses; supersenses with *n* children listed under some other parent have a +*n* designation. S indicates that the supersense maps to an S&R category with the same name; likewise for V (VerbNet) and A (AMR). VerbNet and AMR names differing from the supersense name are written out: ":" names are from AMR and others are from VerbNet. (Some of the above are new in VerbNet, having been added subsequent to the latest published guidelines. VerbNet Pivot and Product are unmapped; roles only in AMR are not shown.) Additionally, a number of S&R categories have been removed or remapped.[4]

2013). Many of the categories in those schemes overlap (or nearly overlap) with S&R labels. Others include semantic categories that are absent from S&R, but appropriate for English prepositions. Table 1 compares the three inventories. The new hierarchy, comprising 73 preposition supersenses, appears in the table, and also in figure 1.

We modified S&R categories where possible to be more closely compatible with the other schemes. On a descriptive level, this allows us to take advantage of the linguistic analyses and explanations motivating

[4] Rough mappings from remapped S&R categories to supersenses: Cause → Causer, Explanation; Co-Participants → Co-Agent, Co-Patient, Co-Theme; Via → Course, Transit; MediumOfCommunication → Via; Numeric → Value; Participant/Accompanier → Accompanier; PartWhole → Partitive, Whole. Means is no longer covered by Instrument. S&R's Experiencer category has been removed (it is substantially different from the supersense and VerbNet categories of the same name). ObjectOfVerb, Opponent/Contrast, PhysicalSupport, and Separation have also been removed.

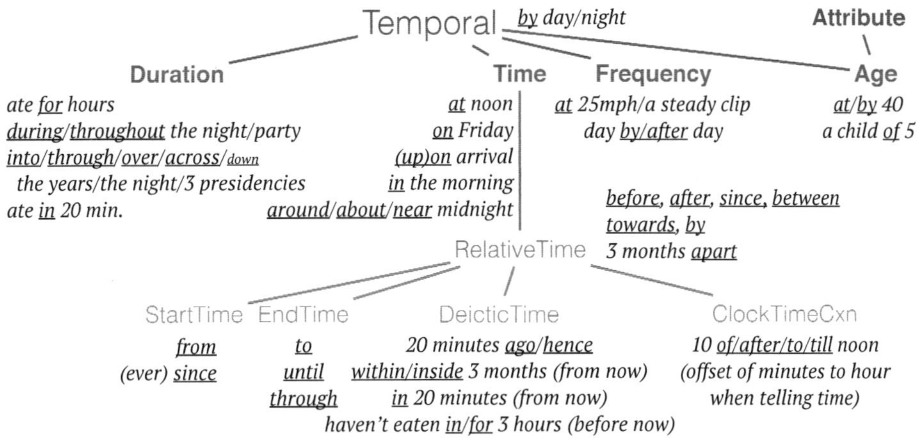

Figure 2: The TEMPORAL subhierarchy, with example preposition usages associated with each supersense.

those categories. On a practical level, this will make it easier to combine resources (lexicons and annotated corpora enriched with semantic role labels).

Following VerbNet, our preposition supersense categories are organized into a hierarchical (multiple inheritance) taxonomy. Not only does this explicate some of the distinctions between related categories that were described textually in S&R (e.g., the relationship between STARTSTATE and SOURCE), but it also provides a practical strategy for annotators who are unsure of how to apply a category—there is often a less specific label to fall back on.

The preposition label set proposed here is noticeably larger than the supersense inventories for other parts of speech (fn. 2). This might warrant concern that it will be too difficult for annotators to learn. However, there are arguments in favor of a larger set when it comes to prepositions. First, because prepositions range from the lexical to the grammatical, they perhaps cover a wider/higher-dimensional semantic space than verbs or nouns. Thus, more categories might be needed for comparable descriptive adequacy. Second, the hierarchy should help guide annotators to the right category or small set of related categories. They will not have to consider all of them one by one. Moreover, the presence of more and less abstract categories gives annotators flexibility when they are uncertain. Finally, because prepositions are closed-class, we envision that the annotation process will be guided (to a much greater extent than for nouns and verbs) by the word type. Having several dozen categories at multiple levels of granularity means that the number of prepositions associated with most categories is small.[5] For TPP prepositions (with fine-grained senses mapped to the new scheme), it will be possible to suggest a filtered list of supersenses to the annotator, and these should suffice for the vast majority of tokens. It may even be desirable to annotate a corpus by type rather than by token, so the annotator can focus on a few supersenses at a time.

Based on preliminary rounds of annotation—a mix of type-driven and token-driven—by several annotators, we are optimistic that the general approach will be successful. The preliminary annotation has also uncovered shortcomings in the annotation guidelines that have informed revisions to the categories and hierarchy. More extensive annotation practice with the current scheme is needed to ascertain its adequacy and usability. Should the size of the hierarchy prove too unwieldy, it will be possible to remove some of the finer-grained distinctions.

Below, we examine some of the areas of the hierarchy that have been overhauled.

3.1 Temporal Refinement

In S&R, all temporal preposition usages fall under a single label, TEMPORAL. VerbNet is slightly more discriminative, with an equivalent TIME supercategory whose daughters are INITIAL_TIME, FINAL_TIME, DURATION, and FREQUENCY.

We have refined this further (figure 2) after coming to the conclusion that the major temporal prepositions

[5]Currently, only 9 preposition types are mapped to more than 10 supersenses: *for* and *by* (20 each), *of* (18), *to* and *in* (16), *with* (15), *at* and *on* (13), and *from* (11). 20 have 4–9 supersenses.

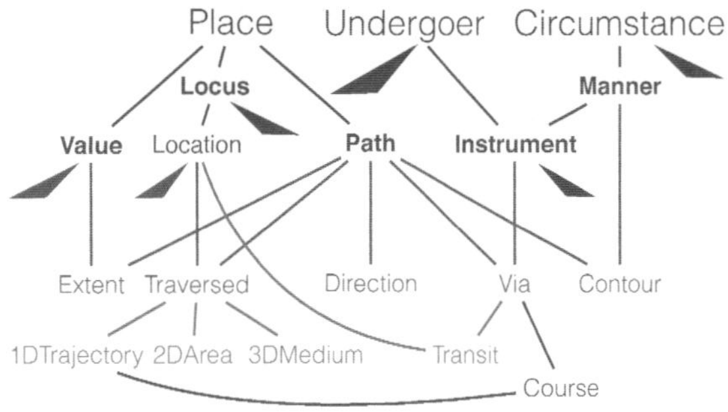

Figure 3: PATH and its subtypes

cluster neatly into finer-grained subcategories. Relations that situate a time as before or after another time are under RELATIVETIME; special cases are STARTTIME, ENDTIME, times implicitly situated relative to the present (DEICTICTIME), and constructions for telling time that express an offset in minutes relative to the hour (CLOCKTIMECXN). We also follow AMR's lead in creating a dedicated AGE category, which inherits from TEMPORAL and ATTRIBUTE.

Given that most of the prepositions in figure 2 are only associated with one or two temporal supersenses (only *in* and *at* are known to occur with three), we do not expect that the subcategories will impose too much of a burden on annotators.

3.2 Paths

Extensive discussion has gone into a section of the hierarchy for *paths*, which were not accounted for to our satisfaction in any of the existing schemes (due to unclear boundaries between the categories). Our analysis draws upon recent studies of caused motion constructions in the context of improving their treatment in VerbNet. Those studies address the basic scenarios of CHANGE OF LOCATION, CHANGE OF STATE, TRANSFER OF POSSESSION, TRANSFER OF INFORMATION, and CHANGE IN VALUE ON A SCALE with regard to their syntactic and semantic argument structures (Hwang et al., 2014; Hwang, 2014, ch. 5). Figure 3 shows our subhierarchy for paths, which is closely related to the approach adopted for VerbNet, but in some respects more detailed. Taking PATH to be the intermediate part of literal or abstract/metaphoric motion, we distinguish subtypes:

- **TRAVERSED:** A stretch of physical space that the mover inhabits during the middle of motion (not necessarily where the event as a whole is located, which would be marked with a simple LOCATION preposition). This category is a subtype of LOCATION as it describes the "where" of the intermediate phase of motion. It is further refined into:
  - **1DTRAJECTORY:** A 1-dimensional region of space that is traversed, such as by following a path or passing a landmark. E.g.: *walk* ***along*** *the river,* ***over*** *the bridge,* ***past*** *the castle*
  - **2DAREA:** The 2-dimensional region of space that is "covered", though there is less of a notion of completeness than with a 1-dimensional trajectory: *I walked* ***about/around*** *the room*
  - **3DMEDIUM:** Volumetric material that the figure moves through, and which may exert a facilitatory or opposing force on the figure: *I waded* ***through*** *the swamp*
- **DIRECTION:** This covers prepositions marking how the motion of the figure, or the figure itself, is aimed/oriented (by contrast with DESTINATION, where the preposition expressly indicates an intended endpoint of motion): *walk* ***toward*** *the door, kick* ***at*** *the wall, toss the ball* ***up***.
- **CONTOUR:** This describes the shape, but not the location, of a path; it is also a kind of MANNER: *walk* ***in*** *a zigzag*
- **EXTENT:** Also a subtype of VALUE, this is the size of a path—the physical distance traversed or the amount of change on a scale: *ran* ***for*** *miles*
- **VIA:** Prepositions in this category mark something that is used for translocation, transfer, or communication between two points/parties. It is a subtype of PATH because it pertains to the intermediate phase of (literal or figurative) motion, and also a subtype of INSTRUMENT because it is something used in order to facilitate that motion. S&R used the label VIA for the spatial domain and MEDIUMOFCOMMUNICATION for communication devices; we instead use the VIA supersense directly for cases that are *not* physical motion, e.g.: *talk* ***by*** *phone*; *talk* ***on/over*** *the phone*; *make an appearance* ***on*** *TV*; *order* ***by*** *credit card* ***via/on*** *the Internet*; *I got the word out* ***via*** *a friend*. Enablers expressed metaphorically as paths, e.g. *Hackers accessed the system* ***via*** *a security hole*, are included as well. There are two subcases:
  - **TRANSIT:** The vehicle/mode of conveyance that facilitates physical motion traversing a path. It is also a subtype of LOCATION because it specifies where the figure was during the motion: *go* ***by*** *plane*
  - **COURSE:** The roadway or route that facilitates physical motion traversing a path. It is also a subtype of 1DTRAJECTORY because it specifies a 1-dimensional path for the figure's motion: *drive* ***via*** *back roads*

For spatial usages of certain prepositions that portray static scenes as motion ("fictive motion"; Talmy, 1996), an argument could be made for either the locative or path categories. Our conventions are:

- **With a figure whose shape/spatial extent is being described with respect to a landmark:**
  - 1DTRAJECTORY for the extent of a 1-dimensional shape: *a cable runs **above** the duct*; *the bridge [that goes] **across** the river*
  - 2DAREA for the extent of a 2-dimensional shape: *Her hair was in plaits **about** her head*
  - INITIALLOCATION for the "starting point": *a road which runs **from** Ixopo into the hills*; *single wires leading **off** the main lines*
  - DESTINATION for the "ending point": *every driveway **to** the castle was crowded*
- **For the spatial orientation of a figure:** DIRECTION: *they faced **away from** each other*
- **Suggesting the spatial path that may be traversed to access a place starting from a reference point (such as the speaker's location):** LOCATION: *in a little street **off** Whitehall*; *He must have parked **around** the front of the motel*; *the auditorium is **through** a set of double doors*
- **For a physical path of perception (line of sight, hearing, etc.):** 1DTRAJECTORY: *Lily peeped **around** the open curtain*; *glance **over** her shoulder*
- **For a perspective in perception or communication:** LOCATION: *I can see Russia **from** my house*; *views **over** Hyde Park*; *she rang him **at** home*

3.3 Communication

English systematically invokes language of motion and transfer to describe communication (Reddy, 1979). S&R includes a specific MEDIUMOFCOMMUNICATION category, but its boundaries are not entirely clear. Similarly, AMR incorporates a :MEDIUM role, though this conflates communicative mediums with what we have called 3DMEDIUM above. Instead, our definition of VIA (§3.2) includes instruments of communication but is slightly more general.

There are also cases where the preposition marks an entity involved in communication, without framing that entity as an intermediary between two parties:

(3) a. I got the scoop **from** a friend/the Internet.
b. I put it down **on** paper.
c. The answer is somewhere **in** this book/room.
d. The rumor spread **around** the school.

Rather than create a proliferation of communication-specific categories, we apply the abstract categories LOCUS, SOURCE, and GOAL for abstract communication, and LOCATION, INITIALLOCATION, and DESTINATION for communication with a concrete component (such as writing).

3.4 Accompaniment vs. Joint Participation

The preposition *with* is frustratingly promiscuous. It often marks an entity that is associated with a main entity or event; what is frustrating is that the nature of the association seems to lie on a continuum from physical copresence to active counterpart in an event:

(4) a. Tim prefers [tea **with** crumpets].
b. Tim sat **with** his computer.
c. Tim walked **with** Lori.
d. Tim talked **with/to** Lori.
e. Tim fought **against/with** Lori.
f. Tim fought **against/#with** the idea.

S&R has PARTICIPANT/ACCOMPANIER and OPPONENT/CONTRAST, but these miss the highly frequent case of *talk with*, which involves a cooperative rather than adversarial activity. VerbNet, on the other hand, has roles CO-AGENT, CO-THEME, and CO-PATIENT for "events with symmetrical participants".[6] We adopt the following supersense conventions:

- ACCOMPANIER applies for (4a–4c), where the two participants are physically colocated or performing the same action in separate (but possibly inferentially related) events. Adding *together* seems more natural for these: *Tim walked/?talked together with Lori.*
- CO-AGENT, CO-PATIENT, and CO-THEME, as in VerbNet, apply where both participants are engaged in the same event in the same basic capacity (4d, 4e).
- THEME applies for (4f), where the thing being fought is not fighting back.

3.5 Values and Comparisons

Many prepositions can be used to express a quantitative value (measuring attributes such as a quantity, distance, or cost), to compare to another value, or to compare to something qualitatively. S&R define a broad category called NUMERIC for preposition senses that mark quantitative values and classify some qualitative comparison senses as OTHER. We have developed a finer-grained scheme.

[6] VerbNet defines CO-AGENT as "Agent who is acting in coordination or reciprocally with another agent while participating in the same event" (VerbNet, p. 20).

COMPARISON/CONTRAST applies to qualitative or quantitative analogies, comparisons, and differentiations: e.g., *he used to have a car **like** mine*; *he was screaming **like** a banshee*; *the club's nothing **to** what it once was*; *the benefits must be weighed **against** the costs*; *the difference **between** income and expenditure*; *these fees are quite distinct **from** expenses*. Where these are relative to a specific scale or ranking, the subcategory SCALAR/RANK is used. Qualitative SCALAR/RANK examples include: *place duty **before** all else*; *at a level **above** the common people*; *warm weather **for** the time of year*.

VALUE captures points on a formal scale—*prices start **at** $10*; *the drunken yobbos who turned up **by** the cartload*; *my car does ten miles **to** the gallon*—plus prepositions used as mathematical operators.

SCALAR/RANK and VALUE share a subtype, VALUECOMPARISON, for comparisons/differentiations on a formal scale—*the hill was **above/below** sea level*. A subtype of this, APPROXIMATOR, is for cases such as *We have **over/about/around/in the vicinity of** 3 eggs left* and *We have **between** 3 and 6 eggs left*.[7] Prepositional expressions *under*, *more than*, *less than*, *greater than*, *fewer than*, *at least*, and *at most* fit into this category as well. Note that these can all be paraphrased with mathematical operators: $\approx < > \leq \geq$. APPROXIMATOR applies regardless of the semantic type of the thing measured (whether it is a spatial extent, temporal duration, monetary value, etc.).

3.6 Manner and Means

In our supersense hierarchy, we place MANNER as a parent of INSTRUMENT (see figure 3). We also propose to distinguish MEANS for prepositions that mark an action that facilitates a goal (S&R include these under INSTRUMENT). We define MEANS as a subtype of both INSTRUMENT and ACTIVITY.

MANNER and its subcategories are for prepositions that mark the "how" of an event: *How did she lecture? **With** enthusiasm* (MANNER); *How did he break up the anthill? **With** a stick* (INSTRUMENT); *How did they retaliate? **With** vicious shootings* (MEANS); *How did we coordinate? **Over** Skype* (VIA); *How did you drive? **In** a zigzag* (CONTOUR).

[7] Dictionaries actually disagree as to whether these senses of *about* and *around* should be considered prepositions or adverbs. Pullum and Huddleston (2002, p. 646) distinguish the syntactic behavior of *over* in "*She wrote [[over fifty] novels]*" vs. "*I spent [over [a year]] here*." Whatever the syntactic evidence, semantically these are all similar: they take a measurement, quantity, or range as an argument and "transform" it in some way into a new measurement, quantity, or range.

3.7 Other Major Changes

Space does not permit a full accounting of our modifications to the S&R scheme, which also include:

- EXPLANATION and RECIPROCATION, two new causal categories with names borrowed from FrameNet. EXPLANATION is for secondary events introduced as contributing to the occurrence of the main event (e.g., *he lied **out of** dishonesty/**for** fear of rejection*), with special cases PURPOSE (what somebody wants to happen) and RECIPROCATION (what is being reacted to: *he was admired/thanked/punished **for** his deeds*).
- CREATOR, a new subtype of AGENT that captures usages such as *stories **by/of** A.A. Milne*.
- STATE, covering (e.g.) ***on** morphine/**off** work*, as a new supertype of STARTSTATE and ENDSTATE.
- CONFIGURATION, a new top-level category for senses marking static configurational relationships between two entities (typically nominals). Subtypes: WHOLE (renamed from S&R's PARTWHOLE), SPECIES, POSSESSOR, and new categories PARTITIVE, SUPERSET, and ELEMENTS.
- LOCATION prepositions can be used with a verb of motion to indicate a *resulting* location: *put the hat **on** the stool*; *go **inside** the house*. S&R list such usages under DESTINATION. We instead deem the preposition's meaning as coerced by the verb, and label the preposition as LOCATION (simplifying documentation and annotation). We reserve the DESTINATION supersense for *to*, *into*, etc., which exclusively mark endpoints of motion when used spatially.

4 Conclusion

English prepositions are a challenging class, given that there are so many of them and they are put to so many uses. We have built on prior work to propose a new hierarchical taxonomy of preposition supersenses, so that their semantics can be modeled in a coarse WSD framework. Our resource documents each supersense with detailed explanations, fine-grained dictionary senses, example sentences, and (where possible) mappings to other resources. The taxonomy will hopefully port well to adpositions and case systems in other languages, though we have not investigated that yet. We have successfully piloted English corpus annotation with our resource, and a full-fledged annotation effort is underway.

Acknowledgments

Improved coarse semantic categories for prepositions are the result of ongoing collaborations; they reflect the efforts of ourselves and others including Tim O'Gorman, Katie Conger, Meredith Green, Archna Bhatia, Carlos Ramírez, Yulia Tsvetkov, Michael Mordowanec, Matt Gardner, Spencer Onuffer, and Nora Kazour, as well as helpful conversations with Ken Litkowski, Orin Hargraves, Michael Ellsworth, Ed Hovy, Lori Levin, the Berkeley FrameNet group, and the AMR design group. We also thank anonymous reviewers for helpful comments. This research was supported in part by a Google research grant for Q/A PropBank Annotation, NSF CAREER grant IIS-1054319, and DARPA grant FA8750-12-2-0342 funded under the DEFT program.

References

Collin F. Baker, Charles J. Fillmore, and John B. Lowe. 1998. The Berkeley FrameNet project. In *Proc. of COLING-ACL*, pages 86–90. Montreal, Quebec, Canada.

Timothy Baldwin and Su Nam Kim. 2010. Multiword expressions. In Nitin Indurkhya and Fred J. Damerau, editors, *Handbook of Natural Language Processing, Second Edition*, pages 267–292. CRC Press, Taylor and Francis Group, Boca Raton, Florida, USA.

Timothy Baldwin, Valia Kordoni, and Aline Villavicencio. 2009. Prepositions in applications: a survey and introduction to the special issue. *Computational Linguistics*, 35(2):119–149.

Laura Banarescu, Claire Bonial, Shu Cai, Madalina Georgescu, Kira Griffitt, Ulf Hermjakob, Kevin Knight, Philipp Koehn, Martha Palmer, and Nathan Schneider. 2013. Abstract Meaning Representation for sembanking. In *Proc. of the 7th Linguistic Annotation Workshop and Interoperability with Discourse*, pages 178–186. Sofia, Bulgaria.

Archna Bhatia, Mandy Simons, Lori Levin, Yulia Tsvetkov, Chris Dyer, and Jordan Bender. 2014. A unified annotation scheme for the semantic/pragmatic components of definiteness. In Nicoletta Calzolari, Khalid Choukri, Thierry Declerck, Hrafn Loftsson, Bente Maegaard, Joseph Mariani, Asuncion Moreno, Jan Odijk, and Stelios Piperidis, editors, *Proc. of LREC*, pages 910–916. Reykjavík, Iceland.

Dwight Le Merton Bolinger. 1971. *The phrasal verb in English*. Harvard University Press, Cambridge, MA.

Claire Bonial, William Corvey, Martha Palmer, Volha V. Petukhova, and Harry Bunt. 2011. A hierarchical unification of LIRICS and VerbNet semantic roles. In *Fifth IEEE International Conference on Semantic Computing*, pages 483–489. Palo Alto, CA, USA.

Melissa Bowerman and Soonja Choi. 2001. Shaping meanings for language: universal and language-specific in the acquisition of spatial semantic categories. In Melissa Bowerman and Stephen Levinson, editors, *Language Acquisition and Conceptual Development*, pages 475–511. Cambridge University Press, Cambridge, UK.

Claudia Brugman. 1981. *The story of 'over': polysemy, semantics and the structure of the lexicon*. MA thesis, University of California, Berkeley, Berkeley, CA. Published New York: Garland, 1981.

Martin Chodorow, Joel Tetreault, and Na-Rae Han. 2007. Detection of grammatical errors involving prepositions. In *Proc. of the Fourth ACL-SIGSEM Workshop on Prepositions*, pages 25–30. Prague, Czech Republic.

Massimiliano Ciaramita and Yasemin Altun. 2006. Broad-coverage sense disambiguation and information extraction with a supersense sequence tagger. In *Proc. of EMNLP*, pages 594–602. Sydney, Australia.

Paul Cook and Suzanne Stevenson. 2006. Classifying particle semantics in English verb-particle constructions. In *Proc. of the Workshop on Multiword Expressions: Identifying and Exploiting Underlying Properties*, pages 45–53. Sydney, Australia.

Daniel Dahlmeier, Hwee Tou Ng, and Tanja Schultz. 2009. Joint learning of preposition senses and semantic roles of prepositional phrases. In *Proc. of EMNLP*, pages 450–458. Singapore.

Dipanjan Das, Desai Chen, André F. T. Martins, Nathan Schneider, and Noah A. Smith. 2014. Frame-semantic parsing. *Computational Linguistics*, 40(1):9–56.

Nicolas Denand and Monique Rolbert. 2004. Contextual processing of locative prepositional phrases. In *Proc. of Coling*, pages 1353–1359. Geneva, Switzerland.

Robert B. Dewell. 1994. *Over* again: Image-schema transformations in semantic analysis. *Cognitive Linguistics*, 5(4):351–380.

Claude Hagège. 2009. *Adpositions*. Oxford University Press, Oxford, UK.

Dirk Hovy, Stephen Tratz, and Eduard Hovy. 2010. What's in a preposition? Dimensions of sense disambiguation for an interesting word class. In *Coling 2010: Posters*, pages 454–462. Beijing, China.

Dirk Hovy, Ashish Vaswani, Stephen Tratz, David Chiang, and Eduard Hovy. 2011. Models and training for unsupervised preposition sense disambiguation. In *Proc. of ACL-HLT*, pages 323–328. Portland, Oregon, USA.

Jena D. Hwang. 2014. *Identification and representation of caused motion constructions*. Ph.D. dissertation, University of Colorado, Boulder, Colorado.

Jena D. Hwang, Annie Zaenen, and Martha Palmer. 2014. Criteria for identifying and annotating caused motion constructions in corpus data. In Nicoletta Calzolari, Khalid Choukri, Thierry Declerck, Hrafn Loftsson, Bente Maegaard, Joseph Mariani, Asuncion Moreno,

Jan Odijk, and Stelios Piperidis, editors, *Proc. of LREC*, pages 1297–1304. Reykjavík, Iceland.

Christian Hying. 2007. A corpus-based analysis of geometric constraints on projective prepositions. In *Proc. of the Fourth ACL-SIGSEM Workshop on Prepositions*, pages 1–8. Prague, Czech Republic.

Julia A. Jolly. 1993. Preposition assignment in English. In Jr. Van Valin, Robert D., editor, *Advances in Role and Reference Grammar*, pages 275–310. John Benjamins, Amsterdam.

Karin Kipper, Anna Korhonen, Neville Ryant, and Martha Palmer. 2008. A large-scale classification of English verbs. *Language Resources and Evaluation*, 42(1):21–40.

George Lakoff. 1987. *Women, fire, and dangerous things: what categories reveal about the mind.* University of Chicago Press, Chicago.

Seth Lindstromberg. 2010. *English Prepositions Explained.* John Benjamins Publishing, Amsterdam, revised edition.

Ken Litkowski. 2013. The Preposition Project corpora. Technical Report 13-01, CL Research, Damascus, MD. URL `http://www.clres.com/online-papers/TPPCorpora.pdf`.

Ken Litkowski. 2014. Pattern Dictionary of English Prepositions. In *Proc. of ACL*, pages 1274–1283. Baltimore, Maryland, USA.

Ken Litkowski and Orin Hargraves. 2005. The Preposition Project. In *Proc. of the Second ACL-SIGSEM Workshop on the Linguistic Dimensions of Prepositions and their Use in Computational Linguistics Formalisms and Applications*, pages 171–179. Colchester, Essex, UK.

Ken Litkowski and Orin Hargraves. 2007. SemEval-2007 Task 06: Word-Sense Disambiguation of Prepositions. In *Proc. of the Fourth International Workshop on Semantic Evaluations (SemEval-2007)*, pages 24–29. Prague, Czech Republic.

Mitchell Marcus, Grace Kim, Mary Ann Marcinkiewicz, Robert MacIntyre, Ann Bies, Mark Ferguson, Karen Katz, and Britta Schasberger. 1994. The Penn Treebank: annotating predicate argument structure. In *Proc. of HLT*, pages 114–119. Plainsboro, NJ, USA.

Antje Müller, Olaf Hülscher, Claudia Roch, Katja Keßelmeier, Tobias Stadtfeld, Jan Strunk, and Tibor Kiss. 2010. An annotation schema for preposition senses in German. In *Proc. of the Fourth Linguistic Annotation Workshop*, pages 177–181. Uppsala, Sweden.

Antje Müller, Claudia Roch, Tobias Stadtfeld, and Tibor Kiss. 2011. Annotating spatial interpretations of German prepositions. In *Proc. of ICSC*, pages 459–466. Palo Alto, CA.

Elizabeth M. O'Dowd. 1998. *Prepositions and particles in English: a discourse-functional account.* Oxford University Press, New York.

Tom O'Hara and Janyce Wiebe. 2003. Preposition semantic classification via Treebank and FrameNet. In Walter Daelemans and Miles Osborne, editors, *Proc. of CoNLL*, pages 79–86. Edmonton, Canada.

Tom O'Hara and Janyce Wiebe. 2009. Exploiting semantic role resources for preposition disambiguation. *Computational Linguistics*, 35(2):151–184.

Geoffrey K. Pullum and Rodney Huddleston. 2002. Prepositions and preposition phrases. In Rodney Huddleston and Geoffrey K. Pullum, editors, *The Cambridge Grammar of the English Language*, pages 579–611. Cambridge University Press, Cambridge, UK.

Gisa Rauh. 1993. On the grammar of lexical and non-lexical prepositions in English. In Cornelia Zelinsky-Wibbelt, editor, *The Semantics of Prepositions: From Mental Processing to Natural Language Processing*, pages 99–150. Mouton de Gruyter, New York.

Michael J. Reddy. 1979. The conduit metaphor: a case of frame conflict in our language about language. In Andrew Ortony, editor, *Metaphor and Thought*, pages 284–324. Cambridge University Press, Cambridge, UK.

Terry Regier. 1996. *The human semantic potential: spatial language and constrained connectionism.* MIT Press, Cambridge, MA.

Roi Reichart and Ari Rappoport. 2010. Tense sense disambiguation: a new syntactic polysemy task. In *Proc. of the 2010 Conference on Empirical Methods in Natural Language Processing*, pages 325–334. Cambridge, MA.

Patrick Saint-Dizier. 2006a. Introduction to the Syntax and Semantics of Prepositions. In Patrick Saint-Dizier and Nancy Ide, editors, *Syntax and Semantics of Prepositions*, pages 1–25. Springer, Dordrecht, The Netherlands.

Patrick Saint-Dizier. 2006b. PrepNet: a multilingual lexical description of prepositions. In *Proc. of LREC*, volume 6, pages 1021–1026. Genoa, Italy.

Nathan Schneider, Behrang Mohit, Kemal Oflazer, and Noah A. Smith. 2012. Coarse lexical semantic annotation with supersenses: an Arabic case study. In *Proc. of ACL*, pages 253–258. Jeju Island, Korea.

Nathan Schneider and Noah A. Smith. 2015. A corpus and model integrating multiword expressions and supersenses. In *Proc. of NAACL-HLT*. Denver, Colorado, USA. To appear.

Vivek Srikumar and Dan Roth. 2013a. An inventory of preposition relations. Technical Report arXiv:1305.5785. URL `http://arxiv.org/abs/1305.5785`.

Vivek Srikumar and Dan Roth. 2013b. Modeling semantic relations expressed by prepositions. *Transactions of the Association for Computational Linguistics*, 1:231–242.

Leonard Talmy. 1996. Fictive motion in language and "ception". In Paul Bloom, Mary A. Peterson, Nadel

Lynn, and Merrill F. Garrett, editors, *Language and Space*, pages 211–276. MIT Press, Cambridge, MA.

Stephen Tratz. 2011. *Semantically-enriched parsing for natural language understanding*. Ph.D. dissertation, University of Southern California, Los Angeles, California.

Stephen Tratz and Dirk Hovy. 2009. Disambiguation of preposition sense using linguistically motivated features. In *Proc. of NAACL-HLT Student Research Workshop and Doctoral Consortium*, pages 96–100. Boulder, Colorado.

Jesse L. Tseng. 2000. *The representation and selection of prepositions*. Ph.D. dissertation, University of Edinburgh, Edinburgh, Scotland, UK. URL `http://citeseerx.ist.psu.edu/viewdoc/download?doi=10.1.1.70.4995&rep=rep1&type=pdf`.

Yulia Tsvetkov, Nathan Schneider, Dirk Hovy, Archna Bhatia, Manaal Faruqui, and Chris Dyer. 2014. Augmenting English adjective senses with supersenses. In Nicoletta Calzolari, Khalid Choukri, Thierry Declerck, Hrafn Loftsson, Bente Maegaard, Joseph Mariani, Asuncion Moreno, Jan Odijk, and Stelios Piperidis, editors, *Proc. of LREC*, pages 4359–4365. Reykjavík, Iceland.

Andrea Tyler and Vyvyan Evans. 2003. *The Semantics of English Prepositions: Spatial Scenes, Embodied Meaning and Cognition*. Cambridge University Press, Cambridge, UK.

VerbNet. n.d. *VerbNet Annotation Guidelines*. `http://verbs.colorado.edu/verb-index/VerbNet_Guidelines.pdf`.

Torben Vestergaard. 1977. *Prepositional phrases and prepositional verbs: a study in grammatical function*. Mouton, The Hague.

Yang Xu and Charles Kemp. 2010. Constructing spatial concepts from universal primitives. In Stellan Ohlsson and Richard Catrambone, editors, *Proc. of CogSci*, pages 346–351. Portland, Oregon.

Patrick Ye and Timothy Baldwin. 2007. MELB-YB: Preposition sense disambiguation using rich semantic features. In *Proc. of SemEval*, pages 241–244. Prague, Czech Republic.

Cornelia Zelinsky-Wibbelt. 1993. Interpreting and translating prepositions: a cognitively based formulation. In Cornelia Zelinsky-Wibbelt, editor, *The Semantics of Prepositions: From Mental Processing to Natural Language Processing*, pages 351–390. Mouton de Gruyter, Berlin.

Joost Zwarts and Yoad Winter. 2000. Vector space semantics: a model-theoretic analysis of locative prepositions. *Journal of Logic, Language and Information*, 9:169–211.

Bilingual English-Czech Valency Lexicon Linked to a Parallel Corpus

Zdeňka Urešová Ondřej Dušek Eva Fučíková Jan Hajič Jana Šindlerová
Charles University in Prague, Faculty of Mathematics and Physics
Institute of Formal and Applied Linguistics
Malostranské nám. 25
CZ-11800 Praha 1
Czech Republic
{uresova,odusek,fucikova,hajic,sindlerova}@ufal.mff.cuni.cz

Abstract

This paper presents a resource and the associated annotation process used in a project of interlinking Czech and English verbal translational equivalents based on a parallel, richly annotated dependency treebank containing also valency and semantic roles, namely the Prague Czech-English Dependency Treebank. One of the main aims of this project is to create a high-quality and relatively large empirical base which could be used both for linguistic comparative research as well as for natural language processing applications, such as machine translation or cross-language sense disambiguation. This paper describes the resulting lexicon, CzEngVallex, and the process of building it, as well some interesting observations and statistics already obtained.

1 Introduction

The present paper describes a cross-language verbal valency mapping between Czech and English and the process of capturing it in an annotated language resource. The result thereof is our Czech-English verbal valency lexicon called CzEngVallex, which explicitly links corresponding verbal senses and their valency arguments. As this mapping is based on the parallel Prague Czech-English Dependency Treebank (PCEDT), which also contains monolingual valency annotation on each side, we are getting a powerful, real-text-based complex of interlinked resources for a comparative description of verb senses and their argument structure in the context of translation equivalents.

While having the aforementioned relations captured in an explicit way will help cross-language linguistic comparison studies, it will also serve as training and testing material for multilingual natural language processing applications, most notably machine translation in systems using deep analysis with semantic elements (such as argument and semantic role labeling).

We are not aware of similar work which links aligned valency lexicons to a parallel dependency treebank, even though the resources as such do exist: a Japanese–English lexicon is described in (Fujita and Bond, 2004b). Similar lexicons have been suggested by Dorr (1997), Uszkoreit (2002) or Baldwin et al. (1999). Fujita and Bond (2004a) suggest an automatic extraction of valency from plain bilingual lexicons, but no subjective evaluation of the valency entries themselves is given.

The overview of the aim of the project described here is given in Sect. 2. In Sect. 3, we introduce the basis for building CzEngVallex—the underlying parallel Prague Czech-English Dependency Treebank and the corresponding monolingual valency lexicons. The CzEngVallex lexicon itself and the process of annotating it is described in Sect. 4, and we conclude with Sect. 5.

2 Comparing Czech and English Valency

This idea of a bilingual valency lexicon linked to a treebank comes from an exploratory and theoretically-oriented project for comparison of valency behavior of Czech and English verbs, which, of course, needs an annotated corpus material. Generalizing over the collected data—several thousand aligned verbs, linked to tens of thousand corpus occurrences—should give us more insight into the basic patterns of cross-language relations.

2.1 Valency in the FGD

This project is based on the valency theory of the Functional Generative Description (FGD) (Sgall et al., 1986) and on its application to the Prague Dependency Treebank (PDT) annotation style (Hajič et al., 2006). In this dependency approach, valency is seen as the ability of some lexical items (in general, not only verbs) to select for certain complementations in order to form larger units of meaning (Panevová, 1974). The governing lexical unit then governs both the morphosyntactic properties[1] of the dependent elements and their semantic interpretation (roles). The number and form of the dependent elements

[1]Morphological properties of verb arguments, or rather constraints on their use specific to every verb/argument combination, are very prominently present in inflectional languages such as Czech.

Proceedings of LAW IX - The 9th Linguistic Annotation Workshop, pages 124–128,
Denver, Colorado, June 5, 2015.

constituting the valency structure of a given verb sense is represented by a *valency frame*, which is listed in a valency lexicon.

According to FGD, the valency relation is a part of deep syntax (*tectogrammatic layer* of linguistic description). Every head-dependent relation is labeled by a *functor* denoting the role of the dependent relative to its head. While the FGD describes two dimensions of valency complementation, we can simplify to say that each verb frame (for a given verb sense) contains both verb arguments as well as adjuncts. The main functors used for verb arguments are Actor/Bearer (ACT), Patient (PAT), Addressee (ADDR), Origin (ORIG) and Effect (EFF).[2] The set of adjuncts (free modifications) is about 50 large (Mikulová et al., 2006; Urešová, 2011a).

3 CzEngVallex Source Data

3.1 The Czech-English Parallel Corpus

The Prague Czech-English Dependency Treebank (PCEDT) (Hajič et al., 2011; Hajič et al., 2012)[3] is a sentence-aligned parallel treebank with automatic word alignments based on the Wall Street Journal (WSJ) section of Penn treebank[4] and its manual translation to Czech. It contains manual annotation of morphology and syntax for Czech and for English on approx. 50,000 sentences (about a million words), i.e., all the usual "merged" 2,312 files of the Penn Treebank WSJ corpus.

It is annotated on several layers, of which the tectogrammatical layer (cf. Sect. 2.1) includes also the annotation of verbal valency relations by referring, for each verb occurrence in the corpus, to the PDT-Vallex and EngVallex valency lexicons (see Sect. 3.2 and 3.3).[5]

3.2 PDT-Vallex – The Czech Valency Lexicon

The Czech valency lexicon PDT-Vallex (Hajič et al., 2003; Urešová, 2011b) has been developed as part of the PDT annotation effort. Valency frames representing verb senses in this lexicon are grouped by headwords (lemmas). Each frame contains the following fields: a unique ID, labeled valency frame members ("slots"), their obligatoriness and required surface forms. The frames are accompanied by example fragments of Czech sentences, taken almost exclusively from the PDT. Additional notes help to distinguish the meaning of the individual valency frames for the same headword.

The version of PDT-Vallex used to build CzEngVallex contains 11,933 valency frames for 7,121 verbs. The verbs and frames come mostly from the data appearing in the latest versions of the PDT and PCEDT.

[2]These would roughly correspond to Arg0, Arg1, etc. in the PropBank style of argument labeling.

[3]`https://catalog.ldc.upenn.edu/LDC2012T08`

[4]`https://catalog.ldc.upenn.edu/LDC99T42`

[5]Both lexicons can be found at `http://ufal.mff.cuni.cz/pcedt2.0` and also online at `http://lindat.mff.cuni.cz/services/PDT-Vallex` and `.../EngVallex`.

```
<frames_pairs owner="...">
 <head>...</head>
 </head>
 <body>
  <valency_word id=... vw_id="ev-w1">
   <en_frame id=... en_id="ev-w1f2">
    <frame_pair id=... cs_id="v-w3161f1">
     <slots>
      <slot en_functor="ACT" cs_functor="ACT"/>
      <slot en_functor="PAT" cs_functor="PAT"/>
     </slots>
    </frame_pair>
    <frame_pair id=... cs_id="v-w9887f1">
     <slots>
      <slot en_functor="ACT" cs_functor="ACT"/>
      <slot en_functor="PAT" cs_functor="PAT"/>
      <slot en_functor="EFF" cs_functor="SUBS"/>
     </slots>
    </frame_pair>
   </en_frame>
  </valency_word>
 </body>
</frames_pairs>
```

Figure 1: Structure of CzEngVallex (part of *abandon* pairing)

3.3 EngVallex – The English Valency Lexicon

EngVallex has been created by a (largely manual) adaptation of an already existing similar resource for English, the PropBank (Kingsbury and Palmer, 2002), to the FGD valency format and to PDT labeling standards (Cinková, 2006). During the adaptation process, arguments were re-labeled, obligatoriness was marked for each valency slot and frames with identical meaning were merged (and some split as well). Links to the original PropBank frame file and roleset have been kept wherever possible.

EngVallex was used for the annotation of the English part of the PCEDT. It contains 7,148 valency frames for 4,337 verbs.

4 Building CzEngVallex

4.1 Structure of CzEngVallex

CzEngVallex builds on all the resources mentioned in Sect. 3. It connects pairs of valency frames in the PCEDT (verb senses) which are translations of each other, aligning their arguments as well. This resource cannot be used independently, since it refers to the valency frame descriptions contained in both PDT-Vallex and EngVallex, and it also relies on the PCEDT.

The structure of this new resource, which is technically a single XML file, is shown in Fig. 1.[6] Aligned pairs of verb frames are grouped by the English verb frame (<en_frame>), and for each English verb sense,

[6]Similar scheme is used in (Hansen-Schirra et al., 2006).

their Czech counterparts are listed (<frame_pair>). For each of such pairs, all the aligned valency slots are listed and referred to by the functor assigned to the slot in the respective valency lexicon. In this example, for the pair *abandon*[7] – *opustit* (lit. *leave [alone]*) the first two arguments match perfectly (ACT:ACT, PAT:PAT) and the third argument in English (EFF) does not match any argument for this particular Czech counterpart, while for the pair *abandon* – *zříci se* (lit. *get rid of [for sth]*), the third English argument maps to a Czech adjunct (SUBS, substitution).

It must be noted here that while all verb–verb pairs have been aligned, annotated, and included in this pairing, there are also many verb–non-verb or non-verb–verb pairs, which have been left aside for this first version of CzEngVallex as none of the underlying lexicons include a complete description of other parts-of-speech.

4.2 The Annotation Process

During the actual annotation process, we have manually aligned English and Czech verbs and their arguments (and in some clear cases also adjuncts). After carefully checking all occurrences of any given valency frame pair in the PCEDT, we included it in CzEngVallex using the structure described in Sect. 4.1, which is based on (Šindlerová and Bojar, 2009; Bojar and Šindlerová, 2010).[8] The process is helped by automatic preprocessing steps.

4.2.1 Preprocessing and Data Preparation

The following steps had been taken before the manual annotation proper started:

- automatic pre-alignment using GIZA++ word alignment (Och and Ney, 2003) and a projection to deep dependency trees (taken from the original PCEDT);
- grouping the occurrences of the same verb sense pairs together to simplify annotation.

4.2.2 Annotation Environment

The annotation interface for manual valency frame alignment[9] has been built as an extension of the TrEd annotation environment (Pajas and Fabian, 2011). TrEd is a fully customizable and programmable graphical editor and viewer for any tree-like structures. It allows displaying and editing sentential tree structures annotated on multiple linguistic layers. The new CzEngVallex TrEd extension uses the data format of the Treex NLP framework (Žabokrtský, 2011; Popel and Žabokrtský, 2010) and pre-existing TrEd extensions for PCEDT, PDT-Vallex, and EngVallex.

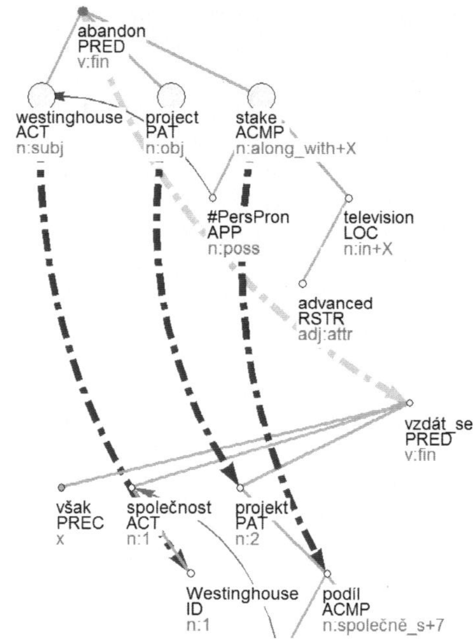

Figure 2: Highlighted alignment in the annotation tool TrEd; color-coding: green for verbs, blue for arguments/adjuncts

The annotation interface includes keyboard macros to change values of individual attributes or to add or delete whole nodes from the structure. Links between English and Czech nodes are added or changed in a drag-and-drop fashion.

4.2.3 Manual Annotation Workflow

The environment described in Sect. 4.2.2 is used to display, edit, collect, and store the alignments between Czech and English valency frames.

Each annotator has their own copy of the treebank, the lexicons, and the valency frame pairing to work on. The changes done by the annotators are merged in the last stage of the process. Any problems encountered, such as wrong annotation in the treebank, or wrong translation, are reported by the annotators through a note system for later corrections.

During the annotation process, the annotator is handed a set of all available sentences for a given verb sense pair. Since verb nodes and their complementations in the PCEDT are automatically pre-aligned (see Sect. 4.2.1), a verb sense pairing suggestion is displayed for each sentence by visually highlighting the pre-alignments (Fig. 2).

The annotator then manually corrects the automatic pre-alignments in the sentence. Then, if the pair is seen for the first time, it is inserted into CzEngVallex by the

[7] Frame ID `ev-w1f2`, which has been created from `abandon.02` in the PropBank, as in *Noriega abandoned command ... for an exile*.

[8] These papers describe only a pilot experiment; the current process differs from their suggestions in several substantial respects.

[9] There are other environments for manual alignment, such as (Melamed, 1998; Samuelsson and Volk, 2007; Ahrenberg et al., 2002), but they work on plain text or phrases, not dependency trees.

annotator (a new CzEngVallex entry is created). For subsequent occurrences, the annotation environment is used to check the pair against the already existing CzEngVallex entry. If any conflict arises, annotators can mark material for further analysis. Typically, errors in either the PCEDT annotation or in the valency lexicons are implied in such cases.

4.3 Lexicon and Corpus: Statistics

Language	Verb types	Frame types	PCEDT Tokens verbs	PCEDT Tokens aligned
English	3,288	4,967	130,514	86,573
Czech	4,192	6,776	118,189	85,606

Table 1: Alignment coverage statistics - CzEngVallex/PCEDT

Table 1 contains some statistics about the new resource. It shows that the financial domain of the WSJ (866,246 English tokens/953,187 Czech tokens) is not very rich in terms of different verbs used: only 4,967 different verb frames (which correspond to a medium-grained sense inventory) on the English side and 6,776 different verb frames on the Czech side have been aligned. However, 19,916 different alignment pairs have been collected: this shows that in translation, even if in a restricted domain, translators use a very rich set of synonyms. The verbs with the highest number of different alignments are *be* (353 different verbs aligned to it in Czech), *make* (203) and *take* (171); conversely, it is *být* (184), *mít* (104) and *získat* (70) (lit. *be, have* and *gain*, respectively).

Comparing the aligned pairs with the complete monolingual valency lexicons (see Sect. 3), about 57% of PDT-Vallex (Czech) verb frames are covered, compared to about 69% of covered EngVallex frames. Token-wise, over 66% of English verb nodes (over 72% Czech ones) have been successfully aligned and match CzEngVallex pairings; the rest are aligned to nouns or other parts-of-speech, or impossible to align at all. These numbers jump to 75/86% (English/Czech) if we discount verbs not aligned to any node.

Statistics for the number of differing members are shown in Table 2. We can see that only about 45% frames match fully, i.e., have the same number of arguments and the same labels. Many frames differ in one or two members (47%) while more divergent pairings are a relatively rare occurrence. The differences can be in part explained by the different behavior of the verbs (i.e., not a full semantic match), but a large number of them can be attributed to a certain degree of ambiguity in label assignments, which could be harmonized in future versions of the valency dictionaries (Šindlerová et al., 2014).

		# Pairs
Full match		9,033
# Differences:	1	6,288
	2	3,135
	3	1,138
	4	261
	5	50
	6	10
	7	1

Table 2: Pairing statistics

5 Conclusions

While the statistics themselves provoke an inquiry into translation practice, the goal is to investigate primarily the cases where the straightforward alignment did **not** happen, i.e., those 25/14% verbs not aligned to a verb, or not matching CzEngVallex pairings. Some of these cases can be extracted by inspecting the data where comments have been added by the annotators, and others by simple technical means (finding verbs with no matching alignment, finding verbs aligned to nouns, adjectives, or other structurally divergent structures).

In addition, we plan to use the newly created resource for NLP tasks, such as MT, or to provide features for cross-language machine learning tasks, such as verb sense disambiguation.

The new resource itself, as described here, after necessary quality check and corrections of the underlying data for consistency reasons, will be published under a Creative Commons license and included with the next edition of the PCEDT.

Acknowledgements

The work described herein has been supported by the Grant No. GP13-03351P of the Grant Agency of the Czech Republic, the Grant No. DF12P01OVV022 of Ministry of Culture of the Czech Republic, and SVV project No. 260 224. It is using language resources hosted by the LINDAT/CLARIN Research Infrastructure, project No. LM2010013 of the Ministry of Education, Youth and Sports of the Czech Republic.

References

Lars Ahrenberg, Mikael Andersson, and Magnus Merkel. 2002. A system for incremental and interactive word linking. In *Proceedings of the 3rd International Conference on Language Resources and Evaluation (LREC-2002)*, pages 485–490.

Timothy Baldwin, Francis Bond, and Ben Hutchinson. 1999. A Valency Dictionary Architecture for Machine Translation.

In *Proceedings of the 8th International Conference on Theoretical and Methodological Issues in Machine Translation (TMI-99)*, pages 207–217, Chester, UK.

Ondřej Bojar and Jana Šindlerová. 2010. Building a bilingual vallex using treebank token alignment: First observations. In *Proceedings of the 7th International Conference on Language Resources and Evaluation (LREC 2010)*, pages 304–309, Valletta, Malta. ELRA, European Language Resources Association.

Silvie Cinková. 2006. From PropBank to EngValLex: Adapting the PropBank-Lexicon to the Valency Theory of the Functional Generative Description. In *Proceedings of the 5th International Conference on Language Resources and Evaluation (LREC 2006)*, pages 2170–2175, Genova, Italy. ELRA.

Bonnie J. Dorr. 1997. Large-scale dictionary construction for foreign language tutoring and interlingual machine translation. *Machine Translation*, 12(4):271–322.

Sanae Fujita and Francis Bond. 2004a. An automatic method of creating valency entries using plain bilingual dictionaries. In *Proceedings of the 10th International Conference on Theoretical and Methodological Issues in Machine Translation (TMI-2004)*, pages 55–64, Baltimore, MD, USA.

Sanae Fujita and Francis Bond. 2004b. A method of creating new bilingual valency entries using alternations. In Gilles Sérasset, editor, *COLING 2004 Multilingual Linguistic Resources*, pages 41–48, Geneva, Switzerland, August 28. COLING.

Jan Hajič, Jarmila Panevová, Eva Hajičová, Petr Sgall, Petr Pajas, Jan Štěpánek, Jiří Havelka, Marie Mikulová, Zdeněk Žabokrtský, Magda Ševčíková-Razímová, and Zdeňka Urešová. 2006. Prague Dependency Treebank 2.0, LDC2006T01.

Jan Hajič, Eva Hajičová, Jarmila Panevová, Petr Sgall, Silvie Cinková, Eva Fučíková, Marie Mikulová, Petr Pajas, Jan Popelka, Jiří Semecký, Jana Šindlerová, Jan Štěpánek, Josef Toman, Zdeňka Urešová, and Zdeněk Žabokrtský. 2011. Prague Czech-English Dependency Treebank 2.0, LDC2012T08.

Jan Hajič, Eva Hajičová, Jarmila Panevová, Petr Sgall, Ondřej Bojar, Silvie Cinková, Eva Fučíková, Marie Mikulová, Petr Pajas, Jan Popelka, Jiří Semecký, Jana Šindlerová, Jan Štěpánek, Josef Toman, Zdeňka Urešová, and Zdeněk Žabokrtský. 2012. Announcing Prague Czech-English Dependency Treebank 2.0. In *Proceedings of the 8th International Conference on Language Resources and Evaluation (LREC 2012)*, pages 3153–3160, İstanbul, Turkey. ELRA, European Language Resources Association.

Jan Hajič, Jarmila Panevová, Zdeňka Urešová, Alevtina Bémová, Veronika Kolářová, and Petr Pajas. 2003. PDT-Vallex: creating a large-coverage valency lexicon for treebank annotation. In *Proceedings of The Second Workshop on Treebanks and Linguistic Theories*, volume 9, page 57–68.

Silvia Hansen-Schirra, Stella Neumann, and Mihaela Vela. 2006. Multi-dimensional annotation and alignment in an english-german translation corpus. In *Proceedings of the 5th Workshop on NLP and XML (NLPXML-2006): Multi-Dimensional Markup in Natural Language Processing, at EACL 2006*, pages 35–42, Trento, Italy.

Paul Kingsbury and Martha Palmer. 2002. From Treebank to Propbank. In *Proceedings of the 3rd International Conference on Language Resources and Evaluation (LREC-2002)*, pages 1989–1993.

I. Dan Melamed. 1998. Manual annotation of translational equivalence: The blinker project. *CoRR*, cmp-lg/9805005.

Marie Mikulová, Alevtina Bémová, Jan Hajič, Eva Hajičová, Jiří Havelka, Veronika Kolářová, Lucie Kučová, Markéta Lopatková, Petr Pajas, Jarmila Panevová, Magda Razímová, Petr Sgall, Jan Štěpánek, Zdeňka Urešová, Kateřina Veselá, and Zdeněk Žabokrtský. 2006. Annotation on the tectogrammatical level in the prague dependency treebank. annotation manual. Technical Report 30, Prague, Czech Rep.

F. J. Och and H. Ney. 2003. A systematic comparison of various statistical alignment models. *Comput. Linguist.*, 29(1):19–51, March.

Petr Pajas and Peter Fabian. 2011. Tred 2.0 – newly refactored tree editor. `http://ufal.mff.cuni.cz/tred`.

Jarmila Panevová. 1974. On verbal frames in Functional generative description I. *Prague Bulletin of Mathematical Linguistics*, (22):3–40.

Martin Popel and Zdeněk Žabokrtský. 2010. TectoMT: modular NLP framework. *Advances in Natural Language Processing*, pages 293–304.

Yvonne Samuelsson and Martin Volk. 2007. Alignment tools for parallel treebanks. In *GLDV Frühjahrstagung*.

Petr Sgall, Eva Hajičová, and Jarmila Panevová. 1986. *The Meaning of the Sentence in Its Semantic and Pragmatic Aspects*. Dordrecht, Reidel, and Prague, Academia, Prague.

Jana Šindlerová and Ondřej Bojar. 2009. Towards English-Czech parallel valency lexicon via treebank examples. In *Proceedings of 8th Treebanks and Linguistic Theories Workshop (TLT)*, pages 185–195, Milano, Italy. Università Cattolica del Sacro Cuore, Università Cattolica del Sacro Cuore.

Jana Šindlerová, Zdeňka Urešová, and Eva Fučíková. 2014. Resources in conflict: A bilingual valency lexicon vs. a bilingual treebank vs. a linguistic theory. In Nicoletta Calzolari (Conference Chair), Khalid Choukri, Thierry Declerck, Hrafn Loftsson, Bente Maegaard, Joseph Mariani, Asuncion Moreno, Jan Odijk, and Stelios Piperidis, editors, *Proceedings of the Ninth International Conference on Language Resources and Evaluation (LREC'14)*, Reykjavik, Iceland. European Language Resources Association (ELRA).

Zdeňka Urešová. 2011a. *Valence sloves v Pražském závislostním korpusu*. Studies in Computational and Theoretical Linguistics. Ústav formální a aplikované lingvistiky, Praha, Czechia.

Zdeňka Urešová. 2011b. *Valenční slovník Pražského závislostního korpusu (PDT-Vallex)*. Studies in Computational and Theoretical Linguistics. Ústav formální a aplikované lingvistiky, Praha, Czechia, ISBN 978-80-904571-1-9, 375 pp.

Hans Uszkoreit. 2002. New chances for deep linguistic processing. In *Proceedings of the 19th International Conference on Computational Linguistics (COLING'02), August 24 - September 1*. Morgan Kauffmann Press.

Zdeněk Žabokrtský. 2011. Treex – an open-source framework for natural language processing. In Markéta Lopatková, editor, *Information Technologies – Applications and Theory*, volume 788, pages 7–14, Košice, Slovakia. Univerzita Pavla Jozefa Šafárika v Košiciach.

Correction Annotation for Non-Native Arabic Texts: Guidelines and Corpus

Wajdi Zaghouani[1], **Nizar Habash**[2], **Houda Bouamor**[1], **Alla Rozovskaya**[3], **Behrang Mohit**[4], **Abeer Heider**[5] **and Kemal Oflazer**[1]

[1]Carnegie Mellon University in Qatar
{wajdiz,hbouamor}@cmu.edu, ko@cs.cmu.edu
[2]New York University Abu Dhabi
nizar.habash@nyu.edu
[3]Center for Computational Learning Systems, Columbia University
alla@ccls.columbia.edu
[4]Ask.com
behrangm@ischool.berkeley.edu
[5]Qatar University
abeer.heider@qu.edu.qa

Abstract

We present our correction annotation guidelines to create a manually corrected non-native (L2) Arabic corpus. We develop our approach by extending an L1 large-scale Arabic corpus and its manual corrections, to include manually corrected non-native Arabic learner essays. Our overarching goal is to use the annotated corpus to develop components for automatic detection and correction of language errors that can be used to help Standard Arabic learners (native and non-native) improve the quality of the Arabic text they produce. The created corpus of L2 text manual corrections is the largest to date. We evaluate our guidelines using inter-annotator agreement and show a high degree of consistency.

1 Introduction

Learner corpora (or L2 corpora) are collections of texts written by non-native learners of the languages of the texts. They are generally marked by a high error rate, i.e., orthographic, lexical, and grammatical errors (Granger, 2003; Hammarberg and Grigonytė, 2014). Learners of Arabic as second language often struggle to produce fluent Arabic text. In addition to the significant structural and conceptual differences between Arabic and other languages (English, French, etc.), vocabulary learning is one of the biggest challenges. Apart from content selection and planning, the writer should find the appropriate words/expressions to express her ideas. Finding the best formulation to integrate within the stylistic context of a discourse, or using the terminology that is more adapted to the context might be more complicated. Learners of Arabic as a second language have to adapt to a different script and different grammatical rules. These factors contribute to the propagation of errors made by L2 speakers that are of different nature than those produced by native speakers (L1 speakers). Hence, in order to model learner language and produce highly efficient error detection and correction methods, it is extremely important to collect a large learner corpus, annotate it and analyze the errors contained in it.

Annotated L2 corpora can provide teachers, learners, second language acquisition researchers, lexicographers and language materials writers, with a valuable data resource. For instance, the annotated corpora can be used for Contrastive Interlanguage Analysis (CIA), since it enables researchers to observe a wide range of instances of under-use, overuse, and misuse of various aspects of the learner language at different levels. Moreover, L2 corpora can be used to compile or improve learner dictionary contents, particularly by identifying the most common errors learners make while providing immediate access to detailed error statistics. This can provide learners with a very useful feedback and help them improve their proficiency level.

Proceedings of LAW IX - The 9th Linguistic Annotation Workshop, pages 129–139,
Denver, Colorado, June 5, 2015. ©2015 Association for Computational Linguistics

These errors may take place in words, phrases, language structures, and the ways words or expressions are used (Granger, 2003). For Arabic, there are few projects that aim at developing Arabic learner corpora and annotating them but most of them are not freely available for users or researchers (Abuhakema et al., 2008; Hassan and Daud, 2011).

In this paper, we present our annotation method and our efforts for extending an L1 large scale Arabic language corpus and its manually edited corrections to include annotated non-native Arabic learner text (L2). This work is part of the Qatar Arabic Language Bank (QALB) project (Zaghouani et al., 2014b), a large-scale error annotation effort that aims to create a manually corrected corpus of errors for a variety of Arabic texts (the target size is 2 million words).[1] Our overarching goal is to use our annotated corpus to develop components for automatic detection and correction of language errors that can be used to help Standard Arabic learners (native and non-native) improve the quality of the Arabic text they produce. The previous version of our annotation guidelines focused on native speaker text. Our extended L2 guidelines are built on the existing L1 guidelines (Zaghouani et al., 2014a) with a focus on the types of errors usually found in the L2 writing style and how to deal with problematic ambiguous cases.[2] Annotated examples are provided in the guidelines to illustrate the various annotation rules and their exceptions. As with the L1 guidelines, the L2 texts should be corrected with a minimum number of edits that produce semantically coherent (accurate) and grammatically correct (fluent) Arabic. The guidelines also devise a priority order for corrections that prefer less intrusive edits starting with inflection, then cliticization, derivation, preposition correction, word choice correction, and finally word insertion. The corpus of L2 text manual corrections we create is the largest to date. We evaluate our guidelines using inter-annotator agreement and show a high degree of consistency.

The remainder of this paper is organized as follows. First, we give an overview of related work in Section 2; then we describe the corpus and the annotation guidelines in Sections 3 and 4. Afterwards, we present our annotation tool and pipeline in Sections 5 and 6. Finally, we present an evaluation of the annotation quality and discuss the L2 annotation challenges in Section 7.

2 Related Work

Currently available manually corrected learner corpora are generally limited when it comes to the language, size and the genre of data. Several corpora of learners of English annotated for errors are publicly available (Rozovskaya and Roth, 2010; Yannakoudakis et al., 2011; Dahlmeier et al., 2013), ranging in size between 60K words and more than one million words. Dickinson and Ledbetter (2012) annotated errors in student essays written by learners of Hungarian at three proficiency levels at Indiana University. The annotation was performed using EXMARaLDA, a freely available tool that allows multiple and concurrent annotations (Schmidt, 2010). Student errors were marked according to various categories of phonological, spelling, agreement and derivation errors.

For Arabic, very few learner corpora annotation project have been built. Abuhakema et al. (2008) annotated a small corpus of 9K words of Arabic written materials produced by native speakers of English in the US who learned Arabic as a foreign language. Part of the learners' texts were written while the learners were studying Arabic in the US, while others were produced when they went to study abroad in Arab countries. A tagset of error annotation based on the FRIDA (French Interlanguage Database) tagset (Granger, 2003) was developed to mark-up the learners' errors.

The Corpus of Malaysian Arabic Learners is another project mainly designed to investigate the incorrect use of Arabic conjunctions among learners. It includes 240K words, produced by various Malaysian university students during their first and second year of Arabic major degree. The corpus includes descriptive and comparative essays produced using Microsoft Word without any help from native speakers (Hassan and Daud, 2011). This corpus is currently not publicly available.

More recently, Farwaneh and Tamimi (2012)

[1] http://nlp.qatar.cmu.edu/qalb/

[2] The L1 guidelines are available at http://reports-archive.adm.cs.cmu.edu/anon/qatar/CMU-CS-QTR-124.pdf

introduced The Arabic Learners Written Corpus (ALWC). This corpus includes around 51K words written by non-native Arabic speakers in the United States and were collected over a period of 15 years. ALWC covers three levels (beginner, intermediate and advanced), and three text styles (descriptive, narrative and instructional). Another notable work in progress has been initiated by Alfaifi and Atwell (2012) aiming at building a $\sim$282K word Arabic learner corpus. The corpus consists of written and spoken materials produced by native and non-native learners of Arabic from pre-university and university levels. Unfortunately, the authors plan to annotate and correct only 10k words of errors in the corpus according to a labeling system inspired by Abuhakema et al. (2008).

3 Corpus Description

Since it was costly to compile our own corpus, we use two freely available L2 Arabic Corpora representing a total of 189K words:

- 51K words from the Arabic Learners Written Corpus (ALWC) (Farwaneh and Tamimi, 2012);
- 139K words from the Arabic Learner Corpus (ALC) (Alfaifi and Atwell, 2012).

The original files of ALWC were in a PDF format. In order to get raw data, we first export the PDF to text, then we manually verified the extracted text to ensure that the data was preserved.

The version of ALC we use is a collection of texts (narrative and discussion) produced by 92 learners of Arabic as a second language in Saudi Arabia and captured in November and December 2012. The corpus is divided according to students' level (beginner, intermediate, advanced).[3]

4 L2 Annotation Guidelines

Essays produced by learners of a Arabic as second language differ from those of natives, not only quantitatively but also qualitatively. Their writings display very different frequencies of words, phrases, and structures, with some items overused and others significantly underused. They also contain varying degrees of grammatical, orthographic and lexical errors. Moreover, sentences written by Arabic L2 speaker have often a different structure and are not as fluent as sentences produced by a native speaker even when no clear mistakes can be found. Therefore, the correction task is complicated by the fact that the acceptability level of a given sentence differs widely within the native speaker annotators as stated by Tetreault and Chodorow (2008). These issues can be related to linguistic factors such as inter-language (L1 interference), the student's teaching and learning methodology, and to the translation effect (conscious interference). Thus, correcting the Arabic L2 essays can be a very challenging task that requires a lot of interpretation efforts by the annotators. This will likely lead to lower inter-annotator agreement as there is often many possible ways to correct the L2 errors.

In order to annotate the L2 corpus, we use our annotation guidelines designed for L1 (Zaghouani et al., 2014b) and add specific L2 annotation rules. Annotation guidelines typically describe the core of the annotation policy. Our annotation guidelines describe the types of errors that are targeted and detail how to correct them, including how to deal with borderline cases. Many annotated examples are provided in the guidelines to illustrate the various annotation rules and exceptions.

As with the L1 guidelines, we adopt an iterative approach to write and improve the L2 guidelines by evaluating various rounds of annotation. The goal is to reach a clear and consistent set of directions for the annotators. For instance, several changes to the guidelines were needed to address the correction of dialectal words and whether or not to correct or ignore certain word categories.

In the following subsections we briefly review the main error types corrected and presented in the guidelines. Then, we detail the L2 specific errors and the L2 correction strategies adopted.

4.1 Guidelines for Error Correction

Errors in any natural language can be defined as a deviation from the standard language norms in word morphology, syntax, punctuation, etc. They can be classified according to basic types such as omis-

[3]A more detailed description of ALC is given at: http://www.arabiclearnercorpus.com/

sion, addition, or substitution errors; or in terms of word order and grammatical form errors. In order to help the annotators understand the types of errors to be corrected, we document them in the annotation guidelines. Furthermore, to reduce over-correction and improve annotation consistency, we instructed the annotators to avoid modifications of any informal or colloquial writing style, which is considered by some to be less acceptable than formal style.

We group the errors to be corrected into seven categories and define them in the guidelines as follows.

Spelling Errors: These occur when at least one of the characters in a word is deleted or substituted by another character, or when an extra character is inserted. Some of these errors result in non-words and some result in other correct words which can not be used in that context.

Word Choice Errors: These include the use of an incorrect word. It was made clear in the guidelines that only wrong word choices are considered for correction, while style changes should not be made since the goal is not to correct or improve the writing style of the text. Word choice errors are particularly frequent in the L2 Arabic student essays.

Morphology Errors: These are usually related to an incorrect derivation or inflection, or incorrect templatic or concatenative morphology. The annotator should be aware of the Arabic morphological inflection rules and their exceptions in order to be able to correct this type of errors.

Syntactic Errors: These include wrong agreement in gender, number, definiteness or case as well as wrong case assignment, wrong tense use, wrong word order, and missing word or redundant/extra words.

Proper Name Errors: These occur in the spelling of persons, organizations, and locations, especially those of foreign origin which could be incorrectly transliterated. If the text uses one of multiple widely acceptable transliterations, the annotators should not modify the word.

Punctuation Errors: Punctuation errors should be corrected according to the commonly accepted Arabic punctuation rules.

Dialectal Usage Errors: In comparison to Standard Arabic, where there are clear spelling standards and conventions, Arabic dialects do not have official orthographic standards partly since they were not commonly written until recently. Today, Arabic dialects are often seen in social media, but also in published novels (and there is even an Egyptian Arabic Wikipedia). Habash et al. (2012) proposed a Conventional Orthography for Dialectal Arabic (or CODA) targeting Egyptian Arabic for computational modeling purposes and demonstrated how to map to it in (Eskander et al., 2013) and (Pasha et al., 2014; Habash et al., 2013). CODAs for other dialects have also been proposed (Zribi et al., 2014; Jarrar et al., 2014). In our current annotation task we neither address dialectal Arabic spelling normalization (Eskander et al., 2013), nor do we systematically translate dialectal words into Standard Arabic (Salloum and Habash, 2013). We recognize that the Arabic language is in a diglossic situation and borrowing is frequent. Most of the texts provided for annotation are in Standard Arabic, but dialectal words are sometimes mistakenly used. We are interested in reducing various spelling inconsistencies that frequently occur. So, as was done in the L1 annotation effort (Zaghouani et al., 2014b), we asked annotators to flag the highly dialectal cases to be reviewed later by the annotation manager. The guidelines classify dialectal word issues into five categories inspired by Habash et al. (2008): dialectal lexical choice, pseudo-dialectal lexical choice, morphological choice, phonological choice and closed class dialectal words. Only the last three categories are considered for correction. For more details, see (Zaghouani et al., 2014a; Zaghouani et al., 2014b).

For more information on Arabic in the context of natural language processing, see (Habash, 2010).

4.2 Additional L2 Annotation Rules

Non-native essays often contain wrong lexical choices or unknown words due to misspelling and it is not easy for annotators to understand these words, interpret the errors and replace them with the correct form (the intended word chosen by the writer). In order to avoid any annotation inconsistency, we extend the general guidelines by adding new rules describing the error correction procedure in texts produced by L2 speakers.

4.2.1 General Correction Rules

First, non-native speaker texts should be corrected with a minimum number of edits.[4] However, correcting errors and making the text semantically coherent and grammatically correct is more important than minimizing the number of edits. Hence, annotators were asked to pay attention to the following three aspects :

- **Accuracy:** The accuracy of the text is very important and any missing meaning observed according to the sentence context should be added to ensure the coherence of the sentence.
- **Fluency:** Spelling, grammatical and agreement errors occur frequently in L2 texts and they should be always corrected. Word reordering is only permitted when it is needed to correct the meaning or the syntax.
- **Style:** L2 texts may be written in a style that is unfamiliar or unnatural to native speakers although the word order is acceptable, and the sentence conveys the meaning correctly. In such cases, the writing style should not be modified to match that of a native speaker.

4.2.2 Correction Priority Order

In order to abide by Arabic's grammatical and spelling rules, it is sometimes necessary to insert new words or do a major correction to unsuitable words selected by the non-native speakers. As the Arabic language is known to have a complex morphology, there is often many ways to correct errors, e.g., by changing the derivation or changing the inflection. To minimize the number of edits and correction, and to avoid any disagreement between annotators, we provide them with the following correction priority guidelines when a correction involving word edits is needed. By following the following predefined correction order, the annotators are more likely to produce a consistent annotation.

1. Correct inflection errors.
2. Correct cliticization errors.
3. Correct derivation errors; but keep root intact.
4. Correct preposition errors (by adding, deleting or substituting a preposition).
5. Correct lexical errors.

Inflection Correction: If the correction is not related to a preposition, the annotator should first try to correct the error by limiting the change to the inflection level (e.g., correction of gender and number). An example of inflection correction is shown in Table 1 in which the verb بدأنا *bdÂnA*[5] 'we started' was replaced by its correct form بدأت *bdÂt* 'I started'.

Cliticization Correction: Adding or changing the clitics.[6] In the example given in Table 1, two clitic corrections are made. In the first case, the annotator added the definite article +ال *Al+* 'the' to مسجد *msjd* 'mosque'. In the second case, the annotator added the missing conjunction +و *w+* 'and'.

Derivation Correction: Here we change the derivation while keeping the same root when possible. The example given in Table 1 shows the derivation of the correct form اغتسلنا *AγtslnA* 'to do a ritual wash' from the the same root of the contextually incorrect word غسلنا *γslnA* – the root is غ س ل *γ s l* 'washing-related'.

Preposition Correction or Insertion: Here we add missing prepositions or correct misused prepositions. An example is shown in Table 1. Prepositions are addressed specifically because they appear often as errors in the preliminary analyses we conducted. Errors in prepositions are not unique to Arabic L2; they are rather common for non-native speakers of other languages such as English (Leacock et al., 2010; Rozovskaya and Roth, 2010).

Lexical Correction: Finally, if it is impossible to fully correct the word using the previous four steps, there is a clear case of word choice errors and the annotator may have to replace the word used. This can be employed to especially correct inadequate lexical choices or unknown words. In the example given in

[4]The minimum edits approach in error correction have already been used in the Error-tagged Learner Corpus of Czech project (Hana et al., 2010)

[5]Arabic transliteration is presented in the Habash-Soudi-Buckwalter scheme (Habash et al., 2007): (in alphabetical order) *Abtθ jHxdðrzsšSDTĎςγfqklmnhwy* and the additional symbols: ' ء, Â أ, Ǎ إ, Ā آ, ŵ ؤ, ŷ ئ, ¯h ة, ý ى.

[6]A clitic is a linguistic unit that is pronounced and written like an affix but is grammatically independent.

	Inflection Error Correction
Original	*knt qd bdÂnA fy AlςAm AlmADy rHl¯hĂlaý mk¯h* كنت قد **بدأنا** في العام الماضي رحلة إلى مكة.
Correction	*knt qd bdÂt fy AlςAm AlmADy rHl¯hĂlaý mk¯h* كنت قد **بدأت** في العام الماضي رحلة إلى مكة.
English	'I had started a trip to Mecca last year.'
	Cliticization Error Correction
Original	وعندما وصلنا **مسجد** الحرام مع زملائي **عددهم** عشرة. *wςndmA wSlnA msjd AlHrAm mς zmlAŷy ςddhm ςšr¯h*
Correction	وعندما وصلنا **المسجد** الحرام مع زملائي **وعددهم** عشرة. *wςndmA wSlnA Almsjd AlHrAm mς zmlAŷy wςddhm ςšr¯h*
English	'And when we got to the Holy Mosque with my ten colleagues.'
	Derivation Error Correction
Original	وقفت الحافلة عند الميقات ونزلنا منها و **غسلنا** ولبسنا ملابس الإحرام. *wqft AlHAfl¯h ςnd AlmyqAt wnzlnA mnhA wγslnA wlbsnA mlAbs AlĂHrAm.*
Correction	وقفت الحافلة عند الميقات ونزلنا منها و **اغتسلنا** ولبسنا ملابس الإحرام. *wqft AlHAfl¯h ςnd AlmyqAt wnzlnA mnhA wAγtslnA wlbsnA mlAbs AlĂHrAm.*
English	'The bus stopped at Miqat and we went down from it and we ritually bathed and we wore ritual clothing.'
	Preposition Correction
Original	*lqd ðhbnA AlHj hðA AlςAm.* لقد ذهبنا الحج هذا العام.
Correction	*lqd ðhbnA Ălý AlHj hðA AlςAm.* لقد ذهبنا **إلى** الحج هذا العام.
English	'We went to the Hajj this year.'
	Lexical Correction
Original	*sÂDς AlmrĀ¯hlky ÂqrÂ AlktAb.* سأضع **المرآة** لكي أقرأ الكتاب.
Correction	*sÂDς AlnĎArAt lky ÂqrÂ AlktAb.* سأضع **النظارات** لكي أقرأ الكتاب.
English	'I will put on the eyeglasses to read the book.'

Table 1: Examples of the different parts of the correction priority order

Table 1, the word المرآة *AlmrĀ¯h*mirror' was replaced by the word النظارات *AlnĎArAt* 'eyeglasses'.

5 The Annotation Tool

In order to ensure the speed and efficiency of the annotation process, as well as better management, we provide the annotators with a web-based annotation framework, originally developed to manually correct errors in L1 texts (Obeid et al., 2013). The annotation interface allows annotators to perform different actions corresponding to the following types of corrections: (a) *edit* misspelled words; (b) *move* words that are not in the right location; (c) *add* missing words; (d) *delete* extraneous words; (e) *merge* words that have been split erroneously; and (f) *split* words that have been merged erroneously.

In our final corpus output format, we record for each annotated file the list of actions taken by the annotator. These actions operate on one or two tokens depending on the action. We also supply token alignments starting from document tokenization to after human annotation.

6 The Annotation Pipeline

The annotation of a large scale corpus requires the involvement of multiple annotators. In our project, the annotation effort is led by an annotation manager, and the team consists of six annotators coming from three Arab countries (Egypt, Palestine and Tunisia) and a programmer. All annotators hold at least a university level degree and they have a strong Arabic language background.

The annotation manager is responsible for the whole annotation task including corpus compilation, the annotation of the gold-standard inter-annotator agreement (IAA) portion of the corpus, writing the annotation guidelines, hiring and training the annotators, evaluating the quality of the annotation, monitoring and reporting on the annotation progress, and designing the annotation tool specifications with the programmer.

The annotation manager assigns tasks to annotators and controls the quality of produced annotations collected. Note that, we give the annotator the possibility to flag a word if he is not certain about its correction. This alerts the annotation manager to check it and correct it.

The annotation manager selects and uploads the text files into the annotation system to create a new annotation project task. Once uploaded, the files are automatically tokenized and processed using MADAMIRA (Pasha et al., 2014), a morphological disambiguation tool that automatically corrects common spelling errors as a side effect of disambiguation. MADAMIRA uses a morphological analyzer to produce, for each input word, a list of analyses specifying every possible morphological interpretation of that word, covering all morphological features of the word. MADAMIRA then applies a set of models to produce a prediction, per word in-context, for different morphological features, such as POS, lemma, gender, number or person. The robust design of MADAMIRA allows it to consider different possible spellings of words, especially relating to Ya/Alif-Maqsura, Ha/Ta-Marbuta and Hamzated Alif forms, which are very common error sources. MADAMIRA selects the correct form in context, thus correcting for these errors which are often connected to lemma choice or morphology.

7 Evaluation

7.1 Inter-Annotator Agreement

Our annotation effort consists of a single annotation pass as commonly done in many annotation projects due to time and budget constraints (Rozovskaya and Roth, 2010; Gamon et al., 2008; Izumi et al., 2004; Nagata et al., 2006). In order to evaluate the quality of our correction annotations, we frequently measure the inter-annotator agreement (IAA) to ensure that the annotators are following the guidelines provided consistently. A high level of agreement between the annotators indicates that the annotation is reliable and the guidelines are useful in producing homogeneous and consistent data. We measure the IAA by averaging WER (Word Error Rate) over all pairs of annotations to compute the AWER (Average Word Error Rate).[7] For the purpose of this evaluation, the WER refers to an annotation error and it is measured against all words in the text. The higher the WER between two annotations, the lower is their agreement.

Table 2 compares the L1 and L2 portions of our corpus in two dimensions. First, we consider the amount of changes done over the whole corpus measured as WER between raw and corrected text. And secondly, we present the IAA numbers in terms of AWER. The IAA results are computed over 200 files (10,288 words) for the L1 corpus and 20 files (3,188 words) for the L2 corpus. Each of these files is corrected by at least three different annotators. We observe that the number of changes in L2 text is 50% more than that in L1, which is consistent with previous studies and our expectation of the complexity of the task. Furthermore, the IAA in L2 is over 10% absolute points worse than in L1. This is particularly disconcerting, but can be explained by the fact that the correction space for L2 text is larger as many different corrections are possible. In order to verify this hypothesis, we performed a second IAA round in which we provide the first IAA round text output to a second pool of three annotators and we measure how much they agree with the correction done by the first round annotator in term of IAA. The low average WER of 3.35 obtained show that there is a high agreement with the corrections done in the first round. We did not do the same second round for our L1 corpus annotations.

We perform a deeper analysis of the annotated corpus. Results are given in Table 3 and show again that there is a correlation between the number of changes and the level of annotators disagreement. It is clear that ALC is less challenging than ALWC as shown in the IAA of the first round and second rounds.

Overall, the high-level of agreement obtained in the second round shows that the annotators produced consistently similar results under the proposed guidelines; and their differences are all within acceptable variation. This of course makes the evaluation of automatic correction harder.[8]

[7] The annotation manager is excluded from this evaluation.

[8] This problem might be solved by considering multiple references in the evaluation process similarly to what is done in machine translation evaluation (Papineni et al., 2002). Unfortu-

Original	انوي ان ساتهي المقالة في عام الانسان قبل الثلاثاء. *Anwy An sAnthy AlmqAl¯lfy ςAm AlAnsAn qbl Alθ lAθA'.* 'I plan I will be-done the article in the year of humanity before Tuesday.'
Annotator 1	أنوي أن أنهي المقالة عن عام الإنسان قبل الثلاثاء. *Ânwy Ân Ânhy AlmqAlħ ςn ςAm AlĂnsAn qbl AlθlAθA'.* 'I plan to finish-off the article about the year of humanity before Tuesday.'
Annotator 2	أنوي أن أنهي المقالة عن عالم الإنسان قبل الثلاثاء. *Ânwy Ân Ânhy AlmqAlħ ςn ςAlm AlĂnsAn qbl AlθlAθA'.* 'I plan to finish-off the article about the human world before Tuesday.'
Annotator 3	أنوي أن أتهي من المقالة في عالم الإنسان قبل الثلاثاء. *Ânwy Ân Ânthy mn AlmqAl¯lfy ςAlm AlĂnsAn qbl AlθlAθA'.* 'I plan to be-done with the article in The Human World before Tuesday.'

Table 4: Example of multiple annotator corrections of an L2 erroneous sentence.

	Changes	IAA$_{Round1}$	IAA$_{Round2}$
L1 corpus	24.45%	3.80%	N/A
L2 corpus	37.64%	14.67%	3.35%

Table 2: Comparison between the L1 and the L2 corpus with the percentage of changes from the RAW source corpus and the inter-annotator agreement (IAA) on "all words" in terms of average WER (Punctuation is ignored). Round1 is basic IAA comparing two annotations starting from raw text. Round2 starts with the output of Round1.

	Changes	IAA$_{Round1}$	IAA$_{Round2}$
ALC corpus	32.65%	13.56%	3.13%
ALWC corpus	51.39%	19.12%	4.20%

Table 3: The percentage of changes from the RAW source corpus and the inter-annotator agreement on "all words" in terms of average WER in the two parts of our L2 corpus (Punctuation is ignored). Round1 is basic IAA comparing two annotations starting from raw text. Round2 starts with the output of Round1.

An analysis of the inter-annotator agreement errors shows that in some cases the annotators did not follow the correction priority order specified in the guidelines (Section 4.2.2) or disagreed on how to apply it. They also either did not pay attention or failed to correct spelling mistakes. In other cases, the disagreement is due to multiple possible interpretations of typos or wrong lexical choices.

In Table 4, we show some examples of disagreement among the annotators. The erroneous L2 sentence has multiple Alif-Hamza errors, an incorrect verb clitic and a confusing phrase في عام الانسان *fy ςAm AlAnsAn* 'in the year of humanity'. All the annotators corrected the Alif-Hamza errors and the verb clitic. However, they disagreed on how to correct the problematic phrase 'in the year of humanity' as (a) 'about the year of humanity', (b) 'about the human world', and (c) 'in the human world'. The different corrections interacted with the form of the main verb after clitic correction اتهي *Anthy* 'be-done' producing two corrections: أنهي *Ânhy* 'finish-off' (derivation change) or أتهي من *Ânthy mn* 'be-done with' (add a preposition). In conversations with the annotators about this case, they expressed strong opinions about what they considered to be the acceptable interpretation that justified their corrections.

nately, such a solution requires more annotations.

7.2 L1 vs L2: Similarities and Differences

We selected a sample of 5K words from both the L1 and L2 corpora to compare their errors. Table 5 highlights the ten most frequent errors found in each corpus. Some errors are corpus-specific while other errors occur in both corpora. For example, the wrong word-order error, the redundant word error and the missing word error are mostly present in the L2 corpus. In contrast, errors such as punctuation errors, incorrect Hamza spelling, and nominal gender/number agreement are present in both corpora.

Err.	Native (L1)	Non-native (L2)
1	Punctuation	Punctuation
2	Hamza	Definiteness
3	Ha/Ta-Marbuta Confusion	Word Choice
4	Alif-Maqsura/Ya Confusion	Hamza
5	Case Endings	Conjunctions, Prepositions
6	Verbal Inflection	Missing Word
7	Agreement	Redundant Word
8	Definiteness	Agreement
9	Conjunctions, Prepositions	Case Endings
10	Word Choice	Word Order

Table 5: Most frequent errors observed in a sample of the L1 and L2 Corpus. The errors are sorted from the most frequent to the least frequent.

8 Conclusion and Future Directions

In this paper, we presented our Arabic L2 correction guidelines and a manually corrected L2 corpus that is the largest to date. We discussed the challenges inherent in learner corpus annotation and we presented our method for efficiently creating an Arabic L2 error corrected corpus. The results obtained in the evaluation suggest that the annotators produced consistently similar results under the proposed guidelines. We believe that publishing this corpus will give researchers a common development and test set for developing related natural language processing applications. A subset of our L2 corpus will be used as part of the Second QALB Shared Task on Automatic Arabic Error Correction in conjunction with the ACL-2015 Workshop on Arabic NLP.[9] This shared task follows the success of the First QALB Shared Task held in conjunction with EMNLP-2014 Workshop on Arabic NLP (Mohit et al., 2014). In the future, we will extend our annotation guidelines to address machine translation output correction (i.e., manual post-editing). We also plan to extend our systems for automatic correction of Arabic language errors (Jeblee et al., 2014; Rozovskaya et al., 2014) to handle L2 data, using the corpus discussed here for training and test purposes.

[9] http://www.arabic-nlp.net/wanlp

Acknowledgements

We thank anonymous reviewers for their valuable comments and suggestions. We also thank all our dedicated annotators: Noor Alzeer, Hoda Fathy, Hoda Ibrahim, Anissa Jrad, Samah Lakhal, Jihene Wafi. We thank Ossama Obeid for his continuous technical support during this project. This publication was made possible by grants NPRP-4-1058-1-168 from the Qatar National Research Fund (a member of the Qatar Foundation).

References

Ghazi Abuhakema, Reem Faraj, Anna Feldman, and Eileen Fitzpatrick. 2008. Annotating an Arabic Learner Corpus for Error. In *Proceedings of The sixth international conference on Language Resources and Evaluation, LREC 2008*, Marrakech, Morocco.

Abdullah Alfaifi and Eric Atwell. 2012. Arabic Learner Corpora (ALC): A Taxonomy of Coding Errors. In *The 8th International Computing Conference in Arabic (ICCA 2012)*, Cairo, Egypt.

Daniel Dahlmeier, Hwee Tou Ng, and Mei Wu Wu. 2013. Building a Large Annotated Corpus of Learner English: The NUS Corpus of Learner English. In *Proceedings of the Eighth Workshop on Innovative Use of NLP for Building Educational Applications*, pages 22–31, Atlanta, Georgia.

Markus Dickinson and Scott Ledbetter. 2012. Annotating Errors in a Hungarian Learner Corpus. In *Proceedings of the Eighth International Conference on Language Resources and Evaluation (LRECâĂŹ12)*, Istanbul, Turkey.

Ramy Eskander, Nizar Habash, Owen Rambow, and Nadi Tomeh. 2013. Processing Spontaneous Orthography. In *Proceedings of the 2013 Conference of the North American Chapter of the Association for Computational Linguistics: Human Language Technologies (NAACL-HLT)*, Atlanta, GA.

Samira Farwaneh and Mohammed Tamimi. 2012. Arabic Learners Written Corpus: A Resource for Research and Learning. *The Center for Educational Resources in Culture, Language and Literacy.*

Michael Gamon, Jianfeng Gao, Chris Brockett, Alexandre Klementiev, William B. Dolan, Dmitriy Belenko, and Lucy Vanderwende. 2008. Using Contextual Speller Techniques and Language Modeling for ESL Error Correction. In *Third International Joint Conference on Natural Language Processing, IJCNLP*, pages 449–456, Hyderabad, India.

Sylviane Granger. 2003. Error-Tagged Learner Corpora and CALL: A Promising Synergy. *CALICO*, 20(3):465–480.

Nizar Habash, Abdelhadi Soudi, and Tim Buckwalter. 2007. On Arabic Transliteration. In A. van den Bosch and A. Soudi, editors, *Arabic Computational Morphology: Knowledge-based and Empirical Methods*. Springer.

Nizar Habash, Owen Rambow, Mona Diab, and Reem Kanjawi-Faraj. 2008. Guidelines for Annotation of Arabic Dialectness. In *Proceedings of the LREC Workshop on HLT & NLP within the Arabic world*, Marrakech, Morocco.

Nizar Habash, Mona Diab, and Owen Rabmow. 2012. Conventional Orthography for Dialectal Arabic. In *Proceedings of the Eighth International Conference on Language Resources and Evaluation (LRECâĂŹ12)*, Istanbul, Turkey.

Nizar Habash, Ryan Roth, Owen Rambow, Ramy Eskander, and Nadi Tomeh. 2013. Morphological Analysis and Disambiguation for Dialectal Arabic. In *Proceedings of the 2013 Conference of the North American Chapter of the Association for Computational Linguistics: Human Language Technologies (NAACL-HLT)*, Atlanta, GA.

Nizar Habash. 2010. *Introduction to Arabic Natural Language Processing*. Morgan & Claypool Publishers.

Björn Hammarberg and Gintarė Grigonytė. 2014. Non-Native Writers' Errors a Challenge to a Spell-Checker. In *1st Nordic workshop on evaluation of spellchecking and proofing tools (NorWEST2014)*, Uppsala, Sweden.

Jirka Hana, Alexandr Rosen, Svatava Škodová, and Barbora Štindlová. 2010. Error-tagged Learner Corpus of Czech. In *Proceedings of The Fourth Linguistic Annotation Workshop (LAW IV)*, Uppsala.

Haslina Hassan and Nuraihan Mat Daud. 2011. Corpus Analysis of Conjunctions: Arabic Learners Difficulties with Collocations. In *Proceedings of the Workshop on Arabic Corpus Linguistics (WACL)*, Lancaster, UK.

Emi Izumi, Kiyotaka Uchimoto, and Hitoshi Isahara. 2004. The NICT JLE Corpus Exploiting the Language Learners' Speech Database for Research and Education. *International Journal of The Computer, the Internet and Management*, 12(2):119–125, May.

Mustafa Jarrar, Nizar Habash, Diyam Akra, and Nasser Zalmout. 2014. Building a Corpus for Palestinian Arabic: a Preliminary Study. In *Proceedings of the EMNLP 2014 Workshop on Arabic Natural Language Processing (ANLP)*, pages 18–27, Doha, Qatar.

Serena Jeblee, Houda Bouamor, Wajdi Zaghouani, and Kemal Oflazer. 2014. Cmuq@ qalb-2014: An smt-based system for automatic arabic error correction. *ANLP 2014*, page 137.

Claudia Leacock, martin Chodorow, Michael Gamon, and Joel Tetreault. 2010. Automated Grammatical Error Detection for Language Learners. *Synthesis Lectures on Human Language Technologies*, 3(1):1–134.

Behrang Mohit, Alla Rozovskaya, Nizar Habash, Wajdi Zaghouani, and Ossama Obeid. 2014. The First QALB Shared Task on Automatic Text Correction for Arabic. In *Proceedings of EMNLP Workshop on Arabic Natural Language Processing*, Doha, Qatar, October.

Ryo Nagata, Atsuo Kawai, Koichiro Morihiro, and Naoki Isu. 2006. A Feedback-Augmented Method for Detecting Errors in the Writing of Learners of English. In *Proceedings of the 21st International Conference on Computational Linguistics and 44th Annual Meeting of the Association for Computational Linguistics*, pages 241–248, Sydney, Australia.

Ossama Obeid, Wajdi Zaghouani, Behrang Mohit, Nizar Habash, Kemal Oflazer, and Nadi Tomeh. 2013. A Web-based Annotation Framework For Large-Scale Text Correction. In *The Companion Volume of the Proceedings of IJCNLP 2013: System Demonstrations*, Nagoya, Japan, October.

Kishore Papineni, Salim Roukos, Todd Ward, and Wei-Jing Zhu. 2002. BLEU: a Method for Automatic Evaluation of Machine Translation. In *Proceedings of the 40th Annual Meeting of the Association for Computational Linguistics*, pages 311–318, Philadelphia, PA.

Arfath Pasha, Mohamed Al-Badrashiny, Ahmed El Kholy, Ramy Eskander, Mona Diab, Nizar Habash, Manoj Pooleery, Owen Rambow, and Ryan Roth. 2014. MADAMIRA: A Fast, Comprehensive Tool for Morphological Analysis and Disambiguation of Arabic. In *In Proceedings of the 9th International Conference on Language Resources and Evaluation*, Reykjavik, Iceland.

Alla Rozovskaya and Dan Roth. 2010. Annotating ESL Errors: Challenges and Rewards. In *NAACL Workshop on Innovative Use of NLP for Building Educational Applications*, Los Angeles, CA.

Alla Rozovskaya, Nizar Habash, Ramy Eskander, Noura Farra, and Wael Salloum. 2014. The columbia system in the qalb-2014 shared task on arabic error correction. In *Workshop on Arabic Natural Language Processing, EMNLP*, page 160.

Wael Salloum and Nizar Habash. 2013. Dialectal Arabic to English Machine Translation: Pivoting through Modern Standard Arabic. In *Proceedings of the 2013 Conference of the North American Chapter of the Association for Computational Linguistics: Human Language Technologies (NAACL-HLT)*, Atlanta, GA.

Thomas Schmidt. 2010. Linguistic Tool Development between Community Practices and Technology Standards. In *Proceedings of the LREC Workshop Lan-*

guage Resource and Language Technology Standards State of the Art, Emerging Needs, and Future Developments.

Joel Tetreault and Martin Chodorow. 2008. Native Judgments of Non-Native Usage: Experiments in Preposition Error Detection. In *Coling 2008: Proceedings of the workshop on Human Judgements in Computational Linguistics*, pages 24–32, Manchester, UK.

Helen Yannakoudakis, Ted Briscoe, and Ben Medlock. 2011. A New Dataset and Method for Automatically Grading ESOL Texts. In *Proceedings of the 49th Annual Meeting of the Association for Computational Linguistics*, pages 180–189, Portland, Oregon, USA.

Wajdi Zaghouani, Nizar Habash, and Behrang Mohit. 2014a. The Qatar Arabic Language Bank Guidelines. Technical Report CMU-CS-QTR-124, School of Computer Science, Carnegie Mellon University, Pittsburgh, PA, September.

Wajdi Zaghouani, Behrang Mohit, Nizar Habash, Ossama Obeid, Nadi Tomeh, Alla Rozovskaya, Noura Farra, Sarah Alkuhlani, and Kemal Oflazer. 2014b. Large Scale Arabic Error Annotation: Guidelines and Framework. In *Proceedings of the Ninth International Conference on Language Resources and Evaluation (LREC'14)*, Reykjavik, Iceland, May.

Inès Zribi, Rahma Boujelbane, Abir Masmoudi, Mariem Ellouze, Lamia Belguith, and Nizar Habash. 2014. A Conventional Orthography for Tunisian Arabic. In *Proceedings of the Ninth International Conference on Language Resources and Evaluation (LREC'14)*, pages 2355–2361, Reykjavik, Iceland.

Balancing the Existing and the New in the Context of Annotating Non-Canonical Language

Ann Bies
Linguistic Data Consortium
University of Pennsylvania
3600 Market Street
Philadelphia, PA 19104, USA
bies@ldc.upenn.edu

Abstract

The importance of balancing linguistic considerations, annotation practicalities, and end user needs in developing language annotation guidelines is discussed. Maintaining a clear view of the various goals and fostering collaboration and feedback across levels of annotation and between corpus creators and corpus users is helpful in determining this balance. Annotating non-canonical language brings additional challenges that serve to highlight the necessity of keeping these goals in mind when creating corpora.

Introduction

Context is important – both the linguistic context of a specific annotation and also the external context of the project as a whole affect what type of annotation scheme can be developed, what kind of annotation can be done, and what the balance of existing and new will need to be in an annotation scheme. Non-canonical language can make the usual linguistic and situational context considerations for annotation even more relevant: how broad the context is (word, sentence, document, conversation, world knowledge), how much that context affects the feature that is being annotated, and whether it is possible for an annotator to take that context into account. In addition, particularly when developing large corpora as part of projects with a short timeline and restricted funding, which is often the case at the Linguistic Data Consortium (LDC), a necessary part of choosing or designing an annotation scheme is considering who the end users of the annotated data will be, what the annotations will be used for, what level of detail is important for the project, and what level of accuracy or consistency is desired.

What are the factors that lead to the adoption of a totally new annotation scheme rather than using an existing annotation scheme?

Since the development of entirely new annotation guidelines is a time-consuming endeavor, it is worth considering whether totally new development is necessary. It may be necessary, if the annotation task is entirely new, or if the goals for using the annotation are entirely new, and neither can take advantage of existing resources.

However, in addition to the potential cost and time to develop entirely new guidelines, several factors could lead positively to the choice of using or adapting existing annotation guidelines for a new task:

- The existence of a large volume of annotated data in an existing annotation scheme that is closely related
- The goal or need to combine existing annotated data with the newly annotated data for statistical, training, or evaluation purposes

Proceedings of LAW IX - The 9th Linguistic Annotation Workshop, pages 140–143,
Denver, Colorado, June 5, 2015. ©2015 Association for Computational Linguistics

- A team of annotators already well trained in an existing annotation scheme
- The feasibility of adapting existing annotation guidelines to meet the goals of a new task
- The existence of a well-designed annotation GUI for an existing task

The non-canonical language that LDC has had experience with includes informal genres (such as SMS/Chat data and speech data) and also dialectal data in languages other than English (such as Egyptian Arabic, which does not have a standardized written form).

When LDC began a project to create English treebank annotations on web text data, we chose to use the existing Penn Treebank guidelines (Bies et al., 1995), but to make additions and adaptations to account for the non-canonical language that appears in internet communication. The existing guidelines addressed most of the syntactic structures that were likely to come up, and the existing annotation tool could handle most of them as well. However, the novel constructions that were present in the data required new guidelines, and some new features also had to be added to the annotation tool. In this case, developing entirely new annotation guidelines and tools would have been prohibitively expensive in both time and effort, and the combination of existing and new worked well for the project (Bies et al., 2012).

Similarly, LDC developed Entities, Relations, and Events (ERE) annotation to support requirements in the DEFT program, including informal genres, and based that development on adapting existing ACE guidelines (Doddington et al., 2004). LDC first defined Light ERE as a simplified form of ACE annotation, with the goal of being able to rapidly produce consistently labeled data in multiple languages (Aguilar et al., 2014), taking advantage of the taxonomy and distinctions developed for ACE. In a second phase of development, Rich ERE expanded entity, relation and event ontologies and also expanded the notion of what is taggable, to provide better support for evaluation tasks in the program. Rich ERE also introduced expanded event coreference with the notion of event hoppers, particularly with respect to event mention and event argument granularity variation (Song et al., 2015).

Treebank and ERE guidelines that have been completed for English have been later adapted for other languages as well – for example, Modern Standard Arabic and also dialectal Arabic treebanks (Maamouri and Bies, 2004; Maamouri et al, 2014; Maamouri et al., 2006; Eskander et al., 2013), as well as Chinese and Spanish ERE (Song et al., 2015). Clearly, new guidelines are necessary to account for language-specific constructions for each language and annotation task, but developing them based on existing guidelines for another language is a considerable head start.

How do you decide on the granularity of the distinctions you choose to annotate? Give examples.

We aim for a level of granularity in annotation distinctions that is

- Consistent with goals of the annotation task and the guidelines
- Useful for downstream users of the data or additional downstream annotation
- Possible for annotators to distinguish reliably

For example, in part-of-speech tagging English web and SMS/Chat text, we make a distinction between emoticons and other decorative uses of punctuation. End users of the data have suggested that the distinction could be useful, since there could be a semantic difference between the two uses, and annotators are able to make the distinction reliably.

In a more structural example from the same data, the syntactic annotation of internet initialisms (such as lol, icymi, rofl, etc.) requires a decision about how much internal structure to give them. Since not every word of the spelled out version is necessarily part of the initials, and since in any case there is often disagreement about what the full spelled out version should be, we do not spell out internet initialisms as part of the annotation. They are left as written and annotated by function in the tree, even if the spelled out version could have internal structure. For example, "atm" for *at the moment* is annotated simply as a one-word temporal adverbial phrase (although the fully spelled out *at the moment* would be a more complex prepositional phrase that includes a noun phrase complement):

```
(ADVP-TMP atm)
```

However, if an initialism takes additional arguments, such as clausal arguments of "idk" for *I don't know*, the argument structure is shown in the tree, so that it is as consistent as possible with other similar structures. The initialism is not spelled out, but at the same time its clausal complement is also annotated:

```
(S (NP-SBJ *PRO*)
   (VP idk
      (SBAR (WHADVP-1 where)
         (S (NP-SBJ I)
            (VP can
               (VP go
                  (ADVP-DIR-1 T*)
   ))))))
```

In developing the concept of event hoppers for Rich ERE, we coreference event mentions at the same level of granularity as ACE (i.e., type and subtype match, and sub-events are treated as separate events), but we allow a greater degree of flexibility in the granularity of the arguments that can be participants in coreferenced event mentions than in ACE (Song et al., 2015). For example,

- Granularity of temporal and spatial expressions (*Attack in Baghdad on Thursday* vs. *Bombing in the Green Zone last week*)
- Trigger granularity (*assaulting 32 people* vs. *wielded a knife*)
- Argument granularity (*18 killed* vs. *dozens killed*)

Relaxing the granularity requirements in this way allows annotators to coreference more event mentions that they know refer to the same event. It more closely matches annotator intuitions, and it gives end users a more complete picture of the annotated events and their participants.

For building new resources for NCLs, is it still worthwhile to invest a huge amount of time and human labour for manual annotation, considering that the annotators spend most of their time making arbitrary decisions, and that the aim of building 'high-quality resources' for NCLs might not be realistic?

Manually annotated resources provide information that may not be possible to determine using automated systems only. High-quality manual annotation of non-canonical language is possible to achieve, given clear annotation guidelines and careful training of annotators.

The premise of the question – that annotators must spend most of their time making arbitrary decisions – seems incorrect to me. It is possible to eliminate or minimize arbitrary decisions in the development of annotation guidelines when that is a priority.

It is also important to keep in mind, however, that different projects and different users may have different requirements regarding quality. "High quality" will not mean the same thing to everybody, and an annotated corpus is valuable if it helps the end users do what they want to do with it. Not all end users require high annotator consistency, and not all end users require a notion of a single right answer.

In addition, not all annotation "improvements" have the same cost, or the same benefit. Some annotation updates may be quite simple or fast but are high value in terms of system performance. Other updates might be difficult or slow and end up not bearing much fruit for the end users. A close feedback loop between corpus creators and corpus users is helpful in terms of selecting what kinds of updates are worthwhile given limited resources. This type of beneficial feedback loop was in place during the development of the Arabic Treebank and Arabic morphological analyzers and parsers (Maamouri et al., 2014; Maamouri et al., 2008; Maamouri et al., 2011; Eskander et al., 2013).

On a related note, what are the considerations when choosing the level of expertise of the annotators? When is crowd sourcing appropriate? When do we need linguistic experts?

The complexity of the annotation task and the required level of consistency for the annotation are the primary considerations in determining the necessary level of linguistic expertise.

Can the concept of "gold annotations" be applied to non-canonical languages where the inherent ambiguity in the data makes it hard to decide on the "ground truth" of an utterance?

For tasks such as syntactic annotation, instances where the inherent ambiguity in the linguistic data makes it impossible to decide on the ground truth of an utterance in context are rare, even in informal genres. If language as it is used were impossibly ambiguous, human communication could not take place. However, the context of the utterance is important, as is giving annotators access to as much of that context as possible. There are certainly situations where the full context may not be available, or where the full context may include non-linguistic factors such as gesture or world knowledge, and those cases will be difficult.

Ambiguity is certainly present in many forms, in non-canonical (and also canonical) language. It may be that allowing or highlighting that ambiguity as part of the "gold annotation" would be valuable. There are also annotation tasks where various gradient phenomena in the data call into question the reality of a single correct answer. When annotating those phenomena is valuable, multiple correct answers or annotated gradients could also be considered as a part of gold annotation.

Acknowledgments

This material is based upon research supported by the Defense Advanced Research Projects Agency (DARPA) Contract No. HR0011-11-C-0145 and Air Force Research Laboratory agreement number FA8750-13-2-0045. The U.S. Government is authorized to reproduce and distribute reprints for Governmental purposes notwithstanding any copyright notation thereon. The views and conclusions contained herein are those of the authors and should not be interpreted as necessarily representing the official policies or endorsements, either expressed or implied, of Air Force Research Laboratory and Defense Advanced Research Projects Agency or the U.S. Government. Portions of this work were supported by a gift from Google, Inc.

References

Jacqueline Aguilar, Charley Beller, Paul McNamee, Benjamin Van Durme, Stephanie Strassel, Zhiyi Song, Joe Ellis. 2014. A Comparison of the Events and Relations Across ACE, ERE, TAC-KBP, and FrameNet Annotation Standards. *ACL 2014: 52nd Annual Meeting of the Association for Computational Linguistics, Baltimore, June 22-27. 2nd Workshop on Events: Definition, Detection, Coreference, and Representation.*

Ann Bies, Mark Ferguson, Karen Katz, Robert MacIntyre. 1995. *Bracketing Guidelines for the Treebank II-style Penn Treebank Project*. University of Pennsylvania, Department of Computer and Information Science Technical Report MS-CIS-95-06.

Ann Bies, Justin Mott, Colin Warner, Seth Kulick. 2012. *English Web Treebank*. Linguistic Data Consortium, LDC Catalog No.: LDC2012T13.

George Doddington, Alexis Mitchell, Mark Przybocki, Lance Ramshaw, Stephanie Strassel, Ralph Weischedel. 2004. The Automatic Content Extraction (ACE) program - tasks, data, and evaluation. In *Proceedings of the Fourth International Conference on Language Resources and Evaluation* (LREC 2004), Lisbon, May 24-30.

Ramy Eskander, Nizar Habash, Ann Bies, Seth Kulick, Mohamed Maamouri. 2013. Automatic Correction and Extension of Morphological Annotations. In *Proceedings of the 7th Linguistic Annotation Workshop & Interoperability with Discourse*, pages 1–10, Association for Computational Linguistics, Sofia, Bulgaria, August 8-9, 2013.

Mohamed Maamouri and Ann Bies. 2004. Developing an Arabic Treebank: Methods, Guidelines, Procedures, and Tools. In *Proceedings of the 20th International Conference on Computational Linguistics* (COLING 2004).

Mohamed Maamouri, Ann Bies, Tim Buckwalter, Mona Diab, Nizar Habash, Owen Rambow, Dalila Tabessi. 2006. Developing and Using a Pilot Dialectal Arabic Treebank. In *Proceedings of the Fifth International Conference on Language Resources and Evaluation* (LREC 2006).

Mohamed Maamouri, Ann Bies, Seth Kulick. 2008. Enhancing the Arabic Treebank: A Collaborative Effort toward New Annotation Guidelines. In *Proceedings of the Sixth International Conference on Language Resources and Evaluation* (LREC 2008).

Mohamed Maamouri, Ann Bies, Seth Kulick, Nizar Habash, Reem Faraj, Ryan Roth. 2011. Arabic Treebanking. In Joseph Olive, Caitlin Christianson and John McCary (Eds.), *Handbook of Natural Language Processing and Machine Translation: DARPA Global Autonomous Language Exploitation*. Springer.

Mohamed Maamouri, Ann Bies, Seth Kulick, Michael Ciul, Nizar Habash, Ramy Eskander. 2014. Developing an Egyptian Arabic Treebank: Impact of Dialectal Morphology on Annotation and Tool Development. In *Proceedings of the Ninth International Conference on Language Resources and Evaluation* (LREC 2014).

Zhiyi Song, Ann Bies, Stephanie Strassel, Tom Riese, Justin Mott, Joe Ellis, Jonathan Wright, Seth Kulick, Neville Ryant, Xiaoyi Ma. 2015. From Light to Rich ERE: Annotation of Entities, Relations, and Events. In *Proceedings of The 3rd Workshop on EVENTS: Definition, Detection, Coreference, and Representation*, at The 2015 Conference of the North American Chapter of the Association for Computational Linguistics - Human Language Technologies (NAACL HLT 2015).

Parsing Learner Text: to Shoehorn or not to Shoehorn

Aoife Cahill
Educational Testing Service
660 Rosedale Rd
Princeton, NJ 08541, USA
acahill@ets.org

1 Introduction

The texts written by language learners can be considered a type of non-canonical text. Language learners tend to make errors when writing in a second language and in this regard, can be seen to violate the canonical rules of a language. The kinds of errors that learners may make include: spelling, grammatical, vocabulary, collocation. The extent and degree to which learners make errors will depend on their proficiency level and this is a factor that should be taken into account when thinking about non-native writing. Highly proficient speakers will make very few errors, and given just a small sample of text it may not even be possible to identify that they are language learners. However, at the same time, the kinds of errors that even highly-proficient language learners make are often very different from the kinds of errors that a native speaker will make. A non-native speaker is likely to have the most trouble with collocations and lexical choice, whereas a native speaker will be less likely to have difficulty here (Leacock et al., 2014).

Our discussions here will focus on the syntactic analysis of English learner data. In particular, we are primarily considering learners at a low to mid-level proficiency. The kinds of mechanical and grammatical errors that these learners make are likely to cause the most difficulty for syntactic analyzers. Syntactic analysis is a key component of attempting to understand the meaning of a text. Therefore, syntactic analysis of learner text is an important step in many applications. The kinds of applications that need to analyze learner text include automated systems that detect and correct grammatical errors, systems that automatically grade texts, native language identification systems, feedback systems, etc.

2 Parsing Learner Text

Geertzen et al. (2013) parse a corpus of 1,000 learner sentences with the Stanford parser and examine the kinds of errors made by the parser. They find that in general the parser is able to recover syntactic dependency relations with high accuracy. In addition, there is only a small amount of variation across proficiency levels. They found that the parser can compensate well for morphological mistakes, but has more difficulty with more complex errors.

Although in this work we are only considering English data, it is worth pointing out some recent related work on German. Ott and Ziai (2010) apply an out-of-the-box German dependency parser to learner text and analyze the impact on down-stream semantic interpretation. They find that core functions such as subject and object can generally be reliably detected, but that when there are key elements (e.g. main verbs) missing from the sentence that the parses are less reliable. They also found that less-severe grammatical errors such as agreement did not tend to cause problems for the parser. Krivanek and Meurers (2011) compare a hand-crafted parser to a statistical parser on German data and find that the parsers are better at detecting complementary dependencies.

The highest-performing NLP tools have all been trained to perform well on well-edited text (often in the newspaper domain). There are two main problems when applying these tools to learner text which

Proceedings of LAW IX - The 9th Linguistic Annotation Workshop, pages 144–147,
Denver, Colorado, June 5, 2015.

may contain many errors. The first is that the state-of-the-art tools are robust to noise and will almost always find some analysis. Depending on the kinds of grammatical errors in the learner text, this analysis can be seriously flawed. The second issue is that often, due to the errors, a traditional linguistic analysis of learner text is not possible or appropriate.

One way of looking at the problem of training statistical NLP tools for learner texts is that learner text is of a different domain to the domain for which the NLP tools were designed. Many unsupervised approaches to domain adaptation have been proposed in the literature, which may be applicable in this scenario. Self-training (McClosky et al., 2006) is one very common and straightforward technique for improving NLP tool performance on text from a new domain. Cahill et al. (2014) showed that it was possible to improve the performance of a baseline constituency parser on learner text by applying self-training.

Another approach to adapting NLP tools to learner text is to train them directly on annotated data. The SALLE project (Syntactically Annotating Learner Language of English) at Indiana University is working towards developing a set of guidelines for annotating syntactic properties (in the form of dependencies) of texts written by learners of English (Ragheb and Dickinson, 2012; Ragheb and Dickinson, 2014). Their goal is to provide accurate syntactic dependency analyses for learner text given the morphological realizations of tokens, and they do not attempt to connect directly to the intended meanings. They plan to release a manually annotated dataset, and are also planning to work on bootstrapping approaches to semi-automatically annotate data.

3 Parsing and Grammaticality

Heilman et al. (2014) argue that grammaticality judgments for sentences should be made on an ordinal scale rather than the binary scale that is often used when talking about grammaticality. They propose a four-point scale where 1 is incomprehensible and 4 is native-sounding.[1] Viewing grammaticality in this way, it is likely that the performance of a syntactic parser will be more or less impacted by the severity of the grammatical error.

In order to briefly test whether different error types impact syntactic parsing to different degrees, we carry out a preliminary experiment with some artificially generated errors. We consider 6 errors that are typical of those made by language learners. These six error types were selected because they can easily be simulated, we do not make any claims about the relative "severity" of these errors here. In general, these errors would not lead to severe difficulties in interpretation for most people, however there are some cases where these errors could lead to ambiguity in interpretation. At the same time, we would predict that some of these errors would cause problems for state of the art parsers (e.g. missing determiner/preposition). We expect tolerance for grammatical errors to differ considerably between parsers and native speakers. The six errors we consider are:

1. missing determiner
2. missing preposition
3. missing pronoun
4. noun number error (plural instead of singular)
5. verb form error (present tense conjugation)
6. incorrect position of adverb

We use the parsed version of WSJ section 23 as our gold standard test corpus and use the GenERRate tool (Foster and Andersen, 2009) to artificially introduce these 6 errors into this well-formed text. The GenERRate tool allows the user to define operations that are applied to well-formed text in order to yield ill-formed text. For example, the operation to introduce a "missing determiner" error is `delete DT`. GenERRate also allows the user to specify the proportion of each error type in the output text. In our experiments, we choose a proportion of 0.03. This means for this error for example, that 3% of the determiners in the original corpus would be deleted.[2]

For each error, we process section 23 to get a version of the text containing that error. We then parse

[1] Non-word spelling errors are ignored in that scheme.

[2] Future work would include experimentation with varying this rate.

	Labeled Bracketing		
	Precision	Recall	F-Score
original	90.23	89.82	90.03
Verb form	89.73	89.24	89.48
Noun number	89.52	89.39	89.45
missing PRP	82.10	79.94	81.01
missing DT	75.49	74.65	75.07
Adverb	71.63	71.41	71.52
missing IN	73.68	68.49	70.99

Table 1: The effect on parser performance on ungrammatical text as measured by labeled constituents.

the original text as well as each modified version of section 23 with ZPar (Zhang and Clark, 2011). We evaluate the output of the parser using SParseval (Roark et al., 2006). This is necessary because the tokens in the gold standard are no longer necessarily in the parser output and standard evaluation software such as `evalb` cannot be applied. The labeled bracket constituency results are given in Table 1. The results show a large difference in parser performance across the 6 error types.

Confusing singular and plural nouns, or confusing the form of the verb lead to only very minor changes in overall constituency structure compared to parsing the original text by Zpar. This is in some ways not that unexpected, since these kinds of errors (at least in the manner they were artificially introduced) only affect the part-of-speech tag of the word. Missing determiners and prepositions lead to large drops in performance. This is expected, since without these key function words, the parser will have difficulty building up NP and PP constituents. Interestingly, the missing pronoun errors do not lead to as dramatic a drop in performance. This may be because pronouns alone form complete NP constituents and their absence will have less of an impact on the construction of the surrounding constituents.

Another important factor to consider is the evaluation metric. Evaluation metrics and annotation schemes can often mask true differences and accentuate other differences by over-counting. Rehbein and van Genabith (2007) compare three different parser evaluation metrics and show that a dependency-based evaluation is best suited to measuring the linguistic information encoded in parse trees. Unfortunately, SParseval does not take the alignment into account when computing dependency scores and so we are unable to report those scores for our experiments at this time.[3]

4 Discussion

Annotating learner text with syntactic analysis, either manually or automatically is problematic for a number of reasons. As shown above, the automatic annotation of texts that contain grammatical errors can have a large impact on parser performance, depending on the kind of error. In the examples above, only one error per sentence was ever introduced.[4] In reality, learner errors interact and can be difficult to disentangle. At the same time, these errors were artificially introduced into relatively long and complex English sentences that a language learner would not necessarily be able to produce. In Geertzen et al. (2013) the naturally occurring errors in their corpus did not seem to cause the parser too much trouble.

Current research has two main approaches: (1) training parsers to produce more accurate trees based on the Penn Treebank style annotation guidelines (e.g. Cahill et al. (2014)) or (2) adapting the underlying annotation schemes to better capture the fact that there may be errors in the text (e.g. Ragheb and Dickinson (2014)). The two approaches have different strengths. The first will produce the kinds of annotated trees that other NLP tools are used to getting as input. Therefore these kinds of trees fit nicely into an already existing NLP pipeline. The second will produce the kinds of annotated trees that will ultimately be more informative when it comes to developing learner-specific applications. Both approaches also have different weaknesses. The Penn Treebank style trees alone cannot provide any insight into potential errors in the sentence, and developing the tools that generate these trees such that they work well on learner text requires more work. On the other hand, a new annotation scheme requires a significant amount of manual effort in order to an-

[3]The dependency scores reported by SParseval will overly-penalize errors involving a change in surface form, as in the noun-number error.

[4]Although the algorithm GenERRate employs to insert errors according to a defined frequency would in theory allow for multiple errors per sentence, we did not see any instances of this in our data.

notate enough data to be able to train a new statistical parser.[5]

Given the encouraging results of Geertzen et al. (2013) and Cahill et al. (2014), the approach of shoehorning existing annotation schemes to fit learner data is the most practical for large-scale applications currently.

References

Aoife Cahill, Binod Gyawali, and James Bruno. 2014. Self-training for parsing learner text. In *Proceedings of the First Joint Workshop on Statistical Parsing of Morphologically Rich Languages and Syntactic Analysis of Non-Canonical Languages*, pages 66–73, Dublin, Ireland, August. Dublin City University.

Jennifer Foster and Oistein Andersen. 2009. Generrate: Generating errors for use in grammatical error detection. In *Proceedings of the Fourth Workshop on Innovative Use of NLP for Building Educational Applications*, pages 82–90, Boulder, Colorado, June. Association for Computational Linguistics.

Jeroen Geertzen, Theodora Alexopoulou, and Anna Korhonen. 2013. Automatic linguistic annotation of large scale L2 databases: the EF-Cambridge Open Language Database (EFCAMDAT). In *Proceedings of the 31st Second Language Research Forum.*

Michael Heilman, Aoife Cahill, Nitin Madnani, Melissa Lopez, Matthew Mulholland, and Joel Tetreault. 2014. Predicting Grammaticality on an Ordinal Scale. In *Proceedings of the 52nd Annual Meeting of the Association for Computational Linguistics (Volume 2: Short Papers)*, pages 174–180, Baltimore, Maryland, June. Association for Computational Linguistics.

Rafiq Abdul Khader, Tracy Holloway King, and Miriam Butt. 2004. Deep call grammars: The lfgot experiment.

Julia Krivanek and Detmar Meurers. 2011. Comparing rule-based and datadriven dependency parsing of learner language. In *Proceedings of the Int. Conference on Dependency Linguistics (Depling 2011)*, pages 310–317.

Claudia Leacock, Martin Chodorow, Michael Gamon, and Joel Tetreault. 2014. Automated Grammatical Error Detection for Language Learners, Second Edition. *Synthesis Lectures on Human Language Technologies*, 7(1):1–170.

[5]There has also been work on extending non-statistical hand-crafted grammars to return structures that indicate the location of grammatical errors (Menzel and Schröder, 1999; Vandeventer Faltin, 2003; Khader et al., 2004).

David McClosky, Eugene Charniak, and Mark Johnson. 2006. Effective self-training for parsing. In *Proceedings of the Human Language Technology Conference of the NAACL, Main Conference*, pages 152–159, New York City, USA, June. Association for Computational Linguistics.

Wolfgang Menzel and Ingo Schröder. 1999. Error diagnosis for language learning systems. *ReCALL*, 11:20–30.

Niels Ott and Ramon Ziai. 2010. Evaluating dependency parsing performance on German learner language. In *Proceedings of the Ninth Workshop on Treebanks and Linguistic Theories (TLT-9)*, pages 175–186.

Marwa Ragheb and Markus Dickinson. 2012. Defining Syntax for Learner Language Annotation. In *Proceedings of COLING 2012: Posters*, pages 965–974, Mumbai, India, December. The COLING 2012 Organizing Committee.

Marwa Ragheb and Markus Dickinson. 2014. Developing a Corpus of Syntactically-Annotated Learner Language for English. In *Proceedings of the Thirteenth International Workshop on Treebanks and Linguistic Theories (TLT13)*, pages 137–148, Tübingen, Germany.

Ines Rehbein and Josef van Genabith. 2007. Evaluating Evaluation Measures. In *Proceedings of the 16th Nordic Conference of Computational Linguistics (NODALIDA-2007)*, Tartu, Estonia.

Brian Roark, Mary Harper, Eugene Charniak, Bonnie Dorr, Mark Johnson, Jeremy G Kahn, Yang Liu, Mari Ostendorf, John Hale, Anna Krasnyanskaya, Matthew Lease, Izhak Shafran, Matthew Snover, Robin Stewart, and Lisa Yung. 2006. Sparseval: Evaluation metrics for parsing speech. In *Proceedings of LREC.*

Anne Vandeventer Faltin. 2003. *Syntactic Error Diagnosis in the context of Computer Assisted Language Learning*. Ph.D. thesis, Université de Genève.

Yue Zhang and Stephen Clark. 2011. Syntactic Processing Using the Generalized Perceptron and Beam Search. *Computational Linguistics*, 37(1):105–151.

Non-canonical language is not harder to annotate than canonical language

Barbara Plank, Héctor Martínez Alonso, Anders Søgaard
Center for Language Technology, University of Copenhagen
Njalsgade 140, Copenhagen, Denmark
bplank@cst.dk, alonso@hum.ku.dk, soegaard@hum.ku.dk

Abstract

As researchers developing robust NLP for a wide range of text types, we are often confronted with the prejudice that annotation of *non-canonical language* (whatever that means) is somehow more arbitrary than annotation of canonical language. To investigate this, we present a small annotation study where annotators were asked, with minimal guidelines, to identify main predicates and arguments in sentences across five different domains, ranging from newswire to Twitter. Our study indicates that (at least such) annotation of non-canonical language is *not* harder. However, we also observe that agreements in social media domains correlate less with model confidence, suggesting that maybe annotators disagree for different reasons when annotating social media data.

1 Introduction

Recently, our research group received the reviews of a paper we submitted to a major, influential journal. The paper included a description of in-house linguistic annotation of Twitter data. One reviewer complained that "the use of Twitter as a corpus might be problematic because of the characteristic use of non-standard/typical language." What the reviewer presumably meant is that linguistic annotation of Twitter data is more arbitrary than annotation of standard or canonical language, e.g., newswire. We believe this premise, or prejudice, is false. "Standard language", as found in newswire and textbooks, for example, is a very biased sample of the linguistic productions in a language community, and the vast majority of the language we process and produce through the course of a day is very different from newswire and textbooks, be it spoken language, literature, or social media text.

Why, then, is newswire considered more standard or more *canonical* than other text types? Obviously, this may simply be because journalists are trained writers and produce fewer errors. But think, for a minute, about languages in which no newspapers are written. What, then, is canonical language? Can spoken language be canonical? Or is newswire called canonical, because, historically, it is what corpora are made of, and the only data that was available to the NLP community for a long time?

This discussion is more than a fight of words. The use of the word 'canonical' alludes to the fact that non-canonical language presents a challenge to the NLP community, but a lot of the reason for NLP tools performing poorly on social media texts and the like seems to be a historical coincidence. Most resources, e.g., syntactic and semantic treebanks, are human-annotated subsets of newswire corpora, simply because most electronic text corpora were newswire corpora when the NLP community began building treebanks. The question is whether annotating non-canonical language, say social media text, is inherently harder than annotating more canonical language, say newswire.

We believe some types of non-canonical language pose interesting *processing* challenges, e.g., with more mixed language, more *ad hoc* spelling conventions, and more texts directed at smaller audiences with more knowledge required during interpretation. However, newswire also comes with its

Proceedings of LAW IX - The 9th Linguistic Annotation Workshop, pages 148–151,
Denver, Colorado, June 5, 2015. ©2015 Association for Computational Linguistics

complexities (headlinese, creative language use, citations, etc.), and if it was not for the skewed distribution of linguistic resources, we do not see why processing social media should be harder than processing newswire.

The skewed distribution underlines the need for new resources, and consequently, raises the important question whether *annotating* non-canonical language, e.g., social media text, is inherently harder than annotating canonical language. There is no priori reason why this should be the case. A full investigation of this question would take a lot of annotation studies, controlling for task, annotator groups, languages, etc.; something which is out of the scope of this squib. Instead, we present a pilot study of a single, specific linguistic annotation task (identifying main verbs and arguments) with two annotators and 50 sentences for each of five different domains (250 annotated sentences in total). Obviously, this is but a toy experiment, and our results should be taken with a grain of salt. However, our design is replicable, the annotated data available,[1] and we hope that others will take up replicating these experiments on a larger scale. Meanwhile, we leave the world with what our toy experiment suggests.

Note that we cannot just compare reported inter-annotator agreement scores across existing projects. Such scores are affected by sample biases, training of annotators, and the completeness of annotation guidelines. Thus, in this position paper we present an annotation study where we asked the *same* annotators to annotate canonical and non-canonical language (over five domains, ranging from newswire to Twitter) with minimal guidelines.

2 Annotating main verbs and arguments

We introduce the simple annotation task of identifying main predicates and arguments in sentences across five different domains.

Annotation Two expert annotators were asked to provide the following three labels:

1. MAINVERB (MV), the main lexical verb of the predicate, e.g., "he was **eating** apples".[2]
2. A0, the subject.
3. A1, which corresponds to two different syntactic functions. A1 is the direct object if there is a MV in the annotated sentence (i.e., "he had been eating **apples**") or the attribute in a copula construction ("he is **happy**").

The only guideline was not to mark auxiliaries, and that the first word in a coordination or multiword unit is the head.

DOMAIN	TOK	TTR	$\overline{SL}$	OOV
WSJ	743	0.56	14.86±2.93	4.2%
Twitter	657	0.67	13.14±3.30	**38.9%**
Answers	674	0.54	13.48±3.00	9.4%
Spoken	646	**0.35**	**12.92±3.05**	6.6%
Fiction	691	0.51	13.82±3.26	8.2%

Table 1: Data characteristics (50 sentences each).

Corpora We selected five different corpora constituting different degrees of perceived canonicity.

1. Wall Street Journal (WSJ): Section 23 from the Ontonotes distribution of the Wall Street Journal dependency treebank (Bies et al., 2012; Petrov and McDonald, 2012).
2. Answers: The Yahoo! Answers test section from the English Web Treebank (Bies et al., 2012; Petrov and McDonald, 2012).
3. Spoken: The Switchboard corpus section of the MASC corpus (Ide et al., 2008).
4. Fiction: The literature subset of the test section of the Brown test set from CoNLL 2008 (Surdeanu et al., 2008), which encompasses the *fiction, mystery, science-fiction, romance* and *humor* categories of the Brown corpus.
5. Twitter: The test section of the Tweebank dependency treebank (Kong et al., 2014).

WSJ is the perceived-of-as-canonical dataset. Answers and Twitter are datasets of social media texts from two different social media. We include Switchboard as an example of spoken language (transcriptions of telephone conversations), and Fiction to incorporate carefully edited (i.e., not user-generated) text that is lexically and syntactically different to newswire. From each corpus, we randomly selected 50 sentences and doubly-annotated them.

[1] `https://bitbucket.org/bplank/predicates`

[2] We follow the Stanford dependency convention in that copulative verbs are not treated as main verbs, and are dependents of the attribute. Thus, here the copula is not marked as MV.

DOMAIN	A0	A1	MV
WSJ	99	76	72
Twitter	88	72	56
Answers	92	79	63
Spoken	100	86	81
Fiction	96	76	78

Table 2: Frequency counts for arguments in the annotated data (50 sentences per domain, two annotators each).

	MATCH		F1			
DOMAIN	EXACT	FRAMES	A0	A1	MV	MICRO
WSJ	66%	82%	0.87	0.66	0.83	0.79
Twitter	52%	66%	0.91	0.69	0.79	0.80
Answers	74%	84%	0.98	0.81	0.88	**0.90**
Spoken	43%	74%	0.91	0.56	0.88	0.79
Fiction	64%	78%	0.83	0.75	0.79	0.80

Table 3: Agreement statistics between the two annotators.

DOMAIN	ρ
WSJ	0.8002
Twitter	0.7019
Answers	**0.6489**
Spoken	0.8165
Fiction	0.8406

Table 4: Correlation (Spearman's ρ) between annotator agreement (how many arguments match out of both) and system confidence (average per-edge confidence).

Table 1 provides statistics for all datasets, namely the amount of tokens (TOK), the type-token ratio (TTR), the average sentence length ($\overline{SL}$), and the out-of-vocabulary rate with regards to the WSJ training section (OOV). We use this last metric as an indicator on how much a domain deviates lexically from newswire. No normalization has been performed. Spoken data has the shortest sentences but the lowest TTR, that is, it is the domain with the highest lexical variation. Nevertheless, the domain with by far the highest OOV is Twitter. $\overline{SL}$ is 13–15 words for the five domains, with slightly longer sentences in newswire. Table 2 provides characteristics of the annotations, i.e., counts for the three annotation labels by both annotators without adjudication (i.e., over the union of the data annotated by two annotators). Subject dropping and imperative mood is common in Twitter, which decreases A0, and fully-formed clauses are also less frequent, thus affecting MV and A1. For completeness, we compare the annotations to the gold dependency trees available in the treebanks. We do so by computing labeled attachment scores for strictly the set of annotated words. The results range from 0.85 LAS on WSJ to 0.56 on Switchboard.

Results Table 3 shows label-wise and micro-averaged F1 scores between annotators for each of the domains. Surprisingly, we see among the lowest agreement on newswire, but all five domains seem about equally hard to annotate, except Answers (which is easier). Again, we remind the reader that this is miniature annotation study, but we think this is an interesting observation.

Newswire may be harder to understand because it is more complex language. For example, we observed that average sentence length was slightly longer for newswire. We measured the correlation between sentence length and sentence-wise agreement for all 250 annotated sentences, however, found the correlation to be low (0.1364). Consequently, it seems unlikely that sentence length had a major effect on our annotations.

We may speculate that annotation disagreements can be due to rare linguistic phenomena and linguistic outliers. In Table 4 we show the correlation per domain between sentence-wise agreement and dependency parsing confidence. We have obtained this confidence from the edge-wise confidence scores provided by an instance of the MST parser (McDonald et al., 2005) trained on WSJ. The parsing confidence for a sentence is obtained from the average of the edges that have received a label (A0, MV, A1) by the annotators, averaged between the two annotators. The correlation for newswire is high, but not the highest, because despite high parsing confidence, annotation agreement is rather low. On the other end, the lowest correlation between parser confidence and agreement is for Answers, which has the highest inter-annotator agreement.

These results, in our view, indicate that what makes annotating social media text hard (at times) is not what makes annotating newswire hard. We leave it for now to validate this finding on a larger scale, as well as to try to understand what makes annotating social media (relatively) hard.

	DOMAIN	FRAME	EXAMPLE
1	Twitter		@user he/A0 better/A1 !! we/A0 buy/MV his stuff/A1 ! haha
2	Spoken	x	those/A1A0 are the ones/A0A1 that I really really hate too
3	Spoken		I/**A0** agree/**MV** with you/A1 on that particular subject there
4	Fiction	x	" I/A0 mean/MV , do you/A0 feel/A1MV like seeing/A1 Kate " ? ?
5	Answers		– sigh – not trying/MV to sounds snooty or stuck up but I/A0 mean/MV really !
6	WSJ	x	Fidelty/**A0** on Saturday opened/**MV** its 54 walk/A1 – in investor centers/A1 across the country .
7	WSJ	x	Nevertheless , he/**A0** says/**MV** a depression does n't appear/A1 likely/A1 .

Table 5: Disagreement examples from all domains, annotator1=blue, annotator2=red, matches=black, Frame (cf., §3).

3 Discussion

Table 5 shows examples of different cases of disagreement from different domains. The native tokenization is kept intact. The FRAME column indicates whether the annotators provided the same valency frame, regardless of which words were said to be the arguments.

In Example 1, we can see a characteristic property of Twitter data, namely that there can be more than one sentence per tweet, and it is therefore often hard to decide what the main predicate is. Example 2 shows a copula case where the same frame is chosen by the two annotators, but they disagree which words satisfy which arguments. In Example 3, the annotators disagree on wether the verb "agree" has a valency-bound preposition ("with"), and thus whether it has a direct object or not. In Example 4, annotators disagree on whether "I mean" is the main clause, and thus the main predicate, or an off-clause satellite that roughly has the function of an interjection. In Example 5, annotators disagree what is the main clause. Example 6 shows disagreement caused by the difficulty to annotate already tokenized text, where it is not straightforward that the adjective "walk-in" has been tokenized apart. In Example 7, there is agreement on whether it is "appear" or "likely" that heads the subordinate clause and fulfills the A1 of the verb say. This disagreement stems from the copulative reading of "appear", which makes it a dependent of "likely" instead of its head in one case. To sum up, the main sources for disagreement stem from choice of main predicate and verb valency.

4 Conclusions

This squib presents a bold opinion and a severely underpowered pilot annotation study. The pilot study, in which we had professional annotators annotate main verbs and arguments with minimal guidelines, indicates that what some refer to as non-canonical language is not harder to annotate than canonical language. Our bold opinion is that the notion of canonical language is absurd and harmful, suggesting that some language, say, newswire, is better suited for linguistic resources than other types of language, say, spoken language or social media texts. What is considered non-canonical language is often the language that we use more often, and often commercially and scientifically more interesting. We believe there is no reason to expect that processing this type of text should be harder, with appropriate training data, and the pilot study presented here suggests that annotation is not harder either.

References

Ann Bies, Justin Mott, Colin Warner, and Seth Kulick. 2012. English web treebank. *Linguistic Data Consortium, Philadelphia, PA.*

Nancy Ide, Collin Baker, Christiane Fellbaum, and Charles Fillmore. 2008. Masc: The manually annotated sub-corpus of american english. In *LREC*.

Lingpeng Kong, Nathan Schneider, Swabha Swayamdipta, Archna Bhatia, Chris Dyer, and Noah A Smith. 2014. A dependency parser for tweets. In *EMNLP*.

Ryan McDonald, Koby Crammer, and Fernando Pereira. 2005. Online large-margin training of dependency parsers. In *ACL*.

Slav Petrov and Ryan McDonald. 2012. Overview of the 2012 Shared Task on Parsing the Web. In *Notes of the First Workshop on Syntactic Analysis of Non-Canonical Language (SANCL)*.

Mihai Surdeanu, Richard Johansson, Adam Meyers, Lluís Màrquez, and Joakim Nivre. 2008. The conll-2008 shared task on joint parsing of syntactic and semantic dependencies. In *CoNLL*.

What I've learned about annotating informal text (and why you shouldn't take my word for it)

Nathan Schneider
School of Informatics
University of Edinburgh
Edinburgh, Scotland, UK
nschneid@inf.ed.ac.uk

1 Introduction

In conjunction with this year's LAW theme, "Syntactic Annotation of Non-canonical Language" (NCL), I have been asked to weigh in on several important questions faced by anyone wishing to create annotated resources of NCLs.

My experience with syntactic annotation of non-canonical language falls under an effort undertaken at Carnegie Mellon University with the aim of building an NLP pipeline for syntactic analysis of Twitter text. We designed a linguistically-grounded annotation scheme, applied it to tweets, and then trained statistical analyzers—first for part-of-speech (POS) tags (Gimpel et al., 2011; Owoputi et al., 2012), then for parses (Schneider et al., 2013; Kong et al., 2014). I will review some of the salient points from this work in addressing the broader questions about annotation methodology.

2 Annotation Scheming

Many annotation schemes have been designed for "canonical" forms of language, such as text in a standard dialect formally edited to meet certain style conventions. In order to annotate non-canonical forms of language, one must determine whether existing schemes should be (a) applied as is, (b) adapted, or (c) avoided in favor of a new scheme. Designing a new annotation scheme is not to be undertaken lightly; on the other hand, if an existing scheme really does not fit the resources, then applying it will likely be a waste of time—because the distinctions it makes are not useful, or because the cost of obtaining the desired number of annotations at the desired level of quality will be too high.

A formula for computing the tradeoffs involved in selecting an annotation scheme would have to involve several variables:

- upfront cost (money, time)—e.g., in writing documentation, building the annotation platform, training annotators
- unit cost (money, time)

interact with

- quality/reliability—will depend on annotator expertise and training, and thoroughness of quality control procedures
- volume
- richness/informativeness—i.e., how many distinctions does the scheme make?
- usefulness/applicability—i.e., how valuable are the annotations for some purpose?

It is clear that higher volume, reliability, and richness will tend to incur higher costs. Usefulness for some downstream application may or may not be clear and measurable during annotation,[1] though frameworks like active learning (Settles, 2012) do take it into explicit consideration to make the annotation process more cost-effective.

We come, then, to the main question: **When is it worth designing a new annotation scheme?** My answer is, *When annotating with an existing scheme would be more painful (costly) than starting afresh.* The second question, **What level of granularity?**, is similarly answered by weighing these tradeoffs: too coarse, and the annotations will not be very informative or useful; too fine, and training annotators will be costly, the annotation will be slow, annotator

[1]And, if a scheme is intended to be general-purpose, usefulness would have to be measured on a battery of tasks to be meaningful.

Proceedings of LAW IX - The 9th Linguistic Annotation Workshop, pages 152–157,
Denver, Colorado, June 5, 2015. ©2015 Association for Computational Linguistics

`the > dog` *or* `dog < the`
unlabeled dependency
`[Barack Obama]`
multiword node
`{a silver} > dollar`
nodes with same head
`(even though)`
underspecified relationship
`so > cool** lolz**`
roots

Texas Rangers are in the World Series ! Go Rangers !!!!!!!!! http://fb.me/D2LsXBJx

```
[Texas Rangers~1] > are** < in
in < (the > [World Series])
Go** < Rangers~2
```

Found the scarriest mystery door in my school . I'M SO CURIOUS D:

```
Found** < (the scarriest mystery door*)
(Found* door in)
in < (my > school)
I'M** < (SO > CURIOUS)
D:**
```

Figure 1: FUDG GFL notation summary and two annotated Twitter examples.

reliability will be low, and some categories may be highly sparse. Estimating these tradeoffs in a particular setting is a qualitative judgment call, so in lieu of a more concrete general principle, I will share some illustrative examples from my own experience.

Twitter POS. Gimpel et al. (2011) introduced (and Owoputi et al., 2012 documented in greater detail) a coarse-grained POS tagset for English tweets. Given that the eventual goal was to build a syntactic parser, we considered extending the Penn Treebank (Marcus et al., 1993) tagset with a few additional tags for social media phenomena (such as emoticons and hashtags). However, we also wanted a "lightweight" tagset to facilitate rapid annotation, and did not feel that the fine-grained inflectional distinctions made in the PTB tags—`VB`, `VBP`, `VBZ`, `VBG`, `VBD`, and `VBN` indicating different forms of verbs, for instance—were an ideal use of annotators' time.

We ultimately decided to craft a tagset coarser grained than the 45 PTB categories, and similar to Petrov et al.'s (2011) "universal" set of 12 categories,[2] but with additional categories suited to tweets: `!` (interjection), `E` (emoticon), `U` (URL), `#` (extrasyntactic hashtag), `@` (at-mention), and `~` (online discourse marker). Finally, we felt that it would be difficult to force a tokenization of nonstandard words like `ima` ("I'm going to"), so we opted for a minimal tokenization and added 5 complex tags for {nominal, proper noun}+{verbal, possessive}, and existential *there* or predeterminer + verbal. This tagset had 20 tags, which proved manageable for a rapid short-term annotation effort. Other Twitter syntax projects, however, chose to adapt the PTB tagset, with the advantage that their data would be more closely compatible with existing resources and tools (Ritter et al., 2011; Foster et al., 2011a,b).

Twitter Treebanking. In annotating a treebank for Twitter, we estimated that a large volume of data at a coarse level of granularity would be more valuable for training parsers than a small amount of data with fine-grained labels. We thus developed Fragmentary Unlabeled Dependency Grammar (FUDG), an annotation scheme for unlabeled dependencies, and applied it to build the TWEEBANK corpus (Schneider et al., 2013; Kong et al., 2014). This scheme does make a couple of special distinctions—it provides special structures for coordination and multiword expressions, which occur in all text genres, and also allows multiple syntactic utterances/sentences per tweet—but by and large, it rests on the assumption that syntactic relations can be characterized as trees of head–modifier dependencies. (Accommodations for cases where it is difficult to determine those dependencies fully are described below.)

3 On Ambiguity

The third question asks: **Can the concept of "gold annotations" be applied to non-canonical languages where the inherent ambiguity in the data makes it hard to decide on the "ground truth" of an utterance?**

First, I think it is important to address the sources of ambiguity. The text that we encounter is (presumably) intended to be understood by someone. Of course, in unedited text there will be occasional errors—accidental misspellings, omitted words, etc.—that might render the utterance uninterpretable, and there may be fewer distinguishing orthographic cues (like capitalization). Even without production errors

[2]Unlike Petrov et al. (2011), we distinguished proper nouns from common nouns, as this distinction is beneficial for named entity recognition.

or orthographic ambiguities, the annotator may lack context that was available to the intended audience, or there may be genuine linguistic differences between the writer and annotator (e.g., unfamiliar slang). On occasion, we have to discard utterly uninterpretable utterances. In other cases we might misinterpret the utterance—but so long as it is a valid human interpetation, this is not necessarily a problem if the goal is to train a parser.

The FUDG framework (Schneider et al., 2013) provides a solution for some forms of syntactic ambiguity: it allows the annotator to **underspecify** parts of the parse. Essentially, the annotation provides a set of constraints which may be consistent with more than one tree. Tokens not mentioned in the constraints are unconstrained—they could be attached to any head in a full analysis consistent with the annotation.

It is also possible to constrain nodes' attachments without specifying their full structure. In Found the scarriest mystery door in my school . (shown with its annotation in the right side of figure 1), there is a subtle PP attachment ambiguity: what was in the school, the door or its discovery?[3] The annotation permits both possibilities via a **fudge expression**: the line `(Found* door in)` imposes the constraint that Found, door, and in must together form a connected subgraph, and (indicated by the asterisk) that Found must be the head of that subgraph. Thus, Found must have as daughters both door and in, or one of them, in which case the other one is the granddaughter to Found.[4]

4 The Annotation Process

When considering the merits of an annotation scheme, it can be easy to forget that the scheme will ultimately be embedded in an annotation process. A full **annotation framework** encapsulates the formal annotation scheme (e.g., tagset, units of annotation), linguistic conventions for its application, documentation, an annotation tool, a means of recruiting and compensating annotators, processes and materials for training annotators, procedures for validation and measuring inter-annotator agreement, etc. As suggested above, the design of the linguistic scheme cannot always be divorced from the practicalities of how it is to be applied to data. Likewise, not all tools and processes are appropriate for all schemes.

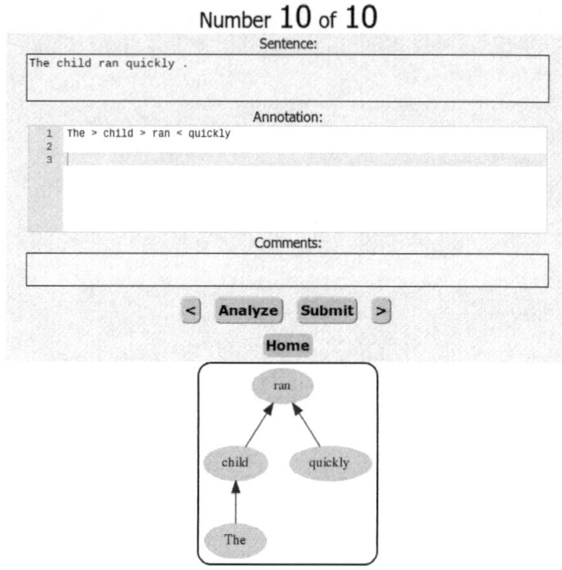

Figure 2: A simple training sentence in the FUDG/GFL annotation tool (Mordowanec et al., 2014).

What are the considerations when choosing the level of expertise of the annotators? When is crowd sourcing appropriate? When do we need linguistic experts?

I find it useful to distinguish annotators along two dimensions. They can be **naïve**, **familiar**, or **expert** at understanding the linguistic phenomena of interest; and they can be **anonymous**—recruited from some general pool of users (such as Amazon Mechanical Turk), and possibly not serious about the task—or **trusted**—honestly willing to do what is asked of them (regardless of their *ability*). While there is crowdsourcing literature on making conventional annotation schemes more cost-effective with anonymous, naïve annotators (e.g., Snow et al., 2008; Hovy et al., 2014), success in this form of crowdsourcing requires the annotation task to be well understood (because it is more difficult to get useful feedback about challenging aspects of the task).

[3]Presumably both, semantically speaking. But this is not merely an issue of annotation conventions: if the scarriest mystery door in my school is a noun phrase, then the PP can be interpreted as expressing the set over which the superlative operates (i.e., 'the scariest out of all the doors in the school'); whereas if the superlative is functioning as an intensifier, it could be the scariest out of all doors in the world.

[4]I.e., `(Found* door in)` is consistent with any of the following: `Found < door < in`, `Found < in < door`, `Found < {door, in}`. The second of these, which is obviously incorrect, is ruled out by the first line of the annotation.

By contrast, the annotation schemes I have discussed above had never been piloted. We instead used a pool of local (trusted) annotators who were, for the most part, familiar with the fundamentals of POS/dependency representations but lacking in advanced training in syntax. Most of them were language technologies graduate students primarily trained as computer scientists. Given their fluency with text-based programming languages, we decided to formulate a similar language for FUDG dependency annotation—the Graph Fragment Language (GFL), whose notation is summarized in figure 1. In initial pilot studies, annotators were asked to annotate the data directly in text files, but this did not scale well because there was no immediate check for well-formedness of their input. Thus, for a larger annotation effort, we built a custom web interface for GFL annotations that produces an immediate graphical visualization of the parse (figure 2; Mordowanec et al., 2014). This framework seemed to work well, though we did not build a point-and-click treebanking interface for comparison.

Kong et al. (2014) present some analyses of the 900-tweet/12k-token TWEEBANK corpus. Most of its annotations were collected in a single a day from two dozen annotators, most of them *familiar* and a few of them *expert* with respect to syntactic representation and English grammar. Several quality measures are reported, but the main finding is that despite some noise in the data, training on TWEEBANK data (instead of out-of-domain training data) produces "a 7.8% gain [in parsing accuracy] with an order of magnitude less annotated data" (Kong et al., 2014, p. 1008). We take this as evidence that trusted non-expert annotations of linguistic structure can be useful. Whether naïve or anonymous annotators could be trained to do dependency annotation is an open question.

For building new resources for NCLs, is it still worthwhile to invest a huge amount of time and human labour for manual annotation, considering that the annotators spend most of their time making arbitrary decisions, and that the aim of building 'high-quality resources' for NCLs might not be realistic?

The Twitter syntactic annotation described above relied on fairly simple schemes distributed among many annotators over a short timeframe. The data produced by this approach has proved beneficial for training Twitter taggers and parsers—at least, relative to no in-domain data. The customization of the annotation schemes for the domain (including permitting underspecification) was intended to reduce the number of arbitrary decisions. (Our dependency annotation guidelines were fairly brief, and annotators were encouraged to avail themselves of underspecification when they encountered syntactic constructions not clearly addressed by the guidelines.)

It is, however, difficult to generalize beyond the framing of the tasks addressed here. I would not, for example, argue that the English Web Treebank (Bies et al., 2012)—a high-quality resource covering five genres of online text in the style of the Penn Treebank—was a wasted effort. But it will, I hope, permit experimentation testing whether the benefits of the full resource (for extrinsic tasks) can be approximated with smaller, less expert, cheaper annotations.

5 Why you shouldn't take my word for it

As with any annotation framework, it is difficult to say exactly which aspects of the setup were successful and which aspects could have been improved. To do so would have required a great many controlled annotation studies, whereas we were focused on producing as much useful data as possible given a limited budget. And of course, it's possible that a more conventional approach to annotation with fewer annotators would have produced more useful data.

In general, it has been my experience that—some well-established best practices notwithstanding—designing an annotation framework involves a mixture of guesswork, intuition, and trial and error. I hope future research will succeed at making this process more empirical and more predictable (see also Hovy and Lavid, 2010; Garrette and Baldridge, 2013). There is a great deal more to discover with regard to understanding the range of text varieties (Baldwin et al., 2013), building statistical models of annotator bias (Snow et al., 2008; Hovy et al., 2013; Passonneau and Carpenter, 2014), automatically detecting inconsistencies in linguistic data (Dickinson and Meurers, 2003; Loftsson, 2009; Kato and Matsubara, 2010), and bringing extrinsic models into the annotation loop (Baldridge and Osborne, 2004; Baldridge and Palmer, 2009; Settles, 2012).

Acknowledgments

I would like to thank the LAW organizers for hosting a panel on this topic, and Noah Smith, Bonnie Webber, and Archna Bhatia for their comments on a draft of this piece.

References

Jason Baldridge and Miles Osborne. 2004. Active learning and the total cost of annotation. In Dekang Lin and Dekai Wu, editors, *Proc. of EMNLP*, pages 9–16. Barcelona, Spain.

Jason Baldridge and Alexis Palmer. 2009. How well does active learning actually work? Time-based evaluation of cost-reduction strategies for language documentation. In *Proc. of EMNLP*, pages 296–305. Suntec, Singapore.

Timothy Baldwin, Paul Cook, Marco Lui, Andrew MacKinlay, and Li Wang. 2013. How noisy social media text, how diffrnt social media sources? In *Proc. of IJCNLP*, pages 356–364. Nagoya, Japan.

Ann Bies, Justin Mott, Colin Warner, and Seth Kulick. 2012. English Web Treebank. Technical Report LDC2012T13, Linguistic Data Consortium, Philadelphia, PA. URL `http://www.ldc.upenn.edu/Catalog/catalogEntry.jsp?catalogId=LDC2012T13`.

Markus Dickinson and W. Detmar Meurers. 2003. Detecting errors in part-of-speech annotation. In *Proc. of EACL*, pages 107–114. Budapest, Hungary.

Jennifer Foster, Özlem Çetinoğlu, Joachim Wagner, Joseph Le Roux, Stephen Hogan, Joakim Nivre, Deirdre Hogan, and Josef van Genabith. 2011a. #hardtoparse: POS tagging and parsing the Twitterverse. In *Proc. of the 2011 AAAI Workshop on Analyzing Microtext*, pages 20–25. San Francisco, CA.

Jennifer Foster, Özlem Çetinoğlu, Joachim Wagner, Joseph Le Roux, Joakim Nivre, Deirdre Hogan, and Josef van Genabith. 2011b. From news to comment: resources and benchmarks for parsing the language of Web 2.0. In *Proc. of IJCNLP*, pages 893–901. Chiang Mai, Thailand.

Dan Garrette and Jason Baldridge. 2013. Learning a part-of-speech tagger from two hours of annotation. In *Proc. of NAACL-HLT*, pages 138–147. Atlanta, Georgia, USA.

Kevin Gimpel, Nathan Schneider, Brendan O'Connor, Dipanjan Das, Daniel Mills, Jacob Eisenstein, Michael Heilman, Dani Yogatama, Jeffrey Flanigan, and Noah A. Smith. 2011. Part-of-speech tagging for Twitter: annotation, features, and experiments. In *Proc. of ACL-HLT*, pages 42–47. Portland, Oregon, USA.

Dirk Hovy, Taylor Berg-Kirkpatrick, Ashish Vaswani, and Eduard Hovy. 2013. Learning whom to trust with MACE. In *Proc. of NAACL-HLT*, pages 1120–1130. Atlanta, Georgia, USA.

Dirk Hovy, Barbara Plank, and Anders Søgaard. 2014. Experiments with crowdsourced re-annotation of a POS tagging data set. In *Proc. of ACL*, pages 377–382. Baltimore, Maryland, USA.

Eduard Hovy and Julia Lavid. 2010. Towards a 'science' of corpus annotation: a new methodological challenge for corpus linguistics. *International journal of translation*, 22(1):13–36.

Yoshihide Kato and Shigeki Matsubara. 2010. Correcting errors in a treebank based on synchronous tree substitution grammar. In *Proc. of ACL*, pages 74–79. Uppsala, Sweden.

Lingpeng Kong, Nathan Schneider, Swabha Swayamdipta, Archna Bhatia, Chris Dyer, and Noah A. Smith. 2014. A dependency parser for tweets. In *Proc. of EMNLP*, pages 1001–1012. Doha, Qatar.

Hrafn Loftsson. 2009. Correcting a POS-tagged corpus using three complementary methods. In *Proc. of EACL*, pages 523–531. Athens, Greece.

Mitchell P. Marcus, Beatrice Santorini, and Mary Ann Marcinkiewicz. 1993. Building a large annotated corpus of English: the Penn Treebank. *Computational Linguistics*, 19(2):313–330.

Michael T. Mordowanec, Nathan Schneider, Chris Dyer, and Noah A. Smith. 2014. Simplified dependency annotations with GFL-Web. In *Proc. of 52nd Annual Meeting of the Association for Computational Linguistics: System Demonstrations*, pages 121–126. Baltimore, Maryland, USA.

Olutobi Owoputi, Brendan O'Connor, Chris Dyer, Kevin Gimpel, and Nathan Schneider. 2012. Part-of-speech tagging for Twitter: word clusters and other advances. Technical Report CMU-ML-12-107, Carnegie Mellon University, Pittsburgh, Pennsylvania. URL `http://www.ark.cs.cmu.edu/TweetNLP/owoputi+etal.tr12.pdf`.

Rebecca J. Passonneau and Bob Carpenter. 2014. The benefits of a model of annotation. *Transactions of the Association for Computational Linguistics*, 2:311–326.

Slav Petrov, Dipanjan Das, and Ryan McDonald. 2011. A universal part-of-speech tagset. *arXiv:1104.2086 [cs]*. URL `http://arxiv.org/abs/1104.2086`, arXiv: 1104.2086.

Alan Ritter, Sam Clark, Mausam, and Oren Etzioni. 2011. Named entity recognition in tweets: an experimental study. In *Proc. of EMNLP*, pages 1524–1534. Edinburgh, Scotland, UK.

Nathan Schneider, Brendan O'Connor, Naomi Saphra,

David Bamman, Manaal Faruqui, Noah A. Smith, Chris Dyer, and Jason Baldridge. 2013. A framework for (under)specifying dependency syntax without overloading annotators. In *Proc. of the 7th Linguistic Annotation Workshop and Interoperability with Discourse*, pages 51–60. Sofia, Bulgaria.

Burr Settles. 2012. *Active Learning*. Number 18 in Synthesis Lectures on Artificial Intelligence and Machine Learning. Morgan & Claypool, San Rafael, CA.

Rion Snow, Brendan O'Connor, Daniel Jurafsky, and Andrew Ng. 2008. Cheap and fast — but is it good? Evaluating non-expert annotations for natural language tasks. In *Proc. of EMNLP*, pages 254–263. Honolulu, Hawaii.

On Grammaticality in the Syntactic Annotation of Learner Language

Markus Dickinson
Indiana University
Bloomington, IN USA
md7@indiana.edu

Marwa Ragheb
Indiana University
Bloomington, IN USA
mragheb@indiana.edu

Abstract

We examine some non-canonical annotation categories that license missing material (ellipses and enumerations). In extending these categories to learner data, the distinctions seem to require an annotator to determine whether a sentence is grammatical or not when deciding between particular analyses. We unpack the assumptions surrounding the annotation of learner language and how these particular phenomena compare to competing analyses, pointing out the implications for annotation practice and second language analysis.

1 Introduction and Motivation

The grammatical principles underlying linguistic annotation are often only implicit. The implicitness and undercommittal to any particular theory can be beneficial, as it: 1) allows multiple users of the annotation to utilize it in different ways; 2) frees annotators to extend existing categories to unforeseen constructions; and 3) treats annotation as indices for others to derive theories from. Without necessarily having to be a theoretically-driven corpus (Oepen et al., 2004), there are cases, however, where a grammatical model for annotation may need to be made more explicit and the annotation categories more precise. For non-canonical data (e.g., historical, second language, and internet data), a thorough definition of language categories should lead to a consistent application throughout a corpus. As one example, knowing whether a hashtag denotes a syntactic unit (e.g., *Got #college admissions questions ?*) is important for obtaining a syntactic tree for Twitter data (Kong et al., 2014). Even for canonical data, annotation categories are not truly meaningful without some specification or guidelines (Rambow, 2010). We here explore *non-canonical categories* for *non-canonical data*, specifically categories that license "missing" material (ellipsis, enumeration) in the context of second language learner data, and we demonstrate that one needs to make clear to what extent the categories in the grammar underlying the annotation extend to novel constructions.

To gauge the impact on second language data of categories designed to cover more "peripheral" phenomena involving missing material requires investigating, first, how these categories apply in general, and, secondly, how they extend to learner data and how they compare to competing, learner-specific analyses. We refer to categories which license missing (or additional) semantic material as *non-canonical categories*. Applying such categories to learner data makes us question to what degree we need to know whether a sentence is grammatical—where *grammatical* refers to being licensed by the grammar underlying the annotation.

Focusing on the data of second language learners and the annotation of syntactic dependencies, the question of grammaticality is compounded, not just by novel constructions, but by various research practices. First, there is a long literature in second language acquisition (SLA) as to the nature of a second language grammar (*interlanguage*) (Selinker, 1972; Adjemian, 1976; Ellis, 1985; Lakshmanan and Selinker, 2001). Secondly, and sometimes competingly, there are many schemes for annotating learner errors in corpora (Díaz-Negrillo and Fernández-

Proceedings of LAW IX - The 9th Linguistic Annotation Workshop, pages 158–167,
Denver, Colorado, June 5, 2015. ©2015 Association for Computational Linguistics

Domínguez, 2006; Granger, 2003; Nicholls, 2003; Lüdeling et al., 2005), where direct or indirect reference is made to target (i.e., native) grammars in the annotation of corrections. Part of the tension between these approaches is to what extent the grammatical categories used for native language are applicable to learner data.

Thus, non-canonical categories are worth investigating not just to improve corpus annotation, but also to provide insight into these traditions. In particular, there has been much discussion in SLA regarding the comparative fallacy (Bley-Vroman, 1983; Lakshmanan and Selinker, 2001; Tenfjord et al., 2006), wherein learner language is (over)compared to the target language, and the degree to which such comparison affects the conclusions drawn. The grammatical annotation of learner language is in some sense ideal for providing insight, as it provides a systematic characterization of everything in the data and thus allows one to assess the degree of over-comparison (Ragheb, 2014).

In section 2 we discuss the aims of linguistic annotation for learner data, which leads directly to a unpacking of the grammaticality assumed in such annotation in section 3—examining both the source of the grammar and the way innovative learner examples do or do not fit within the categories given by that grammar. After setting this stage, we turn to our two main areas of phenomena: 1) ellipsis and missing heads (section 4); and 2) coordination, enumeration, and missing conjunctions (section 5). After seeing the issues involved in these categories and in the decision procedure for annotation (section 6)—at least for one annotation scheme—we conclude in section 7 that the main options for annotation are: 1) apply the native categories even to learner innovations; 2) develop tighter restrictions on the native categories; and/or 3) reference sentence-level grammaticality in the definitions of categories.

This paper will likely raise more questions than it provides answers, as "answers" are ultimately going to be specific to one's particular goals and project. However, we believe the questions are crucial to annotating learner language: indeed, our own motivation for raising these questions stems from syntactically annotating our own learner corpus (Ragheb, 2014; Ragheb and Dickinson, 2014; Dickinson and Ragheb, 2013) and realizing we needed clarification of certain categories, in particular those dealing with missing elements.

We examine phenomena surrounding ellipsis and enumeration because they are the main ones in our annotation scheme that license missing material, and missing material is important to investigate in the context of learner language, as learners often omit structures, e.g., determiners (see (Ragheb, 2014), ch. 7, and references therein). One other category could potentially be confused with categories licensing missing material, namely serial verb (SRL), which licenses a sequence of two verbs without a connector (similar to enumeration). In *come hang with us*, for example, *hang* is a SRL dependent of *come*. We ignore this category because: a) it is restricted to *come* and *go*; b) what we say about distinguishing coordination from enumeration (section 5) can more or less be applied to SRL; and c) we have not noticed it specifically causing confusion.

2 Linguistic Annotation for Learner Data

As argued in (Ragheb and Dickinson, 2011), one way to approach the annotation of learner corpora is by annotating linguistic properties. A starting assumption is that the categories used for learner language are similar enough to those for native language to use native categories. However, one quickly finds that linguistic categories for native speaker data are inadequate to represent the full range of learner productions (Díaz-Negrillo et al., 2010). For example, in (1),[1] the word *he* cannot simply be marked as a nominative or accusative pronoun because in some sense it is both. Thus, one may want to annotate multiple layers, in this case one POS layer for morphological evidence and one for syntactic distributional evidence (i.e., position).

(1) I must play with **he**.

While errors (i.e., ungrammaticalities) can be derived from mismatches between annotation layers, they are not primary entities. The multi-layer linguistic annotation is primarily based on linguistic evidence, not a sentence's correctness.

There are two main wrinkles to separating linguistic annotation from error annotation, however:

[1]Example sentences in this paper come from the SALLE corpus, comprised of essays from an Intensive English Program.

1) annotation categories could employ a notion of grammatical correctness to define; and 2) the decision process for ambiguous cases could reference a sentence's correctness. In the former case, the issue often has to do with using categories that are not always clearly defined for native data, while in the latter case, the issue is in having categories which—even if well-defined on different annotation layers—are insufficient to handle the usage the learner presents. In the next few sections we discuss issues surrounding non-canonical annotation categories and discuss the effect of the decision procedure in section 6.

To make the issues concrete, we rely on the syntactic annotation of the SALLE (Syntactically Annotating Learner Language of English) project (Ragheb, 2014; Ragheb and Dickinson, 2014), which employs multi-layer annotation. The issues are not specific to this annotation, but it illustrates the difficulties in applying native categories to learner data. That is, the SALLE annotation scheme (Dickinson and Ragheb, 2013) helps define questions of what constitutes appropriate linguistic annotation for interlanguage.[2]

3 Grammatical Annotation

When annotating learner data, it is important to know what is meant by *grammatical*. For error annotation, for example, this defines what an error is; e.g., in Korean, a missing postpositional particle may be an error or not depending on the level of formality underpinning grammaticality (Lee et al., 2012). The SALLE framework assumes a grammar based on the target language as an underpinning to the annotation (section 3.1), but, in the face of innovative learner usage, has focused on annotating the language as it appears and not on whether each sentence deviates from that grammar, i.e., is ungrammatical or not (section 3.2).

3.1 Target language grammar

To see the need to make clear the source of grammaticality, consider morphological POS annotation (section 2). In a verbal sequence like *can promotes*, for example, *promotes* intuitively has the morphological evidence of a third person singular verb. But to reference these morphological properties requires some notion of how these properties are defined, e.g., how *-s* stands for third person singular.

One obvious source of information is that "third person singular" comes from the definition of the *-s* morpheme in English. To annotate this way means referencing grammatical concepts from the target language (L2). If a different grammar is chosen to define categories, such as the learner's first language (L1), one might posit, e.g., *-et* as an indicator of "third person singular" (cf. Russian). In (Ragheb and Dickinson, 2012), we argue for using the L2 as the source of the grammar, as learners share many aspects of development in the L2 (Ellis, 2008) and as this can ensure annotation reliability.

3.2 Emerging categories

Annotation deals with the way facts from the grammar interact with phenomena occuring within a sentence. Consider objects, for example: a constellation of properties allows one to specify that two different sentences both contain them. Objects can be defined as: a) occurring, roughly speaking, after a verb (**syntactic distribution**); b) fitting into the argument structure of a verb, typically as a patient/theme (**semantic distribution**); and c) taking accusative case, as appropriate, e.g., *him* (**morphological distribution**). The class of objects emerges from these same patterns occurring across sentences within, in this case, English, and the task of annotation is to see whether a new instance fits into this class.

A distinction between categories—e.g., subjects and objects—arises from them having different sets of (typical) properties. With learner phenomena, there appear to be *new* kinds of emergent categories, ones which may overlap with previously-defined categories. When this happens, one has to specify which of the two categories a particular language instance falls into, and one way may be to say, "Category X is grammatical/native-like; category Y is not." It such cases we cover in the next two sections.

Before examining non-canonical categories, though, consider objects as they relate to the the usage of, for instance, *one* in (2). Does *one* fit the (target) category of object (OBJ), some other target category, or something else entirely?

(2) When I was in my country , I dreamed **one** I

[2]Guidelines at: `http://cl.indiana.edu/~salle/`

can go to a typical American city .

One possible approach (Reznicek et al., 2013; Rehbein et al., 2012) is to say: 1) the usage of *one* is non-native; 2) a native-like target is *I dreamed that one day I could go ...*; and 3) the grammatical annotation of *one* can thus be based upon this target form (e.g., as a type of temporal adjunct of *can go*).

The approach used in SALLE, by contrast, assumes that, after splitting out the linguisitic evidence into different layers (section 2), many learner innovations should be able to fit into an existing target category. In this case, the **morphosyntactic dependency** annotation layer ignores the semantic definition of OBJ and focuses on the fact that *one* occurs as a post-verbal nominal and is consistent with being accusative case. Thus, it can be annotated as conveying the evidence of the target category OBJ.

The point here is that this style of annotation employs definitions from a target grammar, in lieu of creating learner-specific categories or creating target forms that make clear a discrepancy between non-native and native categories, i.e., which deem a sentence ungrammatical. For canonical categories, individual learner instances can be difficult to categorize, but the categories themselves are, generally speaking, relatively well-defined.

4 Ellipsis and Missing Heads

4.1 Ellipsis

Ellipsis concerns omitted material in a sentence. In SALLE, an ELL label marks the relation between two categories that normally would not have a relation, but nonetheless do because of missing material. This ELL label collapses several elliptical relations in the CHILDES project (MacWhinney, 2000) (sec. 12.2), where pairs of labels denote the chain of dependencies that, in a sense, should be present between the two words (e.g., DET-OBJ). ELL is used when no other relation is possible and the dependent relation is not possible to specify locally, i.e., without crossing branches. An example is given in (3).

(3) I am a graduated **Biologist** actually an **Ecologist** .

Here, *Ecologist* restates *Biologist* as an appositive; the adverb *actually*, however, is a verbal modifier. To indicate an elliptical structure (cf. *actually [I am] an Ecologist*), *actually* is annotated as an ELL dependent of *Ecologist*, as in figure 1. The word missing its head takes the ELL label (*actually*) and attaches to the head of the construction (*Ecologist*).[3]

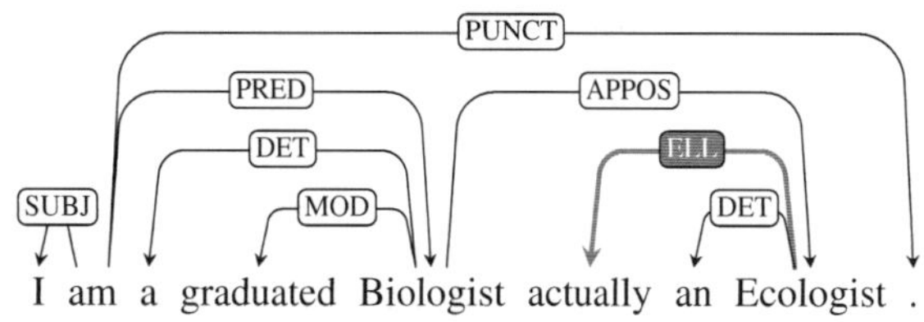

Figure 1: Appositive with an elliptical modifier

4.2 Missing heads

There are other cases of missing heads which are more clearly ungrammatical. One common case for learners concerns the omission of a finite verb in a sentence, as in (4). An analysis which continues the usage of the ELL label would annotate it as in figure 2(a), where the label mitigates the relation between *people* (what would be the subject if *are* were present) and *friendly* (what would be the predicate). Also shown here is a **subcategorization** layer, indicating which arguments each word is selecting for.

(4) Also , the people in it very friendly .

There is something satisfying and dissatisfying about the analysis. On the one hand, it stays in line with the annotation scheme by not marking anything peculiar. On the other hand, it poses two problems: 1) given the general side effect of mismatches between annotation layers when something is ungrammatical, one expects there to be a mismatch here, yet there is not; and 2) given the goal to annotate based on the evidence at hand, one would hope to provide a more informative label than ELL when possible. For example, *people* is a SUBJ of *friendly*, at least in some semantic sense.

Unlike the cases of ellipsis in section 4.1, there is no head recoverable from the context; i.e., unlike in (3) where *am* is present but just non-local, we do not have *are* anywhere in the context. The evidence

[3]Note that the ELL label only concerns missing heads, whereas the term *ellipsis* is generally used more broadly (e.g., (Sag, 1976)); missing dependents are handled differently, as discussed in (Dickinson and Ragheb, 2013) (sec. 5.1.2).

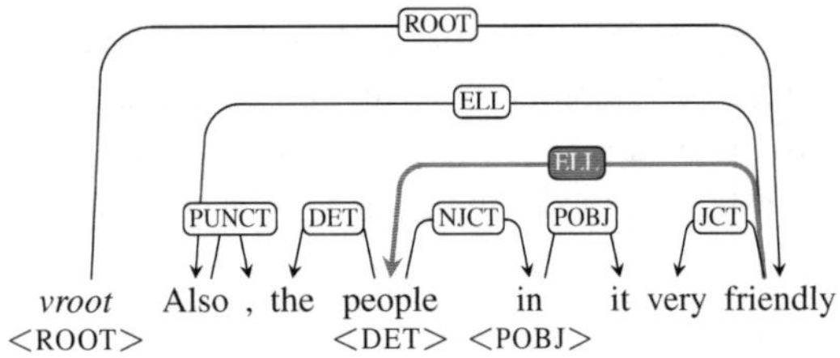

(a) ELL analysis of missing copula

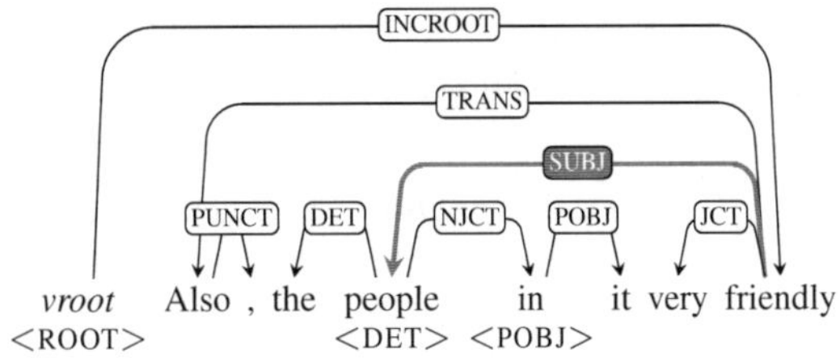

(b) Missing head analysis of missing copula

Figure 2: Example of a missing copula

for this particular case is thus qualitatively different than in the more traditional elliptical cases—and so one may want to treat such cases differently.

There is additional reason for a separate missing head analysis: for some sentences, it is almost unavoidable to posit a missing head. Consider (5), where a purpose clause lacks the infinitive marker *to*. The construction *in order to* is more of a fixed form, and it is clear that a particular function word is missing. While ellipsis is governed by some principles (syntactic or otherwise) (e.g., (Sag, 1976; Goldberg, 2005; Culicover and Jackendoff, 2005)), learners can freely omit heads (and dependents) of various kinds—content or function words, fixed forms or open-ended constructions, etc.—and learner language annotation thus seems to need a separate treatment of missing heads.

(5) . . . I need more natural and friendly place to live with my wife **in order understand** each values and natures . . .

The treatment of (4) in SALLE is shown in figure 2(b). Here, *people* is the SUBJ of *friendly*; unlike ELL, SUBJ is an argument label, meaning it should be subcategorized for, but here it is not (indicated by having no <SUBJ>). Thus, there is a mismatch in annotation, and an informative, evidence-based label (SUBJ) being used. However, the sentence is treated differently than some other cases with missing heads, namely ones deemed elliptical.

4.3 Ellipsis vs. missing head

The details of each particular analysis are less important than noting the decision to make: should ellipsis annotation extend to non-native missing head constructions? There is evidence suggesting that at least some types of these cases are different (e.g., non-local presence/absence of the locally missing head) and thus the ellipsis category may no longer apply.[4] Additionally, there is an open question as to whether one wishes to refer to elliptical constructions as grammatical and missing heads as ungrammatical in determining the distinction.

5 Coordination and Enumeration

Coordination and enumeration feature a similar dichotomy, potentially dependent upon a sentence's grammaticality when no conjunction is present.

5.1 Coordination

Coordination in SALLE is right-branching. In figure 3, for example, *knowledge* serves as the prepositional object (POBJ); *and* is the CCC dependent of *knowledge*; and *personality* is the final coordination (COORD) element. An MCOORD (modificatory coordination) label is used between non-final elements in coordinations of three or more elements. COORD is an argument label and is thus subcategorized for (<COORD>), whereas MCOORD is not.[5]

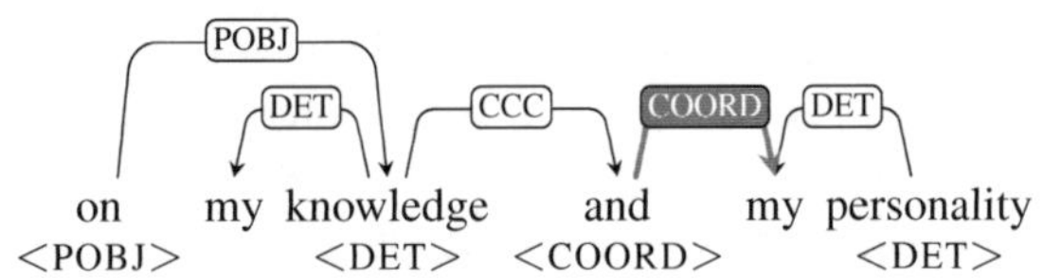

Figure 3: Treatment of basic coordination

[4]There are various other distinctions between figure 2(a) and figure 2(b), owing to other annotation scheme criteria, which we do not delve into here, i.e., ROOT vs. INCROOT, ELL vs. TRANS. See (Dickinson and Ragheb, 2013) for details.

[5]The right-branching analysis handles interactions with subcategorization for learner innovations; nothing hinges on this choice for the current paper, but for more details and argumentation, see (Dickinson and Ragheb, 2011).

5.2 Enumeration

SALLE also includes an enumeration label for lists of things. In line with coordination, they are treated as right-branching, with an ENUM label, as illustrated in figure 4. ENUM is not an argument label and thus does not need to be subcategorized for.

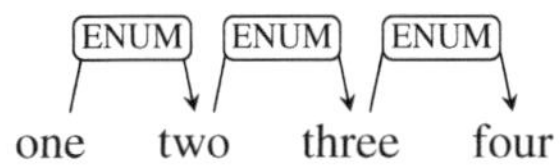

Figure 4: Treatment of an enumerated list (constructed)

This distinction is borrowed from the CHILDES annotation scheme (MacWhinney, 2000; Sagae et al., 2010), but the exact defintion of enumeration is difficult to pin down. Its prototypical properties include not needing a conjunction and often implying a continuation. Otherwise, the semantics are similar to coordination: multiple items are functioning in a parallel fashion. Further, some coordinations in some languages allow for no conjunction (Mithun, 1988), and enumeration might be considered a form of degenerate coordination (Wälchli, 2005).

5.3 Missing conjunction

The question of determining what enumeration refers to has a strong bearing on learner language, where there are constructions which could be either characterized as enumerations or as coordinations without a conjunction. Consider (6), with two separate sequences to consider. Focusing on the sequence of *is*es, there may be something amiss in being able to link them without a conjunction (in addition to the anomalous connection between the noun *Santiago* and the following three adjectives).

(6) I am Chilean , my hometown is Santiago , is beautiful , is big , is nice .

A partial dependency tree for the missing conjunction analysis in SALLE is given in figure 5. The analysis here is to use a COORD relation that is not subcategorized for as the final dependency, thus creating a mismatch indicating ungrammaticality.

It is hard to pinpoint exactly when a missing conjunction analysis should be utilized, and in this case part of the motivation has to do with capturing a formal written register of English. Additionally, garden-variety run-on sentences could be analyzed as missing conjunctions—as the connection between the main clauses in (6) could be. Furthermore, there are sentences where the units being combined are non-parallel, as in the link between *readings* and *swim and running* in (7), again opening the door for a possible missing conjunction analysis.

(7) Besides , I like swim and running , readings

It should be noted that there is also an option of treating the construction as involving two distinct elements with the same function; for example, in *my these tasks*, *tasks* could have two separate determiners. This option can complicate annotation, but does not change the question of how to separate coordination from enumeration, and so we set it aside here.

5.4 Enumeration vs. missing conjunction

Again, the pertinent question is: should enumeration annotation extend to non-native missing conjunctions? As pointed out, there is some evidence suggesting that they are different constructions, and as with missing heads and ellipses (section 4.3), missing conjunction coordinations can thus be defined as not being enumerations. For example, to be an enumeration might mean that no conjunction is required by the context and can be indicated with evidence such as an *etc*, as in (8).

(8) and i sing in church , street , station etc .

Again, an open question is whether one wishes to explicitly reference grammaticality (see, e.g., (Dickinson and Ragheb, 2013), p. 71). Note that such questions could arise for native language annotation, but the greater variability in learner forms exacerbates the problem: a string of items in sequence does not now necessarily mean it is an enumerated list.

6 Annotation Decision Procedure

Learner language can be multi-ways ambiguous—especially when categories license missing material—so annotation needs to provide multiple analyses (Reznicek et al., 2012; Lüdeling et al., 2005), provide enough contextual (meta-data) information to sort through analyses (Ott et al., 2012), and/or have a clear decision procedure for annotation. Due to having minimal meta-data

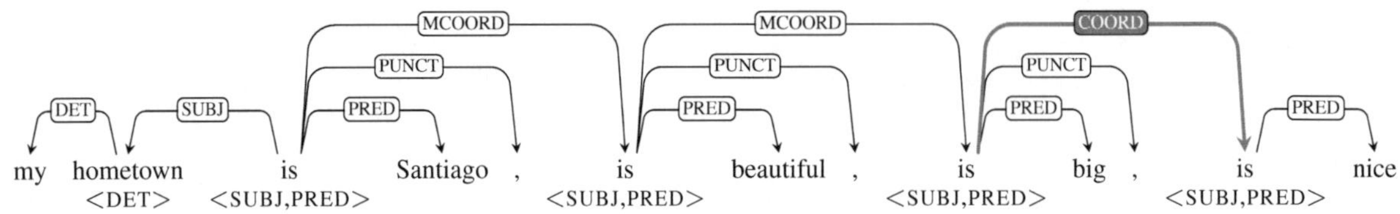

Figure 5: Missing conjunction (secondary SUBJs not shown)

and a small number of annotators, the SALLE project focuses on this last point. The annotation scheme is in some sense independent of the decision procedure involved in assigning the annotation—but the procedure itself could employ a notion of grammaticality in choosing a best analysis.

As mentioned in section 2, the issue here is in having L2 categories that are too specific to handle the usage the learner presents, i.e., no categories fit the usage. For example, in (9), the usage of *what* is not really a (question) determiner (DDQ) and the form is not that of a (subordinating) conjunction (CST).

(9) So when I admit to korea university , I decide **what** i find my own way .

There are a number of possible analyses for handling *what i find my own way*, including:

1. *what* as an extraneous word with no clear function and with a missing auxiliary (e.g., *would*);
2. *what* as a type of infinitival marker, with *i* as an extraneous word; or
3. *what* as a complementizer, albeit lexically anomalous, with the clause as valid (if odd).

A main SALLE heuristic is to "give the learner the benefit of the doubt." This heuristic favors analyses with fewer *mismatches*, i.e., discrepancies between different annotation layers, when no other evidence can distinguish the analyses. In this case, the third analysis is chosen because the lexical anomaly is the only indication of a learner-specific innovation.

Giving the learner the benefit of the doubt stems from treating the learner's language as a system in its own right (section 7.2) and does reduce the ambiguity for annotation. However, to give the benefit of the doubt—in lieu of other evidence—means annotators are arguably aware of how good or bad a sentence is, as they use a lack of errors as a guide. This is still qualitatively different than using explicit target hypotheses—as it is in terms of categories—but the degree to which this procedure references sentence correctness is a question that deserves closer investigation in the future. As mentioned, alternatives are to include more trees or more meta-information to disambiguate, each of which has its own costs.

7 Implications

We have seen non-canonical categories that license missing material (ellipses and enumerations), distinctions which could involve an annotator determining whether a sentence is grammatical when deciding between analyses. The decision procedure to obtain a single annotation may also reference grammaticality. The investigation in this paper and one's particular choices in practice have implications for both annotation practice (section 7.1) and second language analysis (section 7.2).

7.1 Impact on annotation

There are several takeaway points here for annotation of native or non-native data. First, these non-canonical categories seem to require one to consider to what extent annotation labels are merely indices and to what extent they reflect some grammatical properties worth capturing; that is, is there truly a grammar underlying the annotation? One must also consider the effect of annotation heuristics on the definitions in the grammar.

Secondly, when faced with non-canonical data and potentially a new set of competing analyses, one must choose how to apply the non-canonical categories. The main options seem to be the following:

1. Apply the native categories even to learner innovations, thereby extending the original definitions of the categories and making sentences potentially more ambiguous. For example, an

ellipsis category may license nearly any connection between two words.

2. Develop tighter restrictions on the native categories, so that differences in native and non-native instances emerge naturally. For example, ellipsis might be licensed only when the elided words can be literally recovered from the previous context. It should be noted that, in the general case, this option may only be available for data with enough meta-data to consistently distinguish the categories.
3. Reference sentence-level grammaticality in the definitions of categories. In essence, solution #3 is a subtype of solution #2, where the tighter restriction references grammaticality.

We have shied away from #1 because: a) it allows for too many possible analyses, and b) it treats the learner innovations exactly on a par with constructions that seem different. But note that this option seems to be consistent with the annotation practice of extending grammatical categories to new constructions (cf. (Pustejovsky and Stubbs, 2013), ch. 4)), while options #2 and #3 seem to be more in line with treating the underlying grammar as generative, i.e., as defining the set of allowable sentences in a language (cf. work back to (Chomsky, 1965)).

In this light, option #3 could have an unusual interpretation: as we understand it, to say that a missing head is not ellipsis *because it is ungrammatical* is to say that it is not in the target grammar (as ellipsis) because it is not in the grammar. Defining a category in terms of grammaticality may thus be a useful diagnostic for annotation practice, but further work should tease apart how principled this is. In general, being able to properly define a target category so that cases clearly do or do not fit (cf. sections 4.3 and 5.4), i.e., continuing to be evidence-based, seems to be worth pursuing. Option #3 also impacts acquisition research, a point we turn to next.

7.2 Impact on the comparative fallacy

The comparative fallacy in SLA is the notion that a researcher may be over-comparing a learner's interlanguage to the L2, and in that way treating the interlanguage as a corrupt form of the L2 (Bley-Vroman, 1983). (Ragheb and Dickinson, 2011) argue that linguistic annotation avoids the comparative fallacy in a way that error annotation doesn't, but relying on sentence-level grammaticality judgments would make that picture more muddled.

Without delving too deeply into the issue here (including how much one should want to avoid the comparative fallacy), our discussion of non-canonical categories implies that, at least for annotation, the comparative fallacy is not a simple binary distinction. Stemming from section 3, there is a distinction between analyzing target forms and target categories to consider in discussions of comparison, as well as a question of analyzing emerging constructions by making some reference to the correctness of a sentence, irrespective of a specific target. Non-canonical categories such as ellipsis seem to force an investigation into these issues; perhaps not coincidentally, these structures have often been relegated to peripheral phenomena in the theoretical literature (Culicover and Jackendoff, 2005).

8 Outlook

By applying categories appropriate for native language to learner language, we have discovered non-canonical categories that are difficult to apply. Further annotation for English and other languages will likely reveal other nuances, perhaps for distinctions generally difficult for dependency grammar, e.g., relative clauses. An immediate next step is to study categories which license extra arguments, such as topics and appositives.

Learner-specific annotation, such as underspecified categories, may also prove to impact how one sees non-canonical data. In that light, we have only scratched the surface of the implications for second language research, and we have not begun to examine other kinds of non-canonical data (e.g., dialectal). Additionally, one would like to know which categories are indeed useful for acquisition research, and studies utilizing this and other annotation schemes should shed light on this question (Ragheb, 2014; Alexopoulou et al., to appear).

Acknowledgments

We would like to thank Detmar Meurers, Heike Zinsmeister, and James Pustejovsky for discussion surrounding these topics, as well as the three anonymous reviewers for useful comments.

References

Christian Adjemian. 1976. On the nature of interlanguage systems. *Language Learning*, 26(2):297–320.

Theodora Alexopoulou, Jeroen Geertzen, Anna Korhonen, and Detmar Meurers. to appear. Exploring large educational learner corpora for sla research: perspectives on relative clauses. *International Journal of Learner Corpus Research*, 1(1):96–129.

Robert Bley-Vroman. 1983. The comparative fallacy in interlanguage studies: The case of systematicity. *Language Learning*, 33(1):1–17.

Noam Chomsky. 1965. *Aspects of the Theory of Syntax*. MIT Press, Cambrdige, MA.

Peter W. Culicover and Ray Jackendoff. 2005. *Simpler Syntax*. Oxford University Press, Oxford.

Ana Díaz-Negrillo and Jesús Fernández-Domínguez. 2006. Error tagging systems for learner corpora. *RESLA*, 19:83–102.

Ana Díaz-Negrillo, Detmar Meurers, Salvador Valera, and Holger Wunsch. 2010. Towards interlanguage POS annotation for effective learner corpora in SLA and FLT. *Language Forum*, 36(1–2):139–154. Special Issue on New Trends in Language Teaching.

Markus Dickinson and Marwa Ragheb. 2011. Dependency annotation of coordination for learner language. In *Proceedings of the International Conference on Dependency Linguistics (Depling 2011)*, pages 135–144, Barcelona, Spain.

Markus Dickinson and Marwa Ragheb. 2013. Annotation for learner English guidelines, v. 0.1. Technical report, Indiana University, Bloomington, IN, June. June 9, 2013.

Rod Ellis. 1985. Sources of variability in interlanguage. *Applied Linguistics*, 6(2):118–131.

Rod Ellis. 2008. *The Study of Second Language Acquisition*. Oxford University Press, Oxford, second edition.

Lotus Goldberg. 2005. *Verb-Stranding VP Ellipsis: A Cross-Linguistic Study*. Ph.D. thesis, McGill University.

Sylviane Granger. 2003. Error-tagged learner corpora and CALL: A promising synergy. *CALICO Journal*, 20(3):465–480.

Lingpeng Kong, Nathan Schneider, Swabha Swayamdipta, Archna Bhatia, Chris Dyer, and Noah A. Smith. 2014. A dependency parser for tweets. In *Proceedings of the 2014 Conference on Empirical Methods in Natural Language Processing (EMNLP)*, pages 1001–1012, Doha, Qatar, October. Association for Computational Linguistics.

Usha Lakshmanan and Larry Selinker. 2001. Analysing interlanguage: how do we know what learners know? *Second Language Research*, 17(4):393–420.

Sun-Hee Lee, Markus Dickinson, and Ross Israel. 2012. Developing learner corpus annotation for Korean particle errors. In *Proceedings of the Sixth Linguistic Annotation Workshop*, LAW VI '12, pages 129–133, Stroudsburg, PA, USA. Association for Computational Linguistics.

Anke Lüdeling, Maik Walter, Emil Kroymann, and Peter Adolphs. 2005. Multi-level error annotation in learner corpora. In *Proceedings of Corpus Linguistics 2005*, Birmingham.

Brian MacWhinney. 2000. *The CHILDES Project: Tools for Analyzing Talk*. Lawrence Erlbaum Associates, Mahwah, NJ, 3rd edition. Electronic Edition, updated April 25, 2012, Part 2: the CLAN Programs: `http://childes.psy.cmu.edu/manuals/CLAN.pdf`.

Marianne Mithun. 1988. The grammaticization of coordination. In John Haiman and Sandra A. Thompson, editors, *Clause Combining in Grammar and Discourse*, volume 18 of *Typological Studies in Language*, pages 331–359. John Benjamins.

Diane Nicholls. 2003. The cambridge learner corpus - error coding and analysis for lexicography and ELT. In Dawn Archer, Paul Rayson, Andrew Wilson, and Tony McEnery, editors, *Proceedings of the Corpus Linguistics 2003 Conference*, volume 16, pages 572–581, University Centre for Computer Corpus Research on Language, Technical Papers. Lancaster University.

Stephan Oepen, Dan Flickinger, Kristina Toutanova, and Christoper D. Manning. 2004. Lingo redwoods: A rich and dynamic treebank for hpsg. *Research on Language and Computation*, 2(4):575–596.

Niels Ott, Ramon Ziai, and Detmar Meurers. 2012. Creation and analysis of a reading comprehension exercise corpus: Towards evaluating meaning in context. In Thomas Schmidt and Kai Wrner, editors, *Multilingual Corpora and Multilingual Corpus Analysis*, Hamburg Studies in Multilingualism (HSM), pages 47–69. Benjamins, Amsterdam.

James Pustejovsky and Amber Stubbs. 2013. *Natural Language Annotation for Machine Learning*. O'Reilly Media, Inc., Sebastopol, CA.

Marwa Ragheb and Markus Dickinson. 2011. Avoiding the comparative fallacy in the annotation of learner corpora. In *Selected Proceedings of the 2010 Second Language Research Forum: Reconsidering SLA Research, Dimensions, and Directions*, pages 114–124, Somerville, MA. Cascadilla Proceedings Project.

Marwa Ragheb and Markus Dickinson. 2012. Defining syntax for learner language annotation. In *Proceedings of the 24th International Conference on Computational Linguistics (Coling 2012), Poster Session*, pages 965–974, Mumbai, India.

Marwa Ragheb and Markus Dickinson. 2014. Developing a corpus of syntactically-annotated learner language for English. In *Proceedings of the 13th International Workshop on Treebanks and Linguistic Theories (TLT13), Poster Session*, Tübingen, Germany.

Marwa Ragheb. 2014. *Building a Syntactically-Annotated Corpus of Learner English*. Ph.D. thesis, Indiana University, Bloomington, IN, August.

Owen Rambow. 2010. The simple truth about dependency and phrase structure representations: An opinion piece. In *Human Language Technologies: The 2010 Annual Conference of the North American Chapter of the Association for Computational Linguistics*, pages 337–340, Los Angeles, CA, June.

Ines Rehbein, Hagen Hirschmann, Anke Lüdeling, and Marc Reznicek. 2012. Better tags give better trees - or do they? *Linguistic Issues in Language Technology (LiLT)*, 7(10).

Marc Reznicek, Anke Lüdeling, Cedric Krummes, Franziska Schwantuschke, Maik Walter, Karin Schmidt, Hagen Hirschmann, and Torsten Andreas, 2012. *Das Falko-Handbuch. Korpusaufbau und Annotationen Version 2.01*. Humboldt-Universität zu Berlin, Berlin.

Mark Reznicek, Anke Lüdeling, and Hagen Hirschmann. 2013. Competing target hypotheses in the Falko corpus: A flexible multi-layer corpus architecture. In Ana Díaz-Negrillo, Nicolas Ballier, and Paul Thompson, editors, *Automatic Treatment and Analysis of Learner Corpus Data*, pages 101–123. John Benjamins, Amsterdam.

Ivan A. Sag. 1976. *Deletion and logical form*. Ph.D. thesis, Massachusetts Institute of Technology.

Kenji Sagae, Eric Davis, Alon Lavie, and Brian MacWhinney an Shuly Wintner. 2010. Morphosyntactic annotation of CHILDES transcripts. *Journal of Child Language*, 37(3):705–729.

Larry Selinker. 1972. Interlanguage. *International Review of Applied Linguistics*, 10(3):209–231.

Kari Tenfjord, Jon Erik Hagen, and Hilde Johansen. 2006. The hows and whys of coding categories in a learner corpus (or "how and why an error-tagged learner corpus is not *ipso facto* one big comparative fallacy. *Rivista di psicolinguistica applicata*, 6(3):93–108.

Bernhard Wälchli. 2005. *Co-Compounds and Natural Coordination*. Oxford Studies in Typology and Linguistic Theory. Oxford University Press, Oxford.

Across Languages and Genres: Creating a Universal Annotation Scheme for Textual Relations

Ekaterina Lapshinova-Koltunski
Saarland University
Universitat Campus A2.2
66123 Saarbrucken
e.lapshinova
@mx.uni-saarland.de

Anna Nedoluzhko
Charles University in Prague
Malostranske nam. 25,
CZ-11800 Prague 1
nedoluzko
@ufal.mff.cuni.cz

Kerstin Anna Kunz
University of Heidelberg
Ploeck 57a
DE-69117 Heidelberg
kerstin.kunz
@iued.uni-heidelberg.de

Abstract

The present paper describes an attempt to create an interoperable scheme using existing annotations of textual phenomena across languages and genres including non-canonical ones. Such a kind of analysis requires annotated multilingual resources which are costly. Therefore, we make use of annotations already available in the resources for English, German and Czech. As the annotations in these corpora are based on different conceptual and methodological backgrounds, we need an interoperable scheme that covers existing categories and at the same time allows a comparison of the resources. In this paper, we describe how this interoperable scheme was created and which problematic cases we had to consider. The resulting scheme is supposed to be applied in the future to explore contrasts between the three languages under analysis, for which we expect the greatest differences in the degree of variation between non-canonical and canonical language.

1 Aims and Motivation

The aim of the present study is to create a scheme which will allow us to use existing annotations of textual phenomena, and which will be applicable to multiple languages and genres, including non-canonical ones. The annotations were created within two separate projects: German-English Contrasts in Cohesion (GECCo, Lapshinova and Kunz (2014)) whose focus was on English and German on the one hand, and the Prague Dependency Treebank (PDT 3.0, Bejček et al. (2013)) with the analysis of Czech, on the other hand.

The resulting scheme will serve our overarching goal to unify the two approaches in a joint analysis of contrasts between English, German and Czech on the level of discourse. We assume that the greatest differences between these languages lie in the degree of variation between non-canonical and canonical language (here we especially mean spoken language). Previous findings on lexico-grammatical and also cohesive phenomena have evidenced that there is more variation between written and spoken dimensions in German than in English, even though they are closely related, cf. Mair (2006) or Kunz et al. (forthcoming). Studies with respect to spoken and written Czech (see, e.g., Cvrček et al. (2010)) suggest that the differences between written and spoken language are even more pronounced in Czech than in German, at least with respect to lexico-grammar, hence we expect that this also holds for the level of text/ discourse.

We therefore suggest that if we draw a line of differences between spoken and written English, German and Czech, we would observe a continuum in the degree of variation between these languages, as seen in Figure 1. The graph also reflects the above assumption that the differences are less pronounced between English and German than if we compare English and German with Czech. The reasons for this lie in the linguistic heritage of these languages (English and German have a common West-Germanic origin while Czech is a Slavic language) and in sociolinguistic factors that influenced their evolution (for example, Czech purism at the beginning of the 20th century, described, e.g., in Havránek and Weingart (1932)). To our knowledge, there is no

Proceedings of LAW IX - The 9th Linguistic Annotation Workshop, pages 168–177,
Denver, Colorado, June 5, 2015.

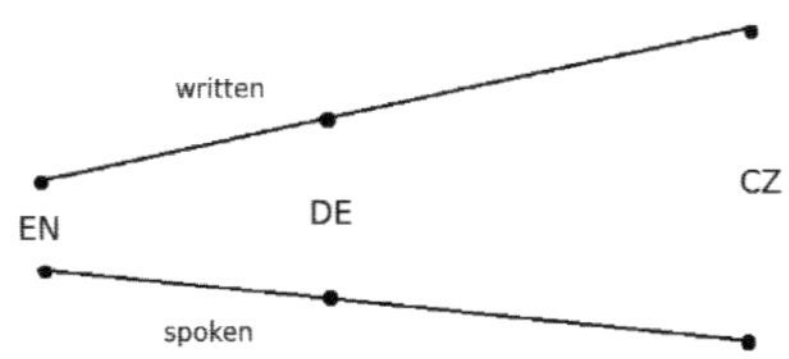

Figure 1: Differences between spoken and written English, German and Czech

research testing these assumptions. We believe that a cross-language analysis based on the interoperable scheme proposed in this work will help to fill this gap.

However, this kind of study requires corpora that are annotated for textual phenomena. As the creation of such corpora is a time-consuming task, we decide to take advantage of existing resources, i.e. corpora, which already contain annotations of these phenomena. However, while capturing the same phenomena, the annotations in the corpora at hand were created in the frame of two different projects (GECCo and PDT, see Section 2). Moreover, both existing annotation schemes only account for the systemic peculiarities and realizational options of the languages analysed and hence are not general enough to permit a comparison across Germanic and Slavic languages. For this reason, we need to unify the categories in these schemes to create an interoperable one which can be applicable to multiple languages and text registers, including spoken ones. The scheme will allow us to profit from the existing annotated resources and at the same time will enable the contrastive analysis of the languages involved. We believe that the resulting scheme will find application not only in our research, but also in further linguistic studies and in cross-language NLP applications. It is beyond the scope of this paper to include the contrastive language analysis, which will follow from the unified scheme in our future work.

2 Theoretical Background

In this section, we describe the frameworks for the analysis of English, German and Czech. They were used in the development of the resources at hand (which are described later in Section 3) and will serve as a basis for our interoperable scheme.

2.1 Frameworks for the analysis of English and German

The analysis of textual phenomena in GECCo is based on the definition of cohesion. The concept was established by Halliday and Hasan (1976) for English, in the frame of Systemic Functional Linguistics. It concerns textual relations between linguistic expressions across grammatical domains. Additionally, the categories under analysis are based on the conceptualisations of de Beaugrande and Dressler (1981), who consider cohesion as an explicit linguistic signal on the text surface to establish coherence or textuality. Cohesion always involves a linguistic trigger (cohesive device) that links up to other linguistic expressions in the same text. The main categories used in the analysis include coreference to create relations of identity, comparative reference, substitution and ellipsis to create relations of comparison between referents belonging to the same type, conjunction for logico-semantic relations between propositions, and lexical cohesion for similarity between different types of referents. The adaptation of these categories and their subcategories to the bilingual comparison of English and German have been described in Kunz et al. (forthcoming). For coreference, ellipsis and lexical cohesion, not only cohesive devices were considered, but also the linguistic expressions they tie up with as well as the cohesive relations. The relations may contain more than just two linguistic expressions and form cohesive chains that stretch over longer passages of text.

2.2 Framework for the analysis of Czech

In the framework for the analysis of Czech, the following textual phenomena are included: ellipses, information structure, grammatical and textual coreference, bridging relations (associative anaphora) and discourse relations. Their definition is based on Functional Generative Description as described in Sgall et al. (1986). The approach uses syntactic as well as semantic criteria for text analysis and considers three layers of text representation: morphological, analytical and tectogrammatical (deep syntactic). At the tectogrammatical layer, the meaning of the sentence is represented as a dependency tree structure, in which nodes represent autosemantic words and are labelled with a large set of attributes. This layer of representation is especially important for elliptical constructions, as they are captured here in reconstructions (Mikulová, 2014). Besides that, the tectogrammatical layer also covers information on structural attributes (in terms of contextually bound or contextually non-bound nodes). The approach to textual phenomena exceeding the sentence boundary is two-fold for the Czech framework. On the one hand, the conception of discourse relations is based on the Penn-style discourse lexically-grounded approach, as described in Prasad et al. (2008). According to this approach, only those relations that are signaled by explicit markers (connectives) are considered as discourse relations. However, in contrast to the Penn-style approach, the set of connectives is an open list, see Poláková et al. (2013), and the treatment of coreference and bridging relations includes both explicit and implicit categories. Language expressions that refer to the same discourse entity are considered to be coreferent. As for bridging relations, their definition has been taken from Clark (1975).

3 Data and Experiment

As already mentioned in Section 1, we aim to take advantage of the existing corpora annotated for textual phenomena to avoid the time-consuming creation of such resources. The existing German and English data are annotated with the GECCo framework described in 2.1, whereas the data for Czech are annotated in the PDT style described in section 2.2 above. The current section provides a brief description of these resources at hand.

3.1 GECCo - German and English corpora

The GECCo corpus annotated for textual phenomena with the framework described in 2.1 represents a continuum of different text types (registers in the sense of Systemic Functional linguistics) from written to spoken discourse. More precisely, it includes English and German texts of ten registers, eight of which represent written discourse and include fictional texts, political essays, instruction manuals, popular-scientific texts, letters to shareholders, prepared political speeches, tourism leaflets and texts from corporate websites. This part contains not only original texts, but also their translations in both directions. The registers of spoken discourse include recorded and transcribed interviews and academic speeches described in Lapshinova-Koltunski et al. (2012), as well as transcriptions of television talkshows, texts from internet forums, medical consultations and sermon texts. The total number of words contained in the corpus comprises ca. 1,6 Mio (including translations). The corpus is annotated on several levels, which include morphological, syntactical, structural and textual information (i.e. information on cohesion as described above). The information on the latter was annotated with the help of semi-automatic procedures described by Lapshinova-Koltunski and Kunz (2014). These result from an integration of the systemic peculiarities of English and German and at the same time account for textual variation in terms of canonical written and non-canonical spoken language. The rich annotation allows capturing information about the structural and syntactic features of cohesive devices (and also antecedents) and about how they are mapped onto information structure. Moreover, it yields information about chain features, e.g. number of elements in chains, distance between chain elements and number of different chains.

3.2 Prague Dependency Treebanks

There is a number of corpora annotated according to the Prague annotation scenario described in section 2.2 above. These include PDT 3.0 – Prague Dependency Treebank (Bejček et al., 2013), PCEDT 2.0 – Prague English Dependency Treebank (Hajič et al., 2012) and PDTSL – Prague Dependency Treebank of Spoken Language (Hajič et al., 2009). All these corpora consist of original texts (Czech and English respectively) extracted from newspaper articles (PDT), Wall Street Journal (PCEDT) and transcribed and reconstructed spontaneous dialogue speech in Czech and English. PCEDT 2.0 also contains translations from English into Czech. The total number of words in written corpora comprises ca. 3,2 Mio (including translations) and spoken corpora for English and Czech total ca. 770 thousand tokens. The written corpora are annotated with morphological, analytical and tectogrammatical information, whereas each sentence is represented as a dependency tree structure. The tectogrammatical layer of PDT 3.0 also contains annotation of information structure attributes and the following discourse phenomena: extended (nominal) textual coreference, bridging relations, discourse connectives and the discourse units linked by them, and semantic relations between these units, see Poláková et al. (2013) for details.

3.3 Experiment settings

The creation of an interoperable scheme requires a comparison of the underlying annotations. We therefore annotate the same data set on the basis of both conceptions, and identify those categories that cover the same phenomena. For this, we have selected texts in English (both originals) belonging to two different genres – journalism and fiction and annotated them in accordance with the guidelines of the Prague and GECCo conceptions. Journalistic texts represent written discourse, whereas the fictional texts we selected are closer to spoken language and other non-canonical genres, e.g., internet blogs or tweets. They are partially narrative and partially dialogic, and hence contain turns, but also reformulations, elaboration and other spoken language features. We believe that this data constellation ensures a good base for our future analysis (aimed at comparison of spoken vs. written dimensions). We decide for texts in English, as English data is available in both underlying resources, hence allowing us to unify the annotated categories afterwards. The journalistic sample contains texts exported from PCEDT 2.0 (see section 3.2), with a size of around 100 sentences. A sample of fictional texts of the same size was exported from the GECCo corpus described in 3.1. For the sake of convenience, we used different annotation tools for the two different frameworks – TrEd (Pajas and Štěpánek, 2008) for the framework described in 2.2, as it allows visualisation of trees, and MMAX2 (Müller and Strube, 2006) for the framework described in 2.1, as this enables visualisation of longer cohesive chains. The annotations were carried out manually by four trained annotators. Then, the parallelly created annotations were compared and analysed qualitatively and quantitatively. The results of this analysis are presented in section 4 below.

4 Analyses

4.1 Overall comparison

Both GECCo and PDT frameworks include annotations of ellipses, coreference relations and discourse connectives. The category of lexical cohesion in the German-English framework (see section 2.1) can be partially mapped to bridging relations in the Czech framework (see 2.2), although lexical cohesion is much more lexically grounded than bridging. Substitution is the only phenomenon which is asymmetric in the frameworks. It is not covered by the definition of textual relations in the framework for Czech, as this device is common for English and (less so) for German but not relevant at all for Czech. We provide a mapping of the phenomena available in both frameworks in Table 1.

GECCo	PDT
coreference	coreference
lexical cohesion	bridging
ellipsis	ellipsis (in dependency trees)
connectives, relations	connectives, arguments, relations
substitution	-

Table 1: Mapping of the phenomena

We count the occurrences of these categories in the experimental dataset and compare absolute numbers for both frameworks, see Figure 2. The numbers in Figure 2 reveal the preferences for certain types of relations in the two approaches involved. At the same time, we are able to observe the similarities between the types.

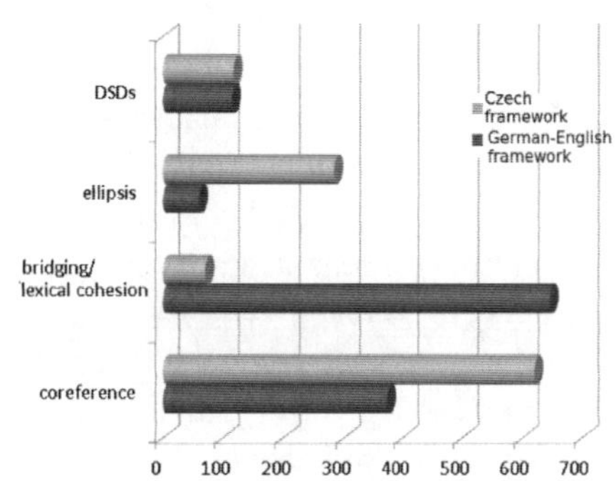

Figure 2: Overall annotation statistics

What is most evident from the figure is that the

number of **discourse relations** expressed by connectives[1] annotated in both approaches is very similar. This is mainly due to the fact that the typology of discourse relations of the main categories is similar in both approaches. Neglecting the terminology, there are four main relations in both approaches: temporal, causal, adversative and additive. In GECCo, also modal DSDs are distinguished (such as *well, sure, of course, surely*, etc.). They are especially frequent in spoken genres. However, they only provide a rather vague link to the two arguments, as they primarily carry an emotional meaning. For this particular reason, this type of textual devices is not included in the PDT framework, where a DSD always requires a clear linkage of two arguments, and in which the scope of discourse arguments is taken into account. If modal DSDs were substracted, the number of connectives for the German-English framework would slightly change. However, it does not change the comparison considerabely. The other difference observed in the approach to discourse relations is that, in the Penn-style, the four main categories are further differentiated into more detailed relations, whereas in the German-English framework, only the general categories are considered.

The numbers for the other textual phenomena reveal more differences. For example, the frequencies of **ellipses** and coreference relations annotated within the PDT framework prevail over those of the other types. This is justified by the representation of the phenomena according to the framework: Apart from textual ellipses (*Did she open the door? No, she did not [open the door]*), it also contains various grammatical types of elliptical constructions, e.g. structural ellipses (ellipses of governing verbs and nouns), different kinds of anaphoric zeros (*Their reaction was 0 to do nothing and 0 ride it out*), including arguments with control constructions (*Peter want to [Peter] sleep*), general arguments (*Jane sells at Bata [what] [to whom]*), etc. These are reconstructed on the deep syntactic level. The GECCo approach is based on signals to textual cohesion, and therefore, ellipses are annotated only in the case of textual relations across grammatical domains. Besides, anaphoric zeros are not reconstructed in syntactic structures.

[1] hereinafter referred to as discourse-structuring devices (DSDs).

For our contrastive analysis, we will consider cases of textual ellipsis only, which are expected to contribute especially to the differences between spoken and written language. We expect textual ellipsis to be more common in spoken genres, as our previous analyses for English and German have already evidenced, cf. Kunz et al. (forthcoming). Example (1) demonstrates a case of textual ellipsis considered in both approaches.

(1) *He'd never even bothered to read it. But Truman had [].*

The difference here lies in the representation of the missing element. In the GECCo approach, this case is annotated as verbal ellipsis. The missing parts of the verbal phrase could either be *bothered to read it* or *read it*. In the PDT approach, the whole verbal phrase is reconstructed in the dependency tree, see Figure 3, connected to the antecedents of verbs by the arrows of grammatical and textual coreference. Note that this type of ellipsis, where only the operator is kept (termed as lexical ellipsis by Hallidday & Hasan (1976)), is available in English, but neither in German nor Czech.

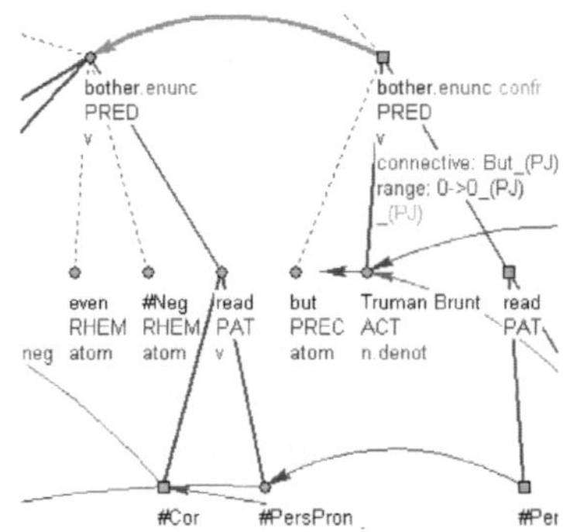

Figure 3: Ellipsis in the dependency tree representation (PDT-style)

The differences in the annotations of **coreference** are due to the diverging definitions of coreferring expressions. In GECCo, only the mentions with an explicit marker, the cohesive device (e.g. definite articles, pronouns, demonstratives, etc.), are taken into account. This implies, for instance, that relations between named entities or between nominal constructions in plural which are not introduced by a determiner are excluded from the annotation of coreference. They are, however, annotated as devices of lexical cohesion (see below). Moreover, as a cohesive relation to the antecedent is indicated by a cohesive device, only this explicit marker is annotated but not the other elements of the anaphoric nominal phrase. Hence, if an anaphoric expression consists of a definite article and a nominal head, the former is annotated as corerential device and the noun as lexical cohesion (see *the* and *manuscript* in example (2)). In the PDT approach, both implicit and explicit relations of coreference are annotated, including indefinite NPs. In addition, the whole anaphoric expression is annotated as one coreferential element, as illustrated in example (2).

(2) *Twenty years I have been working on [this book]," and he leaned over to rap [[the] [manuscript]] with a thick proprietary finger," and you can sit home in Peterskill and read it when it's published.*

Lexical repetitions (which belong to the level of lexical cohesion in GECCo) are also annotated as coreferent if they refer to the same discourse entity.

We assume that the differences in the annotation of coreference are also related to the contrasts that we observe for **bridging/lexical cohesion**, see Figure 2. Although there is a partial intersection of sets of the relations, the different conceptions are clearly seen in the annotations: in lexical cohesion, lexico-semantic properties of mentions in text are important. The semantic relations (e.g., meronymy, hyponymy, synonymy, etc.) assigned to the mentions are based on the context-free sense relations into which lexical words or patterns can enter, whereas their contextual meaning and referential properties are neglected. By contrast, bridging relations are based on the information instantiated in the text, which means that only those conceptual relations are considered which hold between entities mentioned in the same discourse. Nevertheless, we noticed that relations not marked as lexical cohesion are compensated by the annotation of coreference relations in GECCo, and taken together, they are comparable to the relations of bridging and coreference in the PDT framework. For example, repetitions, which are a subcategory of lexical cohesion, are marked as coreference relations in the PDT framework (see above).

Summing up, there are numerous similarities and overlaps in the categories of textual phenomena in both approaches, despite of the differences discussed earlier. This leads us to conclude that textual phenomena are reflected in both approaches in a very similar way although they are annotated with diverging terminology that stems from different theoretical backgrounds. The following section (4.2) illustrates in more detail some of the cases which are especially interesting for a cross-lingual analysis of spoken and written language.

4.2 Case studies

Coreference and bridging / lexical cohesion The interplay between coreference and bridging or lexical cohesion is especially interesting if we compare spoken and written genres, as we expect certain preferences due to contextual settings (short-time memory, presence of all speech participants in the communication situation, etc.). In Table 2, we demonstrate the statistics (numbers are counted for one journalistic text consisting of 43 sentences) for coreference chains identified with both annotation schemes.

	GECCo-style	PDT-style
coref.chains	23	46
aver.chain length1	3,48	4,20
aver.chain length2	6,25	7,05

Table 2: Annotation statistics for coreference chains

We compare the total number of chains and the average chain length[2] which are higher in the PDT framework than in the GECCo approach for German and English. This coincides with the results that we observed in Section 2 above, as the total number of coreference elements is much lower in the GECCo framework.

If we go into detail and analyse the subtypes of anaphora, we find some fine-grained differences in the annotation. For example, event anaphora are annotated in both frameworks. However, the largest

[2]**aver.chain length1** is used for all chains, whereas **aver.chain length2** indicates statistics for chains containing more than two elements.

scope of the antecedent of this anaphora type is limited to the extension of a sentence in the tree-based approach while cohesion-based annotations also include larger textual antecedents.

The above mentioned (see Section 4.1) overlap between coreference and bridging can be illustrated by the example in (3). The relation in (3-a) is covered by a combination of comparative reference and lexical cohesion in the GECCo framework, and by contrastive bridging in the PDT framework. At the same time, comparative reference also includes such cases as (3-b) and (3-c), combined with lexical cohesion in (3-b) and coreference and lexical cohesion in (3-c). Both are cases of bridging anaphora and common textual coreference in the PDT framework.

(3) a. *a presentation – a better presentation, an example – other examples*
b. *some case – such/similar cases.*
c. *one hand – the same hand*

Another illustration of this overlap can be seen in (4), where *she, her children, her war-damaged husband* and *their* are marked as a bridging relation (type subset - set) in one approach, whereas *she, her, her* and *their* are annotated as coreference in the other, *their* with a split antecedent.

(4) *Although [she] was kind and playful to [her] children, she was dreadful to [her war-damaged husband]; she openly brought her lover into [their] home.*

The relation between *The World War II* and *that* in (5) shows how coreference signaled by a demonstrative pronoun in the GECCo approach may coincide with the bridging relation in the PDT approach. In the latter, an explicit anaphor is marked as signalling a bridging and not a coreference relation since it is not entirely clear whether the event (*The World War II* in (5)) is identical with *that time*.

(5) *[The World War II] remained one of the most tragic events in the history. But at [[that] time] nobody thought about it.*

A minor difference between the approaches can be found within the field of event anaphora annotation. In the PDT approach, an antecedent can be explicitly annotated only when it is not longer than one sentence. In the GECCo approach, the scope of the antecedent is annotated independently of the size of the antecedent.

Discourse relations As already mentioned above, the greatest similarities between the two approaches were observed in terms of the total number of identified discourse relations in both schemes. The differences are discovered here on the level of types of relations involved. For example, the connective *and* in (6) is assigned a reason-result relation in the PDT framework, while the GECCo framework considers it as an additive conjunction.

(6) *William Gates and Paul Allen in 1975 developed an early language-housekeeper system for PCs, [and] Gates became an industry billionaire six years after IBM adapted one of these versions in 1981.*

In Table 3, we demonstrate the number of relations identified per approach and per text genre, as we suppose that the detected differences can be genre-sensitive.

	GECCo-style		**PDT-style**	
	journ.	**fict.**	**journ.**	**fict.**
temporal	6	11	5	5
contin./caus.	9	6	19	4
comp./adver.	16	10	15	17
expan./addit.	22	24	19	22
modal	7	4	-	-

Table 3: Annotation statistics for discourse connectives

For instance, both frameworks identify approximately the same number of temporal relations in the journalistic texts. Yet, deviating numbers for this relation are obtained for the fictional texts. The same tendency is observed for relations of contrast (adversative). In case of contingency or causal relations, the situation is different: the number of relations coincide here for fiction rather than journalism.

5 Resulting Scheme and Discussion

Summarising all the cases analysed in the data that were annotated with both frameworks, we create an intersection scheme, covering all overlapping categories. This scheme is illustrated in Table 4. The main categories here are labelled as

IDENTITY, NON-IDENTITY, ELLIPSIS and DISCOURSE RELATIONS. These general categories also include subclasses on a more fine-grained level, e.g. METONYMY or CONTRAST, which can be derived from the existing annotation. For the time being, we exclude the categories without correspondence, i.e. which exist in one approach but not in the other.

As can be seen from the table, the annotation schemes based on both frameworks can be merged even though there are differences in the terminology used for specific features, in the level of granularity and in the method of annotation.

However, without the categories we had to exclude because there was no correspondence between the two approaches, we cannot cover all the cases of textual phenomena. For instance, modal discourse markers, which are especially important for spoken genres cannot be captured by our interoperable scheme for the time being.

One of the main reasons for the incompatibility of the excluded categories lies in the nature of the phenomenon itself: the GECCo approach takes a linguistic signal into account, while the PDT framework includes a more abstract level of coherence. This is especially reflected in the relations of IDENTITY which are not marked by a referring item, e.g. definite article, pronoun, etc. In turn, the GECCo framework captures more semantic relations, e.g. hyponomy, synonymy, etc. that are purely based on sense relations and not on relations between instantiated referents, thus allowing a more fine-grained view on the thematic progression in a text, see Figure 4.

As already stated above, the conceptual dissimilarities discovered in this study seem to result, at least partially, from the systemic differences between Germanic and Slavic languages with respect to the language devices available for expressing textual phenomena. For instance, English uses a very closed class of explicit markers for establishing a relation of comparison, labeled as substitution (*the shirt – the red one*). German is more heterogeneous with respect to the linguistic items available, while Czech has no corresponding structures and makes use of ellipsis instead. We expect that these differences will be even more apparent when integrating the analysis of non-canonical spoken varieties into our trilingual study.

Our future work will include the application of the resulting scheme to our contrastive analysis of naturally occurring texts of English, German and Czech. We are particularly interested in comparing the textual phenomena realized in texts with plain written style with those occurring in non-canonical texts that are produced spontaneously, with a high degree of interaction between varying numbers of speech participants, such as talkshows or private conversation. Moreover, we intend to investigate language production in between spoken and written, such as forums, blogs or interviews. We expect that the most significant differences between languages and genres are tied to varying contextual configurations of mode, e.g. number of speech participants, private vs. public conversation, time laps between production and reception). They may be reflected in textual phenomena with respect to their overall number, the degree of explicitness, as well as the type of textual categories that are preferred. Moreover, we intend to examine variation in the degree of dependence of these textual phenomena on lexicogrammatical constraints or pragmatic peculiarities. The scheme developed in this paper is a first step towards unifying different frameworks that result from separate analyses of Germanic languages and a Slavic language. It therefore reflects a level of generalisation that is applicable to trilingual analysis, which will, however, be broken into more delicate subcategories to permit an identification of fine-grained contrasts.

6 Acknowledgement

This work was made possible by a grant on Short Term Scientific Missions received within the Textlink Action (ISCH COST Action IS1312)[3]. We also acknowledge support from the Grant Agency of the Czech Republic (grant P406/12/0658). This work has been using language resources developed and stored and distributed by the LINDAT/CLARIN project of the Ministry of Education, Youth and Sports of the Czech Republic (project LM2010013). The project GECCo has been supported through a grant from the Deutsche Forschungsgemeinschaft (German Research Society).

[3]http://textlinkcost.wix.com/textlink

	Czech framework	German-English framework
IDENTITY	coreference with pronouns	coreference with pers. and demo. heads (except extended reference)
	pronouns with arrows to segments and events	extended reference
	NP coreference	coreference with pers./ dem. modifiers or def.art.+hyperonymy/ repetition/ synonymy
	coreference of NEs	repetitions of named entities
	coreference with the word same	comp.reference with the word same
	coreference with demonstrative local and temporal adverbs (tam, tehdy)	coreference with demonstrative local and temporal adverbs
NON-IDENTITY	contextual relations of MERONYMY between lexical items	contextual relations of MERONYMY between lexical items
	bridging CONTRAST with comparative adjective	comparative reference excluding cases with the word same
	bridging CONTRAST without comparative adjective	antonyms in lex.coh
DISCOURSE RELATIONS	temporal	temporal
	contingency	causal
	comparison (contrast)	adversative
	expansion	additive
ELLIPSIS	textual ellipsis (nominal, verbal, clausal)	cohesive ellipsis (nominal, verbal, clausal)

Table 4: Categories for the language- and genre-insensitive scheme

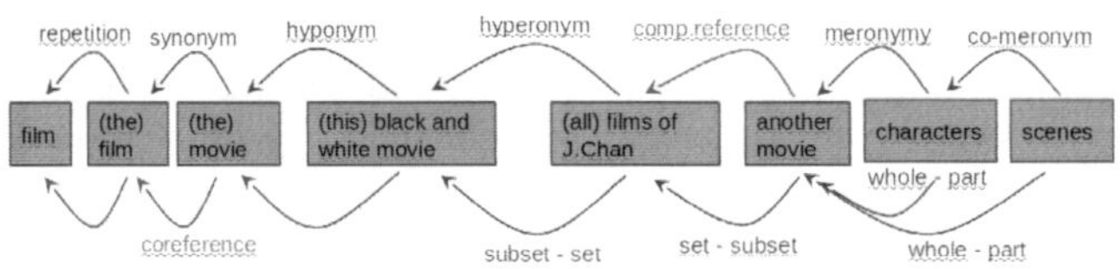

Figure 4: Coreferential and lexical relations in both approaches

References

Robert-Alain de Beaugrande and Wolfgang Ulrich Dressler. 1981. *Einführung in die Textlinguistik*. Niemeyer, Tübingen.

Eduard Bejček, Eva Hajičová, Jan Hajič, Pavlína Jínová, Václava Kettnerová, Veronika Kolářová, Marie Mikulová, Jiří Mírovský, Anna Nedoluzhko, Jarmila Panevová, Lucie Poláková, Magda Ševčíková, Jan Štěpánek, and Šárka Zikánová. 2013. Prague dependency treebank 3.0.

Herbert H. Clark. 1975. Bridging. In *Theoretical Issues in Natural Language Processing*, pages 169–174.

Václav Cvrček, Vileém Kodýtek, Marie Kopivová, Dominika Kováříková, Petr Sgall, Michal Šulc, Jan Táborský, Jan Volín, and Martina Waclawičová. 2010. *Mluvnice současné češtiny/Grammar of Contemporary Czech/*. Karolinum, Prague.

Jan Hajič, Petr Pajas, David Mareček, Marie Mikulová, Zdeňka Urešová, and Petr Podveský. 2009. Prague dependency treebank of spoken language (PDTSL) 0.5.

Jan Hajič, Eva Hajičová, Jarmila Panevová, Petr Sgall, Ondřej Bojar, Silvie Cinková, Eva Fučíková, Marie Mikulová, Petr Pajas, Jan Popelka, Jiří Semecký, Jana Šindlerová, Jan Štěpánek, Josef Toman, Zdeka Urešová, and Zdeněk Žabokrtský. 2012. Announcing Prague Czech-English Dependency Treebank 2.0. In *Proceedings of the 8th International Conference on Language Resources and Evaluation (LREC 2012)*, Istanbul, Turkey. European Language Resources Association.

M.A.K. Halliday and Ruqaiya Hasan. 1976. *Cohesion in English*. Longman, London, New York.

Bohuslav Havránek and Miloš Weingart. 1932. *Spisovná čeština a jazyková kultura / Standard Czech and language culture*. Melantrich, Prague.

Kerstin Kunz, Stefania Degaetano-Ortlieb, Ekaterina Lapshinova-Koltunski, Katrin Menzel, and Erich

Steiner. forthcoming. Gecco – an empirically-based comparison of english-german cohesion. In G. De Sutter, I. Delaere, and M.-A. Lefer, editors, *New Ways of Analysing Translational Behaviour in Corpus-Based Translation Studies*. Mouton de Gruyter. TILSM series.

Ekaterina Lapshinova-Koltunski and Kerstin Kunz. 2014. Annotating cohesion for multillingual analysis. In *Proceedings of the 10th Joint ACL - ISO Workshop on Interoperable Semantic Annotation*, Reykjavik, Iceland, May. LREC.

Ekaterina Lapshinova-Koltunski, Kerstin Kunz, and Marilisa Amoia. 2012. Compiling a multilingual spoken corpus. In Tommaso Raso Heliana Mello, Massimo Pettorino, editor, *Proceedings of the VIIth GSCP International Conference: Speech and corpora*, pages 79–84, Firenze. Firenze University Press.

Christian Mair. 2006. *Twentieth-Century English: History, Variation and Standardization*. Cambridge University Press, Cambridge.

Marie Mikulová. 2014. Semantic representation of ellipsis in the prague dependency treebanks. In *Proceedings of the Twenty-Sixth Conference on Computational Linguistics and Speech Processing ROCLING XXVI (2014)*, pages 125–138, Taipei, Taiwan. Association for Computational Linguistics and Chinese Language Processing (ACLCLP), Association for Computational Linguistics and Chinese Language Processing (ACLCLP).

Christoph Müller and Michael Strube. 2006. Multi-level annotation of linguistic data with MMAX2. In Sabine Braun, Kurt Kohn, and Joybrato Mukherjee, editors, *Corpus Technology and Language Pedagogy: New Resources, New Tools, New Methods*, pages 197–214. Peter Lang, Frankfurt a.M., Germany.

Petr Pajas and Jan Štěpánek. 2008. Recent advances in a feature-rich framework for treebank annotation. In *Proceedings of the 22nd International Conference on Computational Linguistics*, pages 673–680, Manchester, UK. Coling-2008 Organizing Committee.

Lucie Poláková, Jiří Mírovský, Anna Nedoluzhko, Pavlína Jínová, Šárka Zikánová, and Eva Hajičová. 2013. Introducing the prague discourse treebank 1.0. In *Proceedings of the 6th International Joint Conference on Natural Language Processing*, pages 91–99, Nagoya, Japan. Asian Federation of Natural Language Processing, Asian Federation of Natural Language Processing.

Rashmi Prasad, Nikhil Dinesh, Alan Lee, Eleni Miltsakaki, Livio Robaldo, Aravind Joshi, and Bonnie Webber. 2008. The penn discourse treebank 2.0. In *Proceedings of the 6th International Conference on Language Resources and Evaluation (LREC 2008)*, pages 2961–2968, Marrakech, Morocco. European Language Resources Association.

Petr Sgall, Eva Hajicova, and Jarmila Panevovǎ. 1986. *The meaning of the sentence in its semantic and pragmatic aspects*. Reidel, Dordrecht.

Annotating the Implicit Content of Sluices

Pranav Anand & Jim McCloskey
Department of Linguistics
University of California, Santa Cruz
1156 High St., Stevenson Academic
Santa Cruz, CA 95064
{panand,mcclosk}@ucsc.edu

Abstract

This paper reports on an effort to develop a linguistically-informed annotation scheme for *sluicing* (Ross, 1969), ellipsis that leaves behind a *wh*-phrase. We describe a scheme for annotating the elided content, both in terms of a free text representation and its degree of correspondence with its antecedent. We demonstrate that we can achieve reasonable IAA (α between .78 and .88 across eight annotation types) and describe some of the novel patterns that have arisen from this effort.

1 Introduction

Ellipsis is one of the central concerns of modern linguistic theory. Despite its importance, as noted by Bos & Spenader (2011), large-scale annotated corpora of elliptical phenomena are rare. Bos & Spender's own work is part of small group of papers attempting to annotate elliptical phenomena systematically. Much of this work has focused on studying Verb Phrase Ellipsis (VPE), which occurs when a verb phrase is replaced by an auxiliary, as in *I avoided meat, although I didn't have to <avoid meat>*.[1] Here, we consider sluicing (Ross, 1969), a distinct variety of ellipsis in which all but the interrogative phrase of a content question is elided, leaving behind the SLUICE, or *wh*-remnant, subject to an available ANTECEDENT:

(1) It's clear that the University has to change, but in what ways <the University has to change> is less clear.

[1] We follow the convention of indicating the implicit content of ellipsis inside angle brackets.

One of the central debates in the study of ellipsis concerns the various syntactic and semantic mismatches between antecedents and elliptical content, and an animating goal in our research is uncovering a theory-neutral representation of elliptical content that can help sort out the ranges of mismatches. We choose sluicing as our initial target for annotating implicit content for several reasons: it is cross-linguistically common (unlike VPE), it is well studied (which means that we have the makings of a rich annotation system), and it interacts with many other linguistic areas (e.g., the syntax and semantics of questions, discourse dynamics, lexical argument structure).

We describe an effort to extract 4100 sluicing examples from the New York Times subset of the Gigaword Corpus (Graff et al., 2005). We have currently annotated 417 instances in our corpus, and have achieved interannotator α values between .75 and .86 across eight annotators and eight annotation types. We begin in Section 2 with an overview of the theoretical landscape of sluicing and some discussion of previous corpus work. Section 3 lays out our annotation scheme and section 4 provides evaluation of the procedure that led to this scheme. In section 5 we discuss some qualitative observations on the licensing of sluicing that have arisen so far from our annotation. Finally, in section 6 we conclude with areas for future development.

2 Background

2.1 Theoretical Landscape

Following Chung et al. (1995), the literature recognizes two central kinds of sluices. In *merger* sluices (as in (2a)), the antecedent contains a correlate

Proceedings of LAW IX - The 9th Linguistic Annotation Workshop, pages 178–187,
Denver, Colorado, June 5, 2015.

phrase which corresponds to the WH-phrase of the sluice. There are also *sprouting* sluices, in which the context contains no correlate, as in (2b).

(2) a. They've made an offer to one of the candidates, but I'm not sure which one.
b. They were firing, but at what was unclear.

Whether or not the distinction between merger cases and sprouting cases is more than terminological has been a major point of contention: Chung et al. (1995) argue that merger sluices (but not sprouting) are not subject to syntactic island restrictions, a claim Merchant (2001) disputes but which Yoshida et al. (2013) provide experimental evidence for.

At a more basic level, though, the central question in research on sluicing is what, if anything, is the content of the ellipsis site. At one pole, anaphoric theories argue that ellipsis sites have no internal structure, and that resolving elliptical content is a species of anaphora resolution (Hardt, 1993; Darymple et al., 1991; Schieber et al., 1999; Ginzburg and Sag, 2000; Culicover and Jackendoff, 2005; Barker, 2013). At the other, parallelism theories assume that there is syntactic content to ellipsis sites that is somehow parallel to (or recycled from) the linguistic structure of the antecedent (Williams, 1977; Fiengo and May, 1994; Chung et al., 1995; Ross, 1969; Merchant, 2001; Craenenbroeck, 2010). While originally it was thought that parallelism should be defined in purely semantic terms, evidence has steadily accumulated that the availability of sluicing is sensitive to the morphosyntactic structure of the antecedent. First, unlike VPE (Kehler, 2002), sluicing does not tolerate voice mismatches (Merchant, 2001; Chung, 2005; Chung et al., 2011; Anderbois, 2010; Chung, 2013; Merchant, 2007):

(3) a. The candidate was abducted but we don't know who by/by who.
b. Somebody abducted the candidate, but we don't know by who *(he was abducted).

Similarly, bare nominal *wh*-phrases cannot be sluiced in certain cases in which the antecedent clause lacks a crucial preposition (Chung, 2005):

(4) a. They're jealous but it's unclear who *(of).
b. Last night he was very afraid, but he couldn't tell us what *(of).

Nevertheless, the morphosyntactic requirements for parallelism are not absolute, allowing at least for mismatches in finiteness or syntactic category like those below (Merchant, 2001):

(5) a. I can't play quarterback; I don't know how.
b. I remember meeting him but I don't remember when.

This conundrum — the simultaneous sensitivity of parallelism to fine-grained lexical and syntactic structure, alongside its blindness to finiteness or lexical category — highlights how little we still know about the range of potential mismatches. In our research, we aimed to create an annotation scheme that would allow us to bring to light the full variation permitted.

2.2 Related Work

As far as we know, there are precisely seven systematic corpus annotations of ellipsis, four focusing on verb phrase ellipsis (essentially, VPE and a handful of similar verbal processes, like pseudogapping and comparative deletion) (Hardt, 1997; Nielsen, 2005; Bos and Spenader, 2011; Shahabi and Baptista, 2012) and three on sluicing (Fernández et al., 2005; Beecher, 2008; Nykiel, 2010).

The first large-scale study of verbal ellipsis is due to Hardt (1997). 644 cases of VPE were extracted from the Penn Treebank, whose antecedents were then annotated by two coders. Hardt estimates that the tree patterns he looks for have a recall of less than 50%. As a result, two subsequent corpus-driven efforts have involved significant manual examination. Nielsen (2005) read through one million words across two corpora (444K words from the BNC, 680K words from the Penn Treebank), and uncovered 1510 instances of VPE. In addition to coding VPE antecedents, he provides text corresponding to an intuitive paraphrase of the ellipsis site and classifies the kind of mismatch between the antecedent and paraphrase according to thirteen criteria (e.g., tense mismatch, comparatives, inversion, split antecedents, inferred antecedent). In a similar effort, Bos & Spenader (2011) examined the entire WSJ portion of the Penn Treebank, focusing on modals and auxiliaries that "trigger" VPE. They find 580 instances of VPE and related phenomena, which they code for antecedent as well as: the morphosyntactic category of the antecedent, the trigger, and 34 strings connecting the antecedent and elision site. The bilingual VPE corpus of Shahabi & Baptista (2012) is markedly different from the three efforts already mentioned. They examine the Tehran English Persian Parallel Corpus (Pilevar-Taher et al., 2011), an automatically aligned English-to-Persian parallel corpus drawn from Open-subtitles that comprises 3.7 million words in each language. Using a trigger-based search like Bos & Spenader, they find 10,515 instances of VPE in English; they then show that one can straightforwardly quantify the relative poverty of verbal elliptical processes in Persian by determining how many VPE cases are resolved in Persian.

In the case of sluicing, there are three principal efforts, all with very particular and divergent aims. Nykiel (2010), for example, is interested in tracing the relative rates of sprouting and merger in 1689 sluices across five eras of English, from Old English to Present Day English. Beecher (2008) focuses on the particular question of which prepositions support swiping (sluicing in which the wh-expression and a preposition undergo inversion, e.g., *by who*). Using a list of ten question embedding predicates and 38 prepositions from the OED, he uses the Google Search API to extract expressions of the form "predicate who/what P", which he then culls to 3000 sluices. Finally, Fernandez et al. (2005) focuses on 'root' sluices that are isolated sentences (e.g, *Who? Why?*). Using regular expressions, they extract 5343 root sluices from the BNC, which the authors then annotated a portion of for antecedent and sluice type, inspired by Ginzburg and Sag (2000): those asking about an indefinite correlate, those requesting clarification on a presupposition, and statements of general confusion.

What should emerge from this overview is that while there is clearly important antecedent work in this area, the kind of systematic, exhaustive corpus we intend here is novel. Consider the issue of representation. All of the corpora above mark the antecedent and ellipsis site, but the ways they relate the two, if at all, are idiosyncratic. Both Nykiel and Fernandez et al. classify how the sluice wh-expression integrates with the antecedent, but neither of them provides a way of locating other potential (mis)matches. Nielsen additionally provides a text-based resolution and a category for the kind of mismatch, but the categories are quite broad and designed to be mutually exclusive. In addition, as Nielsen alone annotated these sluices, it is unclear whether resolving ellipsis sites in plain text can be done reliably across several annotators. Our goal, in some sense, is to unify all of these efforts.

3 Annotation Scheme Development

3.1 Introduction

The central research questions of this project are the representation schema we will use for resolving sluices and how we will notate mismatch. The representation schema is a tricky eye to thread. On the one hand, as we have seen, the range of representation assumptions is fairly broad. Bos & Spenader notably refrain from following Nielsen in resolving the ellipsis site, precisely because of the theoretical commitments that any choice brings. However, choosing not to resolve in turn means that one cannot catalog mismatches. Instead, our aim is to adopt the minimal representational commitments we must in order to document mismatches.

3.2 Data Selection

Our data comes from the New York Times subset of the English Gigaword Second Edition corpus (Graff et al., 2005). We first parsed the subset with the Stanford parser and then extracted all verb phrases whose final child was a wh-phrase. This yielded 5100 verb phrases. One author manually culled this to 4100 sluices (eliminated expressions were 40% idioms, 40% parsing errors, 15% repetitions we could not remove automatically, and 5% sluicing-like constructions we put aside for the moment). As a final quality check, the other author manually examined all 52,000 wh-phrases in a random 80th of the NYT subcorpus and discovered only one additional sluice.

Table 1 shows the distribution of the extracted sluices by embedding predicate and *wh*-remnant; for clarity, we only break out the top 7 remnants (95% of data) and top 8 predicates (80% of data). While *why* sluices are 44% of the data, somewhat surprisingly, 20% of the data came from degree sluices (*I know*

	oth.	which	where	what	when	how	how much	why	
oth.	58	40	50	67	70	75	132	250	742
figure	1		1			14	1	73	90
ask	4		3	1	1	6	9	79	103
specify	7	21	1	1	13	16	54	5	118
explain	5			1		10	1	189	206
understand	4					5	2	211	222
see	18		2	2		37	3	181	243
say	84	44	49	15	123	47	387	116	865
know	102	33	45	115	146	161	218	728	1548
	283	138	151	202	353	371	807	1832	4137

Table 1: Distribution of Sluices by Embedding Predicate and *wh*-remnant. *Oth.* designates all predicate or remnant types not listed.

he's hurt, but I don't know how bad.). As we discuss in section 5.3, these proved particularly challenging to annotate.

3.3 Scheme Development Procedure

Our annotation scheme was developed on 417 sluice instances over seven rounds of annotation and discussion. Sampling was biased to encourage diversity in *wh*-remnant type: we chose 50 examples randomly from each of the top seven remnant categories (*why*, *how much*, *how*, *when*, *what*, *where*, and *which*; see Table 1 for frequency breakdowns) and 67 randomly from the remaining data. In the first round, the authors first collaboratively annotated 4 sluices chosen for diversity of *wh*-remnant (*why*, *what kind*, *how much*, *what color*) and constructed an initial scheme. In addition to identifying the antecedent, like Nielsen, we resolved the ellipsis site with plain text. We also constructed taxonomies for the types of mismatch, the kind of implicit argument in cases of sprouting, and, in the case of merger, the varieties of correlates. We found that a context window radius of five sentences was sufficient to perform these tasks; crucially, even when the antecedent was nearby, determining the proper antecedent scope and ellipsis resolution often involved understanding the larger questions under discussion in the text. We then each annotated 33 sluices, and adjusted the taxonomies. For the remaining rounds, we recruited six annotators: five advanced undergraduate linguistics students (all with at least two courses in syntax and semantics) and one graduate linguistics student. All eight of us then annotated, in sequence, 40 sluices, followed by two additional rounds of 100 sluices, and one round of 140 sluices. We met weekly to compare and discuss problematic cases, revising the annotation scheme and reannotating all previous material. By round 5, annotators reported being able to annotate 15-20 annotations per hour. Although we considered using the automatic parses in annotation, we found the parsetrees too error-prone to adequately help with the fine-grained constituency analysis we required and elected to use text spans alone.

Annotation was conducted on a modified version of the brat web-based annotation tool (Stenetorp et al., 2012). Existing tools render the annotation of elided content difficult, since those that allow insertion of new markables (e.g., MMAX2 (Mueller and Strube, 2006)) completely alter the document, making inter-annotator comparison difficult. We have minimally modified brat to accept and display a free text paraphrase, but we aim in subsequent versions of this project to allow it to accept new content that can be further annotated as well (i.e, for mismatches with the antecedent).

3.4 Final Annotation Scheme

Our current annotation scheme codebook and a sample of our gold standard annotations in stand-off annotation format are available at http://ohlone.ucsc.edu/SCEC for browsing. Each sluice example is annotated with four obligatory tags: the antecedent, the sluiced expression – including a plain-text paraphrase of the elided content – the main predicate of the antecedent clause, and the correlate, if there is one. The correlate and sluice are also tagged with the taxonomic

MANDATORY TAGS

SLUICE : sluice site.

- TEXT: Free text paraphrase of elided material
- TYPE [Degree, Manner, Reason, Temporal, Locative, Classificatory, Possessive, Passive, PP, Focus, Other]
- ISLAND: whether sluice 'crosses' an island
- Mismatches [Finiteness, Tense, Person, Case, Subject Overtness, Additional Words, Other]

ANTECEDENT : intuitive fill for Ellipsis Site

PREDICATE : main predicate for clause in A .

CORRELATE : material in A replaced or elaborated on by WH-phrase.

- TYPE [Indefinite, Definite, Pronoun, Strong Quantifier, WH-phrase, Name, Disjunction, Temporal/Locative, Degree/Extent]

OPTIONAL TAGS

ELLIPSIS ANTECEDENT : A is elided

ALTERNATIVE ANTECEDENT : Secondary A

E-TYPE : Indefinite in A that is anaphoric in ES

IGNORE : Material not retained in ES

Figure 1: Abridged Sluicing 1.5 Tagset

features mentioned above (type of sluice, type of correlate, and morphosyntactic mismatches). Figure 1 summarizes these features.

In addition, each sluice example may additionally bear six optional tags. Two correspond to cases where there are several possible antecedents. In the case of Alternative Antecedent we observed several cases of antecedent "sandwiching", in which the sluice is buttressed by roughly synonymous potential antecedents, as in (6). Ellipsis Antecedent is used in cases where the antecedent for a sluice is itself elliptical (in all cases we have encountered, VPE).

(6) We lost our focus a little bit somewhere. I don't know where. But we lost it . [27861]

Two additional tags deal with interpretive differences between Antecedent and elided content. EType marks indefinite material in the Antecedent that is interpreted anaphorically in the ellipsis site, as in (7). Ignore marks material that is semantically active in the Antecedent but does not seem to be carried over to the elided content at all, such as parenthetical material (8a) or additive particles (8b).

(7) She said that she would issue a written ruling as soon as possible, but did not say when. [35291]

(8) a. First, though, they must teach. And, before that, figure out how. [36311]

b. He said McDonald also owed federal taxes, but he would not say how much. [5912]

4 Analysis of Annotation Scheme Development

Table 2 provides a condensed measure of interannotator agreement over the tags across the rounds.[2] Because all of the tags are text spans, we use Krippendorff's continuum metric (Krippendorff, 1995) (a special case of Krippendorff's α (Krippendorff, 2014) for spans). In general, IAA rates drop in Round 3, as the additional annotators were introduced, and then rises.

Most of the agreement gains come from conventions about boundaries (e.g., when ignored material at clause-edge should be marked Ignore vs. excluded from the Antecedent, what the predicates of copula and existential sentences are). In addition, the gains for Antecedent in Round 5 are largely due to the introduction of the Elided and Alternative Antecedent tags, which served to resolve a disagreement about what 'the' antecedent was in such unclear

[2]Note that the IAA rates have been computed for the novel instances in each round.

cases. EType's rise involved actual instruction of the annotators about the pragmatics of EType interpretations. Finally, Correlate increases are due both to implicit learning (e.g., what counted as the "real" correlate in an expression), but also due to a growing insight on our part about the complexity of degree sluices (see section 5.3). Agreement on the taxonomic features on Sluice and Correlate, not shown here for reasons of space, were consistently above 95% accuracy.

	Round				
Tag	2	3	4	5	6
Sluice	.83	.75	.78	.88	.86
Ante	.83	.67	.73	.78	.88
Pred	.92	.56	.85	.85	.85
Corr	.72	.58	.60	.74	.78
Elided				.94	.94
AltAnte				.66	.78
EType	.21	.32	.67	.80	.87
Ignore			.43	.74	.78
Text	62.4	48.2	50.4	84.2	84.2
Instances	33	40	100	100	140

Table 2: Inter-Annotator Agreement by Annotation Round. IAA for the first 8 span categories is calculated in Krippendorff's continuum metric and IAA for the free text paraphrases is in BLEU:3. Numbers are computed for new instances annotated in each round, which is provided at the bottom of the table.

4.1 Minimal Tampering and Maximal Omission

A significant portion of our discussions focused on the procedure for resolving the elided content. We found that many of the mismatch types were only clearly apparent on comparison of the free text paraphrase with the antecedent. However, the fact that paraphrases were free text gave annotators a great deal of latitude to modify the form of the antecedent – e.g., introducing an embedding predicate to preserve finiteness or paraphrasing away material to circumvent an island violating structure.

Two best practices arose during the process that increased consistency. First, we adopted a principle of "Minimal Tampering", where annotators were asked to modify the Antecedent text minimally; this was most successful after Round 3, where annotators were given the ability to alter a copy of the Antecedent (as opposed to constructing a paraphrase *de novo*). However, these paraphrases were often unnatural and prolix, because letter of the law Minimal Tampering required an annotator to overtly express material that is more naturally dropped in a typical conversational setting. For example, consider the temporal adjunct *Thursday* in (9a) and the locative adjunct *in the region* in (9b). Should these be explicitly mentioned, and if so, how should the paraphrase be structured (e.g., where should *in the region* go? with the *wh*-remnant or in its original location in the Antecedent?). Similarly, in (9c), the DP *thousands upon thousands of people* is an EType expression. Should that be expressed in the free-text paraphrase as *them, those people, those thousands upon thousands of people*?

(9) a. But Thursday the market for other California municipal bonds recovered a bit. "It's difficult to say how much, because liquidity is relatively low and trading is sporadic," said Ian MacKinnon , senior vice president of fixed-income for the Vanguard Group of mutual funds . [35463]

b. Among the proposals are new power plants in the region, although the report does not specify where. [143606]

c. There was always something new improved equipment, innovative means of transmission, original shows coming down the network line from New York and Chicago and above all, the knowledge that thousands upon thousands of people clustered around a box that sat like a shrine in their living rooms, listening. It didn't really matter to what. [36225]

We adopted Minimal Tampering in part to make links between the Antecedent and ellipsis more automatically recoverable, but after several rounds of unsuccessful additional conventions, we realized by round 5 that a more anaphorically reasonable approach was easier for annotators to reliably implement. We thus introduced a principle of 'Maximal Correlate Omission', which instructed annotators to preserve as little of the Correlate as they could. In the end, this meant that many of the stylistic differences in this kind of redundant content were removed. Correspondingly, there is a spike in agreement rates for Text in Table 2 after round 5 (IAA for paraphrases is provided in BLEU:3 score (Papineni et al., 2002)).

4.2 Unresolved issues

Two issues proved too difficult to annotate reliably. First, because there is controversy in the literature about whether sprouting occurs with 'core' arguments or only adjuncts, we attempted in Round 3 to mark cases of sprouting with their FrameNet roles. However, this task proved too costly for the annotators; fully 30% of the predicates we considered lacked a clear FrameNet entry, and for the remainder, it was often unclear which frame was best suited to the data.[3] This led us to adopt the streamlined sluice TYPE shown in Table 1. In addition, *wh*-remnants that coordinated phrases with distinct types and/or grammatical functions proved too challenging for us to annotate with current tools, since they interacted with the Antecedent in different ways. For example, in (10), the phrases link to different Correlates: *how many* picks up on the amount introduced by the vague partitive *a bunch* and *whom* targets the quantificational DP itself.

(10) To those who have faulted him for not lobbying aggressively for permanent trade relations for China , he said he had called "a bunch" of members of Congress , but would not say how many or whom . [89868]

5 Qualitative Results

Even though our current set of annotated examples is 10% of our extracted data, we are encouraged by the fact we have already encountered phenomena of real theoretical interest, but which one might have feared would be relatively rare – amnestied island-violations, for instance, as in (11) (note that the elided content is ungrammatical, as expected if this is an island amelioration):

(11) The handover took place at a British embassy in one of the newly independent Baltic states. Which one <the handover took place at a British embassy in> has never been confirmed.

In particular, several kinds of mismatch between antecedent and ellipsis site have turned up which have gone undiscussed or underdiscussed in previous work. Here we offer some examples, as an illustration of the potential for discovery that we think our resource holds out.

5.1 Modal mismatches

Since Merchant (2001), it has been known that a finite clause can antecede a nonfinite sluice, triggering attendant realis differences, as in (5a) above. But we have also found many (40) examples of the reverse pattern, where a non-finite (or modal) antecedes a sluice. In 30 of these cases, the precise modality intended inside the sluice is difficult to pin down. In (12), for example, is the intended modal here a simple future, or a future-oriented modal (if so, of what flavor?)? For the moment, we are simply annotating these cases with the expression MODAL, but our eventual goal is to understand why this previously unnoticed kind of vagueness is tolerated in sluicing.

(12) "I want to return (to Peru) some day , but I don't know when < I MODAL return to Peru> ... " [117524]

(13) Texas A&M coach Tony Barone unabashedly predicted that ... the Aggies could be better than a year ago. He just forgot to say when <the Aggies MODAL be better than a year ago>. [88489]

5.2 Compound Correlates

Several of our novel phenomena emerged originally as cases of annotator confusion, including the following:

(14) Despite my inclination toward procrastination, I am determined to send holiday cards this year. It doesn't much matter which holiday. [106579]

[3] An anonymous reviewer asks why we chose FrameNet over Propbank, which is considerably less articulated. As our initial intent was to characterize precisely what the role was, not simply whether it was core, we believed that FrameNet's specificity would be a benefit. The reviewer is right that Propbank may be good enough for the core-distinction, and we plan on following up on this idea.

This example emerged as a problem during annotation precisely because it is unclear what the shape of the analysis is—what the elided content is, what the Antecedent is, how they correspond—and yet all annotators agreed it is grammatical. Three analyses of the elided content are possible: that the *wh*-remnant is sprouted off *holiday cards*; that it is extracted from the compound nominal *holiday cards*, violating numerous constraints on extraction; or that it is extracted from an elided cleft 'pseudo-sluice' (as in (15c)).

(15) a. It doesn't much matter which holiday <I send holiday cards for>

b. It doesn't much matter which holiday <I send [__ cards]>

c. It doesn't much matter which holiday <it is that I send holiday cards for>

Of these options, both the sprouting and compound nominal cases are empirically novel. If sprouting, it should be as ill-formed as **They're jealous but it's unclear who.* If the compound analysis is correct, there are issues for the analysis both of compounds and of correlates.

5.3 Degree Expressions

Among our most vexing (and interesting) cases for annotation were degree sluices, underdiscussed in the theoretical literature, but very common in our data. A degree *wh*-remnant (like *how much*) may have no overt Correlate, as in (16), or may have as correlate a vague indefinite extent, as in (17).

(16) a. They said this would save the government money, though they could not yet say how much <this would save the government money>. [2753]

b. The review, Gilligan acknowledged, delayed the issuance of the notice about Strandflex, but she said she could not estimate by how much <the review delayed the issuance of the notice about Strandflex>. [60122]

(17) a. The Atlanta-based company said Thursday that operating profit would be "substantially below" analysts' estimates but didn't specify how much <operating profit would be below analysts' estimates>. [104088]

b. But Thursday the market for other California municipal bonds recovered a bit. "It's difficult to say how much <the market for other California municipal bonds recovered>, because ... " [35463]

For our annotators, the question was: what is the correlate in cases like (17)? The apparent answer is that the correlates are the vague indefinite extent expressions *substantially* and *a bit.* But these elements are optional and in their absence sluicing with *how much* remains possible, much as in (16b). But that in turn suggests that the 'real' correlates for such cases are not *substantially* or *a bit*, but rather implicit degree expressions which are further restricted by *substantially* or *a bit.* However, if all of that is reasonable, it suggests an account for cases like (16) in which there are also implicit degree correlates—over extents saved, or delayed by.

There is a practical question of annotation here. But as is often the case, annotation dilemmas highlight theoretical puzzles. Cases like those in (16) would naturally be taken to be sprouting cases, while those in (17), because there is an overt indefinite, would naturally be taken to be cases of merger. But that bifurcation obscures important (semantic) commonalities between the two kinds of cases, and suggests once more how useful sluicing can be as a probe for implicit content. And since such cases suggest that at least some apparent cases of sprouting need to be analyzed in terms of implicit correlates, they force the question again of whether or not such interpretations are generally correct—a position which would in turn have important ramifications for theories of implicit content more generally. Vexation for annotators often signals phenomena of particular theoretical interest.

6 Conclusion

In this paper, we have presented a novel, linguistically-informed annotation scheme for tackling the elided content of sluices and have shown that the system can produce annotations with a high degree of reliability. We have also demonstrated that even in the small amount of data we have examined, patterns outside those traditionally talked about are already cropping up. We view the current scheme as stable and are annotating the remainder of our data in earnest. Looking ahead, one crucial question we are still considering is the representational schema for elided content. One key limitation of our present toolkit is the inability to mark correspondences between parts of the overt text and parts of the (annotator-generated) elided content. This has made the annotation of, for example, coordinated sluices, impossible and many other tasks cumbersome. In the future, we plan on adapting brat to allow us to relate parts of the Antecedent and elided content directly, building something akin to a word alignment corpus for ellipsis. Such a method could prove both powerful and reasonably theory-neutral across a range of elliptical constructions. We also are considering incorporating further syntactic and semantic annotation (e.g, lightweight syntactic or semantic dependencies) as an additional layer of representation that can be marshaled to (in)validate various theories of sluicing and ellipsis more generally.

Acknowledgments

We would like to first thank our three anonymous reviewers for helpful comments. We have benefited from conversations with: Sandy Chung, Amy Rose Deal, Dan Hardt, Bill Ladusaw, Jason Merchant, Craige Roberts, Bern Samko, and Matt Wagers. This work has been funded by a UCSC Institute for Humanities Research Grant to the Santa Cruz Ellipsis Consortium and a UCSC Committee on Research grant to Jim McCloskey. Finally, this work would not have been possible without the diligent, incisive labor of annotation-wrangler Bern Samko and our undergraduate annotators at various stages of this project: Philip King, Chelsea Miller, Emma Peoples, Nick Primrose, Michael Titone, Danny de la Vega, Tony Zavala, Jasmine Embry, Jack Haskins, Lily Ng and Rachelle Boyson.

References

Scott Anderbois. 2010. Sluicing as anaphora to issues. Presented at SALT 20, University of British Columbia and Simon Fraser University, April 29–May 1, 2010.

Chris Barker. 2013. Scopability and sluicing. *Linguistics and Philosophy*, 36:187–223.

Henry Beecher. 2008. Pramatic inference in the interpretation of sluiced Prepositional Phrases. In *San Diego Linguistic Papers*, volume 3, pages 2–10. Department of Linguistics, UCSD, La Jolla, California.

Johan Bos and Jennifer Spenader. 2011. An annotated corpus for the analysis of vp ellipsis. *Language Resources and Evaluation*, 45(4):463–494.

Sandra Chung, William Ladusaw, and James McCloskey. 1995. Sluicing and logical form. *Natural Language Semantics*, 3:239–282.

Sandra Chung, William Ladusaw, and James McCloskey. 2011. Sluicing(:) between structure and inference. In Rodrigo Gutiérrez-Bravo, Line Mikkelsen, and Eric Potsdam, editors, *Representing Language: Essays in Honor of Judith Aissen*, pages 31–50. California Digital Library eScholarship Repository. Linguistic Research Center, University of California Santa Cruz, Santa Cruz, California.

Sandra Chung. 2005. Sluicing and the lexicon: The point of no return. In Rebecca Cover and Yuni Kim, editors, *BLS 31, Proceedings of the Thirty-First Annual Meeting of the Berkeley Linguistics Society*, pages 73–91. Department of Linguistics, UC Berkeley, Berkeley, Calif.

Sandra Chung. 2013. Syntactic identity in sluicing: How much and why. *Linguistic Inquiry*, 44:1–44.

Jereon van Craenenbroeck. 2010. *The Syntax of Ellipsis: Evidence from Dutch Dialects*. Oxford University Press, Oxford.

Peter Culicover and Ray Jackendoff. 2005. *Simpler Syntax*. Oxford University Press, Oxford and New York.

Mary Darymple, Stuart M. Schieber, and Fernanda C. N. Pereira. 1991. Ellipsis and higher-order unification. *Linguistics and Philosophy*, 14:399–452.

Raquel Fernández, Jonathan Ginzburg, and Shalom Lappin. 2005. Automatic bare sluice disambiguation in dialogue. In *Proceedings of the IWCS-6 (Sixth International Workshop on Computational Semantics)*, pages 115–127, Tilburg, the Netherlands, January. Available at: http://www.dcs.kcl.ac.uk/staff/lappin/recent_papers_index.html.

Robert Fiengo and Robert May. 1994. *Indices and Identity*. MIT Press, Cambridge, Mass.

Jonathan Ginzburg and Ivan Sag. 2000. *Interrogative Investigations: The Form, Meaning and Use of English Interrogatives*. CSLI Publications, Stanford, Calif.

David Graff, Junbo Kong, Ke Chen, and Kazuaki Maeda. 2005. English gigaword second edition ldc2007t07. Technical report, Linguistic Data Consortium, Philadelphia.

Daniel Hardt. 1993. *Verb Phrase Ellipsis: Form, Meaning and Processing*. Ph.D. thesis, University of Pennsylvania.

Daniel Hardt. 1997. An empirical approach to vp ellipsis. *Computational Lingusitics*, 23(4):525–541.

Andrew Kehler. 2002. *Coherence in Discourse*. CSLI Publications, Stanford, Calif.

Klaus Krippendorff. 1995. On the reliability of unitizing continuous data. In P. V. Marsden, editor, *Sociological Methodology 1995*, volume 25. Blackwell, Cambridge, Massachusetts.

Klaus Krippendorff. 2014. *Content Analysis: An Introduction to its Methodology*. Sage Publications, Thousand Oaks, California, 3rd edition.

Jason Merchant. 2001. *The syntax of silence: sluicing, islands, and the theory of ellipsis*. Oxford University Press, Oxford and New York.

Jason Merchant. 2007. Voice and ellipsis. Manuscript, University of Chicago, available at http://home.uchicago.edu/~merchant/publications.html.

Christoph Mueller and Michael Strube. 2006. Multi-level annotation of linguistic data with mmax2. In *Corpus Technology and Language Pedagogy: New Resources, New Tools, New Methods*.

Leif Arda Nielsen. 2005. A corpus-based study of verb phrase ellipsis identification and resolution.

Johanna Nykiel. 2010. Whatever happened to Old English sluicing. In Robert A. Cloutier, Anne Marie Hamilton-Brehm, and Jr. William A. Kretzschmar, editors, *Studies in the History of the English Language V: Variation and Change in English Grammar and Lexicon: Contemporary Approaches*, pages 37–59. Walter de Gruyter.

Kishore Papineni, Salim Roukos, Todd Ward, and Wei jing Zhu. 2002. Bleu: a method for automatic evaluation of machine translation. pages 311–318.

Mohammad Pilevar-Taher, Heshaam Faili, and Abdol-Hamid Pilevar. 2011. TEP: Tehran English-Persian parallel corpus. In Alexander Gelbukh, editor, *Computational Linguistics and Intelligent Text Processing*, volume 6609 of *Lecture Notes in Computer Science*, pages 68–79. Springer Berlin Heidelberg.

John R. Ross. 1969. Guess who? In Robert Binnick, Alice Davison, Georgia Green, and Jerry Morgan, editors, *CLS 5: Papers from the Fifth Regional Meeting of the Chicago Linguistic Society*, pages 252–286. Chicago Linguistic Society, Chicago, Illinois.

Stuart Schieber, Fernanda Pereira, and Mary Dalrymple. 1999. Interaction of scope and ellipsis. In Shalom Lappin and Elabbas Benmamoun, editors, *Fragments: Studies in Ellipsis and Gapping*, pages 8–31. Oxford University Press, Oxford.

Mitra Shahabi and Jorge Baptista. 2012. A corpus-based translation study on English-Persian verb phrase ellipsis. *ICAME Journal*, 36:95–112.

Pontus Stenetorp, Sampo Pyysalo, Goran Topić, Tomoko Ohta, Sophia Ananiadou, and Jun'ichi Tsujii. 2012. brat: a web-based tool for NLP-assisted text annotation. In *Proceedings of the Demonstrations Session at EACL 2012*. Project Website: http://brat.nlplab.org/about.html.

Edwin Williams. 1977. Discourse and logical form. *Linguistic Inquiry*, 8:101–139.

Masaya Yoshida, Jiyeon Lee, and Michael Walsh Dickey. 2013. The island (in)sensitivity of sluicing and sprouting. In Jon Sprouse and Norbert Hornstein, editors, *Experimental Syntax and Island Effects*, pages 360–376. Cambridge University Press, Cambridge and New York.

Annotating Causal Language Using Corpus Lexicography of Constructions

Jesse Dunietz
Computer Science Department
Carnegie Mellon University
Pittsburgh, PA 15213, USA
jdunietz@cs.cmu.edu

Lori Levin and **Jaime Carbonell**
Language Technologies Institute
Carnegie Mellon University
Pittsburgh, PA 15213, USA
{lsl, jgc}@cs.cmu.edu

Abstract

Detecting and analyzing causal language is essential to extracting semantic relationships. To that end, we present an annotation scheme for English causal language (not metaphysical causality), and discuss two methodologies for annotation. The first uses only a coding manual to train annotators in distinguishing causal from non-causal language. To address low inter-coder agreement, we adopted a second methodology, in which we first created a causal language *constructicon* based on corpus analysis, then required annotators only to annotate instances based on the constructicon. (This resembles the methodology used for annotating the FrameNet and PropBank corpora.) Our contributions, in addition to the annotation scheme itself, are methodological: we discuss when constructicon-based methodology is appropriate, and address the validity of annotation schemes that require expert-level metalinguistic awareness.

1 Introduction

Information extraction relies on identifying and analyzing the semantic relationships expressed in text. One of the most important kinds of relationship to extract is causality: we think about the world around us in terms of causation, and we often consult texts about what causes, enables, or prevents some phenomenon (e.g., medical symptoms, political events, or interpersonal actions). Unsurprisingly, causal language is also ubiquitous; Conrath et al. (2014) found that in French, causation constituted 33% of the relations expressed between verbs.

Despite its centrality to our thought and language, causal relationships are not captured well by standard semantic representations. The linguistic expression of causal relations varies greatly (Wolff et al., 2005), ranging from verbal propositions to discourse relations to arbitrarily complex constructions. There is no one standard representation scheme that can handle all of these types of semantics, making it difficult to analyze and extract causal relationships in a coherent, comprehensive manner.

Filling this gap requires grappling with some of the most difficult issues in language annotation. Causation is a complex concept, heavily discussed in philosophical and psychological circles. Its boundaries are fuzzy: causation is a psychological construct that we use to explain the world around us, and it does not perfectly match either empirical reality or the language we use to describe it (see Neeleman and Van de Koot [2012]). Furthermore, causation is intertwined with many other dimensions of meaning, such as temporal relations, counterfactuals, factivity, and negation. This raises important questions about how to carve out a semantic space for an annotation scheme to meaningfully represent. It also raises practical questions about how to guide annotators to sensible decisions in such a domain.

In this paper, we describe three primary contributions toward coping with the complexity of annotating causal language. First, drawing on principles from construction grammar, we present a new annotation scheme for causal language. The scheme provides a uniform representation for a wide spectrum of causal language, while still allowing for semantically relevant dimensions of variation. It attempts to

Proceedings of LAW IX - The 9th Linguistic Annotation Workshop, pages 188–196,
Denver, Colorado, June 5, 2015.

limit the complexity of annotation by focusing not on the hairy metaphysics of causation, but on the assertions about causation that are explicit in the language. We ultimately plan to use this scheme in an automated causal information extraction system.

Our second contribution is to compare two approaches to annotating causality, one using an annotation manual only and the other using a *constructicon* developed by an expert along with an annotation manual. The constructicon-based methodology is similar to the two-stage methodology used in PropBank (Palmer et al., 2005) and FrameNet (Baker et al., 1998) annotations: an initial phase of corpus lexicography produces a lexicon, followed by a second phase in which annotators identify instances of the lexical frames in a corpus. In our case, the "lexicon" is a list of English constructions that conventionally express causality. We also offer suggestions for when such an approach may be appropriate.

Finally, we discuss the broader implications of our experience for difficult annotation tasks. In particular, we address the concern of arbitrariness in schemes which can only be successfully be applied by experts or highly trained annotators.

2 Related Work

2.1 Annotating Real-World Causal Relations

Several previous projects have attempted to annotate causation in text. Many of these have focused on annotating the causal relations that exist in the real world, rather than causal language.

SemEval 2007 included a task (Girju et al., 2007) concerning classifying semantic relations between nominals, including causal relations. As part of this task, the organizers provided a dataset tagged with noun-noun relations. However, this task relied on a less precise, common-sense notion of real-world causation, and the annotations do not indicate the causal connectives, presumably because real-world causal relationships may not be indicated in the text. The SemEval data also limited the causes and effects to nouns (in our experience, they are often clauses).

Grivaz (2010) finds that human annotators struggle to apply standard philosophical tests to make binary decisions about the presence of causation in a text segment. She suggests alternative criteria, which we take into account in our coding manual. Many of her criteria, however, are concerned with how people identify real-world causal relationships, rather than how speakers or writers explicitly invoke the concept of causality.

The Richer Events Description schema has also incorporated cause/effect relations (Ikuta et al., 2014). This effort, too, is concerned with bringing annotators to agreement on what counts as real-world causation. It is also limited to event-event relations, even though causal language often describes states or objects as causes or effects.

2.2 Annotating Causal Language

Other projects have, to a greater or lesser extent, focused on annotating *stated* causal relationships, much as we have. In general, our scheme attempts to be more precise in its definitions, more general in its scope, and more rich in its representational capacity than these prior works.

The Penn Discourse TreeBank (PDTB; Prasad et al., 2008) includes several relation types that are relevant to causation (primarily CAUSE and REASON). Its representation of causal relations is limited in three important ways that we attempt to overcome. First, it does not capture the subtleties of different types of causal relationships. Second, it is limited to discourse relations, and so excludes other realizations of the relationship (e.g., verb arguments). Finally, its relation hierarchy fails to capture overlaps between the semantics of different discourse phenomena (e.g., hypotheticals may also be causal).

Closer to our work is the scheme proposed by Mirza et al. (2014), who base their representation on Talmy's "force dynamics" model of causation (Talmy, 1988). Their model is rich enough to capture linguistic triggers of causation, as well as causes and effects. It particularly follows Wolff's (2005) taxonomy of expressions of causation. However, like the PDTB, it does not distinguish the different types of causal relationships. It also does not rigorously define what it counts as causal, and like Ikuta's work, it is limited to event-event relations.

The project most similar in spirit to ours is BioCause (Mihăilă et al., 2013), which provides an annotation framework for causal relations in biomedical texts. The BioCause framework, like ours, marks the connective and argument spans and the direction of causality. The primary difference between Bio-

Cause and our project is that ours aims to be more general in scope. As such, our scheme also does not examine some kinds of domain-specific language that BioCause includes (e.g., upregulation). In a sense, our project may be thought of as a generalization of BioCause to broader domains, and also an attempt to pin down more precisely what kinds of relationships to annotate as causal.

3 Causal Language Annotation Scheme

3.1 Annotation Scheme Design Philosophy

For the purposes of this project, we are interested in studying specifically *causal language* – the language used to appeal to psychological notions of causality. We are **not** concerned with identifying relationships that are causal in some "true" metaphysical sense; what characterizes true causation is a highly contentious topic within philosophy (Schaffer, 2014; Dowe, 2008). We believe that focusing on this question has unnecessarily confounded previous attempts at annotating causation in text.

Instead, we are concerned only with *what the text asserts* – causal *language* and what is meant by it. If and only if the text explicitly appeals to some psychological notion of promoting or hindering, then the relationship it asserts is one we want to represent, whether or not it is metaphysically accurate.

Consider, for example, the sentence "She must have met him before, because she recognized him yesterday." Few philosophers would say it expresses a "truly" causal relationship, but it does appeal to the psychological notion of causation. (The category of INFERENCE, described below, was included specifically to handle cases like this.)

Although the boundaries of causality are not well-defined, we wished to study causal language in isolation to the extent we could. We therefore designed the annotation scheme to exclude language that incorporates other elements of meaning beyond causality, as well as language whose causal interpretation is ambiguous or merely suggestive. However, we also designed it to be composable with other components of semantic analysis: negation, aspect, hedging, and so on. We assume that other annotation schemes will represent these aspects, and that this additional information may alter the semantics of the causal relationship as a whole.

Our current focus is English only. We believe that the basic components of the annotation scheme should apply in other languages, but many adjustments to the criteria for inclusion would be needed.

3.2 Defining Causal Language

We use the term *causal language* to refer to clauses or phrases in which one event, state, action, or entity (the cause) is *explicitly presented as* promoting or hindering another (the effect). The cause and effect must be deliberately related by an explicit causal connective. (As emphasized above, the words "presented as" are essential to this definition.)

Causal relations can be expressed in English in many different ways. In this project, we exclude:

- **Causal relationships with no lexical trigger.** We do not annotate implicit causal relationships ("zero" discourse connectives). We expect our work to be compatible with other work on such relationships, such as the implicit relations in the PDTB and systems for recovering those relationships (Conrath et al., 2014).

- **Connectives that lexicalize the means or the result of the causation.** For example, *kill* can be interpreted as "cause to die," but it encodes the result, so we exclude it. This decision was made to allow the scheme to focus specifically on language that expresses causation. If lexical causatives were included, nearly every transitive verb in the English language would have to be considered causal; it would be impossible to disentangle causation as a semantic phenomenon with its own linguistic realizations. It would also be impossible to annotate the cause and effect separately from the connective.[1]

  Omitting lexical causatives is consistent with previous causal language annotation schemes (e.g., Mirza et al. [2014]), though we are not aware of previous attempts to define what must be lexicalized for a verb to be excluded.

- **Connectives that assert an unspecified causal relationship.** "Smoking is linked to cancer"

[1]If lexical connectives are ever desired, the PropBank or FrameNet lexicon could be augmented to indicate which verb senses are causal, and the associated corpus could then act as a supplemental causal language corpus.

does not specify what sort of causal link is present, so we do not annotate it.

- **Temporal language** (e.g., "After I drank some water, I felt much better"). These instances are often extremely ambiguous ("after" can be purely temporal). Even when they are unambiguously causal, the causal relationship is clear not from causal *language*, but from real-world knowledge about the events presented.

3.3 Anatomy of a Causal Language Instance

For each instance of causal language that meets these criteria, we annotate three spans (any of which may be non-contiguous):

- **The causal connective** – the lexical items in the construction signalling the causal relationship. Following the basic ideas of construction grammar (Fillmore et al., 1988), the connective may be any surface linguistic pattern conventionally used to indicate causation. Such constructions generally have at least two open slots (for cause and effect). The connective annotation includes all words whose lemmas appear in every instance of the construction.

- **The cause.** Causes are generally events or states of affairs, expressed as complete clauses or phrases. Sometimes, however, an actor, but not an action, is presented as the cause (e.g., "I prevented a fire."). In such cases, we take the actor to be metonymic for the action, and accordingly annotate the actor as the cause.

- **The effect.** Also generally an event or state of affairs, expressed as a complete clause/phrase.

In general, the spans of the arguments do not overlap with the spans of the connectives (though there are some exceptions).

3.4 Types of Causation

We distinguish four different types of causal relationships, each of which can have subtly different semantics. Examples of each are given in Table 1.

Causation type	Example
CONSEQUENCE	*We are in serious economic trouble* because of **inadequate regulation**.
MOTIVATION	**We don't have much time**, so *let's move quickly*.
PURPOSE	To **strengthen our company**, *we must set clearer policies*.
INFERENCE	*This car was driven recently*, because **the hood is still hot**.

Table 1: Examples of each of the four types of causal language (with **causes** in bold and *effects* in italics).

CONSEQUENCE instances assert that the cause naturally leads to the effect via some chain of events, without highlighting the conscious intervention of any agent. The majority of instances are CONSEQUENCEs (see Table 2).

MOTIVATION instances assert that some agent perceives the cause, and therefore consciously thinks, feels, or chooses something. Again, what is important for this scheme is how the relationship is presented, so an instance is MOTIVATION only if it frames the relationship in a way that highlights an agent's decision or thought.

PURPOSE instances assert that an agent chooses the effect out of a desire to make the cause true. What distinguishes PURPOSEs from MOTIVATIONs is whether the motivating argument is a fact about the world or an outcome the agent hopes to achieve.

Note that there is a confusing duality in PURPOSEs. The desire for a particular outcome (e.g., "to strengthen our company") motivates (causes) the effect ("we must set clearer policies"). But from another perspective, having clearer policies is a cause whose effect may be strengthening the company. We choose to focus on the first of these relationships because we take this to be the primary relationship expressed by language such as "in order to."

INFERENCE instances borrow the language of CONSEQUENCE, but they do not assert an actual chain of events from cause to effect. Instead, they present the cause as evidence or justification for the effect (*epistemic causation*).

3.5 Degrees of Causation

In principle, causal relationships lie on a spectrum from total prevention to total entailment. Wolff et al. (2005) discretize this spectrum into three categories: CAUSE, ENABLE, and PREVENT. In practice, however, we found that annotators were able to reliably

	In subcorpus annotated with:	
	Manual only	**Constructicon**
CONSEQUENCE	66	33
MOTIVATION	18	11
PURPOSE	4	21
INFERENCE	0	4
Total	88	69

Table 2: Number of instances of each causation type in the subcorpora used for IAA. (Counts are from the first author's annotations.)

	Partial overlap:	
	Allowed	**Excluded**
Connectives (F_1)	0.70	0.66
Degrees (κ)	0.87	0.87
Causation types (κ)	0.25	0.29
Argument spans (F_1)	0.94	0.83
Argument labels (κ)	0.92	0.94

Table 3: Inter-annotator agreement for the coding-manual-only approach, showing the middling degree of reliability achieved for connectives and causation types. The difference between the two columns is that for the left column, we counted two annotation spans as a match if at least a quarter of the larger one overlapped with the smaller; for the right column, we required an exact match. κ scores indicate Cohen's kappa. Each κ score was calculated only for spans that agreed (e.g., degrees were only compared for matching connective spans).

distinguish only positive and negative causation. We therefore annotate the degree of each instance as either FACILITATE or INHIBIT. (We hope to return to finer-grained distinctions of degree in future work.)

3.6 Tools and Data

We performed all annotations using BRAT (Stenetorp et al., 2012), a web-based annotation tool. A sample annotation is shown in Figure 1.

For our corpus, we randomly selected documents from the Washington section of the New York Times corpus (Sandhaus, 2008) from the year 2007. We found that the political nature of these documents lent itself to more frequent use of causal language. At present, we have annotated ~1200 sentences in total, containing ~400 instances of causal language.

4 Initial Annotation Process: Coding Manual Only

In the design phase of our project, we developed a coding manual for this annotation scheme, working with three annotators to identify and decide on difficult cases. Once we felt the manual was ready for large-scale annotation, we spent several weeks training a previously uninvolved annotation expert to apply the scheme. The first author's annotations on 201 sentences (containing about 88 instances of causal language) were then compared against the new annotator's to determine inter-annotator agreement. The counts of different causation types are shown in Table 2.

Under this process, annotators were expected to consider all principles and special cases laid out in the manual for each decision: whether something counted as causal language at all, what words should be included in the connective, and what the argument spans should be. Decision trees were provided to determine the degree and type of the instance.

5 Initial Annotation Results and Difficulties

Our initial results (Table 3) did not seem to reflect our many iterations of feedback with the new annotator. For connectives that matched, the argument annotations agreed fairly well, as did the degrees. But the agreement rate for the connectives themselves was only moderately good, and agreement on causation types was abysmal.

Furthermore, the annotator, who had more than 30 years of annotation experience in other tasks, reported that she had found the process torturous and time-consuming, and that she still did not feel confident in her choices. Even to achieve the results in Table 3, the annotator had to ask several clarification questions about specific constructions. This matched the experience of the earlier annotators who had helped us develop the scheme: they felt the guidelines made sense, and for any given annotation they could reach consensus via discussion, but even after working with the scheme for months, annotating still felt difficult and uncertain.

These results raised two important questions. The first was a matter of procedure: what could we do

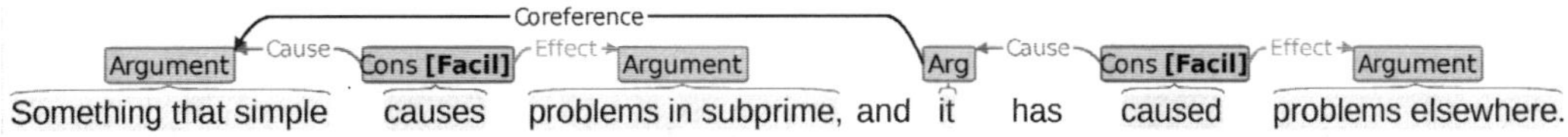

Figure 1: Two fully-annotated instances of causal language in BRAT. Coreference links are included in the annotation only for arguments that consist entirely of a pronoun.

to improve the annotation process and reliability? The second question was more fundamental: even assuming we could improve the agreement scores, how should we interpret the fact that annotators were struggling so? If the scheme was still unintuitive after so much training, was it even meaningful at all?

In the next two sections, we address each of these questions in turn.

6 Modularizing the Annotation Process with Corpus Lexicography

The biggest factor dragging down annotators' comfort seemed to be the sheer number of decisions they had to make. In particular, we were expecting them to mentally redraw for every possible connective the fuzzy line between causal and non-causal, keeping in mind the entire gestalt of guidelines and special cases. It is no surprise that this task felt overwhelming, especially given that even once they had decided an instance was causal, they still faced decisions about annotation spans, causation type, and degree.

Much of this effort is in fact redundant. Most connectives in a text will be familiar, and the uses of any given connective are fairly consistent. Accordingly, once a decision about a linguistic pattern has been made once, that decision can often be applied to future instances of the pattern.

Accordingly, we split the annotation process into two phases. In the first phase, we compiled a *constructicon* – a simple list of known causal constructions – by manually cataloguing all connectives seen so far (including in the original annotation set). This catalog could then be quickly consulted whenever annotators encountered a potential connective. As exemplified in Table 4, the catalog gives the word senses for which each connective pattern applies, as well as possible variants, which words to include in the connective span, the degree the connective indicates, and in some cases restrictions on its causation type. Building the constructicon thus requires the same difficult decisions, but these decisions can be made once in consultation with others, and then applied repeatedly to new instances of each pattern.

Connective pattern	⟨cause⟩ prevents ⟨effect⟩ from ⟨effect⟩
WordNet senses	prevent.verb.01 prevent.verb.02
Annotatable words	prevent, from
Degree	INHIBIT
Type restrictions	Not PURPOSE

Table 4: A sample entry in the constructicon.

The constructicon currently includes 166 constructions, covering 79 lexically distinct connectives (e.g., "prevent __" and "prevent __ from __" are the same connective but distinct constructions).

In the second phase, annotators used the constructicon to label novel text. The task primarily now consisted of recognizing known patterns and making sure that the word senses used in the text matched the senses for which the patterns were defined.

Of course, there is a cycle in this process: if annotators spot a plausible connective that is not in the constructicon, they can propose it to be added. But given the relative rarity of novel connectives, this is not the annotators' primary task.

We expect to release both the constructicon and an expanded corpus based on it at a later date.

6.1 Lexicography-Based Annotation Results

Using this method, we trained another annotator for about a day. After just two rounds of annotation with feedback, the first author and the new annotator both used the constructicon to annotate a new dataset of 260 sentences, drawn from the same corpus, containing 69 instances of causal language.[2]

We expected inter-annotator agreement to decrease compared to our previous attempt. The new

[2]We did not reuse the same dataset because the first author had become too familiar with it and it had informed the constructicon, so it would not have been a meaningful test.

	Partial overlap: Allowed	Excluded
Connectives (F_1)	0.78	0.70
Degrees (κ)	1.0	1.0
Causation types (κ)	0.82	0.80
Argument spans (F_1)	0.96	0.86
Argument labels (κ)	0.98	0.97

Table 5: Inter-annotator agreement results with annotators using the constructicon. See Table 3 for a fuller description of how these statistics were computed.

annotator had far less annotation experience, and he had received a fraction of the training on this task. Additionally, we had fewer coded instances, which tends to cause κ scores to drop, and it seemed likely that the lower density of causal language would make it harder to spot the occasional instance.

In fact, our results (shown in Table 5) improved on our initial results in several important respects. First, there was a modest increase in F_1 for connectives. Second, agreement on causation types was now excellent. Third, all other metrics, even those that had already been high, improved slightly. And perhaps most significantly, these results were achieved with a fraction of the training time – a day instead of weeks – and the annotator found annotating quite painless.

Given that these results were computed on a different dataset, it is possible that the improvements are not as great as they seem. Nonetheless, the difference in annotator comfort was striking, and we believe that both datasets are representative.

Of course, the lexicography work itself still takes significant effort – effort that we were able to shortcut somewhat by mining our existing annotations to build the constructicon. But in general, the lexicography could be done in parallel with refining the scheme itself, as trial datasets are annotated.

6.2 When is Lexicography Appropriate?

The lexicography-based approach to semantic annotation is not new, of course. Several high-profile annotation projects have used it successfully, most notably PropBank and FrameNet. But it is a relatively uncommon approach for projects to take. Our experience suggests that although lexicography may not work well for every annotation effort, it may be more widely useful than current practice would indicate.

The essential question, then, is what characteristics make a project a good fit for corpus lexicography. Our experience here is limited, but one feature of our project seems to have made it particularly amenable to this approach: without a constructicon, annotators had to make the same decisions repeatedly. This was the core reason why the constructicon was useful; a constructicon would not save any work if it did not codify frequently made decisions.

Of course, a lexicography-based approach intensifies concerns about meaningfulness. Adopting a lexicon may increase inter-annotator agreement, but what annotators are agreeing on is more constrained. A generous reading is that that the experts who compiled the lexicon have helped less-expert annotators make more accurate choices. But there is a less charitable reading, as well: if such constraints are needed for agreement, perhaps the annotation scheme fails to capture meaningful semantic categories – perhaps it is merely a fiction of the minds of its designers. It is to this concern that we turn next.

7 What Does Low Non-Expert Agreement Say About Validity?

What imparts validity to an annotation scheme is a fundamental question that haunts every annotation project. Even a well-thought-out scheme can include arbitrary, empirically meaningless decisions, which would seem to undermine the scheme's value as a description of a real linguistic phenomenon.[3]

This risk of arbitrariness is precisely what appears to bother Riezler (2014) in his discussion of circularity in computational linguistics: it is entirely possible that an annotation scheme has high inter-annotator agreement and can even be reproduced by software, and yet the scheme is empirically empty. The agreement can be achieved simply by developing a shared body of implicit, arbitrary theoretical assumptions among expert or intensively trained coders. Meanwhile, the fact that the annotations can be reproduced automatically shows only that the theory can be expressed both as an annotation scheme and as an annotation machine, not that it encapsulates something meaningful.

[3]Similar questions arise in designing and assessing tests for social science research (Trochim, 2006).

Thus, the problem of arbitrary assumptions raises especially serious questions about any scheme for which expertise seems to be required. If a scheme requires expert input or intensive training to reach agreement, that seems to suggest that the scheme is really a "stone soup" of theoretical, possibly arbitrary assumptions among the experts.

One tempting solution is Riezler's first suggestion for breaking circularity: using naive coders, such as crowdsourced annotators. The instructions that convey the scheme to the coders, who do not share the same theoretical assumptions, constitute a second theory that the original theory can be grounded in. This, Riezler implies, would demonstrate the empirical reality of the theory behind the scheme, which he presumably would argue confirms its value.

For many schemes, high agreement among naive coders may indeed break the circularity of the scheme. But as our lexicography-based approach highlights, this solution may not address the deeper problem of arbitrariness. Consider an annotation guide that relies on a lexicon to save the coders decisions. It is debatable whether this would qualify as a sufficiently different description of the theory to break circularity. Either way, though, if the original scheme was arbitrary, the arbitrariness still remains, even if naive coders achieve high agreement. The arbitrary rules are no longer hidden in the heads of the annotators, but instead they are baked directly into the annotation guidelines as pre-made decisions. It seems, then, that the possibility of crowdsourcing (or, more generally, non-expert annotation) is not *sufficient* to make a scheme worthwhile.

Some (though notably not Riezler) have argued that disagreement among naive coders demonstrates the empirical emptiness of a scheme – i.e., that the possibility of crowdsourcing is still a *necessary* condition for a scheme's validity. (The concerns we raised above suggest this argument, as well.) This argument is also problematic, because it assumes that naive coders' explicit knowledge accurately reflects how their language works. That may seem reasonable – after all, naive coders are competent users of the language. But in practice, there is no reason to expect the average person to have meta-linguistic awareness, any more than one would expect a baseball player – a competent user of physics – to correctly identify the physics phenomena at work when he swings. The fact that expertise is required to precisely describe a phenomenon does not mean that the phenomenon is not empirically real.

If, consequently, agreement among naive coders is neither necessary nor sufficient to ascribe value to an annotation scheme, how do we proceed?

One way out is Riezler's second proposal: extrinsic task-based evaluation. If an annotation scheme is useful for a particular downstream NLP task – e.g., information extraction – then in some sense it is irrelevent whether the scheme is arbitrary; it at least correlates with the truth enough to be practically useful. We hope our scheme for causal language will fall into this category by proving useful, both directly to humans seeking causal information and for downstream information extraction.

Another way out is a type of usefulness that Riezler does not discuss. Often, simply attempting to formalize a phenomenon yields insights into some aspect of language, even if the formalization is empirically questionable.

It could be, for example, that our causal language scheme invents empirically meaningless semantic categories. However, it may still suggest hypotheses about how people use certain causal constructions. For instance, how often people talk about inhibiting vs. facilitating may vary dramatically depending on the genre. If validated, such an observation would yield valuable insights about language use and perhaps psychology – insights we would not have even thought to look for without the annotation scheme.

In short, then, we do not believe that low agreement among naive coders (or a need for expert guidance in decision-making, such as a lexicon) necessarily impugns the value of an annotation scheme as a whole. Accordingly, we hope that our suggestion of construction-based lexicography will help others build annotation schemes and corpora that are valuable by the criteria we have outlined. In our own future work, we hope to demonstrate that our causal language scheme meets these criteria, as well.

Acknowledgments

We would like to thank Nora Kazour, Mike Mordawanec, Spencer Onuffer, Donna Gates, Jeremy Doornbos, and Chu-Cheng Lin for all their help with annotations and annotation scheme refinement.

References

Collin F Baker, Charles J Fillmore, and John B Lowe. 1998. The Berkeley FrameNet Project. In *Proceedings of the 17th International Conference on Computational Linguistics-Volume 1*, pages 86–90. Association for Computational Linguistics.

Juliette Conrath, Stergos Afantenos, Nicholas Asher, and Philippe Muller. 2014. Unsupervised extraction of semantic relations using discourse cues. In *Proceedings of COLING 2014, the 25th International Conference on Computational Linguistics: Technical Papers*, pages 2184–2194. Dublin City University and Association for Computational Linguistics.

Phil Dowe. 2008. Causal processes. In Edward N. Zalta, editor, *The Stanford Encyclopedia of Philosophy*. Fall 2008 edition. `http://plato.stanford.edu/archives/fall2008/entries/causation-process/`.

Charles J. Fillmore, Paul Kay, and Mary Catherine O'Connor. 1988. Regularity and idiomaticity in grammatical constructions: The case of let alone. *Language*, 64(3):501–538, September.

Roxana Girju, Stan Szpakowicz, Preslav Nakov, Peter Turney, Vivi Nastase, and Deniz Yuret. 2007. SemEval-2007 task 04: Classification of semantic relations between nominals. In *In Fourth International Workshop on Semantic Evaluations (SemEval-2007)*.

Cécile Grivaz. 2010. Human judgements on causation in French texts. In *Proceedings of the Seventh conference on International Language Resources and Evaluation (LREC'10)*. European Languages Resources Association (ELRA).

Rei Ikuta, Will Styler, Mariah Hamang, Tim O'Gorman, and Martha Palmer. 2014. Challenges of adding causation to Richer Event Descriptions. In *Proceedings of the Second Workshop on EVENTS: Definition, Detection, Coreference, and Representation*, pages 12–20. Association for Computational Linguistics.

Claudiu Mihăilă, Tomoko Ohta, Sampo Pyysalo, and Sophia Ananiadou. 2013. BioCause: Annotating and analysing causality in the biomedical domain. *BMC Bioinformatics*, 14(1):2.

Paramita Mirza, Rachele Sprugnoli, Sara Tonelli, and Manuela Speranza. 2014. Annotating causality in the TempEval-3 corpus. In *Proceedings of the EACL 2014 Workshop on Computational Approaches to Causality in Language (CAtoCL)*, pages 10–19.

Ad Neeleman and Hans Van de Koot, 2012. *The Theta System: Argument Structure at the Interface*, chapter The Linguistic Expression of Causation, pages 20–51. Oxford University Press.

Martha Palmer, Daniel Gildea, and Paul Kingsbury. 2005. The Proposition Bank: An annotated corpus of semantic roles. *Computational Linguistics*, 31(1):71–106.

Rashmi Prasad, Nikhil Dinesh, Alan Lee, Eleni Miltsakaki, Livio Robaldo, Aravind Joshi, and Bonnie Webber. 2008. The Penn Discourse TreeBank 2.0. In Nicoletta Calzolari, Khalid Choukri, Bente Maegaard, Joseph Mariani, Jan Odijk, Stelios Piperidis, and Daniel Tapias, editors, *Proceedings of the Sixth International Conference on Language Resources and Evaluation (LREC'08)*, Marrakech, Morocco, May. European Language Resources Association (ELRA).

Stefan Riezler. 2014. On the problem of theoretical terms in empirical computational linguistics. *Computational Linguistics*, 40(1):235–245.

Evan Sandhaus. 2008. The New York Times annotated corpus. *Linguistic Data Consortium, Philadelphia*.

Jonathan Schaffer. 2014. The metaphysics of causation. In Edward N. Zalta, editor, *The Stanford Encyclopedia of Philosophy*. Summer 2014 edition. `http://plato.stanford.edu/archives/sum2014/entries/causation-metaphysics/`.

Pontus Stenetorp, Sampo Pyysalo, Goran Topić, Tomoko Ohta, Sophia Ananiadou, and Jun'ichi Tsujii. 2012. BRAT: a web-based tool for NLP-assisted text annotation. In *Proceedings of the Demonstrations at the 13th Conference of the European Chapter of the Association for Computational Linguistics*, pages 102–107. Association for Computational Linguistics.

Leonard Talmy. 1988. Force dynamics in language and cognition. *Cognitive Science*, 12(1):49–100.

William M. Trochim. 2006. Reliability & validity. In *The Research Methods Knowledge Base, 2nd Edition*. `http://www.socialresearchmethods.net/kb/relandval.php`.

Phillip Wolff, Bianca Klettke, Tatyana Ventura, and Grace Song. 2005. Expressing causation in English and other languages. In Woo-kyoung Ahn, Robert L. Goldstone, Bradley C. Love, Arthur B. Markman, and Phillip Wolff, editors, *Categorization inside and outside the laboratory: Essays in honor of Douglas L. Medin*, pages 29–48. American Psychological Association, Washington, DC, US.

Author Index